1988

A Bibliography of Chaucer ❧ 1974–1985 ❧

Lorrayne Y. Baird-Lange
and Hildegard Schnuttgen

Stephen G. Smyczynski

*Technical Editor
and Book Designer*

Archon Books
1988

The paper in this publication meets the minimum requirements of
American National Standard for Information Sciences
—Permanence of Paper for Printed Library Materials, ANSI
Z39.48–1984. ∞

Library of Congress Cataloging-in-Publication Data

Baird-Lange, Lorrayne Y., 1927–
A bibliography of Chaucer, 1974–1985.
Includes indexes.
1. Chaucer, Geoffrey, d. 1400—Bibliography.
I. Schnuttgen, Hildegard. II. Title.
Z8164.B275 1988 [PR1905]   016.821′1   87–35157
ISBN 0–208–02134–5

This book is dedicated
to
Calvin Oscar Yates and Orby Craft Yates,
to
Barbara Schnuttgen Jurasek,
and to
the memory of
Karl Schnüttgen

Contents

*See "General Prologue" in the index for the separate pilgrims.

Preface

This twelve-year gathering generally follows the plan of the previous *Bibliography of Chaucer 1964–1973* (1) with the addition of three new categories: Facsimiles, Medieval Women's Studies, and Pedagogy. Index tags within entries, a full subject index, extensive cross-referencing, and the review of scholarship which follows are designed to increase the usefulness and flexibility of this work.

The *tabula gratulatoria* is extensive. We are most grateful for the assistance of regular contributors on the international team of bibliographers listed in the annual *Studies in the Age of Chaucer:* Thomas W. Ross, Virginia E. Leland, Martha S. Waller, Robert P. apRoberts, Sumner Ferris, N. F. Blake, D. F. Chapin, Thomas Hahn, James Wimsatt, Claire Clements Morton, John H. Fisher, Shinsuke Ando, Toshiyuki Takamiya, Keiko Kawachi, Takami Matsuda, Saralyn R. Daly, Juliette Dor, David W. Hiscoe, Raymond E. McGowan, Rebecca S. Beal, Tadahiro Ikegami, Glending Olson, Robert L. Kindrick, Bernard S. Levy, Manuel José Gómez Lara, Margaret J. Daymond, Bege K. Bowers, Gratia M. Murphy, Janet Knapp, Clyde Hankey, Russell A. Peck, Tim D. P. Lally, Stanley R. Hauer, Daniel J. Ransom, Constance Hieatt, Larry Langford, Charles Long, Paul Strohm, Robert Raymo, Paul Clogan, Virginia Scott Zelk, Pat T. Overbeck, Edmund Reiss, David G. Allen, Jerome Mitchell, Judson Boyce Allen, Nancy Rushmore Hooper, Lynn Hunt Levy, Daniel F. Pigg, Joanna Simmers, Christine G. Pearcy, Nan Arbuckle, J. Lane Goodall, Piero Boitani, Tony Colaianne, R. M. Piersol, Thomas H. Seiler, Beverly Taylor, Nanzy Zorn, Werner Beis, Christopher B. Kennedy, Laurence Eldredge, John Fleming, and

Thomas Heffernan. *Ad hoc* and other occasional contributors are also listed in the annual bibliographies in *Studies in the Age of Chaucer.*

In addition to the Youngstown State University faculty members and students listed in the annual *SAC* bibliographies, the following Chaucer students have been helpful over the years in the preparation of the basic card files: Janet Layko, Alice Crosetto, Eileen McClellan, Rosemarie Barbour, Claire Butch, Randy Abraham, Ted Pawcio, Dorothy Simone, Jane Knight, Cathy Baca, Linda Evans, Deborah Greenfield, Norma Ryan, James Villani, Diane MacMurray, Cynthia Bruno, Bill Romanowski, Marilyn Valentino, Anne Davis, John Ryan, Mary Moller, Judy Prebish, Patricia Kutay, John Lencyk, C. E. Moses, Mary Jane Knight, Judy Robinson, and Jean Engle.

To Youngstown State University, Baird-Lange is grateful for support in the form of a year's sabbatical to finish this bibliography, to the University Research Council for financial support for the work in its various stages, to the English Department for xerox, mailings, and careful scheduling of her classes. The biggest debt of gratitude is to Stephen G. Smyczynski, a YSU student who did the word processing and technical editing under her direction, patiently and endlessly correcting and re-doing to overcome technological difficulties. Although all errors are her responsibility, she is grateful to Thomas A. Copeland of Youngstown State University for his helpful reading of the review of scholarship, and to Eleanor M. Beers for help with proofing bibliography entries in the early stages.

For help with library searches and checks, special thanks go to Debra Beronja and Brian Brennan of the Maag Library of Youngstown State University.

L. B.

H. S.

Chaucer Studies: Continuations, Developments, and Prognostications

by
Lorrayne Y. Baird-Lange

The twentieth century has been nominated as "the great age" of Chaucer studies (Rose, 68, p. ix), and the past two decades have seen both increased international interest in Chaucer and increased industry. Since its founding in the late 1970s, first under the executive directorship of Paul G. Ruggiers and later of John H. Fisher, the New Chaucer Society has held five international congresses and planned a sixth for Vancouver in 1988.

In addition to Pennsylvania State University's *Chaucer Review,* edited by R. W. Frank, Jr., two new Chaucer periodicals, both associated with the New Chaucer Society, were launched at the University of Oklahoma in 1979, later to be moved to the University of Tennessee. The annual *Studies in the Age of Chaucer,* edited at first by Roy J. Pearcy and later by Thomas J. Heffernan, publishes articles of high quality, reviews, and a yearly annotated Chaucer bibliography. The *Chaucer Newsletter* includes brief articles, announcements, calendars of events, and reports on the progress of the Variorum Chaucer. The Society also publishes occasional Proceedings of the New Chaucer Society. In addition to journals of English-speaking countries, 102 foreign journals have carried articles on Chaucer since 1974, including journals from South Africa, Pakistan, India, Russia, China, and Japan, as well as from most of the European countries. Contributions from Japanese and Italian scholars have been especially abundant and substantial. New translations have appeared in seven foreign languages.

Second only to the Shakespeare industry, Chaucer scholarship and criticism continue to grow. The present twelve-year gathering contains more than 2,500 entries, including 260 books and 212 dissertations—an average annual twenty-three percent increase in volume over the previous 1964–1973 bibliography in this series (1). Financial support has been plentiful in the form of sabbaticals and grants, some praised, some "proxmired." A wealth of medieval material was made available in the opening of the Rossell Hope Robbins Library, celebrated at University of Rochester in September 1987—this shortly after the appearance of *Chaucer in the Eighties,* edited by Julian N. Wasserman and Robert J. Blanch (Syracuse University Press, 1986), by no means the first collection of essays dedicated to Robbins. Thus, despite the saddening necrology of major Chaucerians, this has been a period of individual and professional celebration.

Basic Studies

Outlining in 1977 the desiderata for Middle English scholarship, George Kane (418) called for more basic studies, especially in Chaucer, needed for the correction and reassessment of texts, chronology, authorship, sources, and influence. His call has not gone unanswered.

Although Crow and Olson's *Chaucer Life-Records* had brought the known facts of **Chaucer's life** up to date in 1966, a few studies since then have uncovered additional data (see *Bibliography of Chaucer 1964–1973* [1], pp. 12–13; and for more selective coverage, *The Riverside Chaucer* [191], p. 774). New details and insights into Chaucer's life published since 1973 and listed in this bibliography are presented by Braddy (76), Ferris (80), the Lelands (82), the Reisners (84), and Yeager (86). Bennett (258) presents evidence of Chaucer's familiarity with Cambridge and Oxford. General reviews of Chaucer's life have been done by Baugh (75), Brewer (77), and DuBoulay (79). Gardner's fictionalized biography (81) is entertaining but not to be used seriously.

The concern expressed by N. F. Blake (190) that **textual studies** lag while criticism develops out of all proportion is widely held and has prompted one of the most heartening developments: the resurgence of interest in textual studies. More than ninety separate studies have appeared dealing with manuscripts, textual matters, and editorial tradition, including important books and articles by N. F. Blake on manuscripts and texts (93), the Hengwrt (94, 96, 97, 99), the textual tradition of the *Canterbury Tales* (99), the Manly-Rickert edition (95), and the *Book of the Duchess* (98). Also included are books by Beverly Boyd on Caxton (103) and on the medieval book (282); an article by Graham D. Caie on glosses in the *Canterbury Tales* (109); and a series of important articles by prominent scholars on the editorial tradition in *Editing Chaucer*, edited by Paul G. Ruggiers (163). The currently strong interest in iconography and manuscript illuminations including portraits of Chaucer is seen in Bentley (92), Davis (113), Fisher (122), Johnson (130), Kelliher (136), McGregor (143), Miskimin (144), Salter and Pearsall (164), Seymour (166), Stevens (169), and Thorpe (170, 171).

Of major importance to textual studies is the Variorum Chaucer, involving forty-two Chaucerians under the general editorship of Paul G. Ruggiers and Donald C. Baker at the University of Oklahoma. By 1986 four of the twenty-five projected volumes in this series had appeared (189, 203, 204, and 207). Seven volumes of the Chaucer Facsimile Series under the editorship of Paul G. Ruggiers and others have been issued by the University of Oklahoma and Pilgrim Books in collaboration with Boydell and Brewer in England (181, 182, 183, 185, 187, 188, and 189); one has been issued by Scolar Press in London (180) and another by D. S. Brewer at Cambridge (184) for a total of nine. More are forthcoming.

In his *The Textual Tradition of the 'Canterbury Tales'* (99), N. F. Blake uses manuscript evidence to argue that of the *Canterbury Tales* only what appears in the Hengwrt manuscript can be attributed to Chaucer. He provides a table of correspondences between Hengwrt and Ellesmere and a bibliography of scholarship on the manuscripts. Elsewhere (94) Blake theorizes that the Hengwrt was probably copied from Chaucer's own copy and is thus the most authentic of the manuscripts. Acceptance of the Robinson edition, he feels, has promoted "assumptions that have become self-justifying, and the text has been amended to conform." The Hengwrt is available in Blake's 1980 edition of the *Canterbury Tales* from the Hengwrt (190) and in the 1979 facsimile, *The Canterbury Tales: A Facsimile and Transcription of the Hengwrt Manuscript, with Variants from the Ellesmere Manuscript* (183). Recognition of the primacy of Hengwrt is sure to revolutionize further editions and criticism of the *Canterbury Tales*.

Three alternatives to the outdated F. N. Robinson text, standard for more than half a century, are *The Riverside Chaucer* (191), an updated Robinson under the general editorship of Larry D. Benson; the 1977 edition of Chaucer's complete works by John H. Fisher (198); and for the *Canterbury Tales,* Robert A. Pratt's edition (206).

In 1978 Rossell Hope Robbins conjectured that Chaucer may have written French poems (510). In 1982 James I. Wimsatt (175) published his edition of fifteen French lyrics marked "Ch" (possibly written by Chaucer) from the University of Pennsylvania MS French 15. The authenticity of these as Chaucer's works is in question, but at least they represent a major addition to Chaucerian apocrypha, and further scholarly studies on their role in the **canon** of Chaucer's works will no doubt follow.

Important editions of primary texts of Chaucer's **sources and literary relations** have also appeared. In his edition, *Chaucer: Sources and Backgrounds* (645), Robert P. Miller assembles a useful collection of Chaucer's classical, patristic and medieval primary sources grouped around themes: Creation and Fall, medieval literary theory, narrative sources, the three estates, antifraternal texts, modes of love, marriage and the good woman, antifeminism, and the Last Judgment.

Barry A. Windeatt's critical edition, *Chaucer's Dream Poetry: Sources and Analogues* (664), gives in translation Chaucer's major French sources and analogues together with relevant matter from Cicero, Boccaccio, and Alanus de Insulis. A. C. Spearing's *Medieval Dream Poetry* (547) deals with fourteenth-century dream poems and Chaucer's sources in Macrobius, Scripture, Christian vision, and *Roman de la Rose.*

Windeatt's edition of *Troilus and Criseyde* with parallel text from *Il Filostrato* (212) has been hailed as "the most important event in Chaucer scholarship for some years" (O'Donoghue review). In this authoritative *Troilus,* Windeatt gives closely scrutinized variant manuscript readings and careful analyses of Chaucer's sources and influences. Also valuable as primary materials are the N. R. Havely edition and translation, *Boccaccio—Sources of 'Troilus' and the Knight's and Franklin's Tales* (625); the Battaglia edition of Boccaccio's *Teseida* (596); and Giuseppi Galigani, ed., *Il Boccaccio nella cultura inglese e anglo-americana* (Florence, 1974).

Sigmund Eisner's edition and translation of the *Kalendarium* of Nicholas of Lynn (617) and Robert E. Lewis's edition of Pope Innocent III's *De miseria condicionis humane* (636) are offered by the University of Georgia in the Chaucer Library series, which is designed to make available in translation classical and medieval texts which Chaucer knew. Texts and translations of fabliaux are provided in Benson and Anderson, *The Literary Context of Chaucer's Fabliaux* (595).

Introductory surveys of source studies appear in Rowland's *Companion* (70): Ruggiers (652) on the Italian influence; Braddy (599) on the French; Hoffman (627) on the classical. Similar surveys also appear in Derek Brewer, ed., *Geoffrey Chaucer* (49): Dronke and Mann, "Chaucer and the Medieval Latin Poets" (614); Harbert, "Chaucer and the Latin Classics" (623); Schless, "Transformations: Chaucer's Use of Italian" (655); Wimsatt, "Chaucer and French Poetry" (662). See also André Crépin, "Chaucer and the French" (607). Useful also for certain of the *Canterbury Tales* is Metlitzki, *The Matter of Araby* (459).

For Chaucer's Italian connections, see especially book-length works by Piero Boitani, *Chaucer and Boccaccio* (597) and his edition of essays by various hands, *Chaucer and the Italian Trecento* (47), with new evidence on economy, law, demography, geography, linguistics; Howard H. Schless, *Chaucer and Dante: A Revaluation* (654); and David Wallace, *Chaucer and the Early Writings of Boccaccio* (659). About 140 other items are available through the subject index under Dante, Boccaccio, and Petrarch.

Several major books examine Chaucer's indebtedness to the Latin poets. John M. Fyler, *Chaucer and Ovid* (618), concentrates on Chaucer's use of Ovid in the dream visions, *Troilus,* and the *Canterbury Tales;* Winthrop Wetherbee, *Chaucer and the Poets* (2451), on literary allusion in *Troilus,* especially from Virgil, Ovid, Statius, Dante, and the *Romance of the Rose.* John P. McCall's *Chaucer Among the Gods* (453) develops Chaucer's aesthetic uses of classical materials to illuminate Chaucerian poetics, showing that Chaucer is the "first humanist" in the literature of England. Humanism in Chaucer, variously interpreted, has also been examined by Ames (248), Tripp (563), and Shigeo (536). In *Chaucer and Pagan Antiquity* (462), Alastair Minnis examines paganism and Chaucer's attitudes toward antiquity in *Troilus* and the *Knight's Tale.* Rudat (525) examines the *Canterbury Tales* for classical allusions, especially from Virgil's *Aeneid.* On mythography, Economou (2171) deals with the tradition of the goddess Nature; Twycross (566) with Venus.

General works on Chaucer's place in the English vernacular tradition include Derek Pearsall, *Old and Middle English Poetry* (493), and P. M. Kean, *Chaucer and the Making of English Poetry* (420). In academic debate Ian Robinson, *Chaucer and the English Tradition* (516), establishes Chaucer as the father of English poetry, originator of the English tradition; Alexander Weiss (577) demonstrates that Chaucer, rather than representing the beginnings, is the culmination of a tradition. J. A. Burrows, *Ricardian Poetry* (309), establishes the last quarter of the fourteenth century as a period in English literature with common characteristics in style, linguistics, and metrics.

In examining **Chaucer's influence** on his followers, A. C. Spearing, *Medieval to Renaissance in English Poetry* (548), challenges the theory of C. S. Lewis that Chaucer "medievalized" his received materials, arguing that Chaucer, himself a "Renaissance" poet, was medievalized by his successors. Frances McNeely Leonard, *Laughter in the Courts of Love* (445), traces the tradition of allegorical love poetry in Chaucer and followers to Spenser. Chaucerian influence on Shakespeare is examined in a book by E. T. Donaldson, *The Swan at the Well: Shakespeare Reading Chaucer* (699); in a collection of essays by various hands edited by Donaldson and Judith J. Kollmann, *Chaucerian Shakespeare: Adaptation and Transformation* (698); and by Ann Thompson, *Shakespeare's Chaucer: A Study in Literary Origins* (811). Chaucerian influence on Spenser and Milton is examined in Kent A. Hieatt, *Chaucer, Spenser, Milton: Mythopoeic Continuities and Transformations*. Alice S. Miskimin, *The Renaissance Chaucer* (761), concentrates on the influence and use of the *Canterbury Tales* and *Troilus* and the changing views regarding Chaucer over the two centuries after his death.

Supplementing Caroline F. E. Spurgeon, *Five Hundred Years of Chaucer Criticism and Allusion, 1357–1900,* and useful in the history of Chaucer **criticism and allusion** is D. S. Brewer, *Critical Heritage* (287) in two volumes, a selection of essays which extends the critical heritage to 1933. Volume 1 (1385–1837) contains comments on Chaucer from Deschamps to Coleridge; volume 2 (1837–1933) from Virginia Woolf to Rosamond Tuve. Carmen J. Dello Buoro, *Rare Early Essays on Chaucer* (327), presents essays from the late nineteenth and early twentieth century.

In **language and word studies**, major books on the English language in Chaucer's day have been done by N. F. Blake, *The English Language in Medieval Literature* (874), which explores the linguistic conditions within which fourteenth-century writers worked; by Arthur O. Sandved, *Introduction to Chaucerian English* (947), which uses the F. N. Robinson edition to examine Chaucer's phonology and morphology; by Gregory Roscow, *Syntax and Style in Chaucer's Poetry* (859), on word order, idiomatic usage, pleonasm, ellipsis, relative clauses, coordination, and parataxis; by John H. Fisher and Diane D. Bornstein, *In Form of Speche Is Chaunge* (898), a historical approach to the language. Other important studies include Udo Fries, *Einführung in die Sprache Chaucers* (899), on phonology, metrics, and morphology; Masa T. Ikegami on rhyme and pronunciation (912); and studies on French loan-words by Juliette de

Caluwé Dor (879, 880, 881), Merete Smith (951), and E. T. Donaldson (889).

General introductory language studies include A. J. Gilbert, *Literary Language from Chaucer to Johnson* (900); Norman Davis, "Chaucer and the English Language" (885); J. Kerkhof, *Studies in the Language of Geoffrey Chaucer* (922); Ralph W. V. Elliott, *Chaucer's English* (891); and Robert A. Peters, *Chaucer's Language* (934). Fifteenth-century chancery English is anthologized by John and Jane Fisher and Malcolm Richardson (896). The social aspects of language use (sociolinguistics) are treated by Johnson (1060), Wilcockson (1570), Dürmüller (1704), and Sola Buil (1146).

David Burnley, *A Guide to Chaucer's Language* (877), concentrates on text, grammar, syntax, usage, style, and the literary potential of Chaucer's language. *Chaucer's Language and the Philosophers' Tradition* (306), by the same author, traces a history of ideas connected with tyranny as represented by some 160 words indexed at the end of the book, giving insights into Criseyde's timidity.

Studies identifying Chaucer's puns are scattered throughout the bibliography. See subject index and especially Larry D. Benson, "The 'Queynte' Punnings of Chaucer's Critics" (260).

Chaucer's **versification** is studied in books by Jack Conner, *English Prosody from Chaucer to Wyatt* (831); by Norman Eliason, *The Language of Chaucer's Poetry* (835); by Ian Robinson, *Chaucer's Prosody* (857); and in various articles—several on the Halle-Keyser theories (823, 829, 839, 844, 845). A general work is Marina Tarlinskaja, *English Verse* (864a). Bibliographic essays on Chaucer's prosody by Tauno F. Mustanoja (850, 851) review the subject.

Of special interest for future studies are the desiderata mentioned in Alan T. Gaylord, "Scanning the Prosodists: An Essay in Metacriticism" (837), which calls for studies of prosody within the contexts of literary and linguistic effects.

Historical Interdisciplinary Studies

A number of studies examine Chaucer's poetry within the contexts of fourteenth-century European culture: philosophy, sociology, economy, politics, religion, and literary backgrounds. George Kane's exemplary introduction, *Chaucer* (413), examines the innovativeness of Chaucer's art within a broad range of cultural contexts.

A major document in **literary sociology**, Terry Jones's astonishing book, *Chaucer's Knight* (1210), draws on well-substantiated historical and sociological contexts to argue that Chaucer's Knight is not a "militant Christian idealist but a shabby mercenary without morals or scruples" (p. 140). Using charts and maps reflecting the realities of warfare in the fourteenth century, Jones traces the Knight's undiscriminating campaigns against both heathen and Christian, and judges that the tale of this ruthless, pillaging mercenary, the *Knight's Tale,* is a "hymn to tyranny." Jones's view should be compared with the positive interpretation of Olson (1296), with Schaefer (532) below, and with Elizabeth Salter's posthumously published *Fourteenth Century English Poetry* (530), which examines social and historical contexts of the *Knight's Tale.* Jones challenges a long tradition of the "ideal" Knight, and is certain to change the course of Knight and *Knight's Tale* criticism.

Literary sociology has likewise been strong among German scholars. In her *Höfische-ritterliche Dichtung und sozialhistorische Realität* (532), Ursula Schaefer examines the knightly ideals of courtly poetry in *Troilus* and the *Knight's Tale* against the historical and social realities of medieval knighthood. N. I. Orme, *From Childhood to Chivalry: The Education of English Kings and Aristocracy* (480), relates to contemporary practice Chaucer's references to the education and upbringing of the noble classes.

In his *Chaucer's Franklin in 'The Canterbury Tales': The Social and Literary Background of a Chaucerian Character* (1253), Henrik Specht presents evidence for the Franklin's high social rank, a corrective to views of him as a social climber of dubious status. Chaucer's middle class is studied by Theodor Wolpers, "Bürgerliches bei Chaucer: Mit einer Skizze des spätmittelalterlichen London" (587). Merchants and craftsmen in late medieval London illuminate the characters and tales of Merchant, Shipman, Miller, and Canon's Yeoman. Chaucer's familiarity with millers, reeves, and clerks is also explored by J. A. W. Bennett, *Chaucer at Oxford and Cambridge* (966), a mixture of historical fact and literary criticism.

Jill Mann, *Chaucer and Medieval Estates Satire* (1196), draws more on traditional literature concerning social classes than on historical social conditions. She studies the social classes represented in the *General Prologue* in the context of medieval estates satire, a genre designed to examine the right relationship between the nobility and the commoners. Chaucer manipulates this tradition to effect an ambivalent reader response to the pilgrims.

In *English Gothic Literature,* Derek Brewer sets fourteenth-century literature, including Chaucer, within the socio-religious context of court and monastery, of city and country. Benedicta Ward, *Miracles and the*

Medieval Mind (2785), establishes an intellectual milieu for the *General Prologue* and *Canterbury Tales* by reviewing records of the miracles at the shrine of Thomas à Becket.

Some sociological studies including Aers (243) and Delany (1006) are examined in terms of Marxist critical theory, discussed below under "Modern Critical Theories."

A historical examination of the social and legal nature of sexuality is found in Vern L. Bullock and James Brundage, *Sexual Practices and the Medieval Church* (2701). Various recent studies have dealt specifically with homosexuality as a psychological factor in literary interpretation. John Boswell (2698) provides a general historical survey; Pierre J. Payer (2702) translates Peter Damian's attack on clerical homosexuality. McAlpine (1266) shows that Chaucer's characterization of the Pardoner as an effeminate, a hermaphrodite, and a eunuch draws in the main medieval perceptions of the homosexual; McVeigh (1267) associates the Pardoner's homosexuality with medieval views of simony and leprosy; Rudat (1739) develops a process of homosexual self-discovery in the *Pardoner's Tale;* Freese (1333), the implicit homoeroticism of the *Miller's* and *Reeve's Tales;* and Clark (990), the scatological elements of homosexuality.

Another social-sexual institution is treated by H. A. Kelly, *Love and Marriage in the Age of Chaucer* (2709). Perhaps legitimate only in literature, courtly love is the subject of several studies: Roger Boas, *The Origin and Meaning of Courtly Love: A Critical Study of European Scholarship* (2603); Larry Benson, "Courtly Love in the Later Middle Ages" (in 821, pp. 237–57); in essays by Eliason, Reiss, Kaske, and Wimsatt in *Chaucer the Love Poet* (466); George Kane, "Chaucer, Love Poetry, and Romantic Love" (415). Comic allegorical love poetry is treated by Leonard, *Laughter in the Courts of Love* (445).

Chaucer's works have also been illuminated through studies in **medieval science**. A general survey of "Chaucer and Science" is given by M. Manzalaoui (2798). Stephan Kohl, *Wissenschaft und Dichtung bei Chaucer* (430) treats science, medicine, the humoral theory, astrology, and dream theory in explications of Chaucer's poetry. Derek Brewer (286) examines Chaucer's use of arithmetic. Chauncy Wood's introduction, "Chaucer and Astrology" (588), in the Rowland *Companion* (70) reviews scholarship; his *Chaucer and the Country of the Stars* (Princeton, 1970) remains the authority on Chaucer's astrology. J. C. Eade (399) analyzes audience expectation and participation regarding astrological matters in the *Canterbury Tales*. Too recent to be included in this bibliography, Laurel Braswell, "The Moon and Medicine in Chaucer's

Time," *SAC* 8 (1986), 145–56, explains the use of lunaries in medieval medicine and Chaucer's allusion to astrological medicine. A bitter "ancient/modern" controversy in the history of medieval medicine and surgery is explored by Infusino and O'Neill (1291): on the treatment of Arcite's wounds, Chaucer adopts the "modern" view; Boccaccio, the "ancient."

A promising field for the application of medieval science to literary explication has been opened by Peter Brown, *Chaucer's Visual World: A Study of his Poetry and the Medieval Optical Tradition* (2788). Brown shows parallels between passages in treatises on optics and passages in Chaucer on vision, light, and space. His study will invite new studies of Chaucer's "realism."

The medieval arts as ancillary disciplines to literary studies have generated important studies. Art and iconography are discussed below under "Critical Theory and Critical Controversies." A major work on **music** in the fourteenth century, Nigel Wilkins, *Music in the Age of Chaucer* (2828), explores the relationship between music and literature in Europe and England, noting Chaucer's references to performance. A companion volume, *Chaucer's Songs* (582), provides a performing edition of fifteen of Chaucer's lyrics, using music by fourteenth-century French composers, and establishing Chaucer's links with contemporary French music and poetry. An article by James I. Wimsatt (2482) analyzes the French lyric element in *Troilus* and a dissertation by Linda Ferguson (2273) analyzes music in *Troilus* and the dream poems. David G. Lanoue's dissertation (437) discusses musical imagery in the *Book of the Duchess* and the *Canterbury Tales*. Gellrich (1335) discovers a parody of medieval music in the *Miller's Tale*.

Critical Theories and Critical Controversies

A. New Criticism and New Historicism

The twentieth century is appropriately called the age of criticism: it has seen a proliferation of critical theories which operate dialectically in reaction, opposition, modification, and correction to each other. The chief positions important to Chaucer studies during this period include historicism, New Criticism, New Historicism (Robertsonianism), a revised New Historicism of Poetics, and a variety of modern literary theories: Russian formalism, linguistic structuralism, anthropological structuralism, deconstruction or post-structuralism, reader response theory, psychoanalytic criticism, Marxist criticism, and feminist criticism.

Concerned with empirically derived facts rather than with ideas, positivism provided a philosophic basis for the principal late nineteenth- and early twentieth-century literary theory, **historicism**. Historicism held that literature can be explained scientifically by reference to its genesis or factual causes: the author's life; his historic, cultural, and social milieu; his sources; historical disciplines ancillary to literature; the conditions of composition; the author's expressed intentions, and so on. Early in this century Chaucer criticism was dominated by this approach, which is still primary, however conscious it may have become of the intervening dialectic of other critical approaches.

In opposition to historicism and other critical theories, an Anglo-American movement, **New Criticism** began in the 1920s with T. S. Eliot and I. A. Richards, to be continued and expanded in both theory and practice from the 1940s onward by Cleanth Brooks, John Crowe Ransom, W. K. Wimsatt, Allen Tate, and a host of practical critics dealing mostly with modern literature. Not an organized critical system, New Criticism consists rather of a set of related attitudes. Although apparently not influenced by the earlier Russian and Czechoslovak formalists (discussed below under "Modern Critical Theories"), Anglo-American New Critics shared with them an insistence upon the autonomy of the literary construct and the centrality of the text, rejecting the historical approach which made literature subservient to other systems. The intrinsic value of literature as a form of knowledge in its own right—the objective theory of art—required privileging of the text. Viewed by most New Critics as a transparent medium between the author and the reader, the text was based upon a dependable, if sometimes ambiguous or complicated relationship between words and things: words point to things; language reflects reality however ironically, indirectly, or subtly. Poetry has a disconcerting quality, but its oppositions, contradictory impulses, and multiplexities are resolved by close reading and textual analysis to arrive at a harmonization of diversities, or a reconciliation of opposites. Thus, poetry (literature) is informed by an organic unity. Meaning dictates structure, which corresponds to reality and to feelings. In 1937 F. R. Leavis had remarked that a critic should "feel into" the text, but later American critics, especially Wimsatt and Beardsley, rejected feeling, as an "affective fallacy."

In the middle of this century arose a school of Chaucerian New Criticism headed by E. T. Donaldson of Yale. "Donaldsonianism" increased appreciation of Chaucer's power and subtlety as a poet by bringing old-style philology into the service of close textual readings, thus rescuing Chaucer from restraints imposed by Kittredgean "realism." The work of the Chaucerian New Critics is characterized at times by intense methodology and semantic analysis designed to reveal the intrinsic worth of Chaucer's poetry accessible through the text and to make it available to intelligent readers. For a more detailed account of early developments, see William R. Crawford, "Introduction: New Directions in Chaucer Criticism," *Bibliography of Chaucer 1954–1963* (Seattle, 1967), pp. xiii–xl, especially pp. xx–xxviii. For a brief sketch see Peter M. Vermeer, "Chaucer and Literary Criticism" (571).

The 1950s also saw the founding of a **New Historicism**, or "Robertsonianism," an exegetical-hermeneutical school of criticism developed by D. W. Robertson, Jr., partly in reaction to Kittredgean "realism," partly in opposition to the New Critics, who underplayed or ignored the historic religious and cultural traditions and milieu of Chaucer's work. This New Historicism begins with an important early essay: "The Doctrine of Charity in Medieval Literary Gardens: A Topical Approach Through Symbolism and Allegory," *Speculum* 26 (1950), 24–49, and is further developed in the classic *Preface to Chaucer* (Princeton, 1962), and in essays appearing over a thirty-year period and collected in 1980 in *Essays in Medieval Culture* (513). A review of Robertson's early career can be found in Eleanor Lewer Courtney (11).

As if to redeem Chaucer from Matthew Arnold's assessment of him as a second-rate poet because of his lack of high seriousness, Robertson sought a medieval system of poetics based in medieval theology within which to interpret Chaucer. He invokes scriptural, especially Pauline doctrine; the allegorists of late classical times; patristic exegetical commentaries; and artistic and iconographic traditions to explain Chaucer's poetic process and meaning. Adherents to this school also examine Chaucer's use of the scriptural, exegetical, and iconographic traditions. Assuming that Chaucer not only accepted the moral universe and seriousness of these traditions between the polarities of *cupiditas/caritas,* but that he also shaped his poetry by allegorical, patristic, exegetical and hermeneutical principles, Robertson pursues Chaucer's meaning by applying these same methods.

Robertson's moral hermeneutics have been criticized as making Chaucer's poetry subservient to religion, as philosophically reductive and inappropriate to a poet of Chaucer's elusiveness, subtlety, ambiguity, multiple perspectives, urbanity, comic vision, and inferred broad humanity—qualities highly prized among the New Critics. Anti-Robertsonian studies in the present period include William E. Rogers (518): on the limits of patristic criticism, he notes that assuming a work to be designed to promote *caritas* is begging the question. Ruth M. Ames

(249) argues that Chaucer's parodies of the Old Testament are as irreverent as they sound; his piety is sincere; and that (contrary to Robertsonianism) he was not deeply moved by either the Old Testament or "current exegetical modes." Derek Pearsall (1881) attacks the allegorization of the *Nun's Priest's Tale,* in favor of a neoclassical or naive reading which distrusts ambiguity and seeks a "literal mimesis of the physical world." Such a reading apprehends "the delightfully uncertain certainties, the fluid transitions of Chaucer's own poem." William Calin (310) argues the inadequacies of the Robersonian view of medieval love. Harriett Hawkins, *Poetic Freedom and Poetic Truth* (1552), rejects Robertson's reading of the *Clerk's Tale* as a moral fable, arguing that poetic truth cannot be historically fossilized.

On the other hand, even among critics of Robertson, few contest the heuristic appropriateness of a great number of illuminating and provocative articles and books which have been inspired by Robertson or which pursue interests parallel to his. Some of these employ the close textual readings demanded by New Criticism, and several have taken their places as classics in Chaucer criticism—as examples, John V. Fleming, "The Summoner's Prologue: An Iconographic Adjustment," *ChauR* 2 (1967), 95–107; Alan Levitan, "The Parody of the Pentecost in Chaucer's Summoner's Tale," *UTQ* 40 (1971), 236–46; Chauncey Wood, "The Sources of Chaucer's Summoner's 'Garleek, Onyons, and eek Lekes,'" *ChauR* 5 (1971), 240–44; and the much quoted Robert P. Miller, "Chaucer's Pardoner, the Scriptural Eunuch, and the Pardoner's Tale," *Speculum* 30 (1955), 180–99. The essays collected by Jeffrey (63), discussed below, continue a direction of Chaucer scholarship, which has made Robertson one of the most influential Chaucerians of the past thirty-five years.

Thus, during the period from the early fifties to the mid-seventies critical controversy was said (though arbitrarily and somewhat inaccurately) to be polarized into two camps: (1) the New Historicists, who brought to bear on Chaucer's poetry a patristic exegetical literary theory external to it and attempted to make Chaucer serve the moral universe represented by that data—a hermeneutical vision of Chaucer as a serious Christian moralist, patristic in his beliefs and poetics, his truth or meaning accessible through allegoresis or other exegetical methods; and (2) the New Critics, who strictly rejected external historical information and confined themselves to close readings of the text, seeking stylistic subtleties and the complexities of multiple perspectives in genre, plot, character, irony, ambiguity, imagery, symbolism, and meaning—insisting on the autonomy of the literary construct and contending that Chaucer's moral universe and poetic vision is to be found exclusively within Chaucer's text itself.

In actual practice on one hand, very few practitioners of New Criticism totally avoid historical facts; on the other, many followers of Robertson work out what they see as Chaucer's moral vision by applying to the study of historical religious or artistic contexts close textual analyses of Chaucer's poetry. Thus the vociferous opposing camps of Robertson and Donaldson have often occupied common grounds.

Robertsonianism in its various mutations still flourishes, Robertson himself having contributed (somewhat more in the mainstream of historicism) several items in this bibliography. Robertson insists that to understand Chaucer we must reconstruct the history and intellectual milieu of his day concerning the Christian tradition (2778); the medieval manor (1203); the medieval franklin and Chaucer's Franklin (1657); the date and purpose of Chaucer's *Troilus* (2378); land tenure and the cloth industry in connection with the Wife of Bath (1488); and the transformation of the Midas tradition in the *Wife of Bath's Tale,* (1489). Still opposing the early mimetic criticism or "realism" of Kittredge and Manly, in "Some Disputed Chaucerian Terminology" (515) he warns that we know too little about the lower classes of the fourteenth century to call Chaucer's portrayal of them "realistic."

Attempts have been made to find a compromise between Kittredge's view of Chaucer's mimetic realism and Robertson's view of Chaucer's moral didacticism; Alfred David is a chief exponent of this *via media.* In *The Strumpet Muse: Art and Morals in Chaucer's Poetry* (326) he examines the conflicting roles of Chaucer as moralist and as entertainer, analyzing various oppositions in Chaucer: authority-experience, intellect-emotion, "ernest-game," "sentence-solaas"—arguing that Chaucer develops from a bookish poetry depending upon authority to a poetry depending upon experience, and that he vacillates between his public moral obligation and his private artistic vision, sometimes running counter to his own intentions. David tacitly accepts Robertson's theological aesthetics, but argues that Chaucer transcended this framework and managed to write about the experiences of real life. In "Chaucerian Comedy and Criseyde" (2257), David also accepts the Robertsonian moral vision, but applies comic lenses to relieve the pervasive gloom of the vision.

Although not necessarily imitating the moral hermeneutics of early Robertsonianism, especially views on *caritas* and *cupiditas,* various books and articles noted in this gathering reflect Robertson's interests, both the scriptural-patristic and the iconographic-artistic. The study of Chaucer's biblical traditions, made popular by Robertson continues to be fruitful. Biblical and exegetical studies are collected in David Lyle Jeffrey, ed., *Chaucer and the Scriptural Tradition* (63), with articles by Wood (1172) on artistic intention; Reiss (1120) on biblical parody; Besserman (970) on *glosynge;* Caie (109) on glosses in the *Canterbury Tales;* Wurtele (1182) on Nicholas of Lyre's *Postillae litteralis et moralis super totam Bibliam;* Jeffrey (629) on biblical and hermeneutic and literary theory; Peck (1112) on St. Paul and the *Canterbury Tales;* Coletti (1760) on the *mulier fortis* motif; Fleming (1175) on Gospel asceticism; Alford (956) on literalism and scriptural testament in the *Canterbury Tales;* Jeffrey (2096) on authority and interpretation in the *House of Fame;* and Robertson himself (2778) on Chaucer and the Christian tradition.

Warren Ginsberg, *The Cast of Character* (368), demonstrates how medieval authors including Chaucer used techniques from theology and biblical exegesis as well as from rhetoric and philosophy as conventions of characterization. Likewise, Siegfried Wenzel (1168) shows how Chaucer borrows plots, images, characterization, motifs, and technical terms from fourteenth-century sermon literature. From a New Critical stance, Stanley S. Hussey (1056) discovers the "objective correlatives" Chaucer used in characterization centuries before T. S. Eliot coined the term.

The Robertsonian insistence upon Chaucer's Christian or moral vision is echoed in *The Elements of Chaucer's Troilus* (2462) by Chauncey Wood, who argues for a moral reading of *Troilus and Criseyde;* and in *Chaucer's Conversion: Allegorical Thought in Medieval Literature* (2525) by Heiner Gillmeister, who claims that *Truth,* a deathbed allegory which hints of Chaucer's conversion to monasticism, is the key to Chaucer's *Retraction* and thus to the *Canterbury Tales.* Another book by Gillmeister, *Discrecioun: Chaucer und die Via Regia* (367), relates Chaucer to the patristic tradition in the concept of *discrecioun* and gives an original allegorization of the *Nun's Priest's Tale* in Robertsonian style. (Compare Derek Pearsall's attack [1881] on allegorizers of the tale.) Analyzing Chaucer's parodies of love, three of the four papers in Mitchell and Provost, eds., *Chaucer the Love Poet* (65), employ the Augustinianism popularized by Robertson and Huppé. J. D. Burnley, *Chaucer's Language and the Philosophers' Tradition* (306), is concerned with Christian moral psychology, arguing that Chaucer shows a distaste for love (passion). A moral reading of medieval literature is supported by Janet Coleman's demonstration in *Medieval Readers and Writers* (321) that most literary works of the fourteenth century were aimed at edification and training in Christian ethics rather than at entertainment, a position also held by Judson Boyce Allen, *The Ethical Poetic of the Later Middle Ages* (246).

The opposite position is taken by Glending Olson, *Literature as Recreation in the Later Middle Ages* (476). In a well researched study depending on primary sources and documented facts, Olson demonstrates that by the late Middle Ages, writers had begun deliberately to write literature for entertainment as well as for moral purposes, a finding which justifies the entertainment value of Chaucer's works and erodes somewhat the basis for Robertsonianism. Olson's expressed aim is "to redress an imbalance in modern scholarship that fosters, intentionally or not, the notion that medieval literary thought had nothing but indifference to or contempt for the purely pleasurable" (p. 13). Olson reinforces his position in "Toward a Poetics of the Late Medieval Court Lyric" (478), showing that late medieval society viewed lyrics as "recreation, as conversation, as personal expression, as music." Olson's book, one among several concerned with Chaucer's poetics, is a major contribution to our knowledge of medieval attitudes toward literature. It is certain to modify the future of Chaucer criticism.

Somewhat less controversial are studies influenced by Robertson's iconographic historicism. Most of these studies are concerned not primarily with Chaucer's visual realism, but with his use of received artistic and iconographic traditions. In his *Chaucer and the Imagery of the Narrative* (1073), V. A. Kolve explores the controlling images—the "language of sign and symbol"—in the *Canterbury Tales*. He establishes the primacy of the visual image. Regarding the *Second Nun's Tale* (1907), Kolve (1907) demonstrates that Chaucer is an iconographic poet, rather than a painterly poet.

Responding also to Robertson's interest in medieval iconography, *Signs and Symbols in Chaucer's Poetry,* edited by Hermann and Burke (61), contains nine essays mostly by Robertson's students and protégés. Chamberlain (311) discusses musical signs and symbols; Gardner (364), signs, symbols, and cancellations; Reiss (501), thematic particulars; Robertson (514), signs from everyday life; Wood (1233), signs in the Prioress's portrait; Gibson (1764), resurrection as an icon in the *Shipman's Tale;* Wimsatt (2063), the question of secular elegy or religious vision in the *Book of the Duchess;* Kolve (2142), iconography in the *Legend of Good Women;* and Huppé (2313), narrative strategy in *Troilus*. In his own essay (514) Robertson reiterates the thesis of *Preface to Chaucer,* that our knowledge of the visual arts Chaucer would have known will enhance our understanding of his figurative language. While most of these essays respond positively to Robertson and develop his philosophies, Gardner (364) voices the typical admiration of and objection to Robertson. While admitting that Robertsonianism has brilliantly illuminated many of Chaucer's works, proving them much richer than we suspected, he contends that Robertson exhibits a certain "tone deafness" that often results in "lunatic readings."

John V. Fleming, "Chaucer and the Visual Arts of His Time" (352), calls for searches for "visual analogues" and for further studies to illuminate both Chaucer's references to the visual arts actually available to him and their possible influence on his style, described as "literary international Gothic." He argues that emphasis on visual rather than moral realism produces unacceptable grotesquery.

Henry A. Kelly (422) contends that Chaucer had a "bad eye for art" and that his references to the visual arts are muddled and bookish. Outside the Robertsonian iconographic tradition, Beryl Rowland's *Blind Beasts: Chaucer's Animal World* (520) reviews Chaucer's received traditions of animal imagery and symbolism.

The impact of New Criticism is pervasive; few will ever again presume to interpret Chaucer without careful attention to the text. Various studies show continuing interest in New Critical concerns as listed in the index: irony, symbolism, ambiguity, imagery, characterization, persona, narration, and so on. Close readings which pay attention to these features include James Winny, *Chaucer's Dream-Poems* (586); Derek Traversi, *The Literary Imagination* (562), and Traversi's *The 'Canterbury Tales': A Reading* (1157), which concerns the validity of poetic fiction and demonstrates the relativity of Chaucer's comic vision and moral assumptions. Stephen Knight, *Ryming Craftily* (429), provides close textual analyses on various stylistic levels. Chaucerian New Criticism and critical practice based on modern literary theory typically deal with antinomies or oppositions, with dialectic complexities and multiple perspectives.

Convinced that Chaucer's poetry can be illuminated by modern dogma, Robert Burlin, *Chaucerian Fiction* (305), proposes a binary structure of the antinomies of experience and authority, tracing through all of the major works Chaucer's developing sophistication in resolving these paradoxes; Alfred David, *The Strumpet Muse* (326), examines the tension between Chaucer's own experience and his felt duty to convey received authority; Donald K. Fry (2088) argues regarding the *House of Fame* that Chaucer distrusted old authorities and their interpreters. In *Laughter in the Courts of Love* (445), Frances McNeely Leonard examines in the dream visions the multiplexity of focus in the coalescence of allegory and comedy.

xxvii

For Charles A. Owen, Jr., "ernest and game" provide the dialectic in *Pilgrimage and Storytelling in the Canterbury Tales* (1106). Renouncing historicism to read the *Canterbury Tales* from modern critical perspective, Donald Howard, *The Idea of the Canterbury Tales* (1052), sees a binary arrangement in a thematic metastructural interlace, in which one tale discredits another. The organizing principle is the memory of experience related by Chaucer the Pilgrim. A unity study, Traugott Lawler, *The One and the Many* (1077), sees the *Canterbury Tales* as a "meta-fabliau" which exposes fraud through professional clashes and integrates the *Parson's Tale* and *Retraction* with the rest of the tales.

Much recent criticism has thus concentrated on the unity of the *Canterbury Tales*, but Derek Pearsall, *The Canterbury Tales* (1110), argues that the separate tale is the primary experience for both reader and critic and encourages eclectic readings.

In *Chaucer's Troilus and Criseyde: A Critical Study* (2233), Ian Bishop examines a dialectic of opposing views of love. Going beyond the formalism of New Critics, Peter Elbow, *Oppositions in Chaucer* (342), argues that in the complexly ironic *Troilus* Chaucer holds in unresolved suspension the logical oppositions of freedom and necessity, either ignoring or transcending them. In the tradition of the medieval *discordia concors* topos, Donald W. Rowe, *O Love, O Charity!: Contraries Harmonized in Chaucer's 'Troilus'* (2380), holds that paradox rather than irony and ambiguity is the chief characteristic of *Troilus*. Psychologically "real," the characters also represent the soul's ascent to God; valid in itself, earthly love also signifies charity; and contraries are harmonized in the unity of earthly tragedy and divine comedy.

Oppositions and contraries in Chaucer are often seen as ironic. Pearsall (1111) points out that irony should be located in the text as an apparent intention of the author, rather than in the reader. Very valuable too are D. H. Green, "On Recognizing Medieval Irony" (2630) and *Irony in Medieval Romance* (2296), which also emphasize the artist's signals; Beryl Rowland, "Seven Kinds of Irony" (in 266); and Edmund Reiss, "Medieval Irony" (502), a study of the *concordantia oppositorum* in literature and art, which shows in "ernest/game" oppositions a pervasive potential for multiplex irony.

Donaldson himself has applied close readings to the *Canterbury Tales* (1010, and 1279), to the *Parliament of Fowls* (2207), to *Troilus* and the tradition of Criseyde (2474). A second edition of his *Chaucer's Poetry* (New York, 1958), appeared in 1975. In "Chaucer's Manuscripts and their Use" (114) he advocates skepticism of printed editions, which falsify items like punctuation. In recent years Donaldson has expanded his interests. He studies Shakespearean uses of Chaucer (698, 699). In "Chaucer's Three Ps" (2263) he gives a psychological interpretation of Chaucer the Poet, thwarted in love, who created Pandarus and the Pardoner as representations of his deep frustrations. Referring to the writings of medieval saints as well as to modern scholars in "Designing a Camel: or, Generalizing the Middle Ages" (334), Donaldson reiterates his opposition to the Robertsonian view regarding Christian motivations of medieval artists.

Similarly, though basing his study on historical evidence, David Aers, *Chaucer, Langland and the Creative Imagination* (243), develops a thesis that the works of Chaucer and Langland do not reflect "closed and given forms of thought and practice" (Robertsonianism) or "dominant attitudes in their ideological and social environment," but rather that both authors engage in "a critical dialectic" with these ideologies and with social customs of the day.

Consciously carrying on the New Critical views of Donaldson, and his opposition to Robertson, is a festschrift in his honor edited by Carruthers and Kirk (52). Here Brewer (292) praises Donaldson as a great textual scholar. Kane (415) discusses Chaucer's satires on courtly love, which Donaldson viewed as a sociological myth; Kirk (2326), the reconciliation of love issues in *Troilus;* Salter (2389), the complexity of Criseyde and Chaucer's benevolence toward her. Bloomfield (1634) argues that in the *Franklin's Tale* Chaucer moves away from the Catholic concept of love and abhorrence of adultery. Leicester (1718) reviews the Augustinian studies of the Pardoner by Miller, Huppé, Patterson, Kittredge, and Robertson, showing that the Pardoner is "the first exegetical critic of his own tale." David (2501) shows the emotionalism of *ABC* as typical religious courtly art; Leach (441) examines ambiguity and metaphor; and Anderson (668a) reflects Donaldson's late interest in Chaucerian continuations.

In his *Chaucer* (413), George Kane's position on evil, his ironic perception of Chaucer's identity as a poet, and his views of the nature of truth in poetry show a critical position similar to Donaldson's, as does P. M. Kean's highly praised two-volume work, *Chaucer and the Making of English Poetry* (420). In her examination of love visions and debates she traces a pattern of narrative development. Refreshingly free from theorizing, she shows how Chaucer worked innovations of a "naturalistic, conversational manner" upon his inherited English tradition. Influenced by Boethius, Macrobius, and the new Aristotelianism, he produced a work infused with Christian philosophy but not fourteenth-century theology.

B. Revised Historicism and Chaucer's Poetics

Also with its roots in the 1950s, the most important current trend in Chaucerian historical criticism is prompted partly by a felt need to provide an alternative both to the Robertsonian view of Chaucerian poetics and to the solipsisms of New Criticism and modern critical theories discussed below.

Typically, English and foreign literary traditions are invoked to illuminate Chaucer's poetics and his meaning. Earlier forerunners in this direction include Charles Muscatine, *Chaucer and the French Tradition,* appearing in 1957; Robert O. Payne, *The Key of Remembrance* in 1963; Robert M. Jordan, *Chaucer and the Shape of Creation* in 1967.

Muscatine analyzes courtly and bourgeois traditions in twelfth- and thirteenth-century French poetry which influenced Chaucer, demonstrating that the medieval mind held views of originality in poetic creation completely different from modern ideas—thus encouraging study of Chaucer in light of medieval aesthetics.

Payne demonstrates that contrary to early twentieth-century opinion, Chaucer's critical attitude is very similar to that of the rhetoricians, for like them he considered poetry a legitimate part of knowledge.

Jordan establishes a system of "Gothic" aesthetics, based on architectural models—a framework within which to analyze Chaucer's inorganic structure of aggregative order. He argues that Chaucer's inconsistencies, shifts in tone and focus, multiple perspectives, and discontinuities are deliberate within the Gothic system. Although opposing Robertson's exegetical emphasis, he recognizes the value of his systematic historical studies.

Among recent studies, **rhetoric** has enjoyed much attention. For a concise review and bibliography of the subject, see Robert O. Payne, "Chaucer and the Art of Rhetoric" (855), which shows the error of early twentieth-century notions (of Manly and others) that medieval literary theory had little influence on Chaucer. He also analyzes Chaucer's development as a rhetor (856). For a general treatment of the *artes praedicandi, artes dictaminis,* and *artes poeticae,* see James J. Murphy, *Rhetoric in the Middle Ages* (2658), and also his edition of essays, *Medieval Eloquence* (2657).

Stephen Knight's *Rymyng Craftily* (429) examines Chaucer's rhetorical and poetical devices as related to his meaning, showing Chaucer's development from the early poetry through the *Canterbury Tales.* He provides a very useful appendix of the Latin names of rhetorical and poetical devices. John P. McCall, *Chaucer Among the Gods* (453), develops Chaucer's use of classical materials to illuminate Chaucerian poetics, showing that Chaucer's poetics of comedy, tragedy, and allegory in his adaptations—his "rhetorics of fragmentation and discontinuity"—convey acceptance of the self and the world.

One of the strongest among these recent trends is the study of **medieval literary theory**, which balances and counters both the Robertsonian system and modern critical theory. A significant figure in the movement, Judson Boyce Allen, *The Ethical Poetic of the Later Middle Ages* (246), studies medieval literary commentators, who commonly conceived of literary works as belonging to ethics. They describe literature in terms of the *forma tractandi* (categories of socially acceptable principles and behavior) and the *forma tractatus* (methods for organizing and dividing the text).

Said to mark the "beginning of a new era" in the criticism and interpretation of medieval literature, A. J. Minnis's *Medieval Theory of Authorship: Scholastic Literary Attitudes in the Later Middle Ages* (465) discovers in materials studied in medieval universities—glosses and prologues of the Latin *auctores* and biblical commentaries and exegeses—a wealth of primary materials for establishing a medieval theory of authorship which emphasizes the relationship between *auctor* and *auctoritas*. The final chapter applies this complex heritage (1100–1400) to Chaucer. In one article (463) Minnis further argues the value of academic prologues in medieval literary criticism; in another (461), referring to theories of alterity (Jauss), he stresses the importance of establishing the "horizon of expectancy" of the medieval audience through medieval literary theory, rather than emphasizing its "modernity." Rosemary Wass (573) also studies Chaucer's relationship to medieval Scholasticism. Future studies of Chaucer's poetics and meaning must recognize these contributions. In fact, interest in medieval rhetoric and literary theory is already generating new critical studies.

Among these should be mentioned Judson Boyce Allen and Theresa Anne Moritz, *A Distinction of Stories* (957). Professing allegiance to historical criticism, they use medieval literary theory, themes, criticism, and structural principles derived from commentaries on Ovid to present a heuristic proposal that the *Canterbury Tales* can be seen as a *distinctio*—a work presenting various aspects of a simple subject. Rejecting the frame-tale theory and the central role of the tellers, they suggest an order and unity based upon thematic interlacing between tales.

Literary genres and topoi which may have influenced Chaucer have similarly been studied. F. Anne Payne, *Chaucer and Menippean Satire* (488) traces a neglected genre demanding complex reader response as a meaningful context for understanding Chaucer's poetics and his work. Peter Yeager (589) examines Chaucer's exempla in light of their distinguishing characteristics, backgrounds, literary traditions, and functions. Within the context of the traditional lament for the dead, Renate Haas (374, 375) studies in Chaucer the laments of lovers and mourners for the dead. Examining the *agere et pati* topos in *The Condition of Creatures* (323), Georgia Ronan Crampton illustrates the use of the suffering and action theme in Chaucer's *Knight's Tale* and Spenser's *Faerie Queene*. The theory of comedy is the subject of an introductory essay by Paul G. Ruggiers, ed., *Versions of Medieval Comedy* (2674).

A. C. Spearing, *Medieval Dream Poetry* (547), traces and analyzes the literary traditions of dreams and dream poetry behind Chaucer's dream visions; James Winny, *Chaucer's Dream Poems* (586), studies medieval dream theory as it relates to Chaucer's dream poems and his development as a poet.

In most of the above studies of medieval literary theory, as well as in others discussed below, Chaucer's development as a poet is a concomitant interest. Joerg O. Fichte, *Chaucer's 'Art Poetical': A Study of Chaucerian Poetics* (348), traces Chaucer's development as he moves through courtly love, morality, order, and conscious concern for the art of poetry—from his early period to his more mature awareness of philosophical, aesthetic, and moral aspects, and to his recognition of poetry as the supreme ordering agent in a chaotic world.

In *Chaucerian Fiction* (305), Burlin traces Chaucer's development from poetic through philosophical to psychological fiction. Through close readings which examine Chaucer's use of his sources, Winthrop Wetherbee's *Chaucer and the Poets: An Essay on 'Troilus and Criseyde'* (2451) traces Chaucer's strategies as he advances from "making" to the art of poetry. Piero Boitani, *Chaucer and the Imaginary World of Fame* (2073), presents the history and meaning of the idea of Fame, Chaucer's sources, and the contemporary tradition.

Legend of Good Women figures prominently in these studies. Derek Brewer, *Towards a Chaucerian Poetic* (297), shows that the *Prologue* is the key to Chaucer's poetics within the medieval tradition. According to Judson Boyce Allen, *The Ethical Poetic of the Later Middle Ages* (246), Chaucer's revision of this "poem about making poems" especially reveals his concern with the philosophy of poetic language. Lisa Kiser, *Telling Classical Tales* (2141), argues that Chaucer subtly contests prevalent medieval theories about the nature and design of poetry. In *The Strumpet Muse* (326), Alfred David shows that Chaucer's search in the *Legend of Good Women* for new poetic subjects is realized in the *Can-*

terbury Tales. Throughout his poetry, argues David, Chaucer the artist wars with Chaucer the moralist, the artist eventually winning out in *Troilus*.

C. Modern Critical Theories

In addition to the school of New Criticism, a number of other modern literary theories have been applied to Chaucer within the recent past. Like New Criticism they address themselves to problems ignored by historicism—problems concerning the nature of the literary as distinguished from the non-literary. Depending upon the aspect privileged, a theory may deal with relationship of author to text, of text to reality, of text to reader, or with the nature of language and form and their relationship to text and meaning. Addressing specific problems in practical criticism but with varying emphases, these theories search for universal principles which hold true for all literature. By its brevity the following discussion ignores many of the subtleties and ramifications of these abstruse and complicated systems, attempting merely to establish a minimum adequate context within which to review recent Chaucerian criticism which reflects or reacts to them.

A previous literary theory with close affinities to New Criticism but unknown to the early New Critics is **formalism**, a rigorous and consistent system developed by Russian and Czechoslovak critics (5. Jefferson, 16–37; 11. Selden, 6–22). Around the figure of Roman Jakobson, arose a Moscow movement (1914–1930) which later influenced the Prague school. Russian formalists assumed that literature is a primary and independent object and that the study of it is an independent science divorced from historicism and from the concomitant mimetic and expressive theories. Concerned with the language of poetry, formalism focuses on the *difference* between literature and other writing, a difference constituted in *defamiliarization,* or "making strange." Dominant elements in a piece of literature are identifiable by their greater degree of defamiliarization. Jakobson defines poetry as "organized violence committed on ordinary speech" (2. Erlich, 219). This tortured quality of language and form revivifies and intensifies vision and experience. Further, Jakobson proposes a "bipolar" structure of language recognizing not only the factors present but also the factors absent. Considering as irrelevant the author as source of the work, formalists see the author as product of the work. The patterned language of poetry is a universe valuable in itself without reference to external reality, or to author, or to historical circumstances; and the history of poetry develops through the constant renewal of language through defamiliarization.

Formalists made a distinction between story and plot: the story (*fabula*) is the raw material; the plot (*sjuzet*) is the literary form of the *fabula*. In the 1980s Gerard Genette refines this theory to accommodate conditions of performance or discourse.

In practical application formalists, like New Critics, recognize intricate multiplex networks of oppositions and equivalences. They differ from New Critics chiefly in their lack of interest in meaning. For them form has priority: content is inextricable from form; indeed, formal devices constitute the content. Their position on referentiality also sets formalists apart from structuralists, with whom they share many other perceptions. In the late twenties and early thirties formalism was deformed by the Marxist-influenced Bakhtin School (see Marxist criticism below) which denied that language works in a semiotic vacuum, that it can be separated from its ideological contexts (compare Foucault below).

The basis for structuralism (10. Robey, 38–64; 11. Selden, 52–71) was provided by the Geneva theorist Ferdinand de Saussure, who developed a sign theory or system of **semiotics** in the first decade of the twentieth century. He hypothesized that the constituents of language are signs, which are related not to reality but to each other. A sign is made up of two parts like two sides of a coin: the *signifier,* spoken or written, and the *signified,* the idea or mental construct. While it functions independently of reality, the *langue,* this self-sufficient closed system of signs, makes possible each instance of communication or *parole;* thought depends upon it, is impossible without it. *Langue* rather than *parole* is the proper object of scientific inquiry. Saussure introduced the important distinction between language study which is *synchronic* (or syntagmatic) and that which is *diachronic* (or associative). The method of traditional philology is largely diachronic, concerned with historical changes. Synchronic study examines the internal functioning of a language system to determine how the language works at a certain point in time. Like the formalists, Saussure was interested in the way language structures the experience of things.

Prague **structuralism** synthesizes Saussurean linguistics and semiotics with Russian formalism (10. Robey, 43–48). All aspects of a literary text, not merely the forms and devices of defamiliarization, become susceptible to "scientific" structural analysis. Not just in literature but in any communication, structuralists recognize a variety of functions: the emotive generated by the author, the conative received by the audience, the metalinguistic coding of grammar, the poetic message, and so on. Thus structuralists do not rule out author and cultural contexts. In agreement with formalism and Saussurean linguistics that literary meaning is a function of a closed system of signs, structuralism goes beyond them, however, in the view that meaning is still *related* to the real world, though literature itself is self-sufficient and non-referential to anything outside itself. Early in the movement structuralists concentrated on the individual text; later, on the structure of literature as a whole. Since they are willing to examine the holistic aesthetic effect of a text, the scope of inquiry is theoretically boundless, and in practice structuralists run into problems of setting limits and the risk of tedium; but the dominant or most highly deformed features of a text (defamiliarization) as well as critical subjectivity prejudice choice and set some boundaries.

In the 1960s, guided by the theories of Lévi-Strauss, French structuralism (6. Jefferson, 85–88) or structural anthropology expanded the linguistic model to encompass non-linguistic systems. **Semiology**, the science of signs, is central to this school. As in language, the individual elements (signs) of social behavior have meaning only within the context of the entire code; thus culture becomes a language and various non-linguistic institutions are subject to analysis on the linguistic model. Only one aspect in the comprehensive scope of structuralism, literary theory encourages a multidisciplinary approach involving such fields as semiotics, philosophy, history, anthropology, and psychoanalysis. The central aim, however, is to master the text. An important figure in structuralist narratology, Vladimir Propp, developed a set of thirty-one functions in Russian fairy tales which proved useful in structuralist studies of various other narrative genres.

Structuralist literary theory differentiates between reading, criticism, and poetics. Shifting focus from the specific text to literature in general, structuralism promotes a "science" of poetics, which assumes textual derivation from a macrocosmic model, the text itself being a microcosm of poetics (6. Jefferson, 97–99). The idea that literature is "metaliterary" in its self-awareness and self-reflexivity weakens distinction between literature and criticism. Further, criticism, itself posing the same sorts of problems as literature, becomes subject to structural analysis. Structuralism thus logically leads to a questioning of critical discourse and of itself. The text is set against itself.

In the 1970s Barthes and Derrida ushered in the age of **post-structuralism** (11. Selden, 74–78, 84–88; 6. Jefferson, 100–10). This movement questions the world as text and our ability to gain control over the text because of the slipperiness of linguistic, historical, or psychological forces involved not only in the production but also in the reception of the text.

Barthes rejected the structuralist microcosmic-macrocosmic view of poetics, objecting to the idea that the structure of literature is modelled upon the structure of language. He sees a contradiction in the structuralist theory that the literary text is self-sufficient and non-referential and the structuralist practice of using a "scientific" referential language to refer to it. The chief subject of poetry, he thinks, is the act of poetry itself, a self-referentiality. Giving prominence to production over meaning, Barthes puts foremost the act of writing and rejects the formalist and structuralist view of the text as a closed system. He sees the process informed by several codes irreducible to structure—codes shared by author and reader, but not referred to by the text. Thus inconclusive, the text does not permit closure, is open-ended. Reality itself is a sort of text; efforts to convey reality (a good example would be the *effictio*) convey instead the problems of representation.

Working within structuralism, Derrida also questions structuralist views of poetics and semiology, by refusing to accept their "logocentrism," i.e., taking texts at face value (6. Jefferson, 104–5; 11. Selden, 85). Opposing the formalist theory which holds that the characterizing principle of defamiliarization sets poetry apart from other discourse, he contends that all language, even that of science, is characterized by *différance,* a word appropriately chosen like many in the Derridean vocabulary for its own ambiguity, multiple meanings, and resistance to definition, but in one aspect suggesting the slippage between signifier and signified. By undermining the reliability of word and text, Derrida undermines structuralist and formalist "scientific" theories which give preeminence to the word or the language of the text. Thus, Derrida replaces structuralism with **deconstruction**. In opposition to Derrida, Paul Zumthor, *La póesie et la voix dans la civilisation médiévale* (2693), objects to Derrida's emphasis on the written word as the chief medium of culture. He sees as a vicious habit of mind the European tradition of sacralizing the written word, and forgetting how much of medieval culture was transmitted orally.

Drawing on the Nietzschean theory of knowledge as a manifestation of the will to power, Michel Foucault (11. Selden, 98–101) also rejects the structuralist reduction of the world to a mere set of texts: man first decides what he wants and then structures a discourse of facts to fit his desires—a discourse with internal censorship, conscious or unconscious, of information that does not fit, a discourse supported by education systems and social pressures. Thus, knowledge is never free from the subjective: we see what we want to see and structure knowledge and discourse accordingly. This holds true for "science" as well as for criticism of the literature of the past.

Since the act of speaking or writing of these matters assumes a process which the theory denies, deconstruction itself is bound to deconstruct, for the only appropriate response to acceptance of the lack of objective knowledge and the indeterminacy of meaning is the solipsism of total silence. And yet its skepticism is a needed corrective to the epistemological arrogance of the partial truths and falsehoods of specialized and analytical "sciences."

The chief **reader-oriented theories** (11. Selden, 106–27), which bring to the front reader consciousness, derive from a philosophical subjectivism which rejects the objective certainties of positivism and nineteenth-century science. T. S. Kuhn has demonstrated that even in science perception of facts depends upon subjective frames of reference. Reader-oriented critical theories assume an active role for the actual reader, who is of course not the same as the author-intended reader.

Phenomenological criticism (11. Selden, 110–12) describes how the consciousness becomes aware of a work of art. These theories draw upon the phenomenology of Husserl, which recognizes the perceiver's centrality in determining meaning. Perceiver consciousness reveals not only itself but the objective reality, or phenomena perceived, and does away with reductive systems. Paul Ricoeur has called Freud, Nietzsche, and Marx "protagonists of suspicion," because all three question consciousness, the origin of all meaning (9. Ricoeur, 99). Phenomenologically oriented critical theory examines a writer's work from the critic's consciousness, which allows him to enter the author's mind and his world. This "logocentric" approach assumes that the meaning of the author can be transferred to the reader. While philosophically and epistemologically more articulate, logocentrism in the final analysis bears some resemblance to the "feeling" approach of the deliberately "naive" reader. Wolfgang Iser's reader theory (5. Lentricchia, 148–50; 11. Selden, 112–14) is phenomenological: although the reader is provided by "response-inviting" clues in the text, he must refer to extra-literary norms (cf. Barthes' codes) to fill in the gaps (compare Jakobson's bipolar theory). The process of reading requires a series of adjustments in expectation as the reader resolves the contradictions presented by the text.

Hans-Georg Gadamer (5. Lentricchia, 150–54; 11. Selden, 111–12) adopts the situational approach of Heidegger, a follower of Husserl. In Heideggerian thinking, the perceiver simultaneously projects and is subjected to the world; he is merged with the object of his perception; he is part of it. Thus, he is never divorced from the historical (though the historical is internal) and meaning depends upon the historical. All interpretations require the critic to enter a dialogue with the past.

Focusing on reader expectations, or *Rezeption-ästhetik,* Hans Robert Jauss (11. Selden, 114–16), also influenced by Heidegger and the **hermeneutics** of Gamader, adds another historical factor to reader response theory. Critics of the literature of any period apply period-specific criteria, or they have in his phrase, "horizon and expectations" regarding such things as genre and poetic characteristics. Recognition of this *alterität,* however, is not the complete range of reader response, which changes through the ages in accordance with reader expectation dictated partly by cultural environment.

Jonathan Culler's identification of the regularities in reader strategy derives from structuralism (1. Cullers, Ch. 1); in a deconstructive reader response theory, Barthes sees the reader as endlessly playing with codes to create his own meanings (6. Jefferson, 100–3). Whatever the philosophic origin, reader-response theories challenge the text-oriented schools of criticism.

As the term suggests, **psychoanalytic criticism** privileges the unconscious (8. Ray, Part II: 13. Wright, 113–33). Freudian psychoanalysis saw literature as a "symptom" of the writer, his fictional characters being images of himself. Whereas classic Freudianism emphasized the writer, some recent theorists apply psychoanalytic analogies to the text, rather than to characters or authors. The structure of desire working among characters of an author's fiction entails rhetorical discontinuities and dislocations. Joel Fineman (349), dealing with concepts of Jakobson, Saussure, Lévi-Strauss, Freud, Heidegger, and Derrida, applies the structure of desire to allegory.

Rejecting Freud's crude phallocentrism, Jacques Lacan (13. Wright, 119–31) reworks Freudianism in structuralist and Derridean terms. While Derrida deconstructs writer and text, Lacan deconstructs reader and text. Even the unconscious is structured by language, which links sounds with thoughts or unconscious fantasies, but language is not fixed and fluctuates with the context. Since desire is never realized in the terms of its imagination, language is not an accurate vehicle for the unconscious.

Certain theorists in the psychoanalytic camp have shifted from the objective paradigm of the text to the subjective paradigm of reader perception. In America the reader response school is represented chiefly by Norman Holland and David Bleich (8. Ray, 62–89). They see the text as a way of revising reader identity through making acceptable socially unacceptable fantasies of the unconscious. Reader perception shapes the object of observation. The reader internalizes the text and, like the analyst, searches for the reality behind fiction. Subjective criticism philosophically denies the existence of objective facts; perception of facts depends upon the perceiver's mental structure, colored by desire. Psychoanalytic reader response theory assumes that the primary drive of the reader is to know himself.

Feminist criticism (1. Culler, 43–64; 11. Selden, Ch. 6) is likewise variously derived and exerts itself in various directions, dealing with such matters as female experience; biological role; sex role, acculturation, and stereotyping; gender theories; political, social, economic and sexual oppression; the language of power (phallologism); and the feminine unconscious. In literary criticism, beginning with Kate Millet, a chief function has been to reveal the male-shaped and male-directed character of literature, to expose and subvert patriarchal sexist ideology. While most feminists violently reject Freud and his view of woman as passive and penis-envying, Juliet Mitchell (11. Selden, 140) accepts Freud, contending that Freudian psychoanalysis is not an advocacy of but an exposure of patriarchy.

Lacan deconstructs Freudian phallocentrism, rejecting biological determinism and metaphorizing the phallus as he recognizes its role in language. Like Lacan, many feminists reject highly abstruse critical theory, and in sympathy with the playfulness and inconclusiveness of Derrida and Lacan, find their most satisfying roles as critical theorists in the debunking of male-produced theories such as those discussed above— identifying as "female" any approach which subverts the arrogance, fraudulence, and partial truth of specialized male "scientific" theories, preferring to male "closure" the play of endless possibility in meaning. Julia Kristeva and Hélène Cixous (11. Selden, 143) believe that the openness to possibility in poetic creativity is related to female sexuality.

While feminist theory has rejected much of the male-produced modern critical theory, much of feminist criticism has yet reflected it. Avant-garde feminists are calling for women to develop their own voice, to reflect their own consciousness and values. Gynocritics deals with the radical difference between men's and women's writing and calls for correcting the omission of the whole tradition of female writing from critical recognition (11. Selden, 135–39). Feminist criticism dealing with social and economic and political factors easily moves into Marxist criticism.

Marxist criticism (3. Forgacs, 134–69; 11. Selden, 23–51) is founded on Marx's idea that social and economic conditions determine consciousness. The theory holds that literature, which ranks alongside philosophy, religion, and politics in the superstructure supported by the socio-economic substructure, can be understood only in terms of the substructure as a reflection of socio-economic realities. Understanding can move both ways: from the substructure to the superstructure or vice versa. The concerns of Russian formalism for linguistic structure in literature were modified in the late twenties by Mikhail Bakhtin (3. Forgacs, 160–65) and followers, who added to these linguistic concerns the denial that language can be divorced from history and from ideology. The chief concern of the Bakhtin School, anti-Stalinist in its persuasion, was the dynamic living social impact of discourse as subversion of authority to bring about change. For Bakhtin the carnival is an attractive image for textual multiplexity and resistance to unity: the normal order is turned upside down; distinctions are blurred; everything authoritative is mocked. In some ways Bakhtin in his emphasis on textual instability is a forerunner of deconstructionism.

Georg Lukács (11. Selden, 28–31) in the 1960s and '70s, however, is recognized as the first important figure in Marxist criticism. Literary works, he believes, are reflections of the realities and contradictions inherent in social systems. A true literary work rises above the common perceptions of reality to allow the reader to see the dialectic in the evolution of socio-economic systems and the complexities and contradictions in the nature of existence. He rejects the closed subjectivity and formalistic innovations of modernism.

While **modern critical theories applied to Chaucer** have rarely resulted in radical new findings, such specialized perspectives focused freshly upon the *idée fixe* or recognized given in Chaucer's work have stimulated a great deal of controversy and a healthy reexamination of traditional approaches, thus contributing substantially to the dialectic which keeps criticism alive. The studies discussed below vary widely in the degree of rigor with which they apply the various critical stances. Many studies indexed under Structure, for example, employ the concept rather casually without extensive or strict reference to structuralist theory. I have tried to select for discussion only those studies deliberately oriented toward or reacting against modern critical schemes.

Peter Haidu, "Repetition: Modern Reflections on Medieval Aesthetics," *MLN* 92 (1977), 875–87, argues that in its self-referentiality the artistic language of poetry represents a loss in primal referential function and a consequent cultural impoverishment. Similarly, in an important study in Chaucerian semiotics, "Mervelous Signals: Poetics, Sign Theory, and Politics in Chaucer's *Troilus*" (2443), Eugene Vance relates verbal signs to social order, arguing a metalinguistic consciousness in the poetics of *Troilus*. Using modern sign theory and theories of Augustine, Aquinas, Ockham, and Duns Scotus, he correlates decadence in language use and the weakening of social fabric. On the other hand, arguing that "we must bring medieval theory to the assistance of modern," Winthrop Wetherbee (578) says that a critical method based on linguistics and sign theory is potentially reductive in its "tendency to contrast the self-betraying convention with the absolute, stable significance of the Word." David Aers (2163) examines reflexivity in *Parliament of Fowls*. Semiotics is also a chief concern of Ingeborg M. Ullman, *Der Erzähler der 'Canterbury Tales'* (1159).

The term "sign" in *Signs and Symbols in Chaucer's Poetry* (61), discussed above, and in Hermann's article (1765), refers mainly to symbols, iconographic motifs, themes, figurative language, and not primarily to semiotic theories. In the same way that Prague structuralists see a metalinguistic structure in all kinds of communication, not just in language, Robert B. Benson (263) studies gesture in Chaucer as a body language modified by genre; Rowland (523) discusses the classical tradition of *pronuntatio* involving voice, gesture, and facial expression, examining its possible semantic role in Chaucer's oral delivery.

A number of modern theorists and critical theories are invoked by Piero Boitani, *La Narrative del Medioeve Inglese* (280)—including Bakhtin and the Russian formalists, Genette and the structuralists—to analyze romance, dream poems, sermons, exempla, etc. He charts the development of narrative from simple story telling for edification or amusement to complex, consciously artistic works like Chaucer's.

In book-length studies the *Canterbury Tales* has been analyzed structurally: in Howard (1052) by the principle of interlacement and the labyrinth; in Helen Cooper (995) by interlacement in a system of Gothic aesthetics; in Allen and Moritz (957) by themes. Elizabeth Salter and Derek Pearsall, "Chaucer's Realism" (529), analyze the balance in the *Canterbury Tales* and *Troilus* between formal structuring, incidental detail, moralizing, exaggeration, and grotesquerie. Drawing upon the societal structuralism and binary oppositions of Lévi-Strauss, Frederick Turner (1305) considers the *Knight's Tale* a closed system myth which encodes cultural norms of its time period. Britton J. Harwood (1340) also analyzes the *Miller's Tale* structurally as a myth; Wallace Martin and Nick Conrad (1768) call upon the Russian formalists, Lévi-Strauss, and Barthes for a formal analysis of traditional fictions and demonstrate that the Lévi-Strauss formula for myth structure applied to its analogues illuminates the *Shipman's Tale*. Thomas D. Cooke, *The Old French and Chaucerian Fabliaux* (993), analyzes structural humor in comic climaxes of the fabliaux. Laury Magnus (1650) applies formalist theory of free and bound motifs to the black rocks digression in the *Franklin's Tale*: a bound motif is essential to the story, but the inessential free motif may provide an essential focus. Michio Masui (1801) examines the interrelatedness of theme, structure, and meaning in the *Prioress's Tale*. Piero Boitani, *Chaucer and the Imaginary World of Fame* (2073), identifies an archetypal structure—labyrinth, castle-palace, cave, desert, flight—for Fame, the goddess of language, myth, and poetry.

Opposing efforts such as these, N. F. Blake (973) argues that given the elusiveness of Chaucer and the fragmentary condition of the *Canterbury Tales,* no structural analysis can be totally valid. In *Towards a Chaucerian Poetic* (297) and "Some Metonymic Relationships in Chaucer" (in 288), D. S. Brewer objects on other grounds. Drawing upon concepts of Jakobson and Propp, he argues a linear metonymic syntagmic operation in Chaucer's works, rather than relationships through vertical structure of similarities or oppositions.

Formalist and structuralist analyses of *Troilus* are reviewed perceptively in Alice Kaminsky, *Chaucer's 'Troilus and Criseyde' and the Critics* (2321). Thomas Elwood Hart (2303) uses medieval structuralism to analyze the five-book design of *Troilus*. William Provost, *The Structure of Chaucer's 'Troilus and Criseyde'* (2374), identifies three structural units: books, narrative units, and time units.

Roland Barthes' idea in "The Death of the Author," in *Image/Music/Text,* trans. Stephen Heath (New York, 1977), is discussed in Denis Walker's argument for structuralist attention to the text (572). Walker notes that the idea follows from the basic premises of structuralism and of the New Critics' abhorrence of the "intentional fallacy." Judith Ferster, "Intention and Interpretation in the *Book of the Duchess*" (2018), says that this perception is inevitable in the very nature of writing, which outlives its author. Wayne C. Booth, *A Rhetoric of Irony* (Chicago, 1974), maintains that the author is never invisible, but always present—not biographically but as a rhetorical construct; and Denis Walker (572) observes that of all interpretive constructs in the act of reading none is more persistent than the author; but H. Marshall Leicester, Jr. (1078), in a deconstructionist argument holds that the only voice is that of the text; hence "Chaucer the maker" gives over to "Chaucer the poem." Carolyn Dinshaw (331) argues that it is necessary to accept two opposing critical views of the author: (1) the commonsense view of the "author behind the text"; and (2) the modern critical view of the author as a "construct" or function of the text designed to limit the "proliferation of meaning."

Anthropological frameworks have been employed by various modern critical theorists. Depending upon such works as Van Gennep, *The Rites of Passage,* studies of liminality involve rituals for important events. Thomas Pison, "Liminality in the *Canterbury Tales*" (1115), sees the pilgrimage as a liminal phase, a rite of passage, in which everyday decorum is in abeyance under the governance of Harry Bailley, the "ritual elder." In a similar study, James R. Andreas (962) shows that the pilgrimage, combining religion and comedy, blurs social hierarchies and sexual distinctions. Morton Bloomfield (1514) suggests that the *Friar's Tale* as a liminal tale reflects the entire experience of the *Canterbury Tales.* Taking as a point of departure the formalist-Marxist Mikhail Bakhtin's study of the medieval folk festival, Edith Kern, *The Absolute Comic* (423), views the characters in the *Miller's Tale* in the grotesquerie and moral vacuum of the folk festival spirit of absolute comedy. Anthropological insights are available in folk literature, as is seen in the collection of essays by Thomas J. Heffernan (60).

Unconvinced of the applicability of anthropological structuralist analyses to Chaucer, Derek Brewer, *Symbolic Stories: Traditional Narratives of the Family Drama in English Literature* (296), examines the motif of the rite of passage into adulthood, in which the individual destroys the image of the parent, replacing it with the image of a beloved equal. He demonstrates that Chaucer is ambivalent or negative toward the motif.

Basic to linguistic structuralism and "deconstructed" in post-structuralism, referentiality occupies the attention of Richard Allen Shoaf in *Dante, Chaucer, and the Currency of the Word* (540). Influenced by Dante, Chaucer developed a late medieval poetics of reference, a theory of mediation or a poetics of exchange whose currency is the word. The economics of exchange is seen in the *Canterbury Tales* in the motif of "quiting." Influenced by Derrida and deconstruction, Shoaf's book is characterized by Derridean playfulness. (Connections between coins and language are also explored in traditional terms by Gerhard Joseph [1766] and Walter Scheps [1742].) In another article (541) Shoaf observes that in the Middle Ages faith in the communion between language and reality was stronger than it is today.

On the contrary, Robert M. Jordon (407) argues that Chaucer, like modern theorists, was concerned with the reliability of language in accounting for reality and that, in fact, Chaucer himself exploits the gap between language and reality. Karla Taylor (2428) similarly theorizes that Chaucer's proverbs in *Troilus* reveal his perceptions of the limitations of language while they simultaneously validate truth. Judith Ferster

(2018) emphasizes the difficulty of communication in *Book of the Duchess*.

Essays by various hands edited by David Lyle Jeffrey, *By Things Seen: Reference and Recognition in Medieval Thought* (2558), deal with medieval ideas regarding referral, referentiality, etc. In his own introduction to the book, Jeffrey identifies a key idea: medieval Christian epistemology was based upon a theory of limited understanding. John M. Fyler, *Chaucer and Ovid* (618), argues that Chaucer had an epistemological skepticism that questioned whether the artist was capable of establishing visions and structures of understanding adequate to effective action.

At the center of modern critical theory, the book, the text, and the act of writing have assumed metaphorical and structural importance, most notably in *The Idea of the Book in the Middle Ages: Language Theory, Mythology, and Fiction* (365), by Jesse M. Gellrich, who uses insights of Lévi-Strauss, Foucault, Barthes, and Derrida to treat the history of textuality from Augustine to Chaucer and to examine the relationship of literature to other medieval cultural forms—architecture, Scholasticism, music, etc.—forms that are often expressed metaphorically as a book. Referring to Curtius, "The Book as Symbol" in *European Literature and the Latin Middle Ages* (New York, 1963); to G. Josipovici, *The World and the Book* (London, 1971); and to the *Poetria Nova* of Geoffry of Vinsauf, Paula Neuss (473) analyzes the architectural image of writing and the book and the equation of "making" and love-making. Judith Ferster examines the topos of the world as text (2174) and characters as texts (346).

Concerned with the linearity of narrative (cf. Brewer, 297, 288 above) and of time, John Ganim, *Style and Consciousness in Middle English Narrative* (2287), revises perceptions of those who see medieval narrative poetry as structured like architecture or other models in the visual arts. (See Gellrich [365], Neuss [473], Cooper [995] and Jordan, *Chaucer and the Shape of Creation*.) Also, according to Richard Lock, *Aspects of Time in Medieval Literature* (448), concepts of time in oral traditions differ from those in literate traditions.

Reader response theories have opened up many shifting and misty areas between Chaucer's own intentions and the impressions of modern readers and critics. Paul Strohm, "Chaucer's Audience(s): Fictional, Implied, Intended, Actual" (557), analyzes the complex problem of ascertaining Chaucer's audiences—which include the fictional *General Prologue* audience, the real audience of Chaucer's day, and today's audience—all of whom can be simultaneously functional. The complexity of reader response is recognized by Alfred David, *The Strumpet Muse* (326).

Impressionistic studies which might be seen as reader response have been ignored in this review when they lack a philosophic or critical framework. The most valuable reader response studies represent thoughtful reactions and insights into modern critical theorists such as Jauss. Distinguishing between "modernity" and Jauss's *alterität,* Alistair J. Minnis, "Chaucer and Comparative Literary Theory" (461), maintains that it is important to establish—through a careful study of late medieval literary theory—the "horizon of expectancy" of *Chaucer's audience.* This horizon changes with each age. John A. Burrow, *Medieval Writers and Their Work* (2610), deals with the ideas behind Middle English literature and with the attitudes to it in later ages.

In "Chaucer and the Modern Reader" (492), Derek Pearsall recognizes the perennial tendency to "hold Chaucer up to the mirror of our own civilization and culture rather than to recognize in him a window . . . into the culture of another age." The fifteenth century praised Chaucer for eloquent rhetoric and sententiousness; the sixteenth, for his attacks on clerical abuse. In the debate of Nature versus Art, the seventeenth century thought he represented Nature. Offering little criticism, the eighteenth century saw the beginnings of Chaucer scholarship. The nineteenth praised him for psychological realism; New Criticism of the twentieth, for his ambiguity, irony, tension, and paradox.

Karla Taylor (2429) points out that since medieval detractors of literature rejected authorial intent as a criterion of moral worth in a text, medieval critics and writers themselves, especially mythographers, located the meaning in the reader. Not what the author intended, but what the reader perceived was important. Concerning fourteenth-century reader reponse, Charlotte C. Morse (1562) gives evidence that the tale of Griselda was understood as exemplary rather than allegorical.

Using the phenomenological hermeneutics of Gadamer and Ricoeur, Judith Ferster, *Chaucer on Interpretation* (346) focuses on the relationship between text and interpreter, identifying the following principles (restated by Joerg O. Fichte) as useful for interpreting Chaucer:

> (1) the subjectivity of the interpreter; (2) the alterity or otherness of the work he confronts; (3) the influence of the tradition on the interpreter's prejudgment . . . ; (4) the resulting hermeneutical cycle of subject-object relationship; (5) the act of interpretation resulting in a process of self-discovery; and (6) interpretation as a never-ending process. (*SAC* 9 [1987], p. 215)

In connection with the *Prioress's Tale,* Terence George Collins (1785) studies reader response to racial literature; Elbow (342), reader response to *Troilus;* Ferster (2174), the phenomenology of reading in the *Parliament of Fowls* and (2017) the epistemology of Chaucer's early dream visions. In his focus on *Troilus* in *Style and Consciousness in Middle English Narrative* (2287), John M. Ganim gives a "revised theory of late medieval literary history based on the relationship of the poet to the reader": the reader of *Troilus* becomes a character in the text and this produces discontinuity and disorientation, limiting the scope of reader response.

The phenomenological theories of perception articulated by Maurice Merleau-Ponty are brought to bear upon the *Miller's Tale* by Patrick J. Gallacher (1334). Merleau-Ponty holds that "the perceived world is an ensemble of routes taken by the body." The three males in the tale have imperfect perceptions and expectations.

The fragmentary state of several of Chaucer's works and the inconclusive nature of others have long occupied critics, but in light of post-structuralist deconstructive and reader response theory, these features have come into new prominence. Such studies are indexed under Inconclusiveness, Closure, Endings, and Indeterminacy. In his study of Chaucer's inconclusive epistemology, *Virtue of Necessity: Inconclusiveness and Narrative Form in Chaucer's Poetry* (544), Larry Sklute argues that in the spirit of the cognitive indeterminacy of late medieval nominalism, Chaucer in his major works avoided closed and authoritative determinations of meaning and moral values. Crampton (324) shows that both Spenser and Chaucer offered their audiences a subtle complex of closures; Holahan (391) argues that doctrine is the "outer limit" of Chaucer's works with unresolved endings. Anne Crehan Stolz (555) argues that Chaucer's unfinishedness, a characteristic of both the fragmentary and the apparently complete works, has a semantic function in the aesthetic vision which he inherited and put to use; the quality of philosophic indeterminacy increases the multiplicity of his meaning and the richness of his vision.

In the opinion of Gellrich (1189) Chaucer questions the nature of poetic structure by leaving the *Canterbury Tales* incomplete. Burnley (306) examines indeterminacy depending on the *pitee* of Theseus in the *Knight's Tale.* Lee W. Patterson (1964), Laurie A. Finke (1956), Gale C. Schricker (1983), and David F. Marshall (1981) deal with the matter of closure in the *Parson's Tale* and *Retraction.* Tony Millns (460) argues that in Chaucer's major works the suspension of judgment, veiled and implicit at the beginnings of tales, is accomplished by Chaucer's splitting the roles of narrator and author. Denis Walker (2062) claims that though art and nature represent harmony, the text of the *Book of the Duchess* leaves the consolatory dialectic unresolved. David Aers (2163) argues that disharmony, multiplicity of authority, and "continuous self-reflexivity" prevent the *Parliament of Fowls* from exhibiting a unified orthodox theodicy, and that the poem ends inconclusively and without closure, the narrator in an open-ended quest for more books. In the *House of Fame,* Jesse Gellrich (2089) examines Chaucer's indeterminacy and transcendence through faith.

Unity theories involving reconciliation of opposites and a sense of closure through thematic resolution are presented by Rosemary Biggio, "Narrative Technique and Closure in Chaucerian Works" (265), and Elmer Jack Fashbaugh, "Chaucer's Troubled Endings" (345). Previously discussed books dealing with reconciliation of opposites—Burlin (305), David (326), Leonard (445), Owen (1106), Bishop (2233), Elbow (342), Rowe (2380)—also search for a sense of closure. Jill Mann (449) argues that Chaucer's open-endedness has its own moral significance and warns against carrying the moralizing of Chaucer to such extremes that the story makes no sense.

Psychological or psychoanalytical studies have seen a fourfold increase over 1964–1973, but only a few of these apply strict psychoanalytic theory. Invoking both Freud and medieval psychology, E. Pearlman (1563) examines the psychological basis of the *Clerk's Tale;* Douglas B. Wilson (2455) and Nikki Stiller (2411) analyze *Troilus* in Freudian terms; Maud Ellmann, "Blanche" (2015), analyzes the *Book of the Duchess* in Freudian and Lacanian terms. Eric D. Brown (1439, 1440) applies archetypal and Jungian principles to the *Wife of Bath's Tale;* Richard Gill (1705) sees the Old Man of the *Pardoner's Tale* as a Jungian archetype. Archetypes are also considered by Piero Boitani (2073), previously mentioned.

Other "psychologizing" studies attempt merely to get into the minds of Chaucer or his characters. Intentionally fictionalized, John Gardner's *The Life and Times of Chaucer* (81) has elements of the "psychobiography," and his *The Poetry of Chaucer* (363), a complementary companion to the biography, presents a reading of Chaucer's poetry "harmonious with the character of Chaucer as his own age knew and understood him" (dust jacket). Chaucer's tales dealing with love offer themselves naturally for such speculation. In *Chaucer's 'Troilus and Criseyde': A Critical Study* (2233), Ian Bishop, in developing the dialectic between *cupiditas* and *caritas,* explores the minds and emotions of the protagonists within a medieval framework. Fritz-Wilhelm Neumann

(2360) examines initiation motifs and archetypes in the *Troilus* story. Alice Kaminski (2321) provides an insightful review of psychologically oriented *Troilus* studies.

In the opinion of Florence Ridley (506), psychological studies are viable only if they are understood as constructs of the critic rather than of Chaucer.

The polemics of prejudice also draw in analyses of psychological matters. Terence George Collins (1785) analyzes the psychology of reader response to racial literature. Feminist criticism applied to Chaucer and the fourteenth century examines the conditions and views of the oppressed and the mythologies, attitudes, rationalizations, and stereotypes justifying oppression. Studies indexed under "Feminism," "Feminist Criticism," "Women," and "Women's Studies," include Arlyn Diamond (1009) on "Chaucer's Women and Women's Chaucer"; Maureen Fries (2279) on Criseyde as feminist and victim; Alkalay-Gut (245) on Chaucer's misconceptions about women; Winthrop Wetherbee (579) on Nature's femininity in medieval poetry; and Judith Ferster (2018), who observes that women are "important because they are absent." Often neglected in ordinary critical studies, but of importance to feminist concerns, the nature and nurture of children in Chaucer is examined by Owen (481).

In the effort to discover authorial prejudices, fantasies, and attitudes toward women, critics sometimes "psychologize" the author or his literary characters. Sheila Delany (1400, 1448, and 1935) presents dark, provocative, and challenging readings of Chaucer and speculations about his psycho-sexual health.

Socio-economic feminist concerns easily merge with Marxist criticism, a position deliberately assumed by Delany in her *Writing Woman* (1006). She argues that the suffering and victimization of women in the Middle Ages was a factor more of hard economic conditions than of patriarchal oppression. Also implicitly Marxist in some respects, *Chaucer, Langland and the Creative Imagination* (243) by David Aers shows that Chaucer and Langland "engage in a critical dialectic with traditional ideologies and social practices" (preface). Chaucer portrays women as victims of the commodity exchange of marriage and of patriarchal militarism.

D. The Controversy About Modern Literary Theories

In a sobering report on the health of the humanities in university curricula, Charles Muscatine in a presidential address to the New Chaucer Society, 1980, asks the question often asked (though not so elegantly) by the growing hordes of anti-intellectuals, by business-minded legislators in control of purse strings, and by the *un*intellectual young who decline to take Chaucer courses: "What Amounteth Al This Wit?" (471). He reminds us of the centrality of literature to culture and recommends that we find readings of Chaucer with modern cultural relevance. It is not yet clear to this writer that modern critical theory relates effectively to the cultural relevance that might interest the *lewed;* it is even less clear, considering the highly philosophical and sophisticated character of many modern critical theories, that they are, as some seem to feel, the province of the *lewed*. And this is not to deny them their province. But Muscatine calls for appropriate *pedagogy.*

The strength of modern literary theory is reflected in the recent establishment of two journals, *NLH* and *Assays* (426). *New Literary History: A Journal of Theory and Interpretation* welcomes "*theoretical articles on literature* that deal with such subjects as the nature of literary history, the reading process, hermeneutics, the relation of linguistics to literature, literary change, literary value, the definitions of periods and their uses in interpretation, the evolution of styles, conventions, and genres, and *articles from other disciplines that help interpret or define the problems of literary study*" (10 [1979], preface). *Assays: Critical Approaches to Medieval and Renaissance Texts,* "a forum for scholarly debate about the connections between contemporary critical theory and early texts," allows "Barthes to meet Beowulf." The journal has published articles on structuralism, deconstruction, Marxism, psychoanalysis, feminism, and so on.

Both Dante and Chaucer voiced concern about reader abuse of their texts, a concern shared by traditionalist Chaucerians, who tend to reject narrow constructions to fit preferred interpretations. Robert O. Payne (855), who questions the ability of studies in semiotics, hermeneutics, and deconstruction to contribute meaningfully to Chaucer, observes that any poet goes "on trial for having produced effects he didn't intend." Also, according to Payne (856), Chaucer himself shows awareness of these problems in his construct of the poet-narrator, who demonstrates in dealing with his sources an awareness of ancient rhetorical concerns: fallibility of persuaders, volatility of audiences, and corruptibility of language through time.

In "Convention and Authority: A Comment on Some Recent Critical Approaches to Chaucer" (578), Winthrop Wetherbee reviews Vance's study on semiotics (2443) and R. Allen Shoaf's "Notes on Chaucer's Poetics of Translation" (542), arguing that these studies are limited and reductive and need to be modified by a more comprehensive approach that would recognize Chaucer's use of the authoritative texts, rather than concentrating on peripheral or dislocated texts.

English Chaucerians are perhaps the staunchest of traditionalists. Derek Pearsall (492) deplores the disappearance of critical consensus and the decline of philology, especially in America, where at the same time the pressure to publish or perish forces scholarly publication before scholar-careerists are ready to produce. Encouraged by the "disappearance of the traditional critical consensus," some Chaucerians, he thinks, produce criticism recommended by nothing better than "hare-brained novelty." Included among these are discoveries of "an infinity of recessive ironies" by Donaldson's followers and the dogmatic orthodoxy of Robertsonianism, which "elevates a particular theological view of literature" into a universal standard. Pearsall urges us (492) to resist the limitations of modern literary critical approaches in favor of more careful study of manuscripts, of medieval literary and stylistic traditions, and of language.

Addressing himself to the above-mentioned problem of subjective irony in critical interpretations in "Epidemic Irony in Modern Approaches to Chaucer's Canterbury Tales" (1111), Pearsall warns that irony must be author-directed, not merely reader-inferred.

Similarly, in a hilarious exposé of over-zealous pun-seekers, "The Queynte Punnings of Chaucer's Critics" (260), Larry D. Benson twits those who see scatological double entendres not supported by philological examination of the text.

Also lamenting the relaxation of academic standards in "The Criticism of Medieval Literature" (336), Mary Dove attacks the misconception that criticism of medieval literature is different from or less satisfactory than criticism of modern. Criticism should seek to discern how the literary work came to be (historical genesis), what it shows us about the period, and how it is independent of its period.

What is it about Chaucer's poetry that invites such a variety of critical theories? In "Chaucer and Modernism" (554), Martin Stevens sees resemblances between medieval and modern aesthetics: both try to dehumanize art; both deform reality; both are self-referential, playful, and ironic. Robert M. Jordan (2097)—relating Chaucer's style to that of Nabokov, Joyce, and Barth—points out that Chaucer was highly accomplished in a solipsistic fictional mode centuries before the post-modernists; and E. T. Donaldson (332) slyly suggests that Chaucer himself is to blame for modern critical confusion because he opens up dilemmas and mysteries and deliberately leaves them unsolved. For similar reasons John H. Fisher (351) believes that Chaucer's poetry easily lends itself to

1

sophisticated modern approaches like reader response theories. In "The Significance of Varying Perspectives" (506), Florence Ridley traces the reception of Chaucer through the centuries, identifying three characteristics of Chaucer's poetry which continue to fascinate and invite critical commentary: "its visuality, its presentation of unchanging human behavior and its deliberate ambiguity. . . ." Hans Jauss (2636) points out that we are drawn to medieval poetry both because of its alterity and because of its modernity or universality.

Also the very nature of literature and literary criticism encourages a variety of approaches. Though he feels that critics have shamelessly distorted Chaucer, Derek Pearsall (1881) admits that "nothing that is said about literature is strictly speaking verifiable, and therefore nothing is falsifiable." Similarly, Glending Olson (476), writing on deconstruction, observes that the ideas about writing, aporias (perplexities), and language can be construed "to justify almost any reading of a text."

Receptive to certain modern critical theories in "Contemporary Literary Theory and Chaucer" (272), Morton Bloomfield distinguishes between approaches appropriate and central to Chaucer studies—rhetoric, theory of literary history, stylistics, literary structuralism, genre theory, literary biography, narratology, and literary hermeneutics—and those peripheral—semiology or semantics, linguistics, phenomenology, or linguistic philosophy, psychology (Jung, Freud), and sociology. Our goal, he says, is "to recreate and undistance the past, and that goal requires every kind of study."

In answer to Bloomfield, Florence Ridley (508) argues for the centrality and usefulness of some critical theories Bloomfield saw as peripheral: psychology, sociology, semiotics (speech-act theory), Heideggerian ontology, theories of Jauss and Iser on reader response—the latter being important to the continued popularity of Chaucer. Elsewhere (507) she suggests that Chaucerians should welcome new techniques to identify what it is about Chaucer's poetry that produces our reader responses, techniques to transcend the cultural differences between medieval and modern times. Bloomfield and Ridley not only reflect but sanction the current state of critical affairs—an acceptance which may serve like a self-fulfilling prophecy to encourage more "modern" studies in the future.

In "The Archaic and the Modern" (in 298), Derek Brewer urges caution: while Chaucer had some of the skepticism of the modern "scientific" mind, his modernism was more nearly related to the neoclassical period. His mentality is "archaic" and timeless: he had perceptions of sacredness and the interrelatedness of everything that are not available to the modern analytic and "scientific" mind. On the other hand, in "The Historicism We Need" (489), Robert O. Payne rejects as contradictory and inappropriate to medieval literature a "negative exclusivist version of historical criticism" which rules out diachronic theory. This "archaeological" view, he contends, is itself a modern view. Using the past, medieval writers were confident that they were writing for the future. We must be free to exercise our own literary judgment.

Brewer (294) calls for a "reconstruction" of Chaucer to recognize the poet's design for oral delivery and his abhorrence of allegory and "glosing"; and to achieve a fuller understanding of "small scale detail of his world." We must reject technical and specialized approaches which prevent us from a "feeling response" and "insulate us from . . . that wide-ranging, anxious, sympathetic, derisive, yet pitying consciousness, which is expressed in the sum total of Chaucer's works."

Bibliographies and Research Tools

Bibliographers have tried to keep pace. The Chaucer Bibliographies, issued by University of Toronto, is an ambitious series begun under the general editorship of A. J. Colaianne and R. M. Piersol and recently assumed by Thomas Hahn. The series is designed to provide comprehensive annotated bibliographies in separate volumes of the scholarship on Chaucer's works, groups of works, and special topics, 1900 to the present. Two in the series have appeared: Russell A. Peck, *Chaucer's Lyrics and 'Anelida and Arcite'* (22) and his *Chaucer's 'Romaunt of the Rose,'* (recently released) with several others forthcoming soon. The volumes of the Variorum Chaucer present a synthesis of Chaucer scholarship from the fifteenth century onward, thus covering about six hundred years as contrasted with less than a century covered by the Toronto series. In the interest of currency, the annual annotated Chaucer bibliographies in *Studies in the Age of Chaucer* were begun by John H. Fisher and later continued by Lorrayne Y. Baird assisted by an international search team. In addition to these new developments, the traditional *MLA, MHRA, YWES, ChauR,* and *NM* annual gatherings continue. Bege K. Bowers (9,10) has assumed the work on "Chaucer Research" and "Chaucer Research in Progress" formerly done by Thomas A. Kirby (17, 18). Two general comprehensive bibliographies cover the ten-year period immediately following William R. Crawford's *Bibliography of Chaucer 1954–1963:* Baird (1) and Fisher (198).

Selected bibliographies covering Chaucer's work are found in Baugh, second ed. (6), *The Riverside Chaucer* (191), Fisher (14), and

Leyerle and Quick's *Chaucer: A Bibliographic Introduction* (Toronto Medieval Bibliographies 10). Leyerle and Quick's bibliography (19), designed for readers relatively unfamiliar with Chaucer, is an annotated guide to more than 1200 items divided into three parts: materials for the study of Chaucer's works, Chaucer's works, and backgrounds. John H. Fisher and Mark Allen, *The Essential Chaucer: An Annotated Bibliography of Major Modern Studies* (Boston: G. K. Hall, 1987) lists and annotates 925 books and articles, most of them published in the last quarter of a century. The bibliography is divided into sections on Chaucer's life, technique, language, themes, and influence, and sections on specific works.

In addition to these general bibliographies, specialized bibliographies and research reviews feature the following: the *Canterbury Tales*, emphasizing major trends of criticism (Courtney, 11); Chaucerian apocrypha (Robbins, 2529) in Albert E. Hartung, ed., *A Manual of Writings in Middle English, 1050–1500*, vol. 4 (28); source and analogue criticism (Morris, 21). Unfortunately discovered too late for inclusion in this bibliography is Will Roger Knedlik, "Chaucer's 'Book of the Duchess': A Bibliographical Compendium of the First 600 Years," a Ph.D. dissertation, University of Washington 1978, which provides annotations through 1969.

With the exception of manuscript and textual studies, Beryl Rowland's revised edition of *Companion to Chaucer Studies* (70) presents sound and comprehensive bibliographic essays or reviews of scholarship by noted Chaucerians on the major categories of Chaucer studies. Also very useful is Derek Brewer, ed., *Geoffrey Chaucer* (49). Florence Ridley (509) presents a brief survey of twentieth-century Chaucer studies up to 1976; Larry D. Benson (261), a general review ending in 1974; Beryl Rowland, in "Contemporary Chaucer Criticism," *English* 22 (1973), 3–10, a survey through the early 1970s. General introductions to Chaucer are found in books by Brewer (285, 293), Kane (413), and Norton-Smith (474).

Several reviews of scholarship are specialized. Kaminsky (2321) gives an evaluation of some five hundred items of criticism on *Troilus and Criseyde* under headings: historical, philosophical, formalistic, and psychological. Lawler (440) reviews the scholarship on Chaucer's prose works—*Boece, Melibee, Astrolabe, Equatorie of Planetis,* and *Parson's Tale*—giving bibliography and noting desiderata for further work. Also outlining desiderata, or what remains to be done, is Görlach (902) on Chaucer's English. Gaylord (837) reviews the scholarly approaches to Chaucer's metrics, and Yeager (821), scholarship on the fifteenth century, including Hoccleve, Henryson, Douglas, Dunbar, and Gower. In addition, various books and articles too numerous to mention provide useful surveys of criticism; a notable example is Robert B. Burlin, *Chaucerian Fiction* (305). Among the basic tools for students and scholars should also be recognized *A Chaucer Dictionary* by Dillon (2831); *A Chaucer Glossary* by Davis et al. (2830); and *Who's Who in Chaucer* by Scott (2836).

Works Consulted

1. Culler, Jonathan. *On Deconstruction: Theory and Criticism After Structuralism* (Ithaca: Cornell University Press, 1982). Ch. 1, "Readers and Reading."

2. Erlich, Victor. *Russian Formalism: History—Doctrine* (The Hague, 1955, 1980).

3. Forgacs, David. "Marxist Literary Theories." In Jefferson and Robey, pp. 134–69.

4. Jefferson, Ann and David Robey, eds. *Modern Literary Theory: A Comparative Introduction* (Totowa, N.J.: Barnes & Noble Books, 1982).

5. Jefferson, Ann. "Russian Formalism." In Jefferson and Robey, pp. 16–37.

6. Jefferson, Ann. "Structuralism and Post-Structuralism." In Jefferson and Robey, pp. 84–112.

7. Lentricchia, Frank. *After the New Criticism* (University of Chicago Press, 1980).

8. Ray, William. *Literary Meanings from Phenomenology to Deconstruction* (Oxford: Basil Blackwell, 1984).

9. Ricoeur, Paul. *The Conflict of Interpretations: Essays in Hermeneutics,* ed. Don Ihde (Evanston, Ill.: Northwestern University Press, 1974).

10. Robey, David. "Modern Linguistics and the Language of Literature." In Jefferson and Robey, pp. 38–64.

11. Selden, Raman. *A Reader's Guide to Contemporary Literary Theory* (Lexington: The University Press of Kentucky, 1985).

12. Steiner, Peter. *Russian Formalism: A Metapoetics* (Ithaca: Cornell University Press, 1984).

13. Wright, Elizabeth. "Modern Psychoanalytic Criticism." In Jefferson and Robey, pp. 113–33.

Master List and Table of Abbreviations

Master List of Periodicals

AArt American Artist (Marion, OH)
A B Bookman's Weekly (Clifton, NJ)
ABR American Benedictine Review (Atchison, KS)
Acta (Binghamton, NY)
AEB Analytical and Enumerative Bibliography (Northern Illinois University, Dekalb)
AHR American Historical Review (Washington, DC)
AI American Imago: A Psychoanalytical Journal for Culture, Science and the Arts (Detroit, MI)
AL American Literature: A Journal of Literary History, Criticism, and Bibliography (Duke University, Durham, NC)
ALLCJ Association for Literary and Linguistic Computing Journal (Cambridge)
Allegorica (University of Texas at Arlington)
AN&Q American Notes and Queries (Lexington, KY)
Anglia: Zeitschrift für Englische Philologie (Tübingen)
AnM Annuale Mediaevale (Dusquesne University, Pittsburgh, PA)
ArAA Arbeiten aus Anglistik und Amerikanistik (Universität Graz, Graz, Austria)
ARBA American Reference Books Annual (Littleton, CO)
Archiv Archiv für das Studium der Neueren Sprachen und Literature (Brunswick, West Germany)
ArchMus Archiv für Musikwissenschaft (Wiesbaden, West Germany)

ARIEL   (Jamshoro, Pakistan)
Ariel: A Review of Arts and Letters in Israel (University of Calgary,
              Alberta, Canada)
ArL   Archivum Linguisticum: A Review of Comparative
              Philology and General Linguistics (University of
              Leeds, Ilkley, Yorks)
ArQ   Arizona Quarterly (University of Arizona, Tucson)
Arts: The Journal of the Sydney Arts Association (Sydney, Australia)
Assays   Assays: Critical Approaches to Medieval and
              Renaissance Texts (Carnegie-Mellon University,
              Pittsburgh, PA)
Atlantis: A Women's Studies Journal/Journal d'Etudes sur la Femme
              (Mount Saint Vincent University, Halifax, Nova
              Scotia, Canada)
AUMLA   Journal of the Association of Australasian Universities
              Language and Literature Association (James Cook
              University of North Queensland, Townsville)
B&B   Books and Bookmen (London, England)
BAM   Bulletin des Anglicistes Médiévistes
Béaloideas: The Journal of the Folklore of Ireland Society (Dublin)
BForum   Book Forum: An International Transdisciplinary
              Quarterly (New York)
BJRL   Bulletin of the John Rylands Library (Manchester)
BkW   Book World (Washington Post, Washington, DC)
Blake: An Illustrated Quarterly (University of New Mexico,
              Albuquerque, NM)
Booklist   (American Library Association, Chicago)
Boundary   Boundary 2: A Journal of Postmodern Literature and
              Culture (SUNY, Binghamton)
British Book News (London)
BRMMLA   Bulletin of the Rocky Mountain Modern Language
              Association (Iowa City, IA; Boulder, CO)
BSUF   Ball State University Forum (Muncie, IN)
Bulletin of Aichi University of Education (Aichigakuin University,
              Aichi, Japan)
Bulletin of Aichi University of Education [Humanities] (Aichi, Japan)
Bulletin of the Faculty of General Education, Utsunomiya University
              (Utsunomiya, Japan)
Bulletin of the Faculty of Liberal Arts, Nagasaki University
              [Humanities] (Nagasaki, Japan)

Bulletin of Faculty of Literature of Tokai University (Tokyo, Japan)
Bulletin of Hirosaki College (Hirosaki, Japan)
Bulletin of Ohtani Women's College (Kyoto, Japan)
Bulletin of Tsuru University (Japan)
Bulletin of Yamaguchi Women's University (Yamaguchi, Japan)
Bulletin of Yamanashi Medical College (Kofu, Japan)
BurM   Burlington Magazine (London)
Business History Review (Boston, MA)
BW   Book World (Chicago Tribune)
C&L   Christianity and Literature (Adrian College, Adrian,
      MI)
C&M   Classica et Mediaevalia (Aarhus University, Roskilde,
      Denmark)
CahiersE Cahiers Elisabéthains: Etudes sur la Pré-Renaissance
      et la Renaissance Anglaises (Univ. Paul Valéry,
      Montpellier)
Caliban   (Toulouse, France)
CanL   Canadian Literature (University of British Columbia,
      Vancouver)
CCTE   Proceedings of Conference of College Teachers of
      English of Texas (Commerce, TX)
CE   College English (National Council of Teachers of
      English, Urbana, IL)
CEA   CEA Critic: An Official Journal of the College
      English Association (Centenary College of
      Louisiana, Shreveport)
Centerpoint: A Journal of Interdisciplinary Studies (New York)
CentR   The Centennial Review (Michigan State University,
      East Lansing, MI)
Centrum: Working Papers of the Minnesota Center for Advanced
      Studies in Language, Style, and Literary Theory
      (University of Minnesota, Minneapolis, MN)
CF   Classical Folia (Holy Cross College, Worcester, MA)
CH   Church History (American Society of Church History,
      Wallingford, PA)
ChauR   Chaucer Review (Pennsylvania State University,
      University Park, PA)
Choice   (Association of College and Research Libraries,
      Middletown, CT)
Christian Science Monitor (Boston, MA)

CHum	Computers and the Humanities (Elmsford, NY)
Cithara: Essays in the Judeo-Christian Tradition (St. Bonaventure University, NY)	
CJItS	Canadian Journal of Italian Studies (McMaster University, Hamilton, Ontario)
CL	Comparative Literature (University of Oregon, Eugene, OR)
CLAJ	College Language Association Journal (Morgan State College, Baltimore, MD)
CLIO: A Journal of Literature, History, and the Philosophy of History (University of Wisconsin-Parkside, Kenosha, WI; Indiana University, Purdue, IN)	
Clio: Rivista Trimestrale di Studi Storici (Rome, Italy)	
CLQ	Colby Library Quarterly (Colby College, Waterville, ME)
CLS	Comparative Literature Studies (University of Illinois, Urbana, IL)
CML	Classical and Modern Literature: A Quarterly (Indiana State University, Terre Haute, IN)
CollL	College Literature (West Chester State College, West Chester, PA)
Comitatus: A Journal of Medieval and Renaissance Studies (University of California, Los Angeles)	
Communiqué	(University of the North, Pietersburg, South Africa)
Comparatist	The Comparatist Journal of the Southern Comparative Literature Association (Clemson University, Clemson, SC)
ConL	Contemporary Literature (University of Wisconson, Madison)
Consort	(Dolmetsch Foundation, Godalming, Surrey, England)
ContempR	Contemporary Review (London, England)
Core	(Doshisha University, Kyoto, Japan)
Costerus: Essays in English and American Language and Literature (Amsterdam, The Netherlands)	
CQ	Cambridge Quarterly (Cambridge)
CRCL	Canadian Review of Comparative Literature/Revue Canadienne de Littérature Comparée (Toronto University)
CR	The Critical Review (Melbourne, Sydney, and Canberra, Australia)

Cresset   (Valparaiso University, IN)
Critic: Journal of Catholic Christian Culture (Chicago)
Critica letteraria (Naples, Italy)
Criticism: A Quarterly for Literature and the Arts (Wayne State
          University, Detroit, MI)
CritQ   Critical Quarterly (Manchester, England)
CritS   Critical Survey (Manchester and Hull, England)
Cronica   (Jassy, Romania)
La Cultura: rivista di filosofia, letterature e storia (Rome, Italy)
CUNY English Forum (The City of New York, New York: AMS
          Press)
DA   Dissertation Abstracts
DAI   Dissertation Abstracts International [supersedes *DA*
          in 1969] (Ann Arbor, MI)
DalR   Dalhousie Review (Dalhousie University, Halifax,
          Nova Scotia)
Delta Epsilon Sigma Bulletin (Dubuque, IA)
DQR   Dutch Quarterly Review of Anglo-American Letters
          (Amsterdam)
DUJ   Durham University Journal, new series (Durham,
          England)
DVLG   Deutsche Vierteljahrsschrift für Literaturwissenschaft
          und Geistesgeschichte (Stuttgart)
E&S   Essays and Studies by Members of the English
          Association, new series (London)
EA   Etudes Anglaises (Vannes, France)
EarlyMus   Early Music (London)
EAS   Essays in Arts and Sciences (University of New
          Haven, West Haven, CT)
EconHistR   Economic History Review (Welwyn Garden City,
          England)
Economist, The (London)
ECS   Eighteenth-Century Studies: An Interdisciplinary
          Journal (Northfield, MN; University of Pittsburgh,
          PA)
ECW   Essays on Canadian Writing (Downsview, Ontario)
EHR   English Historical Review (London)
EIC   Essays in Criticism: A Quarterly Journal of Literary
          Criticism (Oxford, England)
EigoS   Eigo Seinen [The Rising Generation] (Tokyo, Japan)

EiP	Essays in Poetics: The Journal of the British Neo-Formalist School (University of Keele, England)
Éire	Éire-Ireland: A Journal of Irish Studies (St. Paul, MN)
ELH	Journal of English Literary History (Johns Hopkins University, Baltimore, MD)
ELLS	English Literature and Language (Tokyo, Japan)
ELN	English Language Notes (University of Colorado, Boulder)
ELR	English Literary Renaissance (University of Massachusetts, Amherst)
ELWIU	Essays in Literature (Western Illinois University, Macomb, IL)
EM	English Miscellany: A Symposium of History, Literature and the Arts (Rome: Edizioni di Storia e Letteratura)
Encounter	(London, England)

Encyclia: The Journal of the Utah Academy of Sciences, Arts and Letters (Salt Lake City, UT)

English: The Journal of the English Association (London, England)

EngR	English Record (State University College at Oneonta, NY)

Era [Jidia], new series (Hiroshima, Japan; São Paulo, Brazil)

Erasmus: Speculum scientiarum, International Bulletin of Contemporary Scholarship (Wiesbaden, West Germany)

ES	English Studies: A Journal of English Language and Literature (Amsterdam, The Netherlands)
ESA	English Studies in Africa: A Journal of the Humanities (Johannesburg, South Africa)
ESC	English Studies in Canada (University of New Brunswick, Fredericton)
ESELL	Tohoku Gakuin University Review: Essays and Studies in English Language and Literature [Tohoku Gakuin Daigaku Ronshu, Eigo-Eibungaku] (Sendai, Japan)

Essays on Classical Studies (Japan)

Estudios de filologia inglesa (Universidad de Granada, Spain)

Estudios sobre los generos literarios (Universidad de Salamanca, Spain)

Euphorion: Zeitschrift für Literaturgeschichte (Heidelberg, West Germany)

Expl   Explicator (Washington, DC)
Explorations   (Lahore, Pakistan)
Extrapolation: A Journal of Science Fiction and Fantasy (Kent, OH;
            College of Wooster, OH)
Fabula: Zeitschrift für Erzählforschung/Journal of Folktale Studies/
            Revue d'Etudes sur le Conte Populaire (Berlin and
            New York)
FCS   Fifteenth-Century Studies (Detroit, MI)
FForum   Folklore Forum (Bloomington, IN)
Fleur-de-lis Review (Tokyo)
Florilegum: Carleton University Annual Papers on Classical Antiquity
            and the Middle Ages (Ottawa, Canada)
Folklore   (London, England)
FP   Filološki Pregled (Belgrade)
FR   The French Review: Journal of the American
            Association of Teachers of French (Champaign, IL)
FS   French Studies: A Quarterly Review (Oxford,
            England)
FWF   Far Western Forum (Berkeley, CA)
GaR   Georgia Review (University of Georgia, Athens)
Genre   (University of Oklahoma, Norman)
GRM   Germanisch-Romanische Monatsschrift (Heidelberg)
HAR   Humanities Association Review/Association des
            Humanities Revue (Queens University, Kingston,
            Ontario)
Hermathena: A Trinity College Dublin Review (Dublin, Ireland)
History: The Journal of The Historical Association, new series
            (London)
HLQ   Huntington Library Quarterly: A Journal for the
            History and Interpretation of English and American
            Civilization (San Marino, CA)
Horisont: organ för Svenska Osterbottens litteraturvetenskap
            (Stockholm)
HSELL   Hiroshima Studies in English Language and
            Literature (Japan)
HudR   Hudson Review (New York)
HUSL   Hebrew University Studies in Literature and the Arts
            (Jerusalem)
Indian Journal of Applied Linguistics (New Delhi, India)
Innisfree   (Hammond, LA)
Inostrannye yazyki v vysshev shkole (Riga/Moscow)

Interpretations: A Journal of Ideas, Analysis, and Criticism (Memphis, TN)

Isis: International Review Devoted to the History of Science and its Cultural Influences (Smithsonian Institution, Washington, DC)

IS   Italian Studies (Leicester/Hull, England)

ISSQ   Indiana Social Studies Quarterly (Ball State University, Muncie)

Italica   (Columbia University, NY)

JASAT   Journal of the American Studies Association of Texas (Wayland College, Plainview)

JEconHist   Journal of Economic History (Economic History Association, Greenville/ Wilmington, DE)

JEGP   Journal of English and Germanic Philology (University of Illinois at Urbana-Champaign)

JEH   Journal of Ecclesiastical History (London and New York)

JEP   Journal of Evolutionary Psychology (Pittsburgh, PA)

JHI   Journal of the History of Ideas (Temple University, Philadelphia, PA)

JHP   Journal of the History of Philosophy (Washington University, St. Louis, MO)

JMRS   Journal of Medieval and Renaissance Studies (Durham, NC)

JNT   Journal of Narrative Technique (Eastern Michigan University, Ypsilanti)

Journal of English Linguistics: Occasional Monographs (Western Washington University, Bellingham)

Journal of General Education Department, Niigata University (Niigata, Japan)

Journal of the Liberal Arts Department, Kansai Medical University (Osaka, Japan)

Journal of Psychohistory (New York)

Journal of Tenri University (Tenri City/Nara, Japan)

Journal of Tokyo Kasei Gajuin College (Tokyo, Japan)

JRMMRA   Journal of the Rocky Mountain Medieval and Renaissance Association (Northern Arizona University, Flagstaff)

JWCI	Journal of the Warburg and Courtauld Institutes (University of London)
JWH	Journal of World History/Cahiers d'histoire mondiale (Paris)
JWSL	Journal of Women's Studies in Literature (Montreal, Quebec, Canada)
Katahira	(Japan)
Key-Words in Beowulf and Chaucer (Japan)	
Key-Word Studies in Chaucer (Japan)	
KN	Kwartalnik Neofilologiczny (Warsaw, Poland)
Konan Daigaku Kiyo (Kobe, Japan)	
KPAB	Kentucky Philological Association Bulletin (Murray State University, Murray, KY)
KSJ	Keats-Shelley Journal (New York)
L&H	Literature and History: A Journal for the Humanities (London)
L&P	Literature and Psychology (University of Hartford, Teaneck, NJ)
Lagos Review of English Studies (Lagos, Nigeria)	
LangQ	Language Quarterly (University of South Florida, Tampa, FL)
Lang&S	Language and Style: An International Journal (Southern Illinois University, Carbondale)
Latvivyskii gosudarstvennyi universitet (Riga, USSR)	
LauR	Laurel Review (West Virginia Wesleyan College, Buckhannon)
LeedsSE	Leeds Studies in English (University of Leeds, Leeds, England)
Les Bonnes Feuilles (Pennsylvania State University)	
LFQ	Literature/Film Quarterly (Salisbury State College, Salisbury, MD)
LHY	Literary Half-Yearly (University of Mysore, Mysore, India)
Library: Transactions of the Bibliographical Society (London)	
Lingua et Humanitas (Meiji Gakuin University, Japan)	
Linguistics: An Interdisciplinary Journal of the Language Science (The Hague: Mouton)	
LiNQ	Literature in North Queensland (James Cook University, Townsville)
Listener, The	(British Broadcasting Coporation, London)

Literatūra: Lietuvos TSR Aukštųjų Mokyklų Mokslo Darbai (Vilnius, USSR)

LitR	Literary Review: An International Journal of Contemporary Writing (Madison, NJ)
LJ	Library Journal (New York)
LJHum	Lamar Journal of the Humanities (Lamar University, Beaumont, TX)
Lore&L	Lore and Language (University of Sheffield, Sheffield, England)
LRN	Literary Research Newsletter (Manhattan College, Bronx, NY)
Luceafărul	(Bucharest, Romania)
MF	Die Musikforschung (Kassel, West Germany)
M&H	Medievalia et Humanistica (1970-new series Case Western Reserve University; 1973-North Texas State University, Denton, TX)
MA	La Moyen Age: Revue Historique (Brussels, Belgium)
MAE	Medium Aevum (Oxford)

Maledicta: The International Journal of Verbal Agression (Waukesha, WI)

Manuscripta	(St. Louis University Library, MO)
MayR	The Maynooth Review/Reiviú Mhá Nuad: A Journal of the Arts (St. Patrick's College, Kildare, Ireland)
McNR	McNeese Review (McNeese State College, LA)
MCRel	Mythes, croyances et religions dans le monde Anglo-Saxon (Université d'Avignon, France)

Mediaevalia: A Journal of Mediaeval Studies (CEMERS, SUNY, Binghamton, New York)

MedR	Medioevo Romanzo (Bologna)
MeiGR	Meiji Gakuin Ronso [Review] (Tokyo)
MESN	Medieval English Studies Newsletter (Tokyo)

Meta: Journal des Traducteurs/Translators' Journal (Montreal, Quebec, Canada)

MHLS	Mid-Hudson Language Studies (Poughkeepsie, NY)
MichA	Michigan Academician: Papers of the Michigan Academy of Science, Arts, and Letters (Ann Arbor, MI)
MiltonQ	Milton Quarterly (Ohio University, Athens)
Mimesis	(São Paulo, Brazil)
MinnR	The Minnesota Review (Milwaukee, WI)

MissFR	Mississippi Folklore Register (Hattiesburg)
MLN	Modern Language Notes (Baltimore, MD)
MLQ	Modern Language Quarterly (University of Washington, Seattle)
MLR	Modern Language Review (London)
MLS	Modern Language Studies (University of Rhode Island, Kingston)
MoJoResMusEd	Missouri Journal of Research in Music Education (Jefferson City, MO)
Mosaic: A Journal of the Interdisciplinary Study of Literature (University of Manitoba, Winnipeg)	
Mov	Movoznavstvo: Naukovo-Teoretychnyĭ Zhurnal Viddilennia Literatury, Movy i Mystetstvoznavstva Akademiĭ Nauk Ukraïns'koĭ RSR (Kiev, USSR)
Moznayim: Yarhon Agudat ha-Soferim ha-'Ivrim be-Medinat Yiśrael/ Monthly of the Association of Hebrew Writers in Israel (Tel Aviv, Israel)	
MP	Modern Philology: A Journal Devoted to Research in Medieval and Modern Literature (Chicago, IL)
MQ	Midwest Quarterly: A Journal of Contemporary Thought (Pittsburg, KS)
MQR	Michigan Quarterly Review (Ann Arbor, MI)
MS	Mediaeval Studies (Toronto)
MSE	Massachusetts Studies in English (University of Massachusetts, Amherst)
Mus&Let	Music and Letters (London)
Mus&Mus	Music and Musicians (London)
MusQ	Musical Quarterly (New York)
MusT	The Musical Times (London)
N&Q	Notes and Queries, new series (London)
Names: Journal of the American Name Society (State University College at Potsdam, NY)	
NCarF	North Carolina Folklore Journal (N.C. State University at Raleigh)
NCF	Nineteenth-Century Fiction (Berkeley, CA)
NDEJ	Notre Dame English Journal (University of Notre Dame, IN)
Neophil	Neophilologus: An International Journal of Modern and Medieval Language and Literature (Groningen, The Netherlands)

New Republic	(New York)
NLauR	New Laurel Review (Challmette, LA)
NLH	New Literary History: A Journal of Theory and Interpretation (University of Virginia, Charlottesville)
NM	Neuphilologische Mitteilungen: Bulletin of the Modern Language Society (Porthania University, Helsinki, Finland)
NMS	Nottingham Medieval Studies (University of Nottingham)
NNER	Northern New England Review (Franklin Pierce College, Rendge, NH)
NOWELE	North-Western European Language Evolution (Odense University, Denmark)
NRMI	Nuova Rivista Musicale Italiana (Sipra, Torino, Italy)
NS	Die Neueren Sprachen (Frankfurt, West Germany)
NSt	New Statesman (London, England)
NYRB	New York Review of Books
NYTB	New York Times Book Review
Observer	(London)
Ohtani Studies, The	(Kyoto, Japan)
OJES	Osmania Journal of English Studies (Hyderbad, India)
OL	Orbis Litterarum: International Review of Literary Studies (Copenhagen, Denmark)
OPLiLL	Occasional Papers in Linguistics and Language Learning (Coleraine: New University of Ulster)
PAPA	Publications of the Arkansas Philological Association (Fayetteville, AR)
Parergon: The Bulletin of the Australian and New Zealand Association for Medieval and Renaissance Studies	(Dunedin, New Zealand)
Paunch	(SUNY, Buffalo, NY)
PBA	Proceedings of the British Academy (London)
PBSA	Papers of the Bibliographical Society of America (University of Texas, Austin)
PCP	Pacific Coast Philology (California State University, Northridge)
Philologia: Studia Universitatis Babeş-Bolyai, Cluj-Napoca	(Romania)
PhoenixH	(Department of English, Hiroshima University)
Physics Today	(New York, NY)

PLL	Papers on Language and Literature: A Journal for Scholars and Critics of Language and Literature (Southern Illinois University, Edwardsville)
PMLA	Publications of the Modern Language Association of America (New York)
PMPA	Publications of the Missouri Philological Association (University of Missouri-Rolla, Rolla, MO)
PoetT	Poetica: An International Journal of Linguistic-Literary Studies (Tokyo, Japan)
PPMRC	Proceedings of the PMR Conference: Annual Publication of the International Patristic, Mediaeval and Renaissance Conference (Villanova, PA)
PQ	Philological Quarterly (University of Iowa, Iowa City)

Proceedings of the Illinois Medieval Association (Illinois State University, Normal; Western Illinois University, Macomb)

Prose and Poetry (Japan)

QJS	Quarterly Journal of Speech (Falls Church, VA)
QQ	Queen's Quarterly (Kingston, Ontario)
Quarto	(London)
RBPH	Revue Belge de philologie et d'histoire (Brussels, Belgium)
RCEI	Revista Canaria de Estudios Ingleses (Tenerife, Spain)
RdeMus	Revue de Musicologie (Paris)
REL	Review of English Literature (London, 1960–67)
Ren&R	Renaissance and Reformation/Renaissance et Réforme (York University, Downsview, Ontario)

Renditions: A Chinese-English Translation Magazine (Chinese University of Hong Kong, China)

RenQ	Renaissance Quarterly (New York)

Reports of the Keio Institute of Cultural and Linguistic Studies (Tokyo, Japan)

RES	Review of English Studies: A Quarterly Journal of English Literature and the English Language, new series (Oxford)
Rev	Review (Blacksburg/Charlottesville, VA)

Review of Inquiry and Research, The (The Kansai University of Foreign Studies, Suit-shi, Osaka, Japan)

Review of Metaphysics (Catholic University of America, Washington, DC)

RILM	Répertoire International de Littérature Musicale/International Repertory of Music Literature: Abstracts (New York)
RLet	Revista Letras (Paraná, Brazil)
RLM	Rivista di letterature moderne e comparate (Florence)
RLSt	Rackham Literary Studies (Ann Arbor, MI)
RLV	Revue des Langues Vivantes (Brussels, Belgium)
RMRLL	Rocky Mountain Review of Language and Literature (University of Utah, Salt Lake City)
RMSt	Reading Medieval Studies (University of Reading, England)
RomLit	România Literară (Bucharest)
RPh	Romance Philology (University of California, Berkeley)
RPLit	Res Publica Litterarum: Studies in the Classical Tradition (University of Kansas, Lawrence, KS)
RSR	Reference Services Review (Ann Arbor, MI)
RUO	Revue de l'Université d'Ottawa/University of Ottawa Quarterly
RUS	Rice University Studies (Houston, TX)
RUSEng	Rajasthan University Studies in English (Jaipur, India)
SAB	South Atlantic Bulletin: A Quarterly Journal Devoted to Research and Teaching in the Modern Languages and Literature (Knoxville, TN)
SAC	Studies in the Age of Chaucer: The Yearbook of the New Chaucer Society (University of Tennessee, Knoxville)

Samlaren: Tidskrift för Svensk Litteraturvetenskaplig Forskning (Uppsala and Stockholm)

SAQ	South Atlantic Quarterly (Durham, NC)
SAtlR	South Atlantic Review (Knoxville, TN)
SatR	The Saturday Review (New York)
SB	Studies in Bibliography: Papers of the Bibliographical Society of the University of Virginia (Charlottesville, VA)
SCB	see *SCRev*

SCL	Studies in Canadian Literature (Fredericton, New Brunswick, Canada)
SCN	Seventeenth Century News (Pennsylvania State University, University Park, PA)
SCRev	South Central Review: The Journal of the South Central Modern Language Association [formerly *SCB:* South Central Bulletin] (Texas A & M University, College Station, TX)

Secolul: revista de literatura universala (Bucharest, Romania)

SeijoB	Seijo Bungei (Tokyo)
SELit	Studies in English Literature (Tokyo: English Literary Society of Japan)
SELL	Studies in English Language and Literature (Fukuoka, Japan)
SELLA	Shirayuri English Language and Literature Association [Shirayuri Joshi Daigaku Eibungakkai] (Tokyo, Japan)
SES	Sophia English Studies (Tokyo, Japan)
SFQ	Southern Folklore Quarterly (University of Florida, Gainesville)
SGG	Studia Germanica Gandensia (Ghent, Belgium)
Shiron	(Tokyo Joshi Daigaku, Tokyo, Japan)
SHR	Southern Humanities Review (Auburn University, AL)

Shukugawa Studies in Linguistics and Literature (Japan)

Shuru	(Doshisha University, Kyoto, Japan)
SIcon	Studies in Iconography (University of Arizona, Tempe)

Signs: Journal of Women in Culture and Society (Chicago)

SiM	Studies in Medievalism (Oxford, OH)

Sky and Telescope (Cambridge, MA)

SMC	Studies in Medieval Culture (Western Michigan University, Kalamazoo)
SMed	Studi Medievali (Rome)
SN	Studia Neophilologica (Stockholm)
SNNTS	Studies in the Novel (Denton, TX)
SoCR	South Carolina Review (Clemson University)
SoQ	Southern Quarterly: A Journal of the Arts in the South (Hattiesburg, MS)

SoRA	Southern Review: Literary and Interdisciplinary Essays (University of Adelaide, Australia)
Soundings: An Interdisciplinary Journal (Tokyo, Japan)	
SP	Studies in Philology (University of North Carolina, Chapel Hill)
Spectator	(London)
Spectrum	(University of Massachusetts, Amherst)
Speculum: A Journal of Medieval Studies (Cambridge, MA)	
SpenN	Spenser Newsletter (University of Massachusetts, Amherst)
SQ	Shakespeare Quarterly (Washington, DC)
SR	Sewanee Review (University of the South, Sewanee, TN)
SRAZ	Studia Romanica et Anglica Zagrabiensia (Zagreb, Yugoslavia)
SSEng	Sydney Studies in English (Sydney, Australia)
SSF	Studies in Short Fiction (Newberry College, Newberry, SC)
SSI	Social Science Information/Information sur les Sciences Sociales (London)
SSJ	Southern Speech Communication Journal (University of Tennessee, Knoxville)
SSL	Studies in Scottish Literature (University of South Carolina, Columbia, SC)
Standpunte	(Stellenbosch, Republic of South Africa)
StHum	Studies in the Humanities (Indiana, PA)
Studi Inglesi	(Rome)
Studia Mystica	(Sacramento, CA)
Studies: An Irish Quarterly Review (Dublin)	
Studies in Foreign Languages and Literatures (Aichi University of Education, Aichi, Japan)	
Style	(University of Arkansas, Fayetteville)
TCEL	Thought Currents in English Literature (English Literary Society of Aoyama Gakuin University, Tokyo, Japan)
Teaching of English (Sydney Teachers' College, Camperdown, N. S. W., Australia)	
Tenri Daigaku Gakuho (Bulletin of Tenri University, Tambaichi/Nara, Japan)	
Tenri University Journal (Nara, Japan)	

TES   Times Educational Supplement (London)
Thalia: Studies in Literary Humor (University of Ottawa, Ontario)
Theoria: A Journal of Studies in the Arts, Humanities and Social
                Sciences (Natal, South Africa)
THES   Times Higher Education Supplement (London)
Thoth   (Department of English, Syracuse University, NY)
Thought: A Review of Culture and Idea (Fordham University, Bronx,
                NY)
TkR   Tamkang Review: A Quarterly Journal of
                Comparative Studies between Chinese and Foreign
                Literatures (Tamkang College of Arts and Sciences,
                Taipei, Taiwan, China)
TLS   Times Literary Supplement (London, England)
Tokushima Bunri Daigaku Kiyo (Tokushima, Japan)
TPB   Tennessee Philological Bulletin: Proceedings of the
                Annual Meeting of the Tennessee Philological
                Association (Memphis, TN)
Traditio: Studies in Ancient and Medieval History, Thought, and
                Religion (Bronx, NY)
TSE   Tulane Studies in English (Tulane University, New
                Orleans, LA)
TSL   Tennessee Studies in Literature (University of
                Tennessee, Knoxville)
TSLL   Texas Studies in Literature and Language (University
                of Texas at Austin)
TSWL   Tulsa Studies in Women's Literature (University of
                Tulsa, OK)
UDR   University of Dayton Review (Dayton, OH)
UES   Unisa English Studies (University of South Africa,
                Pretoria)
UMS   Unisa Medieval Studies (University of South Africa,
                Pretoria)
Use of English, The (Edinburgh, Scotland)
UTQ   University of Toronto Quarterly (Toronto, Canada)
UWR   University of Windsor Review (Windsor, Ontario)
Viator: Medieval and Renaissance Studies (University of California,
                Berkeley and Los Angeles)
VLang   Visible Language: The Journal for Research on the
                Visual Media of Language (Wayne State University
                Press, c/o Merald E. Wrolstad, Ed. 2643 Eaton
                Rd., Cleveland, OH)

VLU	Vestnik Leningradskogo Universiteta Serii Istorii, Iazyka i Literatury (Leningrad)
Vox Latina	(Saarbrücken, West Germany)
VP	Victorian Poetry (West Virginia University, Morgantown)
VQR	Virginia Quarterly Review (University of Virginia, Charlottesville)
W&L	Women and Literature: A Journal of Women Writers and the Literary Treatment of Women up to 1900 (Rutgers University, New Brunswick, NJ)
Wall Street Journal (New York, NY)	
WCWR	William Carlos Williams Review (Pennsylvania State University, Middleton)
WF	Western Folklore (University of California, Los Angeles)
WGCR	West Georgia College Review (Carrollton, Georgia)
WHR	Western Humanities Review (University of Utah, Salt Lake City)
Wilson Library Bulletin (Bronx, NY)	
WWR	Walt Whitman Review (Wayne State University, Detroit, MI)
XUS	Xavier Review (New Orleans, LA)
YES	Yearbook of English Studies (MHRA, London)
YFS	Yale French Studies (Yale University, New Haven, CT)
YR	Yale Review (New Haven, CT)
YWES	The Year's Work in English Studies (Atlantic Highlands, NJ)
ZAA	Zeitschrift für Anglistik und Amerikanistik (Leipzig)

Miscellaneous Abbreviations

ANSDSL	Australian and New Zealand Studies in German Language and Literature/Australisch-Neuseeländische Studien zur Deutschen Sprache und Literatur
CEMERS	Center for Medieval and Early Renaissance Studies (SUNY, Binghamton, NY)
ME	Middle English
MHRA	Modern Humanities Research Association (London)

MRTS	Medieval and Renaissance Texts and Studies
MS	Manuscript
MSS	Manuscripts
OF	Old French
PPl	*Piers Plowman*
RR	*Roman de la Rose*
SEMA	Southeastern Medieval Association
SUNY	State University of New York
UCPES	University of California Publications, English Studies

Abbreviations of Chaucer's Works

ABC	*An ABC*
Adam	*Adam Scriveyn*
Anel	*Anelida and Arcite*
Astr	*A Treatise on the Astrolabe*
Bal Compl	*A Balade of Complaint*
BD	*The Book of the Duchess*
Bo	*Boece*
Buk	*The Envoy to Bukton*
CkT, CkP, Rv-CkL	*The Cook's Tale, The Cook's Prologue, Reeve-Cook Link*
ClT, ClP, Cl-MerL	*The Clerk's Tale, The Clerk's Prologue, Clerk-Merchant Link*
Compl d'Am	*Complaynt d'Amours*
CT	*The Canterbury Tales*
CYT, CYP	*The Canon's Yeoman's Tale, The Canon's Yeoman's Prologue*
Equat	*The Equatorie of the Planetis*
For	*Fortune*
Form Age	*The Former Age*
FranT, FranP	*The Franklin's Tale, The Franklin's Prologue*
FrT, FrP, Fr-SumL	*The Friar's Tale, The Friar's Prologue, Friar-Summoner Link*
Gent	*Gentilesse*
GP	*The General Prologue*
HF	*The House of Fame*
KnT, Kn-MilL	*The Knight's Tale, Knight-Miller Link*
Lady	*A Complaint to His Lady*
LGW, LGWP	*The Legend of Good Women, The Legend of Good Women Prologue*

ManT, ManP	The Manciple's Tale, The Manciple's Prologue
Mars	The Complaint of Mars
Mel, Mel-MkL	The Tale of Meilbee, Melibee-Monk Link
MercB	Merciles Beaute
MerT, MerE-SqH	The Merchant's Tale, Merchant Endlink-Squire Headlink
MilT, MilP, Mil-RvL	The Miller's Tale, The Miller's Prologue, Miller-Reeve Link
MkT, MkP, Mk-NPL	The Monk's Tale, The Monk's Prologue, Monk-Nun's Priest Link
MLT, MLH, MLP, MLE	The Man of Law's Tale, Man of Law Headlink, The Man of Law's Prologue, Man of Law Endlink
NPT, NPP, NPE	The Nun's Priest's Tale, The Nun's Priest's Prologue, Nun's Priest Endlink
PardT, PardP	The Pardoner's Tale, The Pardoner's Prologue
ParsT, ParsP	The Parson's Tale, The Parson's Prologue
PF	The Parliament of Fowls
PhyT, Phy-PardL	The Physician's Tale, Physician-Pardoner Link
Pity	The Complaint unto Pity
Prov	Proverbs
PrT, PrP, Pr-ThL	The Prioress's Tale, The Prioress's Prologue, Prioress-Thopas Link
Purse	The Complaint of Chaucer to His Purse
Ret	Chaucer's Retraction [Retractation]
Rom	The Romaunt of the Rose
Ros	To Rosemounde
RvT, RvP	The Reeve's Tale, The Reeve's Prologue
Scog	The Envoy to Scogan
ShT, Sh-PrL	The Shipman's Tale, Shipman-Prioress Link
SNT, SNP, SN-CYL	The Second Nun's Tale, The Second Nun's Prologue, Second Nun-Canon's Yeoman Link
SqT, SqH, Sq-FranL	The Squire's Tale, Squire Headlink, Squire-Franklin Link
Sted	Lak of Stedfastnesse
SumT, SumP	The Summoner's Tale, The Summoner's Prologue
TC	Troilus and Criseyde
Th, Th-MelL	The Tale of Sir Thopas, Sir Thopas-Melibee Link
Truth	Truth
Ven	The Complaint of Venus

WBT, WBP,	*The Wife of Bath's Tale, The Wife of Bath's*
WB-FrL	*Prologue, Wife of Bath-Friar Link*
Wom Nob	*Womanly Noblesse*
Wom Unc	*Against Women Unconstant*

A BIBLIOGRAPHY OF CHAUCER, 1974 - 1985

Lorrayne Y. Baird-Lange
&
Hildegard Schnüttgen

Stephen G. Smyczynski

Technical Editor &
Book Designer

BIBLIOGRAPHY

>>> BIBLIOGRAPHIES DEVOTED EXCLUSIVELY TO CHAUCER <<<

1   BAIRD, LORRAYNE Y. A Bibliography of Chaucer, 1964-1973.
    Boston, MA: G. K. Hall; London: Prior, 1977. 287 pp.
    [includes reviews]
    Reviews: Choice 14 (1978), 1477; D. Mehl, Archiv 216
    (1979), 168; Thomas A. Kirby, ES 62 (1981), 383-85.

2   BAIRD, LORRAYNE Y., comp. and ed., et al. "An Annotated Chaucer
    Bibliography, 1981." SAC 5 (1983), 217-76. [includes
    reviews] See also no. 13 below.

3   BAIRD-LANGE, LORRAYNE Y. and CYNTHIA DOBRICH MYERS, comps. and
    eds., et al. "An Annotated Chaucer Bibliography, 1982." SAC
    6 (1984), 233-82. [includes reviews]

4   BAIRD-LANGE, LORRAYNE Y., BEGE BOWERS, and HILDEGARD SCHNÜTTGEN,
    comps. and eds., et al. "An Annotated Chaucer Bibliography,
    1983." SAC 7 (1985), 283-338. [includes reviews]

5   BAIRD-LANGE, LORRAYNE Y., BEGE BOWERS, and HILDEGARD SCHNÜTTGEN,
    comps. and eds., et al. "An Annotated Chaucer Bibliography,
    1984." SAC 8 (1986), 279-341. [includes reviews]

6   BAUGH, ALBERT CROLL. Chaucer. 2nd ed. Goldentree
    Bibliographies. Arlington Heights, IL: AHM Publishing
    Corporation, 1977. 161 pp. [800+ new items]

7   BAZIRE, JOYCE and DAVID MILLS. "Middle English: Chaucer." For
    1972, YWES 53 (1974), 106-20; for 1973, YWES 54 (1975),
    109-23; for 1974, YWES 55 (1976), 148-66; for 1975, YWES 56
    (1977), 118-29; for 1976, YWES 57 (1978), 89-100; for 1977,
    YWES 58 (1979), 107-23; for 1978, YWES 59 (1980), 105-21; for
    1979, YWES 60 (1981), 101-20. See also David Mills and David
    Burnley, no. 20, below.

Bibliography

8   BENSON, L. D.   "Chaucer: A Select Bibliography," in 49, pp.
     352-72.

9   BOWERS, BEGE K. "Chaucer Research, 1984: Report No. 45." ChauR
     20 (1985), 70-78. See also no. 17 below.

10   BOWERS, BEGE K. "Chaucer Research in Progress, 1984-85." NM 86
     (1985), 402-13. See also no. 18 below.

11   COURTNEY, ELEANOR LEWER. "Geoffrey Chaucer's Canterbury Tales:
     An Annotated International Bibliography, 1964-1971." DAI 37
     (1976), 327A. University of Arizona, 1975.

12   EDWARDS, A. S. G., ed. Middle English Prose: A Critical Guide
     to Major Authors and Genres. New Brunswick, NJ: Rutgers
     University Press, 1984. 452 pp. [bibliographic review
     essays; includes prose works of Chaucer] See no. 440 for
     section on Chaucer.
        Reviews: A. J. Colaianne, SAC 7 (1985), 188-91; Albert E.
     Hartung, Speculum 61 (1986), 644-46.

13   FISHER, JOHN H., comp., et al. "An Annotated Chaucer
     Bibliography." 1975-76: SAC 1 (1979), 201-55; 1977-78: SAC
     2 (1980), 221-85; 1979: SAC 3 (1981), 189-259; 1980: SAC 4
     (1982), 193-246. [includes reviews] See also nos. 2-5
     above.

14   FISHER, JOHN H. "English Literature," in The Present State of
     Scholarship in Fourteenth Century Literature. Edited by
     Thomas D. Cooke. Columbia and London: University of
     Missouri Press, 1982, pp. 1-54. [see esp. pp. 32-45]

15   GIACCHERINI, ENRICO. "Chaucer and the Italian Trecento: A
     Bibliography," in 47, pp. 297-304. [Chaucer's Italian
     sources]

16   JOHNSON, JAMES D. "Identifying Chaucer Allusions, 1953-80: An
     Annotated Bibliography." ChauR 19 (1984), 62-86. [follows
     Spurgeon; indexes names and titles]

17   KIRBY, THOMAS A. "Chaucer Research." Report No. 34 (1973):
     ChauR 9 (1974), 80-95; No. 35 (1974): ChauR 9 (1975),
     353-71; No. 36 (1975): ChauR 10 (1976), 260-78; No. 37
     (1976): ChauR 11 (1977), 261-79; No. 38 (1977): ChauR 12
     (1978), 259-77; No. 39 (1978), ChauR 14 (1979), 74-95; No. 40
     (1979): ChauR 15 (1980), 63-84; No. 41 (1980), with Martin
     M. Crow and Charles S. Muscatine, ChauR 15 (1981), 356-79;
     No. 42 (1981): ChauR 16 (1982), 356-77; No. 43 (1982):
     ChauR 17 (1983), 255-77; No. 44 (1983): ChauR 18 (1984),

4

250-72. See also Bege Bowers, no. 9, above.

18   KIRBY, THOMAS A. "Chaucer Research in Progress." 1973-74: NM
      75 (1974), 485-91; 1974-75: NM 76 (1975), 513-21; 1975-76:
      NM 77 (1976), 418-26; 1976-77: NM 78 (1977), 280-86;
      1977-78: NM 79 (1978), 301-06; 1978-79: NM 80 (1979),
      280-86; 1979-80: NM 81 (1980), 307-12; 1980-81: NM 82
      (1981), 346-52; 1981-82: NM 83 (1982), 291-96; 1982-83: NM
      84 (1983), 405-11; 1983-84: NM 85 (1984), 335-43. See also
      Bege Bowers, no. 10, above.

19   LEYERLE, JOHN and ANNE QUICK, eds. Chaucer: A Selected
      Bibliography. Toronto Medieval Bibliographies Series.
      Toronto: University of Toronto Press, 1986. 224 pp.

20   MILLS, DAVID and DAVID BURNLEY. "Middle English: Chaucer." For
      1980, YWES 61 (1982), 100-15; for 1981, YWES 62 (1984),
      127-43; for 1982, YWES 63 (1985), 94-111; for 1983, YWES 64
      (1986), 127-42. See also Joyce Bazire and David Mills, no.
      7, above.

21   MORRIS, LYNN KING. Chaucer Source and Analogue Criticism: A
      Cross-Referenced Guide. Garland Reference Library of the
      Humanities, 454. New York: Garland, 1985. 584 pp.
      [includes four indexes: Chaucer's works, authors, titles,
      and genres of sources] See also no. 646 for DAI citation.
      Reviews: Choice (July-August, 1986), 1660.

22   PECK, RUSSELL A. Chaucer's Lyrics and 'Anelida and Arcite': An
      Annotated Bibliography 1900-1980. Edited by A. J. Colaianne
      and R. M. Piersol. Chaucer Bibliographies. Toronto:
      University of Toronto Press, 1983. 226 pp.
      Reviews: Choice 21 (1983), 255-56; Lorrayne Y. Baird, SAC
      6 (1984), 216-19; Avril Bruten, TLS (6 January, 1984), 20; R.
      T. Lenaghan, Speculum 60 (1985), 709-10.

23   SHIKII, KUMIKO. "Nihon ni okeru Troilus and Criseyde kenkyu"
      [Researches on Troilus and Criseyde in Japan]. SELLA (1984),
      85-97. In Japanese. [critical bibliography of studies on TC
      in Japan on five themes]

24   WEISE, JUDITH. "Geoffrey Chaucer, 1343?-1400," in Research Guide
      to Biography and Criticism 1. Edited by Walton Beacham.
      Washington, DC: Research Publishing, 1985, pp. 218-223.
      [selective]

Bibliography

>>> GENERAL BIBLIOGRAPHIES <<<

25   BOOK REVIEW DIGEST. Edited by Josephine Samudio (1974–76);
     Josephine Samudio and Martha T. Mooney (1977); and Martha T.
     Mooney (1978––). New York: H. W. Wilson Company, 1974––.

26   BOOK REVIEW INDEX. Edited by Mildred Schlientz (1965–68); Gary
     C. Tarbert (1969–84); Gary C. Tarbert and Barbara Beach
     (1985); and Barbara Beach (1986––). Detroit, Book Tower:
     Gale Research Company, 1974––.

27   ESSAY AND GENERAL LITERATURE INDEX. Edited by Norma Freedman
     (1975–79); and John Greenfieldt (1980––). New York: Wilson,
     1934––(1974––).

28   HARTUNG, A. E., ed. Manual of Writings in Middle English
     1050–1500. Hamden, CT: Shoe String Press, 1973. 4 vols.
     See also no. 2529.
        Reviews: R. M. Wilson, MLR 69 (1974), 146; Norman Davis,
     RES 25 (1974), 67–69; Morton W. Bloomfield, Speculum 51
     (1976), 136–37.

29   HUMANITIES INDEX. Edited by Elizabeth E. Pingree (1974–84); and
     Joanna Greenspon (1984––). New York: Wilson, 1974––.

30   AN INDEX TO BOOK REVIEWS IN THE HUMANITIES. Williamston, MI:
     Phillip Thompson, 1960––(1974––).

31   INTERNATIONAL INSTITUTE OF INTELLECTUAL COOPERATION. Index
     translationum: Répertoire international des traductions.
     New series. Paris, 1948––.

32   INTERNATIONALE BIBLIOGRAPHIE DER REZENSIONEN WISSENSCHAFTLICHER
     LITERATUR [International Bibliography of Book Reviews of
     Scholarly Literature]. Edited by Otto Zeller. Osnabrück:
     Felix Dietrich Verlag, 1971––.

33   INTERNATIONALE BIBLIOGRAPHIE DER ZEITSCHRIFTEN–LITERATUR AUS
     ALLEN GEBIETEN DES WISSENS [International Bibliography of
     Periodical Literature Covering All Fields of Knowledge].
     Edited by Otto Zeller. Osnabrück: Felix Dietrich Verlag,
     1974––.

34   JAHRESVERZEICHNIS DER DEUTSCHEN HOCHSCHULSCHRIFTEN, 1885––.
     Bearb. von der Deutschen Bücherei. Leipzig: Verlag für
     Buch– und Bibliothekswesen, 1887––(1974––). [lists German
     dissertations]

35   THE MODERN HUMANITIES RESEARCH ASSOCIATION. <u>Annual Bibliography</u>
      <u>of English Language and Literature</u>. Edited by Derek Roper,
      James B. Misenheimer, Jr., and Mary Jean DeMarr (1974);
      Michael Smith, James B. Misenheimer, Jr., and Mary Jean
      DeMarr (1975–79); and Michael Smith and Mary Jean DeMarr
      (1980–82). Cambridge: Modern Humanities Research
      Association, 1920––(1974––). [notes reviews]

36   THE MODERN HUMANITIES RESEARCH ASSOCIATION. <u>The Year's Work in</u>
      <u>Modern Language Studies</u>. Edited by Glanville Price (1974);
      Glanville Price and David A. Wells (1975–80); David A. Wells
      (1981); and Glanville Price and David A. Wells (1982–84).
      Cambridge: Modern Humanities Research Association,
      1931––(1974––).

37   MODERN LANGUAGE ASSOCIATION OF AMERICA. <u>International</u>
      <u>Bibliography of Books and Articles on the Modern Languages</u>
      <u>and Literatures</u>. Compiled by Harrison T. Meserole, et al.
      New York, 1974––.

38   NATIONAL COUNCIL OF TEACHERS OF ENGLISH. <u>Abstracts of English</u>
      <u>Studies</u>. Urbana, IL: NCTE, 1974–80; Calgary, Alberta,
      Canada: University of Calgary, 1980––.

39   <u>QUARTERLY CHECK–LIST OF MEDIEVALIA: An International Subject</u>
      <u>Index of Current Books, Monographs, Brochures and Separates</u>.
      Darien, CT: American Bibliographic Service, 1974–77.

40   <u>Verzeichnis Lieferbarer Bücher</u> [German Books in Print].
      Frankfurt am Main: Verlag der Buchhandler-Vereinigung GmbH,
      1974–87.

See also: <u>70</u>, 181, 198, 261, 397, 647, 852, <u>2029</u>, <u>2321</u>, 2529, 2536,
           2604, 2612, 2646, 2752.

FESTSCHRIFTEN AND COLLECTIONS

41 ARN, MARY-JO and HANNEKE WIRTJES, eds., with HANS JANSEN.
    Historical and Editorial Studies in Medieval and Early Modern
    English. Festschrift for Johan Gerritsen. Groningen, The
    Netherlands: Wolters-Nordhoff, 1985. See nos. 105, 869,
    2087.

42 BALD, WOLF-DIETRICH and HORST WEINSTOCK, eds. Medieval Studies
    Conference Aachen 1983: Language and Literature. Bamberger
    Beiträge zur Englischen Sprachwissenschaft 15. Frankfurt am
    Main: Verlag Peter Lang, 1984. [seventeen essays on
    language and literature] See nos. 286, 1056, 1212, 2216,
    2496.

43 BENSON, LARRY D., ed. The Learned and the Lewed: Studies in
    Chaucer and Medieval Literature. Harvard English Studies 5.
    Cambridge: Harvard University Press, 1974. 405 pp. [in
    honor of Bartlett Jere Whiting] See nos. 299, 444, 447, 500,
    1559, 1584, 1666, 2006, 2083, 2890.
        Reviews: VQR 51 (1975), lxvi.

44 BENSON, LARRY D. and SIEGFRIED WENZEL, eds. The Wisdom of
    Poetry: Essays in Early English Literature in Honor of
    Morton W. Bloomfield. Kalamazoo, MI: Western Michigan
    University, 1982. 314 pp. See nos. 256, 1792, 2166, 2186,
    2310.
        Reviews: Donald K. Fry, SAC 7 (1985), 163-65.

45 BESSINGER, JESS B., JR. and ROBERT R. RAYMO, eds. Medieval
    Studies in Honor of Lillian Herlands Hornstein. New York:
    New York University Press, 1976. 225 pp. See nos. 122,
    1010, 1131, 2149.

46 BLANCHOT, JEAN-JACQUES and CLAUDE GRAF, eds. Actes du 2^e
    colloque de langue et de littérature écossaises (Moyen Age et
    Renaissance). Univ. de Strasbourg 5-11 juillet 1978.
    Strasbourg: Univ. de Strasbourg. 429 pp. See nos. 732,
    760, 764, 776, 804, 832.

8

47   BOITANI, PIERO, ed. Chaucer and the Italian Trecento.
      Cambridge: Cambridge University Press, 1983. 313 pp. See
      nos. 15, 281, 315, 320, 438, 594, 598, 602, 658, 1178, 1179,
      1239, 1311, 1574, 2154, 2484.
         Reviews: Avril Bruten, TLS (6 January, 1984), 20; James
      Simpson, MAE 54 (1985), 306–08; Ian Bishop, RES, n. s., 36
      (1985), 557–58; Howard H. Schless, SAC 7 (1985), 170–71;
      Madison U. Sowell, JRMMRA 6 (1985), 173–82.

48   BOITANI, PIERO and ANNA TORTI, eds. Medieval and Pseudo-Medieval
      Literature. Tübinger Beiträge zur Anglistik 6. Tübingen:
      Narr, 1984. See nos. 607, 1111, 1273, 2496.
         Reviews: Noted in Speculum 60 (1985), 471.

49   BREWER, DEREK [S.], ed. Geoffrey Chaucer. Writers and Their
      Background. London: Bell, 1974; Athens: Ohio University
      Press, 1975. 401 pp. See nos. 8, 79, 114, 261, 291, 431,
      614, 623, 655, 662, 886, 2780, 2798.
         Reviews: Derek Pearsall, MLR 70 (1975), 846–49; TLS (14
      February, 1975), 177; Peter M. Vermeer, DQR 5 (1975), 138–45;
      Marjory Rigby, RES 27 (1976), 193–96; P. M. Kean, MAE 45
      (1976), 221–22.

50   BURGESS, GLYN S., A. D. DEYERMOND, W. H. JACKSON, A. D. MILLS,
      and P. T. RICKETTS, eds. Court and Poet: Selected
      Proceedings of the Third Congress of the International
      Courtly Literature Society, Liverpool, 1980. ARCA:
      Classical and Medieval Texts, Papers, and Monographs, Vol. 5.
      Liverpool: Cairns, 1981. See nos. 322, 1640, 1824.
         Reviews: H. F. Williams, JHP 6 (1982), 159.

51   BURROW, J. A. Essays on Medieval Literature. Oxford: Clarendon
      Press, 1984. [12 essays on English and Scottish writings,
      some previously printed, one new on Chaucer] See no. 1273.
         Reviews: Denton Fox, TLS (6 July, 1984), 759; M. M.
      Dubois, EA 38 (1985), 314; Derek Pearsall, ES 66 (1985),
      80–82; G. A. Lester, Lore&L 4 (1985), 90–91.

52   CARRUTHERS, MARY J. and ELIZABETH D. KIRK, eds. Acts of Inter-
      pretation: The Text in Its Contexts, 700–1600: Essays on
      Medieval and Renaissance Literature in Honor of E. Talbot
      Donaldson. Norman, OK: Pilgrim Books, 1982. 385 pp. See
      nos. 292, 415, 441, 668a, 1634, 1718, 2326, 2389, 2501.
         Reviews: William F. Pollard, SAC 6 (1984), 181–86;
      Speculum 60 (1985), 215.

53   COCOZZELLA, PETER, ed. The Late Middle Ages. Binghamton:
      Center for Medieval and Early Renaissance Studies, 1984 (for
      1981). See nos. 247, 1534.

Festschriften and Collections

54 CUMMINS, PATRICIA, PATRICK W. CONNER, and CHARLES W. CONNELL, eds. Literary and Historical Perspectives of the Middle Ages: Proceedings of 1981 SEMA Meeting. Morgantown: West Virginia University Press, 1982. See nos. 316, 575, 661.
Reviews: Alison Goddard Elliott, Speculum 59 (1984), 471-72.

55 DELLO BUORO, CARMEN J. Rare Early Essays on Geoffrey Chaucer. Rare Early Essays Series. Darby, PA: Norwood Editions, 1981. 219 pp. [late nineteenth-, early twentieth-century essays]

56 DIAMOND, ARLYN and LEE R. EDWARDS, eds. The Authority of Experience: Essays in Feminist Criticism. Amherst: University of Massachusetts Press, 1977. 304 pp. See nos. 1009, 2279.
Reviews: Mary Ellman, TLS (15 April, 1977), 452; N. Auerbach, NCF 32 (1977), 340-45.

57 EBIN, LOIS, ed. Vernacular Poetics in the Middle Ages. Studies in Medieval Culture 16. Kalamazoo: Western Michigan University, Medieval Institute Publications, 1984. See nos. 478, 2109, 2137, 2453.
Reviews: Paul Barrette, SAC 7 (1985), 183-88; Rita M. Verbrugge, C&L 35 (1985), 81-82.

58 ECONOMOU, GEORGE D., ed. Geoffrey Chaucer: A Collection of Original Articles. Contemporary Studies in Literature. New York: McGraw-Hill, 1975. 148 pp. See nos. 300, 340, 379, 580, 633, 1008, 1118, 1164.

59 GRAY, DOUGLAS, and E. G. STANLEY, eds. Middle English Studies Presented to Norman Davis in Honour of His Seventieth Birthday. Oxford: Clarendon Press, 1983. See nos. 132, 428, 686, 946, 953, 1279, 2139.
Reviews: Helen Neuss, TLS (6 July, 1984), 759; N. F. Blake, ES 65 (1984), 367-68; M. Rigby, RES, n. s., 36 (1985), 553-54; D. Mehl, N&Q 32 (1985), 92-93; F. Chevillet, EA 38 (1985), 314; Speculum 60 (1985), 479.

60 HEFFERNAN, THOMAS J., ed. The Popular Literature of Medieval England. Tennessee Studies in Literature 28. Knoxville: The University of Tennessee Press, 1985. See 350, 503, 709, 1067.

61 HERMANN, JOHN P. and JOHN J. BURKE, eds. Signs and Symbols in Chaucer's Poetry. University: University of Alabama Press, 1981. See nos. 311, 364, 501, 514, 1233, 1764, 2063, 2142,

2313.
Reviews: Glending Olson, Speculum 58 (1983), 263–64;
Cecily Clark, ES 64 (1983), 570–71; David C. Fowler, MP 81
(1984), 407–14; Ian Bishop, RES 35 (1984), 357–59; Dieter
Mehl, Anglia 102 (1984), 214–18.

62 HEYWORTH, P. L., ed. Medieval Studies for J. A. W. Bennett.
Oxford: Clarendon Press, 1981. See nos. 96, 106, 126, 994,
1366, 1985, 2238.
Reviews: A. V. C. Schmidt, MAE 51 (1982), 234–37; Larry D.
Benson, Speculum 58 (1983), 555; Piero Boitani, SAC 5 (1983),
166–73.

63 JEFFREY, DAVID LYLE, ed. Chaucer and Scriptural Tradition.
Ottawa, Ontario: University of Ottawa Press, 1984. See nos.
109, 629, 956, 970, 1112, 1120, 1172, 1175, 1182, 1760, 2096,
2778.
Reviews: Marianne G. Briscoe, C&L 34 (1985), 74–75;
Speculum 60 (1985), 746; M. T. Tavormina, JEGP 85 (1986),
99–102.

64 KINSMAN, ROBERT S., ed. The Darker Vision of the Renaissance:
Beyond the Fields of Reason. UCLA Center for Medieval and
Renaissance Studies Contributions, 6. Berkeley: University
of California Press. 320 pp. See nos. 2311, 2720, 2825.
Reviews: D. P. Walker, TLS (24 September, 1976), 1218;
Wayne Shumaker, RenQ 29 (1976), 263.

65 MITCHELL, JEROME and WILLIAM PROVOST, eds. Chaucer the Love
Poet. Athens: Georgia University Press, 1973. 117 pp.
[listed in no. 1, item no. 56] See also no. 466.
Reviews: Choice 11 (1974), 762; D. W. Robertson, SAB 39
(1974), 136–43; F. Diekstra, ES 57 (1976), 367–69; Martin
Lehnert, ZAA 24 (1976), 357–62; Charles Muscatine, Speculum
51 (1976), 522–24; G. C. Britton, N&Q 222 (1977), 82–86.

66 PEARSALL, DEREK, ed. Essays in Memory of Elizabeth Salter.
LeedsSE, n. s., 14 (1983). See nos. 976, 1202, 1751, 2333.

67 ROBBINS, ROSSELL HOPE. Chaucer at Albany. Middle English Texts
and Contexts, no. 2. New York: Franklin, 1975. See nos.
405, 489, 554, 1042, 1107, 1960, 2069, 2088, 2112, 2131.
Reviews: Speculum 52 (1977), 767; Marjorie Rigby, RES 29
(1978), 194–96; Heiner Gillmeister, Archiv 218 (1981),
166–70.

68 ROSE, DONALD M., ed. New Perspectives in Chaucer Criticism.
Norman, OK: Pilgrim, 1981. 248 pp. See nos. 94, 272, 352,
416, 422, 461, 508, 541, 578, 889, 897, 1907, 2066, 2400.

11

Festschriften and Collections

Reviews: David C. Fowler, MP 81 (1981), 407–14; Barry Windeatt, SAC 5 (1983), 202–07; Richard B. Marks, Speculum 58 (1983), 1133.

69   ROWLAND, BERYL, ed. Chaucer and Middle English Studies in Honour of Rossell Hope Robbins. London: Allen & Unwin; Kent, OH: Kent State University Press, 1974. 424 pp. See nos. 80, 168, 561, 600, 632, 653, 718, 851, 1099, 1117, 1139, 1362, 1433, 2352, 2366, 2436, 2629, 2753.
Reviews: E. Talbot Donaldson, TLS (28 February, 1975), 212; Morton Bloomfield, Speculum 51 (1976), 163–64; Janet M. Cowen, RES 27 (1976), 57–59; R. Derolez, ES 57 (1976), 260–62; Gisela Guddat-Figge, Anglia 95 (1977), 510–15.

70   ROWLAND, BERYL, ed. Companion to Chaucer Studies. rev. ed. New York: Oxford University Press, 1979. 516 pp. See nos. 75, 242, 403, 521, 588, 599, 627, 652, 850, 855, 981, 1094, 1104, 1119, 1140, 1194, 2047, 2114, 2128, 2164, 2348, 2490.

71   SALU, MARY and ROBERT T. FARRELL, eds. J. R. R. Tolkien, Scholar and Storyteller: Essays in Memoriam. Ithaca: Cornell University Press, 1982. 325 pp. See nos. 370, 1173, 1401, 2113.
Reviews: Emerson Brown, Jr., SAC 2 (1980), 204–07; M. Godden, RES, n. s., 32 (1981), 488–93; André Crépin, EA 34 (1981), 109; Charles Lloyd, SR 89 (1981), 281–87, esp. 286–87.

72   STROHM, PAUL and THOMAS J. HEFFERNAN, eds. Studies in the Age of Chaucer Proceedings 1, 1984: Reconstructing Chaucer. Papers presented at the Fourth International Congress of the New Chaucer Society, the University of York, August 6–11, 1984; selected and revised. Knoxville, TN: The New Chaucer Society, 1985. See 260, 294, 407, 583, 608, 660, 1093, 1101, 1291, 1431, 1465, 1589, 1888, 2055, 2101, 2204, 2304, 2354, 2486, 2783.

72a SZARMACH, PAUL E. and BERNARD S. LEVY, eds. The Fourteenth Century. Acta 4. Binghamton: Center for Medieval & Early Renaissance Studies, State University of New York at Binghamton, 1977. 135 pp. See nos. 418, 960, 1580, 1742, 2754.

73   VASTA, EDWARD and ZACHARIAS P. THUNDY, eds. Chaucerian Problems and Perspectives: Essays Presented to Paul E. Beichner, C. S. C. Notre Dame: University of Notre Dame Press, 1979. 264 pp. See nos. 284, 504, 663, 1122, 1257, 1411, 1412, 1513, 1621, 1812, 1835, 1856, 2165, 2474, 2505, 2523, 2530.
Reviews: Donald C. Baker, ELN 19:1 (1981), 56–59; J. D.

Festschriften and Collections

Burnley, <u>RES</u>, n. s., 33 (1982), 455–56.

74   WILKES, G. A. and A. P. RIEMER, eds. <u>Studies in Chaucer</u>. Sydney
      Studies in English. Sydney: University of Sydney, 1981.
      See nos. 1352, 1499, 1607, 1717, 1876.

LIFE

75   BAUGH, ALBERT C. "Chaucer the Man," in 70, pp. 1-20.

76   BRADDY, HALDEEN. "Chaucer, Alice Perrers, and Cecily
     Chaumpaigne." Speculum 52 (1977), 906-11.

77   BREWER, DEREK. Chaucer and His World. New York: Dodd, Mead;
     London: Eyre Methuen, 1978. 224 pp. [+historical, social
     backgrounds, illus.]
        Reviews: A. C. Spearing, TLS (24 November, 1978), 1372;
     John H. Fisher, SAC 1 (1979), 170-77; R. T. Davies, MLR 75
     (1980), 357-58.

78   CLOGAN, PAUL M. "Literary Criticism in William Godwin's Life of
     Chaucer." M&H, n. s., 6 (1975), 189-98.

79   DuBOULAY, F. R. H. "The Historical Chaucer," in 49, pp. 33-57.

80   FERRIS, SUMNER. "Chaucer, Richard II, Henry IV, and 13 October,"
     in 69, pp. 210-17.

81   GARDNER, JOHN [CHAMPLIN]. The Life and Times of Chaucer. New
     York: Knopf, 1976; London: Cape, 1977. 328 pp.
     [nominalism; Neoplatonism]
        Reviews: New Yorker 53 (25 April, 1977), 149-50; Time 109
     (16 May, 1977), 96, 98; James Hitchcock, Critic 36 (1977),
     74-76; Robert W. Hanning, GaR 31 (1977), 732-35; Theodore
     Morrison, BkW (27 March, 1977), E5; Anthony Quinton, SatR 4
     (16 April, 1977), 46, 48; Charles Muscatine, NYTB (24 April,
     1977), 13, 38-39; Sumner Ferris, Speculum 52 (1977), 970-74;
     Marvin Mudrick, HudR 30 (1977), 426-36; Gabriel Josipovici,
     NYRB 28 (1977), 18-22; Terrence A. McVeigh, America 136 (21
     May, 1977), 469-70; A. N. Wilson, NSt 94 (25 November, 1977),
     735-37; Choice 14 (1978), 1644; VQR 54 (1978), 14, 16; Janet
     M. Cowen, RES 29 (1978), 471-72; Beryl Rowland, QQ 85
     (1978-79), 719-20; John H. Fisher, SAC 1 (1979), 170-77; P.
     J. Frankis, N&Q 27 (1980), 248.

82   LELAND, VIRGINIA E. with JOHN L. LELAND. "'According to the Law

14

Life

of the Marsh and Our Realm of England': Chaucer as
Commissioner of Dikes and Ditches, 1390." MichA 14 (1981),
71-79. [+RvT, GP]

83   MacRAE, ANNETTE WATSON. "Geoffrey Chaucer: A New View of His
'Dismissal' from the Customs House." East Carolina
University M. A. Thesis, 1975. 87 pp.

84   REISNER, THOMAS A. and MARY E. REISNER. "Lewis Clifford and the
Kingdom of Navarre." MP 75 (1978), 385-90. [on a possible
acquaintance of Chaucer's]

85   TAKAHASHI, GENJI. "Chaucer's England--A Study of Godwin's Life
of Chaucer." MeiGR 380 (1985), 1-51.

86   YEAGER, R. F. "British Library Additional MS 5141: An Unnoticed
Chaucer Vita." JMRS 14 (1984), 261-81. [16th-century
account of Chaucer's life and works]

See also: 24, 258, 261, 285, 293, 319, 396, 413, 493, 605, 609, 791,
938, 1631, 1847, 2116, 2528, 2871.

MANUSCRIPT AND TEXTUAL STUDIES

87 ALDERSON, WILLIAM L. "John Urry," in 163 below, pp. 93–115.

88 AMY, ERNEST F. The Text of Chaucer's 'Legend of Good Women'.
    [1918]. New York: Haskell, 1965.

89 BAKER, DONALD C. "Frederick James Furnivall (1825–1910)," in 163
    below, pp. 157–169. [+Henry Bradshaw]

90 BATESON, F[REDERICK] W. "Could Chaucer Spell?" EIC 25 (1975),
    2–24.

91 BENSON, C. DAVID and DAVID ROLLMAN. "Wynkyn de Worde and the
    Ending of Chaucer's Troilus and Criseyde." MP 78 (1981),
    275–79.

92 BENTLEY, G. E., JR. "Comment Upon the Illustrated
    Eighteenth-Century Chaucer." MP 78 (1981), 398. See no. 144
    below.

93 BLAKE, N. F. "Chaucer Manuscripts and Texts." Rev 3 (1981),
    219–232. See no. 183. [review article]

94 BLAKE, N. F. "Chaucer's Text and the Web of Words," in 68, pp.
    223–40. [superiority of Hengwrt; questionable readings in
    CT: KnT, ParsT, ParsP, ClT, ShT, GP, RvT, MilT, NPT]

95 BLAKE, N. F. "The Editorial Assumptions in the Manly-Rickert
    Edition of The Canterbury Tales." ES 64 (1983), 385–400.

96 BLAKE, N. F. "On Editing the Canterbury Tales," in 62, pp.
    101–119. [superiority of Hengwrt]

97 BLAKE, N. F. "The Relationship Between the Hengwrt and the
    Ellesmere Manuscripts of the Canterbury Tales." E&S 32
    (1979), 1–18.

98 BLAKE, N. F. "The Textual Tradition of The Book of the Duchess."
    ES 62 (1981), 237–48. [spurious lines in Thynne]

16

99   BLAKE, N. F. The Textual Tradition of the 'Canterbury Tales'.
      London, Caulfield East, and Baltimore: Edward Arnold, 1985.
      Reviews: S. S. Hussey, THES (6 December, 1985), 17.

100   BLODGETT, JAMES E[DWARD]. "Some Printer's Copy for William
      Thynne's 1532 Edition of Chaucer." Library 1 (1979), 97–113.

101   BLODGETT, JAMES EDWARD. "William Thynne and His 1532 Edition of
      Chaucer." DAI 36 (1976), 5311A. Indiana University, 1975.

102   BLODGETT, JAMES E[DWARD]. "William Thynne (d. 1546)," in 163
      below, pp. 35–52. [textual variants; manuscript study]

103   BOYD, BEVERLY, ed. Chaucer According to William Caxton: Minor
      Poems and 'Boece', 1478. Lawrence, KS: Allen Press, 1978.
      202 pp.
      Reviews: Traugott Lawler, Speculum 55 (1980), 861; Richard
      R. Griffith, SAC 2 (1980), 151–53.

104   BOYD, BEVERLY. "William Caxton (1422?–1491)," in 163 below, pp.
      13–34. [+manuscript study]

105   BREWER, DEREK. "Middle English Romance and Its Audiences," in
      41, pp. 37–47. [Corpus Christi College, Cambridge, MS 61]

106   BREWER, DEREK. "Observations on the Text of Troilus," in 62, pp.
      121–38. [emends three Corpus readings]

107   BROWN, EMERSON, JR. "Thoughts on Editing Chaucer: The
      'Electronic-Information Revolution' and a Proposal for the
      Future." Chaucer Newsletter 2:2 (University of Oklahoma,
      1980), 2–3.

108   BROWN, EMERSON, JR. "Thoughts on the Variorum Chaucer." Chaucer
      Newsletter 2:1 (1980), 4–6.

109   CAIE, GRAHAM D. "The Significance of Marginal Glosses in the
      Earliest Manuscripts of The Canterbury Tales," in Papers from
      the First Nordic Conference for English Studies, Oslo, 17–19
      September, 1980. Edited by Stig Johansson and Bjorn Tysdahl.
      Oslo: University of Oslo, Institute of English Studies,
      1981, pp. 25–34. Reprinted in 63, pp. 75–88. [Ellesmere,
      Hengwrt, and Cambridge Dd. 4.24; Innocent III, De miseria
      humane conditionis]

110   CLOGAN, PAUL. "The Textual Reliability of Chaucer's Lyrics: 'A
      Complaint to His Lady'." M&H 5 (1974), 183–89.

Bibliography of Chaucer, 1974 - 1985

Manuscript and Textual Studies

111   COOK, DANIEL. "The Revision of Chaucer's Troilus: The Beta
       Text." ChauR 9 (1974), 51-62.

112   COWEN, JANET M. "Eighteenth-Century Ownership of Two Chaucer
       Manuscripts." N&Q 28 (1981), 392-94. [British Library MS
       Add. 12524, MS Add. 9832; +LGW]

113   DAVIS, R. EVAN. "The Pendant in the Chaucer Portraits." ChauR
       17 (1982), 193-95. [+St. Thomas of Canterbury, ampulla
       containing blood; iconography]

114   DONALDSON, E. T. "Chaucer's Manuscripts and Their Use," in 49,
       pp. 85-108.

114a   DOYLE, A. I. "Early 15th-Century Copies of Gower's Confessio
       Amantis and Chaucer's Canterbury Tales," in Buch und Text im
       15. Jahrhundert. Arbeitsgespräche in der Herzog August
       Bibliothek Wolfenbüttel vom 1. bis 3. März 1978. Hamburg:
       Hauswedell, 1981, pp. 47-50.

115   DOYLE, A. I. and GEORGE B. PACE. "Further Texts of Chaucer's
       Minor Poems." SB 28 (1975), 41-61. [ABC from Melbourne MS.;
       Truth from Nottingham ME LM I; Wom Unc from Bodleian Fairfax
       16]

116   DOYLE, A. I. and M. B. PARKES. "The Production of Copies of the
       Canterbury Tales and the Confessio Amantis in the Early
       Fifteenth Century," in Medieval Scribes, Manuscripts, &
       Libraries: Essays Presented to N. R. Ker. Edited by M. B.
       Parkes and A. G. Watson. London: Scolar, 1979, pp. 163-210.
       [Trinity College, Cambridge, MS R. 3.2]

117   DRIVER, MARTHA WESTCOTT. "The Early Editions of Chaucer's
       Troilus." DAI 41 (1981), 4391A. University of Pennsylvania,
       1980.

118   EDWARDS, A. S. G. "Variant Texts of 'The Parliament of Birds'."
       PBSA 69 (1975), 77-79.

119   EDWARDS, A. S. G. "Walter Skeat (1835-1912)," in 163 below, pp.
       171-89.

120   EDWARDS, A. S. G. and J. HEDLEY. "John Stow, The Craft of Lovers
       and T.C.C. R. 3.19." SB 28 (1975), 265-68. [Stow's edition
       of the Craft of Lovers, in the 1561 edition of Chaucer from
       Trinity College Cambridge R. 3.19]

121   ELLIOTT, CHARLES. "The Reeve's Prologue and Tale in the
       Ellesmere and Hengwrt Manuscripts." N&Q 11 (1964), 167-70.

18

122   FISHER, JOHN H. "The Intended Illustrations in MS Corpus Christi
       61 of Chaucer's Troylus and Criseyde," in 45, pp. 111-21.

123   FLETCHER, BRADFORD Y. "Printer's Copy for Stow's Chaucer." SB
       31 (1978), 184-201.

124   GARBÁTY, THOMAS J. "Wynkyn de Worde's 'Sir Thopas' and Other
       Tales." SB 31 (1978), 57-67. [+Caxton; Hengwrt; PrT, Mel,
       MkT]

125   HANNA, RALPH, III. "Robert K. Root (1877-1950)," in 163 below,
       pp. 191-205. [+McCormick]

126   HEYWORTH, P. L. "The Punctuation of Middle English Texts," in
       62, pp. 140-57. [+CT, ClT, TC; Usk, Testament of Love]

127   HUDSON, ANNE. "John Stow (1525?-1605)," in 163 below, pp. 53-70.
       [+Thynne]

128   HUTMACHER, WILLIAM FREDERICK. "A Transcription and Collation of
       Wynkyn de Worde's 1498 Edition of The Canterbury Tales with
       Cx^2, The General Prologue through The Franklin's Tale.
       (Volumes I-III.)" DAI 38 (1977), 779A. Texas Tech
       University, 1976.

129   HUTMACHER, WILLIAM F. Wynkyn de Worde and Chaucer's 'Canterbury
       Tales' with Caxton^2 from the General Prologue through The
       Knight's Tale. Amsterdam: Rodopi, 1978. 223 pp.
       Reviews: N. F. Blake, N&Q 26 (1979), 160-61.

130   JOHNSON, FRIDOLF, introd. William Morris Ornamentation and
       Illustrations from the Kelmscott Chaucer. New York: Dover
       Publications; London: Constable, 1973. 112 pp.
       Reviews: Doris Grumbach, New Republic 170 (26 January,
       1974), 33; American Artist 36 (1974), 15.

131   KANE, GEORGE. "John M. Manly (1865-1940) and Edith Rickert
       (1871-1938)," in 163 below, pp. 207-229. [+Ellesmere]

132   KANE, GEORGE. "The Text of The Legend of Good Women in CUL MS
       Gg.4.27," in 59, pp. 39-58.

133   KEISER, GEORGE R. "The Collation of the Cardigan Chaucer
       Manuscript." PBSA 73 (1979), 333-34.

134   KEISER, GEORGE R. "In Defense of the Bradshaw Shift." ChauR 12
       (1978), 191-201.

135   KEISER, GEORGE R. "Revision in Group E of The Canterbury Tales."

Manuscript and Textual Studies

Manuscripta 17 (1973), 159-77.

136 KELLIHER, HILTON. "The Historiated Initial in the Devonshire
     Chaucer." N&Q 24 (1977), 197. [representation of young
     Chaucer?]

137 KILLOUGH, GEORGE B[OYD]. "Punctuation and Caesura in Chaucer."
     SAC 4 (1982), 87-107.

138 KILLOUGH, GEORGE BOYD. "The Virgule in the Poetry of the
     Canterbury Tales. DAI 39 (1979), 5496A. Ohio University,
     1978.

139 KNIGHT, STEPHEN. "Textual Variants: Textual Variance." SoRA 16
     (1983), 44-54.

140 KUHN, SHERMAN M. "The Language of Some Fifteenth-Century
     Chaucerians: A Study of Manuscript Variants in the
     Canterbury Tales." SMC 4 (1974), 472-82. [+Manly-Rickert]

141 LERER, SETH. "An Unrecorded Proverb from British Library MS
     Additional 35286." N&Q 32 (1985), 305-06. [Mel]

142 LUCAS, PETER J. "Eighteenth-Century Ownership of Two Chaucer
     Manuscripts." N&Q 28 (1981), 392-98. [+LGW, The Tale of
     Guiscardo and Ghismonda]

143 McGREGOR, JAMES H. "The Iconography of Chaucer in Hoccleve's De
     Regimine Principum and in the Troilus Frontispiece." ChauR
     11 (1977), 338-50. [funerary iconography]

144 MISKIMIN, ALICE. "The Illustrated Eighteenth-Century Chaucer."
     MP 77 (1979), 26-55. [George Vertue's illustrations in Urry;
     Thomas Stothard's in Bell; William Blake] See no. 92 above.

145 MOORMAN, CHARLES. "Computing Housman's Fleas: A Statistical
     Analysis of Manly's Landmark Manuscripts in the General
     Prologue to the Canterbury Tales." ALLCJ 3 (1982), 15-35.
     [+Rickert]

146 MOSSER, DANIEL W. "Manly and Rickert's Collation of Huntington
     Library Chaucer Manuscript HM 144 (Hn)." PBSA 79 (1985),
     235-40. [Ellesmere MS, Cardigan MS, HM 144]

147 NEWTON, JUDITH MAY. "Another Text of Troilus: Kynaston's
     Version of Book II." ESELL 72 (Japan, 1981), 41-55. [Latin
     language translation]

148 NOKES, DAVID. "Pope's Chaucer." RES 27 (1976), 180-82.

Manuscript and Textual Studies

149   OWEN, CHARLES A., JR. "The Alternative Reading of The Canterbury
       Tales: Chaucer's Text and the Early Manuscripts." PMLA 97
       (1982), 237-50.

150   OWEN, CHARLES A., JR. "A Note on the Ink in Some Chaucer
       Manuscripts." Chaucer Newsletter 2:2 (University of
       Oklahoma, 1980), 14. [Ellesmere, Hengwrt]

151   OWINGS, FRANK N., JR. "Keats, Lamb, and a Black-Letter Chaucer."
       PBSA 75 (1981), 147-55. [+Speght]

152   PACE, GEORGE B. and LINDA E. VOIGTS. "A 'Boece' Fragment." SAC
       1 (1979), 143-50.

153   PAUL, JAMES. "A Defense of the Ellesmere Order." RLSt 5 (1974),
       118-20.

154   PEARSALL, DEREK. "Editing Medieval Texts: Some Developments and
       Problems," in Textual Criticism and Literary Interpretation.
       Edited by Jerome J. McGann. Chicago: University of Chicago
       Press, 1985, pp. 92-106. [Hengwrt, +Manly and Rickert,
       Robinson eds.]

155   PEARSALL, DEREK. "Thomas Speght (ca. 1550-?)," in 163 below, pp.
       71-92. [+Stow, Thynne]

156   PEAVLER, JAMES M. "Analysis of Corpora of Variations." CHum 8
       (1974), 153-59. [on programming for a variorum edition,
       lyrics]

157   PETTI, ANTHONY G. English Literary Hands from Chaucer to Dryden.
       London: Edward Arnold, 1977.
       Reviews: Johan Geritsen, ES 62 (1981), 92-93.

158   PRATT, ROBERT A. "Chaucer's Title: The Tales of Caunterbury."
       PQ 54 (1975), 19-25. [evidence from fifteenth century]

159   RAMSEY, ROY VANCE. "The Hengwrt and Ellesmere Manuscripts of the
       Canterbury Tales: Different Scribes." SB 35 (1982), 133-54.
       See Samuels, no. 165, below.

160   REINECKE, GEORGE F. "F. N. Robinson (1872-1967)," in 163 below,
       pp. 230-51.

161   ROOT, ROBERT K. The Textual Tradition of Chaucer's 'Troilus'.
       [Chaucer Society, 1916.] New York: Johnson Reprint, 1967.

Manuscript and Textual Studies

162   ROSS, THOMAS W. "Thomas Wright (1810-1877)," in 163 below, pp.
        145-56.

163   RUGGIERS, PAUL G., ed. Editing Chaucer: The Great Tradition.
        Norman, OK: Pilgrim, 1984. 301 pp. [discusses editions
        (1478-1957)] See nos. 87, 89, 102, 104, 119, 125, 127, 131,
        155, 160, 162, 178.
        Reviews: A. I. Doyle, Speculum 61 (1986), 700-04.

164   SALTER, ELIZABETH and DEREK PEARSALL. "Pictorial Illustration of
        Late Medieval Poetic Texts: The Role of the Frontispiece or
        Prefatory Picture," in Medieval Iconography and Narrative: A
        Symposium. Edited by Flemming G. Andersen, Esther Nyholm,
        Marianne Powell, and Flemming Talbo Stubkjaer. Odense:
        Odense University Press, 1980, pp. 100-23. [Troilus
        frontispiece in Corpus Christi College Cambridge MS 61]

165   SAMUELS, M. L. "The Scribe of the Hengwrt and Ellesmere
        Manuscripts of The Canterbury Tales." SAC 5 (1983), 49-65.
        [+linguistic approach] Challenges Ramsey, no. 159, above.

166   SEYMOUR, MICHAEL. "Manuscript Portraits of Chaucer and
        Hoccleve." BurM 124 (1982), 618-23. [Ellesmere, Harley
        4866; Corpus Christi College, Cambridge, MS 61]

167   SHERBO, ARTHUR. "A Lost MS of Chaucer's Legend of Good Women?"
        SB 35 (1982), 154-55. [+British Library Additional MS 9832,
        Samuel Pegge]

168   SILVIA, DANIEL S. "Some Fifteenth-Century Manuscripts of the
        Canterbury Tales," in 69, pp. 153-63.

169   STEVENS, MARTIN. "The Ellesmere Miniatures as Illustrations of
        Chaucer's Canterbury Tales." SIcon 7-8 (1981-82), 113-34.

170   THORPE, JAMES. Chaucer's 'Canterbury Tales': The Ellesmere
        Manuscript. 2nd ed. San Marino, CA: Huntington Library,
        1978. 24 pp. [rev. illus. ed. of A Noble Heritage, 1974]

171   THORPE, JAMES. "Chaucer's Canterbury Tales: The Ellesmere
        Manuscript," in Gifts of Genius: Treasures of the Huntington
        Library. San Marino, CA: The Huntington Library, 1981, pp.
        13-16. [popular treatment; includes color plates]

172   TSCHANN, JUDITH. "The Layout of Sir Thopas in the Ellesmere,
        Hengwrt, Cambridge Dd.4.24, and Cambridge Gg.4.27
        Manuscripts." ChauR 20 (1985), 1-13.

173   TURNER, ROBERT K., JR. "'The Two Noble Kinsmen' and Speght's

Manuscript and Textual Studies

Chaucer." N&Q 27 (1980), 175-76.

173a   WALLACE D[AVID] J. "Some Amendments to the Apparatus of
       Robinson's Works of Chaucer." N&Q 30 (1983), 202.

174   WHITE, JACK HAMMONS. "A Collation of Richard Pynson's 1492
       Edition of The Canterbury Tales and William Caxton's 1485
       Edition, with a Study of Pynson's Variants (Volumes I-III)."
       DAI 39 (1978), 2926A. Texas Tech University.

175   WIMSATT, JAMES I. Chaucer and the Poems of "Ch" in University of
       Pennsylvania MS French 15. Woodbridge, Suffolk: D. S.
       Brewer; London: Rowman and Littlefield, 1982. 136 pp.
       [fifteen French poems; early Chaucer?]
          Reviews: Susan Dannenbaum, SAC 6 (1984), 226-28; F. N. M.
       Diekstra, ES 65 (1984), 562-64; Bernard O'Donoghue, TLS (18
       May, 1984), 555; Karl Reichl, Anglia 103 (1984), 187-89;
       Claude Thiry, MA 91 (1985), 149-51.

176   WIMSATT, JAMES I. "Froissart, Chaucer, and the Pastourelles of
       the Pennsylvania Manuscript," in 72, pp. 69-79.
       [Pennsylvania MS French 15]

177   WINDEATT, B. A. "The Scribes as Chaucer's Early Critics." SAC 1
       (1979), 119-41.

178   WINDEATT, B. A. "Thomas Tyrwhitt (1730-1786)," in 163 above, pp.
       117-43.

179   YEAGER, R. F. "Literary Theory at the Close of the Middle Ages:
       William Caxton and William Thynne." SAC 6 (1984), 135-64.

See also: 86, 189, 190, 196, 261, 321, 344, 759, 824, 837, 878, 946,
            968, 1004, 1047, 1061, 1110, 1220, 1366, 1371, 1406, 1414,
            1434, 1442, 1607, 1767, 1917, 1953, 1992, 2139, 2238, 2359,
            2366, 2369, 2499, 2503, 2511, 2522, 2528, 2531, 2632, 2833.

FACSIMILES

180   Bodleian Library MS Fairfax 16. Introduction by John
       Norton-Smith. London: Scolar Press, 1979. 688 pp.
       [contains BD, HF, Anel, Mars, PF]
         Reviews: T. A. Shippey, TLS (7 March, 1980), 272; Donald
       C. Baker, SAC 3 (1981), 165-69; Pamela Gradon, RES 33 (1982),
       308-09.

181   MS Bodley 638. Introduction by Pamela Robinson. The Chaucer
       Facsimile Series, 2. General Editors, Paul G. Ruggiers and
       Donald M. Rose. Norman, OK: Pilgrim Books, 1981; Suffolk:
       Boydell-Brewer, 1982. 480 pp. [contains HF, BD, Anel, LGW,
       PF, Pity, ABC, For, Compl d'Am; +biblio.]

182   Cambridge Library MS GG.4.27. Introduction by Malcolm Parkes and
       Richard Beadle. The Chaucer Facsimile Series. Norman, OK:
       Pilgrim Books; Suffolk: Boydell-Brewer, 1980. 3 vols. 1034
       pp. [vol. 1 contains The Minor Poems, TC, part of CT; vol.
       2, remainder CT; vol. 3, LGW, PF, Lydgate's Temple of Glass,
       color plates, studies by Parkes and Beadle on the manuscript
       and illuminations]

183   The 'Canterbury Tales': A Facsimile and Transcription of the
       Hengwrt Manuscript, with Variants from the Ellesmere
       Manuscript. Introduction by Donald C. Baker, A. I. Doyle,
       and M. B. Parkes. The Variorum Edition of the Works of
       Geoffrey Chaucer, Vol. 1. Edited by Paul G. Ruggiers and
       Donald C. Baker. Norman: University of Oklahoma Press;
       Woodbridge: Boydell & Brewer, 1979. 1024 pp. [manuscripts
       of CT; introductions on historical, biographical, literary,
       and textual information]
         Reviews: Choice 16 (1979), 662; LJ 104 (15 April, 1979),
       951; George Kane, Mediaevalia 5 (1979), 283-89; William C.
       McAvoy, Manuscripta 25 (1981), 183-85; N. F. Blake, "Chaucer
       Manuscripts and Texts," Rev 3 (1981), 219-32; E. G. Stanley,
       N&Q, n. s., 29 (1982), 426-28; Derek Pearsall, ES 63 (1982),
       568-70.

184   Corpus Christi College Cambridge MS 61. Introduction by M. B.

Parkes and Elizabeth Salter. Cambridge: D. S. Brewer, 1978. 368 pp. [earliest extant text of TC?; paleographical description of the manuscript by Parkes; iconographical study of the illustration by Salter]
Reviews: Choice 15 (1979), 1514; Donald C. Baker, SAC 1 (1979), 187-93; M. C. Seymour, Library 4 (1982), 190-91.

185 St. John's College, Cambridge, MS L.1. Introduction by Richard Beadle and J. J. Griffiths. The Chaucer Facsimile Series, 3. General Editor, Paul G. Ruggiers. Norman, OK: Pilgrim Books, 1983. [TC, Henryson's Testament of Cresseid]

186 ROBINSON, DUNCAN. William Morris, Edward Burne--Jones and The Kelmscott Chaucer. London: Basilisk, 1975. [facsimile rpt. 1st ed., 1896; includes essay by D. Robinson on the work of William Morris] See no. 576.

187 Manuscript Pepys 2006, A Facsimile, Magdalene College, Cambridge. Introduction by A. S. G. Edwards. The Chaucer Facsimile Series, 6. General Editor, Paul G. Ruggiers. Norman, OK: Pilgrim Books; Woodbridge and Suffolk: Boydell & Brewer, 1986. [LGW, ABC, HF, Mars, Ven, For, PF, Mel, ParsP, ParsT, Ret, Anel, Scog, Purse, Truth, MercB]

188 MS Tanner 346: A Facsimile, Bodleian Library Oxford University. Introduction by Pamela Robinson. The Chaucer Facsimile Series, 1. General Editors, Paul G. Ruggiers and Donald M. Rose. Norman, OK: Pilgrim Books; Suffolk: Boydell-Brewer, 1980. 290 pp. [establishes the canon of the minor poems Anel, Mars, Ven, Pity; contains BD, PF, LGW, poems by Lydgate and Hoccleve]
Reviews: N. F. Blake, ES 63 (1982), 71-73.

188a The Pierpont Morgan Library MS M.817. Introduction by Jeanne Krochalis. The Chaucer Facsimile Series, 4. General Editor, Paul G. Ruggiers. Norman, OK: Pilgrim Books, 1986. 255 pp.

128,858

EDITIONS WITH NOTES

189   BAKER, DONALD C., ed. The 'Canterbury Tales', Part Ten: The
       Manciple's Tale. The Variorum Edition of the Works of
       Geoffrey Chaucer. Gen. Ed. Paul G. Ruggiers and Assoc. Ed.
       Donald C. Baker. Vol. 2. Norman: University of Oklahoma
       Press, 1984. 146 pp. [based on Hengwrt, collates ten
       manuscripts and twenty-one printed editions with critical
       commentary, survey of the criticism, and bibliographic index]
           Reviews: John Scattergood, SAC 7 (1985), 161-63.

190   BLAKE, N. F., ed. Geoffrey Chaucer: The 'Canterbury Tales',
       Edited from the Hengwrt Manuscript. London: Arnold, 1980.
       707 pp. [omits CYT and links joining SqT/MerT and
       MerT/FranT]
           Reviews: T. A. Shippey, TLS (16 January, 1981), 60; John
       H. Fisher, AEB 5 (1981), 160-62; L. Chaskalson, UES 19
       (1981), 36-38; E. G. Stanley, N&Q, n. s., 29 (1982), 428-29;
       Johan Kerling, ES 64 (1983), 91-92; Christina von Nolcken,
       RES 34 (1983), 56-58; Donald C. Baker, ELN 22:3 (1985),
       72-73.

191   BENSON, LARRY D., gen. ed., et al. The Riverside Chaucer. 3rd
       ed. [Based on The Works of Geoffrey Chaucer. Edited by F.
       N. Robinson.] Boston: Houghton Mifflin, 1987. 1327 pp.

192   BROWN, CARLETON, ed. The 'Pardoner's Tale' [by] Chaucer.
       [1935]; Oxford: Clarendon, 1974. 63 pp.

193   BROWN, EMERSON, JR. "Thoughts on Editing Chaucer: The
       'Electronic-Information Revolution' and a Proposal for the
       Future." Chaucer Newsletter 2:2 (1980), 2-3.

194   CAWLEY, A. C. Chaucer, 'Canterbury Tales'. rev. ed. (1958).
       London: A. Strahan, 1975.
           Reviews: ContempR 226 (1975), 280.

195   CIGMAN, GLORIA, ed. The Wife of Bath's Prologue and Tale and the
       Clerk's Prologue and Tale from the 'Canterbury Tales'. The
       London Medieval & Renaissance Series. London: University of

London Press, 1975; New York: Holmes & Meier, 1976. 194 pp.
Reviews: Choice 13 (1976), 977-78; Dorothy Colmer, YES 7
(1977), 208-09.

196   CLARK, WILLIAM BEDFORD. "Special Feature: An Interview with
       Paul G. Ruggiers on the Variorum Chaucer." SCRev 1 (1984),
       141-56. [on editing]

197   DONALDSON, E. T., ed. Chaucer's Poetry: An Anthology for the
       Modern Reader. 2nd ed. New York: Ronald, 1975; New York:
       Scott Foresman, 1984. [first edition, 1958]

198   FISHER, JOHN H., ed. The Complete Poetry and Prose of Geoffrey
       Chaucer. New York; London: Holt, Rinehart & Winston, 1977.
       1032 pp. [includes bibliography]
          Reviews: Derek S. Brewer, TSL 23 (1978), 119-22; Ralph
       Hanna III, Rev 1 (1979), 61-71; Roy Vance Ramsey, SAC 1
       (1979), 163-70.

199   HAVELY, N[ICHOLAS] R., ed. The Friar's, Summoner's and
       Pardoner's Tales from the 'Canterbury Tales'. London
       Medieval & Renaissance Series. London: University of London
       Press, 1975; New York: Holmes & Meier, 1976. 165 pp.
          Reviews: Choice 13 (1976), 977; Dorothy Colmer, YES 7
       (1977), 208-09.

200   HOWARD, DONALD R. and JAMES DEAN, eds. 'Troilus and Criseyde'
       and Selected Short Poems. The Signet Classic Poetry Series.
       New York: New American Library; London: New English
       Library, 1976. 327 pp.
          Reviews: Choice 14 (1977), 61.

201   MORGAN, GERALD, ed. Geoffrey Chaucer: The Franklin's Tale from
       The 'Canterbury Tales'. London Medieval and Renaissance
       Series. London: Hodder & Stoughton, 1980; Holmes & Meier,
       1981. 116 pp.
          Reviews: J. D. Burnley, Lore&L 3 (1980), 140-41; Jill
       Mann, Encounter (1980), 60-64; Choice 19 (1981), 75; Nicholas
       Jacobs, MAE 52 (1983), 126-30.

202   MORRISON, THEODORE, ed. The Portable Chaucer. Viking Portable
       Library. [1949]; New York: Viking Press, 1975;
       Harmondsworth: Penguin, 1977. 611 pp. [rev. ed.]

203   PACE, GEORGE B. and ALFRED DAVIS, eds. Geoffrey Chaucer: The
       Minor Poems: Part One. The Variorum Edition of the Works of
       Geoffrey Chaucer. Gen. Ed. Paul G. Ruggiers and Assoc. Ed.
       Donald C. Baker. Vol. 5. Norman: University of Oklahoma
       Press, 1982. 223 pp. [Part One contains Truth, Gent, Sted,

Editions with Notes

Form Age, For, Purse, Adam, Buk, Scog, Ros, MercB, Wom Nob, Wom Unc, Prov; texts and collations by Pace, critical introductions and notes by Davis]
Reviews: Paul Clogan, SAC 5 (1983), 179–83; R. T. Lenaghan, Speculum 59 (1984), 379–83; N. F. Blake, ES 65 (1984), 175–76.

204   PEARSALL, DEREK, ed. The 'Canterbury Tales', Part Nine: The Nun's Priest's Tale. The Variorum Edition of the Works of Geoffrey Chaucer. Gen. Ed. Paul G. Ruggiers and Assoc. Ed. Donald C. Baker. Vol. 2. Norman: University of Oklahoma Press, 1983/1984. 284 pp.
Reviews: AB Bookman's Weekly 75 (10 June, 1985), 4484–85; N. F. Blake, SAC 7 (1985), 229–33.

205   PHILLIPS, HELEN, ed. The Book of the Duchess. Durham and Saint Andrews Medieval Texts, Vol. 3. Scotland: Universities of Durham and Saint Andrews, 1983. 238 pp.
Reviews: J. Lawlor, MAE 54 (1985), 308–10; J. D. Burnley, RES 36 (1985), 409–10; John Frankis, DUJ 46 (1985), 264–65; A. Inskip Dickerson, Speculum 61 (1986), 128–30.

206   PRATT, ROBERT A., ed. The Tales of Canterbury Complete. Boston: Houghton Mifflin, 1974. 587 pp.
Reviews: Derek S. Brewer, YES 7 (1977), 205–08; R. T. Davies, N&Q 222 (1977), 170–71; F. Diekstra, ES 59 (1978), 370–72.

207   ROSS, THOMAS W., ed. The 'Canterbury Tales', Part Three: The Miller's Tale. The Variorum Edition of the Works of Geoffrey Chaucer. Gen. Ed. Paul G. Ruggiers and Assoc. Ed. Donald C. Baker. Vol. 2. Norman: University of Oklahoma Press, 1983. 273 pp. [based on Hengwrt, collates ten manuscripts and twenty printed editions with full critical apparatus]
Reviews: Choice 21 (1984), 702; Christian K. Zacher, Rev 6 (Charlottesville, 1984), 49–62; N. F. Blake, ES 65 (1984), 177–79; Jeremy Griffiths, SAC 7 (1985), 237–42.

208   SCHMIDT, A[UBREY] V. C., ed. The General Prologue to the 'Canterbury Tales', and the Canon Yeoman's Prologue and Tale." London Medieval and Renaissance Series. London: London University Press, 1974; New York: Holmes & Meier, 1976. 175 pp.
Reviews: W. D. Maxwell-Mahon, UES 14 (1976), 94–95; Choice 13 (1976), 977–78.

209   SPEARING A. C. and J. E. SPEARING, eds. The Reeve's Prologue and Tale with the Cook's Prologue and the Fragment of His Tale. Cambridge: Cambridge University Press, 1979. 128 pp.

BIBLIOGRAPHY OF CHAUCER, 1974 - 1985

[introduction, 1-65; with notes and glossary]

210   WILKINS, NIGEL. Chaucer Songs. Cambridge: D. S. Brewer, 1980.
       29 pp. [see also Wilkins, Music in the Age of Chaucer, no.
       2828]
          Reviews: Richard Rastall, EarlyMus 8 (1980), 547-48; David
       Fallows, MusT 124 (1983), 679-80.

211   WINDEATT, B[ARRY] A. "An Edition of Books 4 and 5 of Chaucer's
       Troilus and Criseyde." Ph.D. Thesis, University of
       Cambridge, 1975.

212   WINDEATT, BARRY [A.], ed. Geoffrey Chaucer: 'Troilus and
       Criseyde'. A New Edition of 'The Book of Troilus'. London:
       Longman, 1984. [TC text is side by side with Boccaccio's Il
       Filostrato]
          Reviews: Judith Ferster, "What Chaucer Really Did," EIC 35
       (1985), 345-50; B. O'Donoghue, TLS (12 April, 1985), 416.

213   WINNY, JAMES, ed. The Miller's Prologue and Tale from the
       'Canterbury Tales'. Selected Tales from Chaucer. London:
       Cambridge University Press, 1971. 108 pp.
          Reviews: V. E. Watts, DUJ 35 (1973), 108-09.

214   WINNY, JAMES, ed. The Prioress' Prologue and Tale from the
       'Canterbury Tales' by Geoffrey Chaucer. With Introduction,
       Glossary, and Notes. London and Cambridge: Cambridge
       University Press, 1975. 64 pp.
          Reviews: Dieter Mehl, Anglia 95 (1977), 233.

215   ZACHER, CHRISTIAN K. "Editorial Presence in the Variorum
       Chaucer." Rev 6 (1984), 49-62. [review article] See no.
       207 above.

See also: 95, 154, 163, 183, 1594, 2481.

MODERNIZATIONS AND TRANSLATIONS

216   BEIDLER, PETER G. "Chaucer and the Trots: What to Do about
       Those Modern English Translations." ChauR 19 (1985),
       290–301.

217   BERGNER, HEINZ, trans. Chaucer, Geoffrey: The Canterbury
       Tales/Die Canterbury-Erzählungen. Stuttgart: Reclam, 1982.
       560 pp. [dual language: Middle English/German]
       Reviews: AN&Q 21 (1982), 28.

218   CALUWÉ-DOR, JULIETTE DE, trans. Geoffroy Chaucer: Les Contes de
       Cantorbéry Ière partie. Ktemata 5. Ghent: Editions
       Scientifiques Story-Scientia, 1977. 147 pp. [Le Prologue
       général, Le Conte du chevalier, Le Conte du meunier, Le Conte
       du prêtre des nonnes]
       Reviews: H. Suhamy, EA 32 (1979), 462; Roy J. Pearcy, SAC
       3 (1981), 128–34.

219   CALUWÉ-DOR, JULIETTE DE. "Translating Chaucer into French, a
       Continuation." Chaucer Newsletter 5:1 (1983), 1, 7.

220   CHAN, MIMI. "On Translating Chaucer into Chinese." Renditions 8
       (1977), 39–51.

221   COGHILL, NEVILL. Geoffrey Chaucer, 'The Canterbury Tales': An
       Illustrated Selection. Rendered into Modern English.
       Harmondsworth, Middlesex, England: Penguin, 1978. [based on
       Coghill's 1951 translation]
       Reviews: B&B 23 (1978), 32; Martyn Wakelin, TES 10 (1978),
       24.

222   COGHILL, NEVILL, trans. The Prologue to 'The Canterbury Tales'
       by Geoffrey Chaucer in the Original Text from Caxton's First
       Edition with a Translation into Modern English. Salisbury:
       Perdix Press, 1984. 83 pp.
       Reviews: Bernard O'Donoghue, TLS (12 April, 1985), 416.

223   DONOHUE, JAMES J., ed. Chaucer's 'Canterbury Tales' Complete, in
       Present-Day English. Dubuque, IA: Loras College Press,

1979. 626 pp.

224   DONOHUE, JAMES J., trans. Chaucer's Lesser Poems Complete in
       Present-Day English. Dubuque, IA: Loras College Press,
       1974. 275 pp. [in verse]
       Reviews: Choice 12 (1975), 530.

225   DONOHUE, JAMES J., trans. Chaucer's 'Troilus and Cressida':
       Five Books in Present-Day English. Dubuque, IA: Loras
       College Press, 1975. 201 pp.
       Reviews: Choice 13 (1976), 816.

226   DUŢESCU, DAN. "Trei poeme în prezentarea şi tălmăcirea lui
       . . ." [Three Poems (by Chaucer) Presented and Translated by
       Dan Duţescu]. Secolul 20 (1978), 97-99. [Ros, Scog, Purse]

227   DUŢESCU, DAN. Troilus şi Cresida. Bucharest: Univers, 1978.
       With introduction, pp. 7-22.

228   EBI, HISATO, KEIKO HAMAGUCHI, and KAZUO YOSHIDA, trans. "The
       Wife of Bath's Prologue. Part 2." Shuru 44 (1983), 119-30.
       In Japanese.

229   EKRONI, AVIV. "Sippurei Canterbury." Moznayim 52 (1981),
       429-30. [analysis of Simon Sandback's Hebrew translation of
       CT]

230   HAGIWARA, FUMIHIKO. "Chaucer's ABC--A Japanese Translation."
       Prose & Poetry 35 (1980), 5.

231   HIRA, TOSHINORI. "The Romaunt of the Rose (Fragment A),
       Translated into Japanese." Bulletin of the Faculty of
       Liberal Arts, Nagasaki University, Humanities 21 (1981),
       75-88.

232   HIRAOKA, TERUAKI. "A Japanese Translation of The House of Fame,
       III, 1091-1656." Mimesis 12 (1980), 41-50.

233   JOHNSON, W. B., trans. Chaucer: La Rakontoj de Canterbury,
       Prologo. Glasgow: Eldonejo Kardo, 1980. 80 pp. [Esperanto
       trans. of GP]
       Reviews: Marjorie Boulton, N&Q, n. s., 28 (1981), 277.

234   KASHKINA, I. Introductory article to Russian translation of
       Canterbury Tales. Moscow: Khudozhestvennaya literature,
       1973. 527 pp.

235   LEHNERT, MARTIN, ed. and trans. Die Canterbury-Erzählungen.
       Leipzig, DDR: Insel-Verlag Anton Kippenberg, 1981. 696 pp.

Modernizations and Translations

Reviews: Georg Seehase, ZAA 31 (1983), 353-55.

236   LEHNERT, MARTIN, ed. and trans. Die Canterbury Tales. By
        Geoffrey Chaucer. Winkler Weltlit Werkdruckausq. Munich,
        BRD: Winkler Verlag, 1985. 696 pp.

237   SHIGEO, HISASHI, trans. "The Merchant's Tale (IV, 1213-2440)."
        MeiGR 337 (1983), 1-40. [Japanese prose translation with
        notes]

238   SHIGEO, HISASHI. "The Pardoner's Prologue and Tale, Fragment VI,
        11. 329-966." MeiGR 384 (1985), 1-24. In Japanese.

239   SHIGEO, HISASHI, trans. "The Wife of Bath's Prologue." MeiGR
        335 (1982), 1-32. [translation into Japanese with notes]

240   STONE, BRIAN, trans. Love Visions: 'The Book of the Duchess';
        'The House of Fame'; 'The Parliament of Birds'; 'The Legend
        of Good Women'. Harmondsworth, Eng.: Penguin, 1983. 262
        pp.
          Reviews: V. J. Scattergood, British Book News (1983), 640.

241   WRIGHT, DAVID, trans. The 'Canterbury Tales': A Verse
        Translation. By Geoffrey Chaucer. New York: Oxford
        University Press, 1985.
          Reviews: N. F. Blake, Lore&L 4 (1985), 95.

See also: 147, 745, 770, 2392.

GENERAL CRITICISM

242 ACKERMAN, ROBERT W. "Chaucer, the Church, and Religion," in 70, pp. 21–41. [in CT, ABC, For, Truth, Gent, TC, BD, HF, PF]

243 AERS, DAVID. Chaucer, Langland, and the Creative Imagination. London: Routledge & Kegan Paul, 1979. 236 pp. [criticism of the ecclesiastical in PP1, WBP, CT, TC
       Reviews: Paul Strohm, Criticism 22 (1980), 376–77; Victoria Rothschild, TLS (8 August, 1980), 901; Choice 17 (1980), 668; Jill Mann, Encounter (1980), 60–64; J. J. Anderson, CritQ 23 (1981), 82–83; Elton D. Higgs, SAC 3 (1981), 121–24; J. D. Burnley, RES 33 (1982), 309–11; Barbara Nolan, Speculum 58 (1983), 139–41; A. V. C. Schmidt, EIC (1983), 238–46.

244 ALDERSON, WILLIAM L. and ARNOLD C. HENDERSON. Chaucer and Augustan Scholarship. UCPES, 35. Berkeley: University of California Press, 1970. 284 pp.
       Reviews: T. A. Birrell, Neophil 47 (1973), 426–27.

245 ALKALAY-GUT, KAREN. "Problems in Literary Herstory: Chaucerian Msconceptions." RCEI 6 (1983), 73–78. [feminist criticism]

246 ALLEN, JUDSON BOYCE. The Ethical Poetic of the Later Middle Ages: A Decorum of Convenient Distinction. Toronto: University of Toronto Press, 1982. [in CT, LGW]
       Reviews: A. J. Colaianne, SAC 5 (1983), 137–40; A. J. Minnis, Speculum 59 (1984), 363–66; Gerald Morgan, MAE 53 (1984), 110–11.

247 AMES, RUTH M. "Corn and Shrimps: Chaucer's Mockery of Religious Controversy," in 53, pp. 71–88. [predestination; Lollardy; clerical celibacy; TC, CT]

248 AMES, RUTH M. God's Plenty: Chaucer's Christian Humanism. Chicago: Loyola University Press, 1984. [sex, love, marriage; Jews, OT; feminism; paganism]

249 AMES, RUTH M. "Prototype and Parody in Chaucerian Exegesis."

General Criticism

Acta 4 (1977), 87–105.

250   ANDŌ, SHINSUKE. "Chaucer no Joseitachi," in Eikoku Renaissance
      Bungaku no Joseizō. Edited by Peter Milward and Ishii
      Shōnosuke. Tokyo: Aratake, 1982, pp. 51–75. [women]

251   ANDŌ, SHINSUKE. "The Ideal of Feminine Beauty: A Comparative
      Note." PoetT 12 (Tokyo, 1981), 3–9. In English.

252   ANDŌ, SHINSUKE. "Kenkyū no Genkyō to Kadai: Chaucer." EigoS
      128 (1983), 722–23. In Japanese. [rev. article; women]

253   ANDŌ, SHINSUKE. "Women in Chaucer's Works," in The Images of
      Women in English Renaissance Literature. Edited by Institute
      of Renaissance Studies. Tokyo: Renaissance Library, 1982,
      vol. 13, pp. 51–75. In Japanese. [irony, humor, parody]

254   BACHMAN, WILLIAM BRYANT, JR. "Idealistic–Materialistic
      Opposition as an Informing Principle in Chaucer's
      Philosophical Narratives." DAI 36 (1976), 6696A. Syracuse
      University, 1975. [determinism; CT, TC]

255   BARDARIO, JOSÉ. "Chaucer: en torno a cuatro 'poemas mayores'"
      [Chaucer: A Reappraisal of Four 'Major Poems']. Estudios de
      filología inglesa 3 (1977), 19–39. [BD, PF, HF, LGW]

256   BARNEY, STEPHEN A. "Chaucer's Lists," in 44, pp. 189–223. [in
      TC, Anel, Rom, CT, BD, LGW, HF, PF, Pity]

257   BEIDLER, PETER G. "Chaucer and the Trots: What to Do about
      Those Modern English Translations." ChauR 19 (1985),
      290–301.

258   BENNETT, J. A. W. Chaucer at Oxford and Cambridge. Alexander
      Lectures, 1970. London and Oxford: Clarendon; University of
      Toronto Press, 1974. 131 pp. [Strode; Bradwardine; CT,
      mills, MilT, RvT]
         Reviews: James K. McConica, UTQ 45 (1975), 91–92; Robert
      B. Burlin, QQ 82 (1975), 636; Janet Coleman, MAE 44 (1975),
      307–11; Joseph E. Grennen, Thought 51 (1976), 110–11; E. T.
      Donaldson, MLR 71 (1976), 626–27; Martin Lehnert, ZAA 24
      (1976), 357–62; Norman Davis, RES 27 (1976), 336–37; Martin
      M. Crow, Speculum 52 (1977), 347–49; Peter M. Vermeer, ES 59
      (1978), 261–65; Karl Reichl, Anglia 100 (1982), 498–99.

259   BENNETT, J. A. W. "Chaucer, Dante, and Boccaccio," in Geoffrey
      Chaucer: Conferenze organizzate dall'Accademia Nazionale dei
      Lincei in Collaborazione con la British Academy. Problemi
      Attuali di Scienza e di Cultura, Quaderno 234. Roma:

Accademia Nazionale dei Lincei, 1977, pp. 3–22.

260   BENSON, LARRY D. "The 'Queynte' Punnings of Chaucer's Critics,"
       in 72, pp. 23–47.

261   BENSON, LARRY D. "A Reader's Guide to the Writings on Chaucer,"
       in 49, pp. 321–51. [general review]

262   BENSON, ROBERT G. "Gesture in Chaucer's Poetry." DAI 35 (1974),
       3670A. University of North Carolina, Chapel Hill. [TC]

263   BENSON, ROBERT G. Medieval Body Language: A Study of Use of
       Gesture in Chaucer's Poetry. Anglistica, 21. Copenhagen:
       Rosenkilde and Bagger, 1980. 170 pp. [CT, TC, PF, HF, Anel,
       LGW, BD, Rom, lyrics]
           Reviews: Edmund Reiss, SAtlR 46:1 (1981), 100–01; Werner
       Habicht, Anglia 100 (1982), 500–501; Helen S. Houghton, MAE
       51 (1982), 261–62; Barry Windeatt, SAC 4 (1982), 144–46; R.
       T. Davies, N&Q 29 (1982), 158; Alasdair A. MacDonald, ES 63
       (1982), 474–75.

264   BICKFORD, CHARLES G. "The Influence of Rhetoric on Chaucer's
       Portraiture." DAI 34 (1974), 5091A. University of
       Pennsylvania. [Geoffrey of Vinsauf, Matthew of Vendome, and
       Rhetorica ad Herennium; CT, TC, For, BD]

265   BIGGIO, ROSEMARY. "Narrative Technique and Closure in Chaucerian
       Works." DAI 44 (1983), 164A. St. John's University.
       [structuralism; symbolism; closure; CT, TC, PF, BD, HF, TC,
       CT]

266   BIRNEY, EARLE. Essays on Chaucerian Irony. Ed. Beryl Rowland.
       Toronto: University of Toronto Press, 1985. [previously
       published essays, including "Seven Kinds of Irony" by
       Rowland]

267   BISHOP, IAN. "Chaucer and the Rhetoric of Consolation." MAE 52
       (1983), 38–50. [BD, TC, CT]

268   BLAKE, N. F. "Geoffrey Chaucer: The Critics and the Canon."
       Archiv 221 (1984), 65–79. [unfinished works; HF]

269   BLAMIRES, ALCUIN. "Chaucer's Revaluation of Chivalric Honor."
       Mediaevalia 5 (1979), 245–269. [Truth, Mars, Th, KnT, Mel]

270   BLOOM, HAROLD, ed. Geoffrey Chaucer. New York: Chelsea, 1985.
       [nine previously published essays]

271   BLOOMFIELD, MORTON W. "Chaucer and Reason." UES 11:1 (March,

Bibliography of Chaucer, 1974 - 1985

General Criticism

1973), 1-3. [HF, LGW, CT]

272   BLOOMFIELD, MORTON W. "Contemporary Literary Theory and
       Chaucer," in 68, pp. 23-36. [semiotics; narrative;
       structuralism] See also nos. 461, 508.

273   BLOOMFIELD, MORTON W. "Essays on Chaucer." YR 60 (1971),
       438-40. [review article]

274   BLOOMFIELD, MORTON W. "Fourteenth-Century England: Realism and
       Rationalism in Wyclif and Chaucer." ESA 16 (1973), 59-70.

275   BOARDMAN, PHILLIP C. "The Role of the Poet in Chaucer's Early
       Dream Visions." DAI 35 (1974), 394A. University of
       Washington. [BD, HF, PF]

276   BOITANI, PIERO. "Chaucer and Lists of Tress." RMSt 2 (1976),
       28-44. University of Reading. [PF, KnT]

277   BOITANI, PIERO. "Chaucer's Temples of Venus." Studi Inglesi
       (Rome) 2 (1975) 9-31. [Boccaccio; HF, PF, KnT]

278   BOITANI, PIERO, ed. J. A. W. Bennett: The Humane Medievalist
       and Other Essays in English Literature and Learning from
       Chaucer to Eliot. Rome: Edizioni di storia e letteratura,
       1982. [previously published essays, two on Chaucer]

279   BOITANI, PIERO and A. TORTI, eds. Literature in Fourteenth
       Century England. Tübinger Beiträge zur Anglistik, 5.
       Germany: G. N. Verlag, 1983. [essays by various hands on
       poetry, drama, lyrics]
          Reviews: Noted in Speculum 60 (1985), 471.

280   BOITANI, PIERO. La Narrativa del Medioeve Inglese. Biblioteca
       di Studi Inglesi, 36. Bari: Adriatica Editrice, 1980.
       Trans. Joan Krakover Hall as English Medieval Narrative in
       the 13th and 14th Centuries. Cambridge: Cambridge
       University Press, 1982. [exempla; legends; comic tales;
       modern critical theory; BD, HF, PF, TC, LGW, CT]
          Reviews: N. F. Blake, ES 64 (1983), 77-78; John H. Fisher,
       SAC 5 (1983), 152-55; Helen Cooper, MAE 53 (1984), 121-23;
       Velma Bourgeois Richmond, Speculum 59 (1984), 623-25;
       Dorothea Siegmund-Schultze, ZAA 32 (1984), 359-61.

281   BOITANI, PIERO. "Style, Iconography, and Narrative: The Lesson
       of the Teseida," in 47, pp. 185-99. [HF, Anel, TC, LGW, CT]

282   BOYD, BEVERLY. Chaucer and the Medieval Book. San Marino, CA:
       Huntington Library, 1973. 176 pp.

Bibliography of Chaucer, 1974 - 1985

General Criticism

Reviews: Velma Bourgeois Richmond, FWF 1 (1974), 273-75;
N. F. Blake, Speculum 51 (1976), 314-16.

283   BOYD, BEVERLY. "Whatever Happened to Chaucer's Renaissance?"
       FCS 1 (1978), 15-21.

284   BREWER, DEREK [S]. "The Arming of the Warrior in European
       Literature and Chaucer," in 73, pp. 221-43. [Th, KnT, GP,
       TC]

285   BREWER, D[EREK] S. Chaucer. 3rd ed. London and New York:
       Longman, 1960, 1973. [life; romances; Boethius; PF, HF, A&A,
       CT, TC, LGW]

286   BREWER, DEREK [S]. "Chaucer and Arithmetic," in 42, pp. 111-19;
       and in 2064, pp. 155-64. [BD, HF, PF, TC, Astr, CT]

287   BREWER, D[EREK] S., ed. Chaucer: The Critical Heritage.
       London: Routledge & Kegan Paul, 1978. 2 vols. 342 pp. and
       510 pp. [references to Chaucer from Deschamps to Rosamond
       Tuve]
          Reviews: A. G. Rigg, RES 30 (1979), 336-38; R. T. Davies,
       N&Q 26 (1979), 62-63; T. A. Shippey, TLS (30 November, 1979),
       73; Choice 15 (1979), 1662; J. M. Maguin, CahiersE 19 (1981),
       101; Derek Pearsall, MLR 76 (1981), 158-59.

288   BREWER, DEREK [S]. Chaucer the Poet as Storyteller. London:
       Macmillan Press, 1984. 150 pp. [Chaucer's sources; genre of
       PF; comic tales; fabliaux; rationalism]
          Reviews: Bernard O'Donoghue, TLS (12 April, 1985), 416.

288a   BREWER, D[EREK] [S]. "Chaucer's Attitudes to Music." PoetT
       15/16 (1983), 128-35.

289   BREWER, DEREK [S]. "Children in Chaucer." REL 5:3 (1964),
       52-60.

290   BREWER, DEREK [S]. English Gothic Literature. History of
       Literature Series. New York: Schocken Books, 1983. [court,
       monastery; works of Chaucer]
          Reviews: Helen Cooper, MAE 54 (1985), 295-96.

291   BREWER, DEREK S. "Gothic Chaucer," in 49, pp. 1-32.

292   BREWER, DEREK [S]. "The Grain of the Text," in 52, pp. 119-27.
       [TC; versification; scribes]

293   BREWER, DEREK [S]. An Introduction to Chaucer. London:
       Longman, 1984.

Bibliography of Chaucer, 1974 - 1985

General Criticism

        Reviews: Bernard O'Donoghue, TLS (12 April, 1985), 416.

294   BREWER, DEREK [S]. "The Reconstruction of Chaucer," in 72, pp.
       3-19. [BD, HF, PF, LGW, NPT]

295   BREWER, D[EREK] S. "Structures and Character-Types of Chaucer's
       Popular Comic Tales," in Estudios sobre los géneros
       literarios, I: Grecia clásica e Inglaterra. Edited by
       Javier Coy and Javier De Hoz, eds. Acta Salmanticensia,
       Filosofía y Letras 89. Salamanca: Universidad de Salamanca,
       1975, pp. 107-18. [in CT]

296   BREWER, DEREK [S]. Symbolic Stories: Traditional Narratives of
       the Family Drama in English Literature. Cambridge: D. S.
       Brewer; Totowa, NJ: Rowman and Littlefield, 1980. 190 pp.
       [chapter on Chaucer]
          Reviews: W. R. J. B., CritQ 23 (1981), 92; R. W. Hanning,
       Speculum 57 (1982), 864-67; C. Gauvin, EA 35 (1982), 439.

297   BREWER, DEREK S. Towards a Chaucerian Poetic. Sir Israel
       Gollanez Memorial Lecture, British Academy, 1974. From the
       Proceedings of the British Academy, 60. London: Oxford
       University Press, 1974. 36 pp.
          Reviews: Götz Schmitz, Anglia 95 (1977), 515-18.

298   BREWER, DEREK [S]. Tradition and Innovation in Chaucer.
       Atlantic Highlands, NJ: Humanities Press; London and
       Basingstoke: Macmillan Press, 1982. 181 pp. [collection of
       Brewer's articles]
          Reviews: A. S. G. Edwards, Speculum 59 (1984), 716.

299   BROOKHOUSE, CHRISTOPHER. "In Search of Chaucer: The Needed
       Narrative," in 43, pp. 67-80. [BD, HF, PF, TC, CT]

300   BROWN, EMERSON, JR. "Chaucer and the European Literary
       Tradition," in 58, pp. 37-54. [CT]

301   BROWN, P. Chaucer's Visual World: A Study of His Poetry and the
       Medieval Optical Tradition. England: University of York,
       D.Phil, 1981. 2 vols. [CT] See also no. 2788.

302   BUCKMASTER, ELIZABETH MARIE. "'Caught in Remembraunce': Chaucer
       and the Art of Memory." DAI 42 (1981), 2136A. University of
       Delaware. [HF, GP, KnT]

303   BURCHFIELD, ROBERT. "Realms and Approximations: Sources of
       Chaucer's Power." E&S 35 (1982), 1-13.

304   BURCHMORE, DAVID WEGNER. "Through Secret Sense: The

Transformations of Myth in Medieval and Renaissance Literature." DAI 40 (1980), 5044A. University of Virginia. [TC, MerT, WBT]

305   BURLIN, ROBERT B. Chaucerian Fiction. Princeton: Princeton University Press, 1977. 294 pp. [poetic; philosophical; psychological]
        Reviews: Earl F. Guy, Ariel 9 (1978), 97-99; Derek S. Brewer, TLS 15 (16 June, 1978), 669; Gloria Cigman, RES 24 (1978), 469-70; R. T. Davies, N&Q 25 (1978), 356-58; Donald Howard, JEGP 77 (1978), 267-70; Judson Boyce Allen, Speculum 54 (1979), 116-18; Lee W. Patterson, UTQ 48 (1979), 236-82; A. J. Minnis, MAE 49 (1980), 145-49; Robert M. Jordan, Rev 2 (1980), 46-69; Russell A. Peck, SAC 2 (1980), 154-58; J. M. Maguin, CahiersE 19 (1981), 99.

306   BURNLEY, J. D. Chaucer's Language and the Philosophers' Tradition. Chaucer Studies, 2. Cambridge: D. S. Brewer; Totowa, NJ: Rowman and Littlefield, 1979. 196 pp. [tyrant topos; Senecan antitypes; CT, TC]
        Reviews: Choice 17 (1980), 526-27; Jill Mann, Encounter (1980), 60-64; T. A. Shippey, TLS (7 March, 1980), 272; John H. Fisher, Speculum 56 (1981), 448-49; A. V. C. Schmidt, MAE 50 (1981), 344-46; Peter Mack, MLR 77 (1982), 404-405; Götz Schmitz, Anglia 100 (1982), 183-85; Phillipa Hardman, RES 33 (1982), 71-73; Doreen M. E. Gilliam, ES 63 (1982), 360-63; John M. Hill, SAC 5 (1983), 156-60.

307   BURNLEY, J. D. "Chaucer's Termes." YES 7 (1977), 53-67. [comparisons with contemporaries]

308   BURROW, J. A. "The Poet as Petitioner." SAC 3 (1981), 61-75. [For, Purse, Scog, HF, LGW]

309   BURROW, J. A. Ricardian Poetry: Chaucer, Gower, Langland, and the Gawain Poet. New Haven, CT: Yale University Press, 1971. 174 pp.
        Reviews: M. C. Seymour, ES 54 (1973), 274-75; Theodore A. Stroud, MP 71 (1973), 71-73; Albert B. Friedman, ELN 11:2 (1983), 126-28; G. C. Britton, N&Q 20 (1973), 29-30; Morton W. Bloomfield, Speculum 48 (1973), 345-47.

310   CALIN, WILLIAM. "Defense and Illustration of Fin'Amor: Some Polemical Comments on the Robertsonian Approach," in 2678, pp. 32-48.

311   CHAMBERLAIN, DAVID. "Musical Signs and Symbols in Chaucer: Convention and Originality," in 61. [CT, PF, BD, HF, TC, Boece, LGW, Mars]

Bibliography of Chaucer, 1974 - 1985

General Criticism

312   CHANCE, JANE. "Chaucer and Mythology." Chaucer Newsletter 6:1
        (1984), 1-2. [Virgil, Lucan, Statius, Martianus Capella,
        Boethius, Ovid]

313   "Chaucer's Audience: Discussion." ChauR 18 (1983), 175-81.
        [symposium by thirteen Chaucerians]

314   CHERCHI, PAOLO. "The First German Essay on Chaucer." ChauR 13
        (1978), 80-85. [Karl Flögel]

315   CHILDS, WENDY. "Anglo-Italian Contacts in the Fourteenth
        Century," in 47, pp. 65-87.

316   CHISNELL, ROBERT E. "Chaucer's Neglected Prose," in 54, pp.
        156-73.

317   CHRISTIANSON, PAUL. "Chaucer's Literacy." ChauR 11 (1976),
        112-27. [TC II, 255-73]

318   CLARK, GEORGE. "Chaucer's Third and Fourth of May." RUO 52
        (1982), 257-65. [TC, NPT, KnT; medieval lunaria]

319   CLOGAN, PAUL M. "Literary Criticism in William Godwin's Life of
        Chaucer." M&H 6 (1975), 189-98.

320   COLEMAN, JANET. "English Culture in the Fourteenth Century," in
        47, pp. 33-63.

321   COLEMAN, JANET. Medieval Readers and Writers, 1350-1400. New
        York: Columbia University Press, 1981. 337 pp. [reform and
        edification; references to CT]
          Reviews: Fred C. Robinson, SR (1982), 608-12; Thomas John
        Heffernan, SAC 5 (1983), 160-64; Charles R. Young, SAQ
        (1983), 109.

322   COLLINS, MARIE. "Love, Nature, and Law in the Poetry of Gower
        and Chaucer," in 50, pp. 113-28. [animal imagery; metaphor]

323   CRAMPTON, GEORGIA R[ONAN]. The Condition of Creatures:
        Suffering and Action in Chaucer and Spenser. New Haven and
        London: Yale University Press, 1974. 207 pp. [KnT]
          Reviews: A. Kent Hieatt, SpenN 6 (1975), 1-3; John M.
        Steadman, RenQ 29 (1976), 268-71; D. S. Brewer, N&Q 23
        (1976), 560; Hugh A. Maclachlan, Ren&R 12 (1976), 55-56;
        Peter M. Vermeer, DQR 6 (1976), 74-78; P. L. Bayley, RES 27
        (1976), 197-98; Helen Cooper, MLR 72 (1977) 887-88; A. C.
        Hamilton, MAE 46 (1977), 155-57; Götz Schmitz, Anglia 96
        (1978), 511-13; Morton W. Bloomfield, RBPH 59 (1981), 740-41.

324   CRAMPTON, GEORGIA R[ONAN]. "Other Senses of Ending," in 778, pp.
       132-42. [closure; +Spenser]

325   DAVID, ALFRED. "An Iconography of Noses: Directions in the
       History of a Physical Stereotype," in Mapping the Cosmos.
       Edited by Jane Chance and R. O. Wells. Houston, TX: Rice
       University Press, 1985, pp. 76-97. [GP Miller, Prioress;
       RvT]

326   DAVID, ALFRED. The Strumpet Muse: Art and Morals in Chaucer's
       Poetry. Bloomington: Indiana University Press, 1976. 280
       pp. [TC, CT, LGW]
          Reviews: Gabriel Josipovici, NYRB (28 April, 1977), 18-22;
       Marvin Mudrick, HudR 30 (1977), 426-36; Victoria Rothschild,
       TLS (13 January, 1978), 43; Howell Chickering, Jr., Speculum
       53 (1978), 565-67; Chauncey Wood, JEGP 77 (1978), 423-25; Lee
       W. Patterson, UTQ 48 (1979), 263-82; Charles Owen, Jr., SAC 1
       (1979), 158-63; Larry M. Sklute, ELN 16:4 (1979), 325-28.

327   DELLO BUORO, CARMEN J. Rare Early Essays on Geoffrey Chaucer.
       Rare Early Essays Series. Darby, PA: Norwood Editions,
       1981. 219 pp. [late nineteenth, early twentieth century
       essays]

328   DeNERVILLE, CATHERINE J. M. "An Analysis and Classification of
       Four Critical Approaches to Chaucer in the Twentieth
       Century." DAI 35 (1974), 1619A. Catholic University.

329   DIEKSTRA, F. N. M. "Some Recent Books on Chaucer." ES 65
       (1984), 555-569. [review article] See nos. 175, 462, 586,
       625, 922, 2390, 2467, 2828.

330   DILLARD, NANCY F. "The English Fabular Tradition: Chaucer,
       Spenser, Dryden." DAI 34 (1974), 7186A. University of
       Tennessee. [PF, CT]

331   DINSHAW, CAROLYN LOUISE. "Chaucer and the Text: Two Views of
       the Author." DAI 43 (1983), 2342-43A. Princeton University,
       1982. [TC, LGW, HF, LGWP]

332   DONALDSON, E. TALBOT. "Chaucer in the Twentieth Century." SAC 2
       (1980), 7-13. [twentieth-century conflict of opinions; TC]

333   DONALDSON, E. TALBOT. "Chaucer's Three 'P's': Pandarus,
       Pardoner and Poet." MQR 14 (1975), 282-301. [TC, CT]

334   DONALDSON, E. TALBOT. "Designing a Camel; or, Generalizing the
       Middle Ages." TSL 22 (1977) 1-16. [CT]

BIBLIOGRAPHY OF CHAUCER, 1974 - 1985

General Criticism

335 DONALDSON, E. TALBOT. "The Presidential Address, 1979: Chaucer
     in the Twentieth Century." SAC 2 (1980), 7-13. [TC]

336 DOVE, MARY. "The Criticism of Medieval Literature: A Sermon
     and an Exemplum." CR 21 (1979) 36-44. [GP: Yeoman]

337 DUMITRESCU-BUŞULENGA, ZOE. "Un om între vremuri: Geoffrey
     Chaucer" [A Man Between Ages: Geoffrey Chaucer], in Valori
     şi echivalenţe umanistice [Humanistic Values and
     Equivalences]. Bucharest: Editura Eminescu, 1973, pp.
     331-59.

338 DUNĂREANU, LUCIAN. "Naratorii Geoffrey Chaucer şi Ion Creangă"
     [Geoffrey Chaucer and Ion Creangă, Narrators]. Philologia 25
     (1980), 71-74 (Studia Universitatis Babeş-Bolyai,
     Cluj-Napoca).

339 EADE, J. C. "'We Ben to Lewed or to Slowe': Chaucer's Astronomy
     and Audience Participation." SAC 4 (1982), 53-85. [CT]

340 ECONOMOU, GEORGE D. "Introduction: Chaucer the Innovator," in
     58, pp. 1-14. [CT]

341 ECONOMOU, GEORGE D. "The Two Venuses and Courtly Love," in The
     Pursuit of Perfection: Courtly Love in Medieval Literature
     by Joan M. Ferrante and George D. Economou. National
     University Publications Series in Literary Criticism. Port
     Washington, NY: Kennikat, 1975, pp. 17-50. [CT, PF, TC,
     Ros]

342 ELBOW, PETER. Oppositions in Chaucer. Middletown: Wesleyan
     University Press, 1975. 180 pp. [+Boethius]
       Reviews: Frank C. Gardiner, AN&Q 16 (1977), 60-62; Colin
     Wilcockson, MAE 48 (1979), 146-48.

343 ERZGRÄBER, WILLI, ed. Geoffrey Chaucer. Wege der Forschung,
     253. Darmstadt: Wissenschaftliche Buchgesellschaft, 1983,
     pp. 447-69. [prev. pub. essays]

344 EVANS, GILLIAN. Chaucer. Authors in Their Age. Glasgow:
     Blackie, 1977. 150 pp. [introductory]

344a FAROOQI, KHALIDA SALEEM. "Chaucer's Religion in His Art." ARIEL
     7 (Jamshoro, 1981-82), 13-21.

345 FASHBAUGH, ELMER JACK. "Chaucer's Troubled Endings." DAI 44
     (1983), 1082A. Ohio State University.

346 FERSTER, JUDITH. Chaucer on Interpretation. Cambridge and New

York: Cambridge University Press, 1985. [KnT, BD, PF, ClT, WBP, WBT, CT; Harry Bailly]
Reviews: A. C. Spearing, EIC 36 (1986), 68-75.

347 FERSTER, JUDITH. "What Chaucer Really Did." EIC 35 (1985), 345-50. [review art.] See no. 212.

348 FICHTE, JOERG O. Chaucer's "Art Poetical": A Study in Chaucerian Poetics. Studies and Texts in English, 1. Tübingen: Gunter Narr, 1980. [BD, PF, HF, KnT]
Reviews: Alan T. Gaylord, Speculum 56 (1981), 608-11; Dieter Mehl, Anglia 100 (1982), 181-83; Thorlac Turville-Petre, YES 13 (1983), 296-97; Phillipa Hardman, RES 34 (1983), 55-56.

349 FINEMAN, JOEL. "The Structure of Allegorical Desire," in Allegory and Representation. Edited by Stephen J. Greenblatt. Baltimore, MD; London: Johns Hopkins University Press, pp. 26-60. [Levi-Strauss; Saussure; Jakobson; Freud; Heidegger; Derrida]

350 FISHER, JOHN H. "Chaucer and the Written Language," in 60, pp. 237-51. [CT]

351 FISHER, JOHN H. "Chaucer's Prescience." SAC 5 (1983), 3-15. [reader response theories; ClT]

352 FLEMING, JOHN V. "Chaucer and the Visual Arts of His Time," in 68, pp. 121-36. [iconography; GP Summoner; RvT, FrT]

353 FORD, BORIS, ed. Medieval Literature: Chaucer and the Alliterative Tradition. London: Penguin Press, 1982. [a revised version of The Age of Chaucer, vol. 1 of the Pelican Guide to English Literature]
Reviews: J. J. A[nders], CritQ 23 (1982), 92; James Simpson, MAE 53 (1984), 307-11; Avril Bruten, TLS (6 January, 1984), 20.

354 FOWLER, DAVID C. "Additions to the Golden Mountain: Four Recent Books on Chaucer." MP 81 (1984), 407-14. [review article] See nos. 61, 68, 859, 1253.

355 FREIWALD, LEAH ZEVA. "Chaucer's Use of Classical Mythology: The Myths in the Context of the Medieval Audience." DAI 44 (1984), 2467-68A. [BD, LGWP, KnT, TC]

356 FRIEDMAN, JOHN BLOCK. "Another Look at Chaucer and the Physiognomists." SP 78 (1981), 138-52. [affective compared to humoral; Aristotle]

BIBLIOGRAPHY OF CHAUCER, 1974 - 1985

General Criticism

357   FRIES, MAUREEN. "The 'Other' Voice: Woman's Song, Its Satire and Its Transcendence in Late Medieval British Literature," in Vox Feminae: Studies in Medieval Woman's Songs. Studies in Medieval Culture, 15. Edited by John F. Plummer. Kalamazoo: Medieval Institute, Western Michigan University, 1981, pp. 155-78. [CT, TC]

358   FRIMAN, ANNE. "Of Bretherhede: The Friendship Motif in Chaucer." Innisfree 3 (1976), 24-36. [CT]

359   GALANTIC, ELIZABETH JOYCE. "Chaucer's Dream-Visions: His Evolving Critical Perspective." DAI 43 (1983), 2996-97A. Harvard University, 1982.

360   GARBÁTY, THOMAS J. "Chaucer and Comedy." Genre 9 (1976), 451-68. [comedy, tragedy, fabliau]

361   GARBÁTY, THOMAS J. "Chaucer and Comedy," in Versions of Medieval Comedy. Edited by Paul G. Ruggiers. Norman: University of Oklahoma Press, 1977, pp. 173-90. [comedy, tragedy, fabliaux]

362   GARBÁTY, THOMAS J. "The Degradation of Chaucer's 'Geffrey'." PMLA 89 (1974), 97-104. [BD, PF, HF, CT, LGW, Th]

363   GARDNER, JOHN CHAMPLIN. The Poetry of Chaucer. Carbondale: Southern Illinois University Press, 1977. 408 pp. [Chaucer's development: BD, PF, TC, HF, LGW, CT]
        Reviews: Charles Muscatine, NYRB (24 April, 1977), 38-39; Robert W. Hanning, GaR 31 (1977), 732-35; Theodore Morrison, BkW (27 March, 1977), E5; Gabriel Josipovici, NYRB (28 April, 1977), 18-22; Joseph E. Milosh, Cithara 17 (1977), 58-60; Marvin Mudrick, HudR 30 (1977), 426-36; Victoria Rothschild, TLS (13 January, 1978), 43; Lee W. Patterson, UTQ 48 (1979), 263-82; John H. Fisher, SAC 1 (1979), 170-77; R. A. Shoaf, MP 77 (1980), 317-20.

364   GARDNER, JOHN. "Signs, Symbols, and Cancellations," in 61, pp. 195-207. [CT, BD, PF, LGW, TC, Anel]

365   GELLRICH, JESSE M. The Idea of the Book in the Middle Ages: Language Theory, Mythology, and Fiction. Ithaca, NY: Cornell University Press, 1985. [+Levi-Strauss, Foucault, Barthes, Derrida, St. Augustine; music, architecture, scholasticism] See nos. 1189, 2089, 2133.

366   GILLIARD, FRANK D. "Chaucer's Attitude Towards Astrology." JWCI 36 (1973), 365-66.

44

367 GILLMEISTER, HEINER. Discrecioun: Chaucer und die Via Regia.
     Studien zur englischen Literatur 8. Bonn: Bouvier, 1972.
     250 pp. [CT]
        Reviews: Derek S. Brewer, Anglia 94 (1976), 228-32.

368 GINSBERG, WARREN. "The Cast of Character: Chaucer and the
     Conventions of Reality," in The Representation of Personality
     in Ancient and Medieval Literature. Toronto: University of
     Toronto Press, 1983. 202 pp. [BD, CT, LGW, MLT, ClT]
        Reviews: Elaine Tuttle Hansen, MLQ 44 (1983), 314-17; Mark
     Allen, SAC 6 (1984), 192-96; Robert W. Hanning, Speculum 60
     (1985), 404-06.

369 GRAHAM, PAUL TREES. "The Meaning of Structure in Chaucerian
     Narrative." DAI 40 (1980), 5045A. University of
     Missouri-Columbia, 1979. [BD, CT]

370 GRAY, DOUGLAS. "Chaucer and 'Pite'," in 71, pp. 173-203. [TC,
     CT, Pity, PF]

371 GREEN, RICHARD FIRTH. "Women in Chaucer's Audience." ChauR 18
     (1983), 146-54.

372 GROSS, LAILA. "The Heart: Chaucer's Concretization of
     Emotions." McNR 21 (1974-75), 89-102. [medieval physiology]

373 GROSSMAN, JUDITH. "The Correction of a Descriptive Schema: Some
     'Buts' in Barbour and Chaucer." SAC 1 (1979), 41-54. [char.
     of Criseyde; TC, CT]

374 HAAS, RENATE. "Chaucer's Use of the Lament for the Dead," in
     Chaucer in the Eighties. Edited by Julian N. Wasserman and
     Robert J. Blanch. Syracuse, NY: Syracuse University Press,
     1986, pp. 23-37. [Pity, BD, SqT, LGW, MLT, PhyT, ManT, TC,
     NPT]

375 HAAS, RENATE. Die mittelenglische Totenklage: Realitätsbezug,
     abendländische Tradition und individuelle Gestaltung.
     Regensburger Arbeiten zur Anglistik und Amerikanistik, 16.
     Frankfurt: Lang, 1980. [lament for the dead; Pity, BD, LGW,
     CT]
        Reviews: Martin Lehnert, ZAA 29 (1981), 167-68; Wolfgang
     Schulze, Vox Latina 17 (1981), 454-55.

376 HANNA, RALPH, III. "A New Edition of Chaucer." Rev 1 (1979),
     61-74. [review article] See no. 198.

377 HANNING, ROBERT W. "Chaucer and the Dangers of Poetry." CEA 46

General Criticism

(1984), 17-26. [dream visions; pryvetee; BD, PF, HF, CT, MilT, WBP, WBT, ManT, Ret]

378   HANNING, ROBERT W. "From Eva and Ave to Eglentyne and Alisoun: Chaucer's Insight into the Roles Women Play." Signs 2 (1977), 580-99. [CT, HF, TC, LGW]

379   HANNING, ROBERT W. "The Theme of Art and Life in Chaucer's Poetry," in 58, pp. 15-36. [HF, BD, TC, CT]

380   HASKELL, ANN S. "A Pirandellian Perspective of Chaucer." NM 76 (1975), 236-46. [Chaucer's anti-illusionism]

381   HASKELL, ANN S. "The Portrayal of Women by Chaucer and His Age," in What Manner of Woman: Essays on English and American Life and Literature. Ed. Marlene Springer. New York: New York University Press, 1977, pp. 1-14. [CT, TC]

382   HAWKINS, HARRIETT. Poetic Freedom and Poetic Truth: Chaucer, Shakespeare, Marlowe, Milton. Oxford: Clarendon Press, 1976. 136 pp. [CT]
        Reviews: David Norbrook, English 25 (1976), 233-37; TLS (24 December, 1976), 1619; MiltonQ 11 (1977), 58-59; S. Gorley Putt, EIC 27 (1977), 171-74; Imogene De Smet, RenQ 30 (1977), 401-02; W. W. Robson, RES 28 (1977), 342-44; M. C. Bradbrook, MLR 74 (1979), 157-58; Karina Williamson, N&Q 26 (1979), 448-49; Marianne Novy, SCN 37 (1979), 11-12.

383   HEFFERNAN, CAROL FALVO. "Wells and Streams in Three Chaucerian Gardens." PLL 15 (1979), 339-56. [CT, PF]

384   HELLSTRÖM, PÄR. "Perspektiv på Chaucerforskningen." Samlaren 103 (1982), 90-111. [criticism]

385   HENDRICKSON, RHODA MILLER MARTIN. "Chaucer's Proverbs: Of Medicyne and of Compleynte." DAI 42 (1981), 1140-41A. Emory University, 1980. [For, Buk, Scog, TC, CT]

386   HERACOURT, WILL. Die Wertwelt Chaucers: Die Wertwelt einer Zeitwende. Heidelberg: Carl Winter, 1939. [virtues, values, ideals of Chaucer's day]

387   HIEATT, A. KENT. Chaucer, Spenser, Milton: Mythopoeic Continuities and Transformations. London: McGill-Queen's University Press, 1975. 292 pp.
        Reviews: John Mulryan, Cithara 16 (1976), 75-76; Claes Schaar, RenQ 29 (1976), 439-40; Arnold Stein, SR 84 (1976), 695-706; MiltonQ 11 (1977), 23-24; Hugh McLean, UTQ 46 (1977), 180-82; Mario Praz, ES 58 (1977), 160-62; Elizabeth

General Criticism

Dipple, MLQ 38 (1977), 304-06; John Buxton, RES 28 (1977), 345-46.

388   HILARY, CHRISTINE RYAN. "The 'Confessio' Tradition from Augustine to Chaucer." DAI 41 (1980), 242A. University of California, Berkeley, 1979. [Augustine; WBP]

389   HIRA, TOSHINORI. "A Love 'Par Amour', Conventionalized and Satirized, in Chaucer." Bulletin of the Faculty of Liberal Arts, Nagasaki University 20 (1980), 69-81. In English.

390   HIRA, TOSHINORI. "Two Phases of Chaucer, Moral and Mortal," in Maekawa Shunichi Kyoju Kanreki Kinen-ronbunshui: Essays in Commemoration of S. Maekawa. Tokyo: Eihosha, 1968.

391   HOLAHAN, MICHAEL. "'Swich fyn . . . swich fyn': Senses of Ending in Chaucer and Spenser," in 778, pp. 116-31. [closure]

392   HOLLEY, LINDA TARTE. "Chaucer and the Function of the Word." DAI 36 (1976), 8075A. Tulane University, 1975. [glosing; CT]

393   HORNSBY, JOSEPH ALLEN. "Studies in Chaucer's Use of Law." DAI 45 (1985), 1275A. University of Toronto, 1984.

394   HOWARD, DONALD R. "Chaucer's Idea of an Idea." E&S 29 (1976) 39-55. [HF, CT]

395   HOWARD, DONALD R., BERYL ROWLAND, E. TALBOT DONALDSON, FLORENCE RIDLEY, and DANIEL SYLVIA. "Thwarted Sexuality in Chaucer's Works." Florilegium 3 (1981), 239-267.

396   HUDSON, KATHERINE. The Story of Geoffrey Chaucer. London: Oxford University Press, 1974.
        Reviews: TLS (29 March, 1974), 335.

397   HUSSEY, S. S. Chaucer: An Introduction. 2nd ed. London and New York: Methuen, 1982. 245 pp. [revised, expanded notes, bibliography]
        Reviews: Martin Lehnert, ZAA 23 (1975), 64-67; J. J. A[nders], CritQ 24 (1982), 93.

398   IKEGAMI, TADAHIRO. "Chaucer and His Age," in Introduction to English Literature--Society and Literature. Edited by Bishu Saito. Tokyo: Shuppan Publishing, 1978, pp. 57-66. In Japanese.

399   IKEGAMI, TADAHIRO. "Kenkyū no Genkyō to Kadai: Chaucer." EigoS

47

Bibliography of Chaucer, 1974 - 1985

General Criticism

128 (1983), 722-23. [current Chaucer scholarship]

400   IKEGAMI, TADAHIRO. "'Parliament' of Chaucerians." EigoS 125 (1979), 214-17.

401   IKEGAMI, TADAHIRO. "Present State of Chaucer and Arthurian Studies." EigoS 130 (1985), 496-97. In Japanese.

402   JENNINGS, MARGARET, C. S. J. "Chaucer's Beards." Archiv 215 (1978), 362-68. [physiognomy; iconography; beards; TC, CT, BD]

403   JORDAN, ROBERT M. "Chaucerian Narrative," in 70, pp. 95-116.

404   JORDAN, ROBERT M. "Chaucerian Romance?" YFS 51 (1974), 223-34. [structural analysis; CT, TC]

405   JORDAN, ROBERT M. "The Question of Genre: Five Chaucerian Romances," in 67, pp. 77-104. [TC, CT]

406   JORDAN, ROBERT M. "Romantic Unity, High Seriousness, and Chaucerian Fiction." Rev 2 (1980), 49-69. [review article] See no. 305.

407   JORDAN, ROBERT M. "Vision, Pilgrimage, and Rhetorical Composition," in 72, pp. 195-200. [HF, ManT, TC, Ret, BD, PF, CT]

408   JOSIPOVICI, GABRIEL. "The Temptations of Chaucer." NYRB (28 April, 1977), 18-22. [review article] See nos. 81, 326, 363, 1052.

409   JULIUS, PATRICIA WARD. "Appearance and Reality in Chaucer's Early Dream-Visions." DAI 37 (1976), 3606-07A. Michigan State University. [BD, PF, HF]

410   JUSTMAN, STEWART MARTIN. "Abuse of Authority in Chaucer." DAI 37 (1976), 3607A. Columbia University. [irony; HF, CT, Mel]

411   JUSTMAN STEWART [MARTIN]. "Medieval Monism and Abuse of Authority in Chaucer." ChauR 11 (1976), 95-111.

412   KAMOWSKI, WILLIAM F. "Chaucer's Bifocals: The Poet's Simultaneous Strategies for Fourteenth-Century Reading and Listening Audiences." DAI 45 (1985), 3645A. Washington State University, 1984. [TC, LGW, CT]

413   KANE, GEORGE. Chaucer. New York: Oxford University Press, 1984. [HF, PF, TC, CT]

Reviews: B. O'Donoghue, TLS (12 April, 1985), 416; N. F. Blake, Lore&L 4 (1985), 105; Theoharis C. Theoharis, Christian Science Monitor (22 February, 1985), 25.

414   KANE, GEORGE. "Chaucer and the Idea of a Poet," in Geoffrey Chaucer: Conferenze organizzate dall' Accademia Nazionale dei Lincei in Collaborazione con la Bristish Academy. Problemi Attuali di Scienza e di Cultura, Quaderno 234. Roma: Accademia Nazionale dei Lincei, 1977, pp. 35-49.

415   KANE, GEORGE. "Chaucer, Love Poetry, and Romantic Love," in 52, pp. 237-55. [fin amour; eroticism; satire]

416   KANE, GEORGE. "Langland and Chaucer: An Obligatory Conjunction," in 68, pp. 5-19. [Bradleian fallacy; CT]

417   KANE, GEORGE. The Liberating Truth: The Concept of Integrity in Chaucer's Writings. John Coffin Memorial Lecture, 1979. London: Athlone Press, 1980. 34 pp. [trouthe; CT, A&A, HF, lyrics]

418   KANE, GEORGE. "Outstanding Problems of Middle English Scholarship," in 72a, pp. 1-17.

419   KAWASAKI, MASATOSHI. "Chaucer no Menzaijōuri no Seikaku to Imi ni tsuite," in Bungaku to Ningen: Nakajima Kanji Kyōju Tsuito Ronbunshu. Tokyo: Kinseido, 1981, pp. 21-40. [Chaucer's characters]

420   KEAN, P. M. Chaucer and the Making of English Poetry. London: Routledge and Kegan Paul, 1972. 2 vols. 486 pp. Reviews: B. H. Loof, DQR 3 (1973), 191-92; G. C. Britton, N&Q 21 (1974), 270-71; E. Talbot Donaldson, ELN 12:2 (1974), 126-28; Dieter Mehl,Anglia 92 (1974), 444-51; Morton W. Bloomfield, MAE 43 (1974), 193-95; E. R. Hatcher, Speculum 50 (1975), 323-37; P. M. Vermeer, ES 56 (1975), 53-55.

421   KELLOGG, A. L. Chaucer, Langland, Arthur. New Brunswick, NJ: Rutgers University Press, 1972. 385 pp. Reviews: Barbara Raw, N&Q, n. s., 20, (1973), 437-39; R. M. Wilson, YES 4 (1975), 245-47.

422   KELLY, HENRY ANSGAR. "Chaucer's Arts and Our Arts," in 68, pp. 107-20. [liberal arts; visual arts]

423   KERN, EDITH. The Absolute Comic. Bloomington: Indiana University Press, 1980. [Mikhail Bakhtin, carnivalesque spirit; CT] See no. 1069.

General Criticism

424   KIM, SUN SOOK. "Chaucer and Gower: A Comparative Study." DAI
        36 (1975), 3732A. University of South Carolina.

425   KLENE, JEAN, C. S. C. "Chaucer's Contributions to a Popular
        Topos: The World Upside-Down." Viator 11 (1980), 321-34.
        [BD, A&A, CT, TC, Boece, Host]

426   KNAPP, PEGGY A. Assays: Critical Approaches to Medieval and
        Renaissance Texts. Vol. 2. Pittsburgh, PA: University of
        Pittsburgh Press, 1983.
        Reviews: Daniel J. Ransom, SAC 6 (1984), 199-202.

427   KNIGHT, STEPHEN. "Chaucer and the Sociology of Literature." SAC
        2 (1980), 15-51. [Pierre Macherey, structure, mimesis; BD,
        HF, PF, TC, CT]

428   KNIGHT, STEPHEN. "Politics and Chaucer's Poetry," in The Radical
        Reader. Edited by Stephen Knight and Michael Wilding.
        Sydney: Wild & Woolley, 1977, pp. 169-92. [Marxist
        approach; dichotomies in Chaucer]

429   KNIGHT, STEPHEN. Rymyng Craftily: Meaning in Chaucer's Poetry.
        New York: Humanities, 1974. 247 pp. [A&A, PF, TC, CT]
        Reviews: Choice 11 (1975), 1777; Martin Lehnert, ZAA 24
        (1976), 357-62; F. Diekstra, ES 58 (1977), 58-61.

430   KOHL, STEPHAN. Wissenschaft und Dichtung bei Chaucer:
        Dargestellt hauptsächlich am Beispiel der Medizin.
        Studienreihe Humanitas. Frankfurt: Akademische
        Verlagsgesellschaft, 1973. 401 pp. [science; medicine;
        humoral theory; dreams; alchemy; astrology; Chaucer's
        sources; TC, CT, ABC]
        Reviews: Heiner Gillmeister, Anglia 94 (1976), 502-05.

431   KOLVE, V. A. "Chaucer and the Visual Arts," in 49, pp. 290-320.

432   KOOPER, E. S. "Love, Marriage and Salvation in Chaucer's Book of
        the Duchess and Parlement of Foules." Utrecht Dissertation,
        1985. [+Aelred of Rievauly, Jean de Meun, Thomas Aquinas,
        Aristotle]

433   KREISLER, NICOLAI A. VON. "The Achievement of Chaucer's
        Love-Visions." DA 29 (1968), 1882A. University of Texas.

434   KROG, FRITZ. Studien zu Chaucer und Langland. Anglistische
        Forschungen, 65. Heidelberg: Carl Winter, 1928. [Chaucer's
        development]

435   KUHL, E. P. Studies in Chaucer and Shakespeare. Beloit, WI:

Belting, 1971. 440 pp.
Reviews: R. T. Davies, N&Q, n. s., 20, (1973), 30-32.

436   LAKSHMI, VIJAY. "The Antiquarian as Literary Analyst: Virginia Woolf on Chaucer." OJES 17 (1981), 19-25.

437   LANOUE, DAVID G. "Musical Imagery in the Poetry of Juan Ruíz, Guillaume de Machaut, and Chaucer: A Comparative Study." DAI 42 (1981), 1141-42A. University of Nebraska-Lincoln. [BD, CT, GP: Summoner, GP: Pardoner]

438   LARNER, JOHN. "Chaucer's Italy," in 47, pp. 7-32.

439   LAWES, ROCHIE WHITTINGTON. "The Heaven of Fourteenth-Century English Poets: An Examination of the Paradisaical References in the English Works of Chaucer, Gower, Langland, and the Pearl Poet." DAI 45 (1984), 1111A. University of Mississippi.

440   LAWLER, TRAUGOTT. "Chaucer," in Middle English Prose: A Critical Guide to Major Authors and Genres. Edited by A. S. G. Edwards. New Brunswick: Rutgers University Press, 1984, pp. 291-313. [rev. of scholarship; desiderata; Bo, Astr, Equat, CT]

441   LEACH, ELEANOR WINSOR. "Morwe of May: A Season of Feminine Ambiguity," in 52, pp. 299-310. [KnT, LGW]

442   LEFFINGWELL, WILLIAM CLARE, JR. "Some Versions of Chaucerian Irony." DAI 41 (1981), 3592A. University of Maryland, 1980. [CT, TC, PF; Macrobius; Alain de Lille]

443   LEHNERT, MARTIN. "Geoffrey Chaucer--Der Dichter der Liebe." ZAA 32 (1984), 5-18. [TC, CT]

444   LENAGHAN, R. T. "The Clerk of Venus: Chaucer and Medieval Romance," in 43, pp. 31-43. [TC, CT]

445   LEONARD, FRANCES McNEELY. Laughter in the Courts of Love: Comedy in Allegory from Chaucer to Spenser. Norman, OK: Pilgrim Books, 1981. 192 pp. [figura, referent] Reviews: George D. Economou, Speculum 58 (1983), 773-74; John Bugge, SAC 5 (1983), 177-79; Douglas A. Northrop, MP 81 (1984), 306-08.

446   LEWIS, ROBERT E. Handbook for Contributors to the Chaucer Library. Athens: University of Georgia Press, 1973. 21 pp.

447   LEYERLE, JOHN. "The Heart and the Chain," in 43, pp. 113-45.

Bibliography of Chaucer, 1974 - 1985

General Criticism

[BD, CT, PF]

448   LOCK, RICHARD. Aspects of Time in Medieval Literature. Garland Publications in Comparative Literature. New York and London: Garland, 1985. [ShT, pp. 234-39]

449   MANN, JILL. "Now Read on: Medieval Literature." Encounter (1980), 60-64. [rev. art.; open-endedness] See nos. 243, 1210.

450   MANNING, STEPHEN. "Rhetoric as Therapy: The Man in Black, Dorigen, and Chauntecleer." KPAB (1978), 19-25.

451   MARSHALL, LINDA E. "Osbern Mentions a Book." PQ 56 (1977), 407-13. [Osborne of Gloucester; Liber derivationum; PF, HF, BD]

452   MASUI, MICHIO. Chaucer no Sekai. Tokyo: Iwanami Shinsho, 1976. 244 pp. [Chaucer's world]

453   McCALL, JOHN P. Chaucer Among the Gods: The Poetics of Classical Myth. University Park: Pennsylvania State University Press, 1979. 200 pp. [comedy, tragedy, allegory; Virgil, Ovid, Lucan, Dante, Graunson, Boccaccio, Froissart] Reviews: George D. Economou, SAC 3 (1981), 152-56.

454   McGANN, JEROME J. "The Text, the Poem, and the Problem of Historical Method." NLH 12 (1981), 269-88. [Chaucer's "publishing options"]

455   McGREGOR, JAMES HARVEY. "Tragedy in Medieval and Renaissance Ovidian Imitations." DAI 37 (1976), 276-77A. Princeton University, 1975. [Ovid; Chaucerian parody; Caxton; Spenser; Dante; Greek tragedy]

456   MEHL, DIETER. "Chaucer's Audience." LeedsSE 10 (1978), 58-74.

457   MEHL, DIETER. Geoffrey Chaucer: eine Einführung in seine erzählenden Dichtungen. Grundlagen der Anglistik und Amerikanistik, 7. Berlin: Erich Schmidt Verlag, 1973. 226 pp.
Reviews: Martin Lehnert, ZAA 24 (1976), 357-62; P. J. Frankis, MAE 46 (1977), 335-36; Karl Heinz Göller, GRM 27 (1977), 248-50; Willi Erzgräber, Archiv 215 (1978), 403-06; Peter M. Vermeer, ES 59 (1978), 261-65.

458   MERLO, CAROLYN. "Chaucer's 'Broun' and Medieval Color Symbolism." CLAJ 25 (1981), 225-26. [TC, BD, Rom, HF, CT].

General Criticism

459   METLITZKI, DOROTHEE. The Matter of Araby in Medieval England.
       New Haven and London: Yale University Press, 1977. 320 pp.
       [SqT, CYT, WBP, WBT, Th, KnT]
       Reviews: Edgar Hill Duncan, SAC 2 (1980), 181-87.

460   MILLNS, TONY. "Chaucer's Suspended Judgements." EIC 27 (1977),
       1-19. [TC, PF, HF, CT]

461   MINNIS, ALASTAIR J. "Chaucer and Comparative Literary Theory,"
       in 68, pp. 53-69. [Aristotle; Jauss, Hans Robert, alterity]
       See also nos. 272, 508.

462   MINNIS, A[LASTAIR] J. Chaucer and Pagan Antiquity. Chaucer
       Studies, no. 8. Woodbridge, Suffolk: Boydell and Brewer;
       Totowa, NJ: Rowman and Littlefield, 1982. [TC, KnT]
       Reviews: C. D. Benson, SAC 6 (1984), 205-208; F. N. M.
       Diekstra, ES 65 (1984), 559-62; Bernard O'Donoghue, TLS (18
       May, 1984), 555; A. G. Rigg, N&Q, n. s., 31 (1984), 258; Götz
       Schmitz, Archiv 221 (1984), 369-71 (in German); Vincent J.
       DiMarco, Anglia 103 (1984), 189-94; P. J. Mroczkowski, RES 36
       (1985), 406-08; Winthrop Wetherbee, Speculum 60 (1985),
       440-43; Hugh White, MAE 54 (1985), 305-06.

463   MINNIS, ALASTAIR J. "The Influence of Academic Prologues on the
       Prologues and Literary Attitudes of Late-Medieval English
       Writers." MS 43 (1981), 342-83. [MkT, Mel, NPT, TC]

464   MINNIS, A[LASTAIR] J. "Medieval Discussions of the Role of the
       Author: A Preliminary Survey, with Particular Reference to
       Chaucer and Gower." DAI 37 (1976-77), 1534C. Queen's
       University, Belfast. [theologians' commentaries on auctores]

465   MINNIS, A[LASTAIR] J. Medieval Theory of Authorship: Scholastic
       Literary Attitudes in the Later Middle Ages. London: Scolar
       Press, 1984. [+Gower, Chaucer]
       Reviews: Helen Cooper, TLS (6 July, 1984), 759; R. F.
       Yeager, SAC 7 (1985), 218-21.

466   MITCHELL, JEROME and WILLIAM PROVOST, eds. Chaucer the Love-
       Poet. Athens: University of Georgia Press, 1973. 126 pp.
       See also no. 65.
       Reviews: Choice 11 (1974), 762; Lee Ramsey, Cithara 15
       (1975), 112-14; Jerome Mandel, SoCR 7 (1975), 69-70.

467   MORI, YOSHINOBU. "Chaucer to Tenmon Senseijutsu." EigoS 120
       (1974), 261-62, 324-25, 373-75. [astrology]

468   MUDRICK, MARVIN. "The Blind Men and the Elephant." HudR 30
       (1977), 426-36. [rev. art.; psychocriticism] See nos. 81,

Bibliography of Chaucer, 1974 - 1985

General Criticism

326, 363, 1052.

469   MURPHY, FRANCIS X., C.SS.R. "Chaucer's Patristic Knowledge." PPMRC, 1 (1976), 53–57. [Augustine]

470   MUSCATINE, CHARLES. Poetry and Crisis in the Age of Chaucer. Notre Dame: University of Notre Dame Press, 1972.
Reviews: John H. Fisher, SAQ 72 (1973), 609–11; E. Talbot Donaldson, CL 25 (1973), 262–63; Joseph E. Milosh, Jr., Cithara 13 (1973), 86–88.

471   MUSCATINE, CHARLES. "'What Amounteth Al This Wit?'—Chaucer and Scholarship." SAC 3 (1981), 3–11.

472   NAKAO, YOSHIYUKI. "Allegory and Realism in Chaucer." HSELL, 29 (1984), 15–26. [+personification; English abstr., 66]

473   NEUSS, PAULA. "Images of Writing and the Book in Chaucer's Poetry." RES 32 (1981), 385–397.

474   NORTON-SMITH, JOHN. Geoffrey Chaucer. London and Boston: Routledge & Kegan Paul, 1974. 274 pp. [BD, Ven, Pity, Mars, HF, LGW, CT, TC, Scog, Buk]
Reviews: F. Diekstra, ES 57 (1976), 552–54; Dieter Mehl, Anglia 94 (1976), 224–28; Derek Brewer, RES 27 (1976), 55–57; G. C. Britton, N&Q 222 (1977), 82–86.

475   OLHOEFT, JANET ELLEN. "Division and Connection: Mediation in Chaucer." DAI 44 (1984), 2143–44A. SUNY, Buffalo, 1983. [CT, BD]

476   OLSON, GLENDING. Literature as Recreation in the Later Middle Ages. Ithaca, NY, and London: Cornell University Press, 1982. 245 pp. [includes "Recreation in the Canterbury Tales," pp. 155–63.]
Reviews: John Bliese, QJS 70 (1984), 217–18; A. J. Minnis, MAE 53 (1984), 109–10; Richard M. Piersol, SAC 6 (1984), 213–16; Winthrop Wetherbee, Speculum 59 (1984), 429–31.

477   OLSON, GLENDING. "Making and Poetry in the Age of Chaucer." CL 31 (1979), 272–90. ["makere"/"poete"; vernacular versifiers/Latin Christian humanists]

478   OLSON, GLENDING. "Toward a Poetics of the Late Medieval Court Lyric," in 57, pp. 227–248. [+Aristotle; Nicomachean Ethics; TC, BD, GP, BuK, Purse, Truth, Sted; Machaut; Froissart]

479   ORME, NICHOLAS. "Chaucer and Education." ChauR 16 (1981), 38–59. [WBT, SqT]

480 ORME, NICHOLAS. From Childhood to Chivalry: The Education of
     the English Kings and Aristocracy, 1066-1530. London and New
     York: Methuen, 1984. [+Chaucer's references to aristocratic
     upbringing]

481 OWEN, CHARLES A., JR. "A Certein Nombre of Conclusions: The
     Nature and Nurture of Children in Chaucer." ChauR 16 (1981),
     60-75. [CT, Astr]

482 OWEN, CHARLES A., JR. "Undergraduate and Graduate Courses: New
     Patterns." Chaucer Newsletter 2:2 (1980), 7-10. [CT]

483 PALMER, DAVID ANDREW. "Chaucer and the Nature of Chivalric
     Ideas." DAI 37 (1977), 6507-08A. McMaster University, 1976.
     [CT, TC, Mars]

484 PALOMO, DOLORES. "Alpha and Omega: Of Chaucer and Joyce."
     Mosaic 8:2 (1975), 19-31. [Catholic ethos; CT; comedy]

485 PALOMO, DOLORES. "Chaucer, Cervantes, and the Birth of the
     Novel." Mosaic 8:4 (1975), 61-72. [self-conscious narrator;
     TC, HF]

486 PANZARELLA, PATRICK JOSEPH. "Chaucer and Literary Genre." DAI
     38 (1977), 1375A. State University of New York at Buffalo.
     [romance; fabliau]

487 PATTERSON, LEE W. "Writing about Writing: The Case of Chaucer."
     UTQ 48 (1979), 263-82. [review article] See nos. 305, 363,
     1052.

488 PAYNE, F. ANNE. Chaucer and Menippean Satire. Madison:
     University of Wisconsin Press, 1981. 290 pp. [Lucian,
     Petronius, Apuleius, Boethius, Consolatione Philosophiae;
     KnT, NPT, TC, Bo]
         Reviews: Valerie Adams, TLS (15 January, 1982), 56; David
     Staines, SN 55 (1983), 206-09; William Frost, CL 35 (1983),
     382-84; Helen Cooper, MAE 52 (1983), 134-36; Cecily Clark, ES
     64 (1983), 189; Russell A. Peck, SAC 5 (1983), 187-92;
     Christina von Nolcken, RES 35 (1984), 355-56; Jan Ziolkowski,
     CLS 21 (1984), 235-37.

489 PAYNE, ROBERT O. "The Historical Criticism We Need," in 67, pp.
     179-92. [+audience]

490 PEARCY, ROY J. "Chaucer, Deschamps, and Le Roman de Brut."
     Arts: The Journal of the Sydney University Arts Association
     12 (1984), 35-59. [+Purse]

General Criticism

491   PEARCY, ROY J., ed. Studies in the Age of Chaucer. Vol. 2.
       Norman, OK: The New Chaucer Society, 1980.
       Reviews: J. A. Burrow, RES 34 (1983), 203-205.

492   PEARSALL, DEREK. "Chaucer and the Modern Reader: A Question of
       Approach." DQR 11 (1981), 258-66. [opposition to modern
       approaches]

493   PEARSALL, DEREK. Old English and Middle English Poetry. London
       and Boston: Routledge & Kegan Paul, 1977. [+Chaucer's life,
       language, sources]
       Reviews: Przemyslaw Mroczkowski, ES 61 (1980), 457-62.

494   PECK, RUSSELL A. "Chaucer and the Nominalist Questions."
       Speculum 53 (1978), 745-60. [+Ockham]

495   PELEN, MARC MAITLAND. "The Marriage Journey." DAI 34 (1974),
       7242A. Princeton University, 1973.

496   PONOVA, M. K. "Razvitie zarubezhnoĭ literaturno-kriticheskoĭ
       mysli XIX-XX vekov i problemy izucheniia" [The Development of
       Foreign Literary-Critical Thought of the Nineteenth and
       Twentieth Centuries and the Problems of Literary Study] in
       Realizm i Khudozhestvennye iskanniia v zarubezhnoi literatur
       XIX-XX vekov [Realism and the Artistic Quest in Foreign
       Literature]. Voronezh: Voronezh University, 1980, pp.
       79-92. [Chaucer criticism]

497   RALSTON, MICHAEL EARL. "A Typology of Guides in Medieval
       Literature." DAI 45 (1984), 1111A. Auburn University. [HF,
       TC, CT]

498   REDWINE, BRUCE, III. "Decorum and Expression of Intention in
       Beowulf, Njals Saga, and Chaucer." DAI 45 (1985), 2869A.
       University of California-Berkeley, 1984. [+body language]

499   REISS, EDMUND. "Chaucer and His Audience." ChauR 14 (1980),
       390-402. [+FranT]

500   REISS, EDMUND. "Chaucer's Courtly Love," in 43, pp. 95-111.

501   REISS, EDMUND. "Chaucer's Thematic Particulars," in 61, pp.
       27-42. [CT, SNT, TC]

502   REISS, EDMUND. "Medieval Irony." JHI 42 (1981), 209-226.
       [concordantia oppositorum, Chrétien; Chaucer's "game" and
       "mirth"]

503   REISS, EDMUND. "Romance," in 60, pp. 108-30. [KnT, WBT, CT

structure]

504 RENOIR, ALAIN. "The Inept Lover and the Reluctant Mistress:
     Remarks on Sexual Inefficiency in Medieval Literature," in
     73, pp. 180–206. [TC, MilT]

505 RICHMOND, VELMA BOURGEOIS. "Pacience in Adversitee: Chaucer's
     Presentation of Marriage." Viator 10 (1979), 323–54. [CT,
     TC]

506 RIDLEY, FLORENCE H. "Chaucerian Criticism: The Significance of
     Varying Perspectives." NM 81 (1980), 131–41.

507 RIDLEY, FLORENCE H. "Questions without Answers—Yet or Ever?
     New Critical Modes and Chaucer." ChauR 16 (1981), 101–106.

508 RIDLEY, FLORENCE H. "A Response to 'Contemporary Literary Theory
     and Chaucer'," in 68, pp. 37–51. See also nos. 272, 461.

509 RIDLEY, FLORENCE H. "The State of Chaucer Studies: A Brief
     Survey." SAC 1 (1979) 3–16.

510 ROBBINS, ROSSELL HOPE. "Geoffroi Chaucier, poète français,
     Father of English Poetry." ChauR 13 (1978), 93–115. [+BD]

511 ROBBINS, ROSSELL HOPE. "The Vintner's Son: French Wine in
     English Bottles," in Eleanor of Aquitaine: Patron and
     Politician. Edited by William W. Kibler. Symposia in Arts
     and the Humanities 3. Austin: University of Texas Press,
     1976, pp. 147–72. [+Eleanor of Aquitaine]

512 ROBERTSON, D. W., JR. "Chaucer Criticism." M&H 8 (1977),
     252–55. [review article] See no. 1052.

513 ROBERTSON, D. W., JR. Essays in Medieval Culture. Princeton,
     NJ: Princeton University Press, 1980. 404 pp. [24 essays
     previously published]
     Reviews: Valerie Adams, TLS (9 January, 1981), 38; Maxwell
     Luria, SAC 4 (1982), 181–89; R. T. Davies, N&Q, n. s., 29
     (1982), 157–58.

514 ROBERTSON, D. W., JR. "Simple Signs from Everyday Life in
     Chaucer," in 61, pp. 11–26. [visual arts; GP, WBT, RvT]

515 ROBERTSON, D. W., JR. "Some Disputed Chaucerian Terminology."
     Speculum 52 (1977), 571–81. [+realism]

516 ROBINSON, IAN. Chaucer and the English Tradition. Cambridge and
     New York: Cambridge University Press, 1972. 296 pp.

Bibliography of Chaucer, 1974 - 1985

General Criticism

> Reviews: Donald Davie, EIC 22 (1972), 429–36; Peter G. Beidler, Italica 50 (1973), 446–8; Bernard Huppé, Criticism 15 (1973), 69–70; Donald K. Fry, ELN 11:2 (1973), 123–6; Raymond P. Tripp, Jr., PoetT 2 (1974), 127–38; Peter M. Vermeer, DQR 4 (1974), 97–110; Peter M. Vermeer, ES 55 (1974), 464–7; William Provost, GaR 28 (1974), 361–5; E. Talbot Donaldson, MP 71 (1974), 413–15; Lee Ramsey, Cithara 14 (1975), 118–22; Derek Pearsall, DUJ 37 (1975), 100–2; P. M. Kean, MLR 72 (1977), 655–56.

517 ROBINSON, SHARON PATTYSON. "Narrative Voice in Chaucer's Dream Visions." DAI 37 (1977), 4375–76A. University of Toledo, 1976. [BD, HF, PF]

518 ROGERS, WILLIAM E. "The Raven and the Writing Desk: The Theoretical Limits of Patristic Criticism." ChauR 14 (1980), 260–77.

519 ROSENBERG, BRUCE A. "The Oral Performance of Chaucer's Poetry: Situation and Medium." FForum 13 (1980), 224–37.

520 ROWLAND, BERYL. Blind Beasts: Chaucer's Animal World. Kent, OH: Kent State University Press, 1971. 204 pp.
     Reviews: Edmund Reiss, Speculum 49 (1974), 151–53; C. Schaar, SN 46 (1974), 547–51.

521 ROWLAND, BERYL. "Chaucer's Imagery," in 70, pp. 117–42. [transcendence of realism]

522 ROWLAND, BERYL. "Haldeen Braddy." ChauR 14 (1980), 191–98. [bibliography]

523 ROWLAND, BERYL. "Pronuntiatio and Its Effect on Chaucer's Audience." SAC 4 (1982), 33–51. [+gestures]

524 RUBEY, DANIEL ROBERT. "Literary Texts and Social Change: Relationships Between English and French Medieval Romances and their Audiences." DAI 42 (1982), 3153–54A. Indiana University, 1981. [Chaucer's romances, Ch. 4]

525 RUDAT, WOLFGANG E. H. The Mutual Commerce: Masters of Classical Allusion in English and American Literature. Heidelberg: Carl Winter Universitätsverlag, 1985. [KnT, CT; Virgil's Aeneid] See Chapters 2 and 5.

526 RUGGIERS, PAUL G. "Platonic Forms in Chaucer." ChauR 17 (1983), 366–81. [food; sex; play; art; religion]

527 RUNDE, JOSEPH. "Magic and Meaning: The Poetics of Romance."

General Criticism

DAI 41 (1980), 2128A. Pennsylvania State University. [+WBT; magic]

528   SAITO, ISAMU. "Tsumi o tazunete: Igirisu chusei sekkyo bungaku to Chaucer" [In Quest of Sins: Chaucer and Medieval Homiletic Literature], in Chaucer to Kirisutokyo [Chaucer and Medieval Christianity]. Symposium Series of Medieval English Literature 1. Tokyo: Gaku-shobo, 1984. In Japanese. [exempla]

529   SALTER, ELIZABETH and DEREK PEARSALL. "Chaucer's Realism," in English Poetry. Edited by Alan Sinfield. London: Sussex, 1976, pp. 36-51. [a dialog]

530   SALTER, ELIZABETH. Fourteenth-Century English Poetry: Contexts and Readings. Oxford: Clarendon Press; New York: Oxford University Press, 1983. 224 pp. [KnT, sources]
      Reviews: Denton Fox, TLS (17 February, 1984), 172; Tesma Outakoski, NM 85 (1984), 376-78; Ann Squires, DUJ, n. s., 46 (1984), 112-13; Anne Middleton, Speculum 60 (1985), 112-13.

531   SAPORA, ROBERT. "Charles A. Owen, Jr.: A Bibliography." ChauR 17 (1983), 284-85.

532   SCHAEFER, URSULA. Höfisch-ritterliche Dichtung und sozialhistorische Realität: Literatursoziologische Studien zum Verhältnis von Adelsstruktur, Ritterideal und Dichtung bei Geoffrey Chaucer. Neue Studien zur Anglistik and Amerikanistik 10. Frankfurt: Peter Lang, 1977. 397 pp. [in BD, PF, CT, TC]
      Reviews: Howell Chickering, SAC 2 (1980), 207-11.

533   SCOTT, A. F. Who's Who in Chaucer. London: Elm Tree Books; New York: Taplinger, 1974. 145 pp. See also no. 2836.

534   SHERMAN, JOHN STORRS. "Some Chaucerian Traditions." DAI 37 (1976), 995A. University of Washington, 1975. [in PF, Purse, HF, PardT]

535   SHIGEO, HISASHI. "Chaucer and Arthurian Romances." Lingua et Humanitas 3 (1985), 57-65. In Japanese.

536   SHIGEO, HISASHI. "Chaucer ni okeru Humanism" [Humanism in Chaucer], in Renaissance ni okeru Dōkebungaku [Fools in Renaissance Literature]. Edited by Shōnosuke Ishii and Peter Milward. Renaissance Literature Series, 14. Tokyo: Aratake-Shuppan, 1983, pp. 22-55. In Japanese. [humanism; fool; CT, TC; Italian influence; comedy]

General Criticism

537   SHIGEO, HISASHI. "Kami no setsuri to jiyuishi" [God's Providence
       and Man's Free Will]" in Chaucer to Kirisutokyo [Chaucer and
       Medieval Christianity]. Symposium Series of Medieval English
       Literature 1. Tokyo: Gaku-shobo, 1984, pp. 133-53. In
       Japanese. [free will; Providence]

538   SHIKII, KUMIKO. "Chaucer and Catholicism," in Shirayuri Joshi
       Daigaku Eibungakka. SELLA 10 (1981), 26-31. In Japanese.

539   SHIPPEY, T. A. "Catching Up: English Literature 1: From Alcuin
       to Chaucer." TLS (30 November, 1979), 73-74. [criticism of
       modern interpretation]

540   SHOAF, R. A. Dante, Chaucer, and the Currency of the Word:
       Money, Images, and Reference in Late Medieval Poetry.
       Norman, OK: Pilgrim, 1983. 312 pp. [language/coinage
       referentiality; Dante; CT, TC, HF]
          Reviews: Piero Boitani, SAC 7 (1985), 242-45; Madison U.
       Sowell, JRMMRA 6 (1985), 173-82.

541   SHOAF, R. A. "Dante's Commedia and Chaucer's Theory of
       Mediation: A Preliminary Sketch," in 68, pp. 83-103.

542   SHOAF, R. A. "Notes toward Chaucer's Poetics of Translation."
       SAC 1 (1979), 55-66. [in CT, PF, LGW]

543   SINGH, BRIJRAJ. "Chaucer as a Poet of Love." RUSEng 6 (1972),
       1-11. [TC, CT, lyrics, PF]

544   SKLUTE, LARRY. Virtue of Necessity: Inconclusiveness and
       Narrative Form in Chaucer's Poetry. Columbus: Ohio State
       University Press, 1984. [indeterminacy, nominalism, dream
       visions, TC, CT]
          Reviews: N. B. Atwater, Choice 23 (October, 1985), 300.

545   SOUTHMAYD, DAVID EDWARD. "Chaucer and the Medieval Conventions
       of Bird Imagery." DAI 41 (1981), 3596A. McGill University,
       1980. [HF, NPT, PF]

546   SOWELL, MADISON U. "Chaucer and the Three Crowns of Florence
       (Dante, Petrarch, and Boccaccio): Recent Comparative
       Scholarship." JRMMRA 6 (1985), 173-82. [review article]
       See nos. 47, 540, 654.

546a   SPEARING, A. C. "Chaucerian Authority and Inheritance," in 2064,
       pp. 185-202. [father figures in Chaucer]

547   SPEARING, A. C. Medieval Dream Poetry. Cambridge: Cambridge
       University Press, 1976. 256 pp. [Macrobius, Guillaume de

Lorris and Jean de Meun; <u>BD</u>, <u>HF</u>, <u>PF</u>, <u>LGW</u>]
Reviews: David Aers, <u>EIC</u> 27 (1977), 157–62; Derek
Pearsall, <u>TLS</u> (19 August, 1977), 999; W. A. Davenport,
<u>English</u> 26 (1977), 228–33; Domenico Pezzini, <u>SMed</u> 18 (1977),
188–91.

548   SPEARING, A. C. <u>Medieval to Renaissance in English Poetry</u>.
Cambridge: Cambridge University Press, 1985. [Ch. 2: <u>HF</u>,
<u>TC</u>, <u>Th</u>, <u>KnT</u>, <u>WBT</u>, <u>SqT</u>, <u>FranT</u>; Ch.3: Lydgate, Hoccleve, and
Chaucer; Ch.4: Scottish Chaucerians—Henryson and Dunbar]
Reviews: T. A. Shippey, <u>THES</u> (29 November, 1985), 20.

549   SPEARING, A. C. "Renaissance Chaucer and Father Chaucer."
<u>English</u> 34 (1985), 1–38. [condenses no. 548 above]

550   SPECHT, HENRIK. "The Beautiful, the Handsome, and the Ugly:
Some Aspects of the Art of Character Portrayal in Medieval
Literature." <u>SN</u> 56 (1984), 129–146. [ugliness, beauty]

551   SPECHT, HENRIK. "Some Aspects of the Art of Portraiture in
Medieval Literature, with Special Reference to the Use of
<u>Ethopoeia</u> or <u>Adlocutio</u>," in <u>Proceedings from the Second</u>
<u>Nordic Conference for English Studies</u>. Edited by Råken
Ringbom and Matti Pissanen. Åbo: Åbo Akademi, 1984, pp.
403–13.

552   SPISAK, JAMES WILLIAM. "Medieval Marriage Concepts and Chaucer's
Good Old Lovers," in <u>Human Sexuality in the Middle Ages and</u>
<u>Renaissance</u>. Edited by Douglas Radcliffe–Umstead.
University of Pittsburgh Publications on Middle Ages and
Renaissance 4. Pittsburgh: Center for Medieval and
Renaissance Studies, University of Pittsburgh, 1978, pp.
15–26. [Jerome, Augustine, Peter Lombard, Finnian, Halitgar;
<u>CT</u>]

553   STANFORD, W. N. "Guido Cavalcanti's 'Canzone'; Perfection and
the Soul in Love: Some Implications for the Medieval
'World-view'." <u>SoRA</u> 10:1 (1977), 43–58. [<u>caritas</u>,
<u>cupiditas</u>]

554   STEVENS, MARTIN. "Chaucer and Modernism: An Essay in
Criticism," in 67, pp. 193–216.

555   STOLZ, ANNE CREHAN. "The Artifice of Temporality: A Study of
Unfinishedness in Chaucer." <u>DAI</u> 39 (1979), 5498–99A.
University of California, Berkeley, 1978. [<u>CT</u>, <u>HF</u>, <u>A&A</u>, <u>LGW</u>,
<u>Astr</u>]

556   STROHM, PAUL. "Chaucer's Audience." <u>L&H</u> 5 (1977), 26–41.

Bibliography of Chaucer, 1974 - 1985

General Criticism

557   STROHM, PAUL. "Chaucer's Audience(s): Fictional, Implied,
      Intended, Actual." ChauR 18 (1983), 137-45.

558   STROUD, THEODORE A. "Genres and Themes: A Reaction to Two Views
      of Chaucer." MP 72 (1974), 60-70. [review article] See no.
      2408. Also reviews Norman Eliason, The Language of Chaucer's
      Poetry (1972).

559   SWART, FELIX. "Chaucer and the English Reformation." Neophil 62
      (1978), 616-19.

560   SYLVIA, DANIEL, DONALD R. HOWARD, BERYL ROWLAND, E. TALBOT
      DONALDSON, and FLORENCE RIDLEY. "Thwarted Sexuality in
      Chaucer's Works." Florilegium 3 (1982), 239-56. [erotic in
      PF, TC, CT]

561   TALBOT, CHARLES H. "The Elixir of Youth," in 69, pp. 31-42.
      [alchemy, Ramon Lull; CYT]

562   TRAVERSI, DEREK. The Literary Imagination: Studies in Dante,
      Chaucer, and Shakespeare. Newark: University of Delaware
      Press, 1982. 266 pp. See nos. 1663, 1947.
        Reviews: Avril Bruten, TLS (6 January, 1984), 20;
      Christina von Nolcken, RES 36 (1985), 401-02.

563   TRIPP, RAYMOND P., JR. Beyond Canterbury: Chaucer, Humanism and
      Literature. Church Stretton, England: Orny; Denver:
      Society for New Language Study, 1977. [KnT, BD]
        Reviews: Alan T. Gaylord, SAC 2 (1980), 211-18.

564   TRIPP, RAYMOND P., JR. "The Criticism of 'Wonder': A Review and
      Commentary upon Chaucer and the English Tradition by Ian
      Robinson . . ." PoetT 2 (1974), 127-38. [review article]
      See no. 516.

565   TUPAN, MARIA-ANA. "Inceput de ev în poezia englezã" [Start of an
      Era in English Poetry]. Luceafãrul 21:46 (1978), 8. In
      Romanian.

566   TWYCROSS, MEG. The Medieval Anadyomene: A Study in Chaucer's
      Mythography. Medium Aevum Monographs, n. s., 1. Oxford:
      Basil Blackwell, for The Society for the Study of Medieval
      Languages and Literature, 1972. 119 pp. [Ven, KnT, HF]
        Reviews: TLS (15 March, 1974), 261; S. S. Hussey, MLR 70
      (1975), 387-89.

567   UHLIG, CLAUS. Chaucer und die Armut: Zum Prinzip der
      kontextuellen Wahrheit in den 'Canterbury Tales'. Akademie

62

der Wissenschaften und der Literatur, Abhandlungen der geistes- und sozialwissenschaftlichen Klasse, Jahrgang 1973, Nr. 14. Mainz: Verlag der Akademie der Wissenschaften und der Literatur, 1974. 54 pp. [NPT, MLT]
Reviews: Dieter Mehl, Anglia 94 (1976), 501–02; Martin Lehnert, ZAA 24 (1976), 357–62.

568   VARNAITĖ, IRENA. "Dž. Čoseris ir prerenesanso problems" [Chaucer and the Problem of the Pre-Renaissance]. Literatūra 16:3 (1974), 23–33. [sums. in English and Russian; TC, PF, Th]

569   VARNAITĖ, I[RENA]. "Kai kurios Čoserio kūrybos problemos amerikiečių kritikoje." Literatūra 17:3 (1975), 89–100. [American criticism of Chaucer]

570   VARNAITĖ, IRENA. "Problemy izučenija poèm Čosera" [Problems of the Analysis of Chaucer's Poems]. Literatūra 15:3 (1973), 19–33.

571   VERMEER, PETER M. "Chaucer and Literary Criticism." DQR 4 (1974), 97–110. [review article on modern critics] See no. 516 above.

572   WALKER, DENIS. "The Structure of Literary Response in Chaucerian Texts." Parergon 3 (1985), 107–14. [CT, GP, PF NPT]

573   WASS, ROSEMARY THÉRÈSE ANN. "Chaucer and Late Medieval Scholasticism: A Preliminary Study of Individuality and Experience." DAI 34 (1974), 5128A. University of Cincinnati, 1973.

574   WATERHOUSE, RUTH and JOHN STEPHENS. "The Backward Look: Retrospectivity in Medieval Literature." SoRA 16 (1983), 356–373. [Malory; Gower; TC, BD, WBT]

575   WEISS, ALEXANDER. "Chaucer's Early Translations from French: The Art of Creative Transformation," in 54, pp. 174–82.

576   WEISS, ALEXANDER. "Chaucer's Native Heritage." DAI 35 (1974), 2958–59A. University of California, Berkeley. [in CT, TC, LGW, Rom, ABC, Buk]

577   WEISS, ALEXANDER. Chaucer's Native Heritage. American University Studies, Series 4. English Language and Literature 11. New York and Berne: Lang, 1985. [style; KnT, CT, TC, HF, MilT, Rom]
Reviews: L. B. Hall, Choice 22 (1985), 1636.

578   WETHERBEE, WINTHROP. "Convention and Authority: A Comment on

Bibliography of Chaucer, 1974 - 1985

General Criticism

Some Recent Critical Approaches to Chaucer," in 68, pp. 71–81. [TC; Dante]

579 WETHERBEE, WINTHROP. "Some Implications of Nature's Femininity in Medieval Poetry," in Approaches to Nature in the Middle Ages: Papers of the Tenth Annual Conference of the Center for Medieval and Early Renaissance Studies. Edited by Lawrence D. Roberts. Medieval and Renaissance Texts and Studies 16. Binghamton: MRTS, 1982, pp. 47–62. [PF, WBT]

580 WETHERBEE, WINTHROP. "Some Intellectual Themes in Chaucer's Poetry," in 58, pp. 75–91. [philosophy]

581 WHITLARK, JAMES S. "Chaucer and the Pagan Gods." AnM 18 (1977), 65–75. [in CT, TC, HF, BD; demons]

582 WILKINS, NIGEL. Chaucer Songs. Cambridge: D. S. Brewer, 1980. 29 pp. [in LGW, Ros, For, Venus, TC, PF] See also no. 2828.

583 WIMSATT, JAMES. "Froissart, Chaucer, and the Pastourelles of the Pennsylvania Manuscript," in 72, pp. 69–79. [Pennsylvania MS French 15; +influence on GP, MilT, RvT, CYT, PF, TC]

584 WINDEATT, BARRY. "Gesture in Chaucer." M&H 9 (1979), 143–61. [in CT, LGW, TC, BD]

585 WINDEATT, BARRY. "Handmade Literature: Chaucer's Narrative." Encounter 63 (1984), 55–59, [rev. art.] See nos. 877, 995, 1073.

585a WINDEATT, BARRY. "Pace in Chaucer: 'The proverb seith: He hasteth wel that wisely kan abyde'." PoetT 14 (1983), 51–65.

586 WINNY, JAMES. Chaucer's Dream-Poems. New York: Harper; London: Chatto and Windus, 1973. 158 pp. [PF, HF, BD, CT; Host; pilgrim-poet]
     Reviews: Donald K. Fry, LJ 99 (1974), 660; Colin Wilcockson, MAE 44 (1975), 311–13; Constance Hieatt, Speculum 52 (1977), 186–88.

587 WOLPERS, THEODOR. "Bürgerliches bei Chaucer: Mit einer Skizze des spätmittelalterlichen London," in Über Bürger, Stadt und städtische Literatur im Spätmittelalter: Bericht über Kolloquien der Kommission zur Erforschung der Kultur des Spätmittelalters, 1975–1977. Edited by Josef Fleckenstein and Karl Stackmann. Abhandlungen der Akademie der Wissenschaften, Phil.-Hist. Klasse, third series, 121. Göttingen: Vandenhoeck and Ruprecht, 1980, pp. 216–288. (Rpt. as separate monograph by the same publisher, 1980. 73

64

pp.) [CT, GP, TC]
   Reviews: Karl Heinz Göller, SAC 4 (1982), 190-92.

588   WOOD, CHAUNCEY. "Chaucer and Astrology," in 70, pp. 202-20.

589   YEAGER, PETER L. "Chaucer's Exempla: A Study of their
      Backgrounds, Characteristics, and Literary Functions." DAI
      35 (1974), 3780A. University of North Carolina, Chapel Hill.
      [rhetoric; artes praedicandi; Machaut; DeMeun; astronomy;
      religion; CT, TC, HF]

590   ZANONI, MARY-LOUISE. "Divine Order and Human Freedom in
      Chaucer's Poetry and Philosophical Tradition." DAI 42
      (1982), 5115A. Cornell Univeristy. [scholasticism; TC, CT]

See also: 24, 2778, 2780, 2864, 2865.

LITERARY RELATIONS AND SOURCES

591 ANDREAS, JAMES R. "The Noble Rhetor: Chaucer and Medieval
        Poetic Tradition." DAI 34 (1974), 5088A. Vanderbilt.
        [mythography; rhetoric; Geoffrey de Vinsauf]

592 BASWELL, CHRISTOPHER CHARLES. "'Figures of Olde Werk': Visions
        of Virgil in Later Medieval England." DAI 44 (1984), 2761A.
        Yale University, 1983. [Aeneid, HF, LGW; allegory]

593 BENNETT, J. A. W. "Chaucer, Dante and Boccaccio," in Geoffrey
        Chaucer: Conferenze organizzate dall' Accademia nazionale
        dei Lincei. Rome: Accademia nazionale dei Lincei, 1977.

594 BENNETT, J. A. W. "Chaucer, Dante and Boccaccio," in 47, pp.
        89-113. [Boccaccio; Dante; TC, KnT]

595 BENSON, LARRY D. and THEODORE M. ANDERSON. The Literary Context
        of Chaucer's Fabliaux: Texts and Translations.
        Indianapolis, IN; New York: Bobbs-Merrill, 1971. 395 pp.
        Reviews: R. Derolez, ES 56 (1975), 87-88.

596 BOCCACCIO. Teseida. Ed. S. Battaglia. Florence: Accademia
        della Crusca, 1938. Trans. Bernadette M. McCoy. The Book of
        Theseus. New York: Medieval Text Association, 1974.

597 BOITANI, PIERO. Chaucer and Boccaccio. Medium Aevum Monographs,
        n. s., 8. Oxford: Society for the Study of Medieval
        Languages and Literature, 1977. 210 pp. [Teseida,
        Filostrato, TC, PF, KnT, lyrics, Anel]
        Reviews: Brian Murdoch, SMed 19 (1978), 752-56; R. D. S.
        Jack, MLR 74 (1979), 713-15; Patrick Boyde, MAE 50 (1981),
        167-68; P. Calì, IS 34 (1981), 141-43; Howard H. Schless,
        Speculum 60 (1985), 644-46.

598 BOITANI, PIERO. "What Dante Meant to Chaucer," in 47, pp.
        115-39. [Purgatorio, Paradiso, LGW, HF, TC]

599 BRADDY, HALDEEN. "The French Influence on Chaucer," in 70, pp.
        143-59.

Literary Relations and Sources

600   BREWER, D. S. "Chaucer and Chrétien and Arthurian Romance," in
        69, pp. 255-59. [CT]

601   CARPENTER, ANN. "The Loathly Lady in Texas Lore." JASAT 5
        (1974), 48-53.

602   CHILDS, WENDY. "Anglo-Italian Contacts in the Fourteenth
        Century," in 47, pp. 65-87. [Italian culture]

603   CLOGAN, PAUL M. "Literary Genres in a Medieval Textbook." M&H,
        n. s., 11 (1982), 199-209. [ethics; Liber Catonianus]

604   COGGESHALL, JOHN M. "Chaucer in the Ozarks: A New Look at the
        Sources." SFQ 45 (1981), 41-60.

605   COLEMAN, WILLIAM E. "Chaucer, the Teseida, and the Visconti
        Library at Pavia: A Hypothesis." MAE 51 (1982), 92-101.
        See also no. 609.

606   COLEY, JOHN SMARTT, trans. Le Roman de Thèbes: The Story of
        Thebes. Garland Library of Medieval Literature 44. New York
        and London: Garland, 1985. [TC, KnT]

607   CRÉPIN, ANDRÉ. "Chaucer and the French," in 48, pp. 55-77.

608   DAVID, ALFRED. "Recycling Anelida and Arcite: Chaucer as a
        Source for Chaucer," in 72, pp. 105-15. [KnT, LGWP, SqT,
        MerT, PF, Anel]

609   DELASANTA, RODNEY K. "Chaucer, Pavia, and the Ciel d'Oro." MAE
        54 (1985), 117-21. See Coleman, no. 605, above.

610   DIAS-FERREIRA, JULIA. "Another Portuguese Analogue of Chaucer's
        Pardoner's Tale." ChauR 11 (1977), 258-60.

611   DIEKSTRA, F. "Chaucer's Way with His Sources: Accident into
        Substance and Substance into Accident." ES 62 (1981),
        215-36. [Jean de Meun; CT, BD, Rom, Reason]

612   DiMARCO, VINCENT. "Richard Hole and the Merchant's and Squire's
        Tales: An Unrecognized Eighteenth-Century (1797)
        Contribution to Source and Analogue Study." ChauR 16 (1981),
        171-80. [pear-tree, healing-sword]

613   DOLAN, MICHAEL JAMES. "Chaucer and the Continental Tradition: A
        Study in Neoplatonic Influences." DAI 35 (1975) 4511-12A.
        Cornell University, 1974. [influence of Plato; Chalcidius;
        Boethius; Macrobius; Silvestris; de Lille; de Meun]

Literary Relations and Sources

614   DRONKE, PETER and JILL MANN. "Chaucer and the Medieval Latin
      Poets," in 49, pp. 154-83. [cosmological; Trojan; satiric]

615   EHRHART, MARGARET JEAN. "Chaucer's Contemporary, Guillaume de
      Machaut: A Critical Study of Four Dits amoureux." DAI 35
      (1975), 7299-300A. University of Illinois at
      Urbana-Champaign, 1974.

616   EISNER, SIGMUND. "Chaucer's Use of Nicholas of Lynn's Calendar."
      E&S 29 (1976), 1-22. [in CT, Astr]

617   EISNER, SIGMUND, ed. and trans., and GARY MAC EOIN, trans. The
      'Kalendarium' of Nicholas of Lynn. The Chaucer Library.
      London: Scolar Press; Athens: University of Georgia Press,
      1980. 248 pp.
          Reviews: Ron B. Thompson, AEB 5 (1981), 237-38; T. A.
      Shippey, TLS (27 February, 1981), 236; J. C. Eade, MAE 51
      (1982), 251-54; M. A. Manzalaoui, Speculum 57 (1982), 646-48;
      Owen Gingerich, SAC 4 (1982), 149-51.

618   FYLER, JOHN M. Chaucer and Ovid. London; New Haven: Yale
      University Press, 1979. 206 pp. [in HF, BD, PF, LGW, TC,
      KnT, NPT]
          Reviews: T. A. Shippey, TLS (30 November, 1979), 73; John
      H. Fisher, Speculum 55 (1980), 866; James J. Wilhelm, CL 32
      (1980), 331-33; R. W. Hanning, SAC 2 (1980), 159-65; Elaine
      Tuttle Hansen, MLQ 41 (1980), 90-93; Lisa J. Kiser, MP 78
      (1980), 167-69; Richard L. Hoffman, JEGP 80 (1981), 231-34;
      Phillipa Hardman, RES 32 (1981), 204-05; C. Gauvin, EA 34
      (1981), 462; Götz Schmitz, Anglia 100 (1982), 186-89; R. T.
      Davies, MLR 77 (1982), 403-04.

619   GIBSON, MARGARET, ed. Boethius: His Life, Thought, and
      Influence. Oxford: Basil Blackwell, 1981. See no. 646
      below.
          Reviews: Andrew Hughes, Mus&Let 64 (1983), 267-69; Russell
      A. Peck, Speculum 59 (1984), 903-05.

620   GINSBERG, WARREN STUART. "Le grant translateur: Chaucer and His
      Sources." DAI 36 (1975), 2843-44A. Yale University.

621   GUILLAUME DE LORRIS and JEAN DE MEUN. Le Roman de la Rose. Ed.
      Felix Lecoy. Paris: Champion, 1965-70. 3 vols. Trans. H.
      W. Robbins and C. W. Dunn. New York: Dutton, 1962. Trans.
      Charles Dahlberg. Princeton: Princeton University Press,
      1971.

622   HALABY, RAOUF J. "Arabic Influences on Chaucer: Speculative

Literary Relations and Sources

Essays on a Study of Literary Relationship." DAI 34 (1974), 5911-12A. East Texas State University. [SqT, PardT, FrT, MancT, TC, KnT, CT]

623 HARBERT, BRUCE. "Chaucer and the Latin Classics," in 49, pp. 137-53. [general; +Ovid]

624 HARTY, KEVIN J. "Chaucer and the Fair Field of Anglo-Norman." Les Bonnes Feuilles 5 (1975), 3-17 (Pennsylvania State University). [Anglo-Norman sources: Trevet; MLT, FranT]

625 HAVELY, N. R., ed. and trans. Boccaccio--Sources of 'Troilus' and the Knight's and Franklin's Tales. Chaucer Studies, 5. Cambridge: D. S. Brewer; Totowa, NJ: Rowman and Littlefield, 1980. 225 pp.
     Reviews: Gay Clifford, TLS (16 January, 1981), 80; Valerie Adams, TLS (29 May, 1981); Derek Pearsall, THES (27 February, 1981), 14; Thomas A. Van, SAC 4 (1982), 159-61; G. H. McWilliam, MLR 78 (1983), 133-35; F. N. M. Diekstra, ES 65 (1984), 558.

626 HIEATT, CONSTANCE B. "Un Autre Fourme [Another Form]: Guillaume de Machaut and the Dream Vision Form." ChauR 14 (1979), 97-115. [SqT, PF]

627 HOFFMAN, RICHARD L. "The Influence of the Classics on Chaucer," in 70, pp. 185-201. [Ovid; Virgil; Statius]

628 HOY, JAMES F. "A Twentieth-Century Analogue to Chaucer's Merchant's Tale." ChauR 14 (1979), 155-57.

629 JEFFREY, DAVID LYLE. "Chaucer and Wyclif: Biblical Hermeneutic and Literary Theory in XIVth Century," in 63, pp. 109-40. [Lollards John of Gaunt; Gent, Truth, Form Age, Mel, HF, CT, ParsT]

630 KALLICH, PAUL EUGENE. "Chaucer's Translation Technique." DAI 44 (1984), 2143A. University of Pennsylvania, 1983. [in BD, ABC, Bo, Mel, MerT]

631 KEAN, P. M. "Chaucer an Englishman Elusively Italianate." RES 34 (1983), 388-394. [Italian sources; style]

632 KIRBY, THOMAS A. "An Analogue (?) to the Reeve's Tale," in 69, pp. 381-83.

633 KIRK, ELIZABETH D. "Chaucer and His English Contemporaries," in 58, pp. 111-27. [frame tales; symbols; word play; conventions]

Literary Relations and Sources

634   KOOIJMAN, JACQUES. "Envoi de fleurs: A propos des échanges
        littéraires entre la France et l'Angleterre sous la Guerre de
        Cent Ans," in Etudes de langue et de littérature françaises
        offertes à André Lanly. Edited by Bernard Guidoux. Nancy:
        Universite de Nancy, 1980, pp. 173-83. [Eustache Deschamps]

635   LERER, SETH. Boethius and Dialogue: Literary Method in the
        Consolation of Philosophy. Princeton: Princeton University
        Press, 1985. [+Cicero, Augustine, Fulgentius]

636   LEWIS, ROBERT E., ed. De miseria condicionis humane by Lotario
        dei Segni (Pope Innocent III). The Chaucer Library. Athens:
        University of Georgia Press, 1978; London: Scolar Press,
        1980. 303 pp. [MLT, LGW; lost works]
            Reviews: Daniel Silvia, SAC 2 (1980), 167-72; T. A.
        Shippey, TLS (27 February, 1981), 236; Vincent Gillespie, MAE
        50 (1981), 309-10; Derek Pearsall THES (27 February, 1981),
        14.

637   LONGO, JOHN DUANE. "Literary Appropriation as Translatio in
        Chaucer and the Roman de la Rose." DAI 42 (1982), 4444A.
        Princeton University. [LGWP, BD, TC, FranT]

638   LUNDBERG, MARLENE HELEN COOREMAN. "The Chaucer-Gower Analogues:
        A Study in Literary Technique." DAI 42 (1982), 3993A.
        Indiana University, 1981. [LGW, WBT, PhyT]

639   LURIA, MAXWELL. A Reader's Guide to the 'Roman de la Rose'.
        Hamden, CT: Archon, 1982.
            Reviews: Alfred David, Speculum 59 (1984), 404-06.

640   MANN, NICHOLAS. "Dal moralista al poeta: Appunti per la fortuna
        del Petrarca in Inghilterra," in Convegno internazionale
        Francesco Petrarca. Roma-Arezzo-Padova--Arquà Petrarca,
        24-27 aprile 1974. (Atti dei Convegni Lincei, 10), pp.
        59-69.

641   McGRADY, DONALD. "Chaucer and the Decameron Reconsidered."
        ChauR 12 (1977), 1-26. [parallels in CT]

642   McGRADY, DONALD. "Were Sercambi's 'Novelle' Known from the
        Middle Ages on?" Italica 57 (1980), 3-18.

643   MEIER, HANS H. "Middle English Styles in Translation: The Case
        of Chaucer and Charles," in So Meny People, Longages and
        Tonges: Philological Essays in Scots and Mediaeval English
        Presented to Angus McIntosh. Edited by Michael Benskin and
        M. L. Samuels. Edinburgh: Authors, 1981, pp. 367-76.

Literary Relations and Sources

644   MILLER, LUCIEN. "Marital Love in Two Early Chinese Narrative
       Ballads--with Analogues from Chaucer's Canterbury Tales."
       TkR 13 (1982), 37-53.

645   MILLER, ROBERT P., ed. Chaucer: Sources and Backgrounds. New
       York: Oxford University Press, 1977. 507 pp. [in BD, CT,
       lyrics, HF, LGW, PF, TC; anthology of texts]
         Reviews: Choice 14 (1977), 1357; Gabriel Josipovici, NYRB
       (28 April, 1977), 18-22; Bruce A. Rosenberg, SAC 2 (1980),
       187-90; J. M. Maguin, CahiersE 19 (1981), 99-100.

646   MINNIS, ALASTAIR. "Aspects of the Medieval French and English
       Traditions of the De Consolatione Philosophiae," in 619, pp.
       312-61. [MkT, Bo, KnT, TC]

647   MORRIS, LYNN CAMPBELL KING. "Chaucer Source and Analogue
       Criticism." DAI 44 (1984), 3681A. SUNY-Stonybrook, 1983.
       [bibliography] See no. 21 for printed version.

648   MURPHY, MICHAEL. "Chaucer's Devil Among the Irish." Eire 19
       (1984), 133-38.

649   PECK, RUSSELL A. Kingship and Common Profit in Gower's
       'Confessio Amantis'. Carbondale: Southern Illinois
       University Press, 1978. 204 pp. [+CT, WBT]
         Reviews: Anthony E. Farnham, Speculum 55 (1980), 166-69;
       Y. F. Yeager, MLR 76 (1981), 654-56.

650   PEDEN, ALISON M. "Macrobius and Mediaeval Dream Literature."
       MAE 54 (1985), 59-73. [PF, HF, BD, NPT]

651   PISANTI, TOMMASO. "Influssi danteschi nell' Europa del Trecento
       e del Quattrocento." Critica letteraria 3 (1975), 637-61.

652   RUGGIERS, PAUL G. "The Italian Influence on Chaucer," in 70, pp.
       160-84. [Dante; Petrarch; Boccaccio]

653   SCHLAUCH, MARGARET. "A Polish Analogue of the Man of Law's
       Tale," in 69, pp. 372-80.

654   SCHLESS, HOWARD H. Chaucer and Dante: A Revaluation. Norman,
       OK: Pilgrim Books, 1984. 268 pp.
         Reviews: Donald C. Baker, ELN 23:2 (1985), 71-72; Madison
       U. Sowell, JRMMRA 6 (1985), 173-82; Winthrop Wetherbee, MP 83
       (1986), 419-30; Janet L. Smarr, JEGP 85 (1986), 97-99.

655   SCHLESS, HOWARD [H]. "Transformations: Chaucer's Use of
       Italian," in 49, pp. 184-223. [general; Boccaccio; Dante]

Literary Relations and Sources

656 SHAW, JUDITH DAVIS. "Lust and Lore in Gower and Chaucer." ChauR
     19 (1984), 110-22. [ParsT, CT]

657 UTLEY, FRANCIS L. "Boccaccio, Chaucer and the International
     Popular Tale." WF 33 (1974), 181-201. [Decameron, TC, CT]

658 WALLACE, DAVID. "Chaucer and Boccaccio's Early Writings," in 47,
     pp. 141-62. [Guillaume de Lorris; Cortesia; Machaut; BD, HF;
     Dante]

658a WALLACE, DAVID. "Chaucer and the Early Writings of Boccaccio."
     Doct. diss., University of Cambridge, 1983. See no. 659.

659 WALLACE, DAVID. Chaucer and the Early Writings of Boccaccio.
     Chaucer Studies 12. Woodbridge, Suffolk: D. S. Brewer,
     1985. 209 pp. [HF, TC]
        Reviews: C. D. Benson, Speculum 62 (1987), 217-19.

660 WALLACE, DAVID. "Chaucer and the European Rose," in 72, pp.
     61-67. [RR: influence on Brunetto Latini, Dante, Boccaccio,
     Petrarch, Chaucer]

661 WEISS, ALEXANDER. "Chaucer's Early Translations from French:
     The Art of Creative Transformation," in 54, pp. 174-82.

662 WIMSATT, JAMES I. "Chaucer and French Poetry," in 49, pp.
     109-36. [RR; Macrobius; Machaut; Boccaccio--general
     treatment]

663 WIMSATT, JAMES I. "Chaucer, Fortune, and Machaut's 'Il m'est
     avis'," in 73, pp. 119-31. [in BD, Bo, Sted, MerT, For]

664 WINDEATT, B[ARRY] A., ed. and trans. Chaucer's Dream Poetry:
     Sources and Analogues. Chaucer Studies, 7. Cambridge,
     England: D. S. Brewer; Totowa, NJ: Rowman and Littlefield,
     1982. 168 pp. [includes translations--Machaut, Froissart,
     Jean de Condé, Cicero, Alanus de Insulis--PF, HF, LGW]
        Reviews: Derek Pearsall, N&Q 30 (1983), 248-50; David
     Staines, Speculum 58 (1983), 1143-44; James I. Wimsatt, SAC 5
     (1983), 210-12; F. N. M. Diekstra, ES 65 (1984), 558-59.

See also Source Studies under separate works: 1174-82, 1209, 1234-35,
1237, 1243, 1246, 1309-18, 1389, 1421-25a, 1512-13, 1527-29, 1539-40,
1572-76, 1619-22, 1629-31, 1666-73, 1688-90, 1754-57, 1776-1780, 1808-10,
1836-37, 1849, 1894-1901, 1912-15, 1950-51, 1973-78, 1992, 2065-69,
2119-22, 2153-62, 2207-2209, 2467-2484. Further cross references follow
these numbers. Under some works [Miller's Tale, Sir Thopas, Canon's
Yeoman's Tale, Anelida and Arcite, Boethius, Lyrics (General)], Source

Bibliography of Chaucer, 1974 - 1985

Literary Relations and Sources

Studies contain only cross references. For completeness, all numbers should be consulted.

See also: 15, 21, 175, 176, 212, 259, 264, 277, 283, 293, 300, 307, 350, 413, 414, 432, 451, 453, 463, 488, 493, 497, 511, 536, 550, 562, 576, 580, 583, 589, 735, 828, 835, 855, 856, 897, 1065, 1088, 1096, 1097, 1098, 1100, 1162, 1173, 1181, 1239, 1425a, 1900a, 2068a, 2487, 2496, 2498, 2518, 2519, 2520, 2528.

INFLUENCE AND ALLUSIONS

665   AINSWORTH, JEANNETTE THERESE. "The Welsh Troelus A Cresyd:
        Toward a Better Understanding." DAI 40 (1980), 4015-16A.
        Rutgers University, 1979. [Cresyd as tragic heroine]

666   ALEKSEEV, M. P. Pushkin i Choser [Pushkin and Chaucer].
        Sravnitel'no-istorich-eskie issledovania [Comparative
        Historical Researches]. Leningrad: Nauka, 1972. 467 pp.

667   ANDERSON, JUDITH H. "'A Gentle Knight was Pricking on the
        Plaine': The Chaucerian Connection." ELR 15 (1985), 166-74.
        [Th; Spenser]

668   ANDERSON, JUDITH H. "'Not Worth a boterflye': 'Muipotmos' and
        'The Nun's Priest's Tale'." JMRS 1 (1971), 89-106.

668a   ANDERSON, JUDITH H. "What Comes After Chaucer's But:
        Adversative Constructions in Spenser," in 52, pp. 105-18.
        [+GP]

669   ARN, MARY-JO. "Fortunes Stabilnes: The English Poems of Charles
        of Orleans in their English Context." FCS 7 (1983), 1-18.

670   BAIRD, JOSPEH L. "God's Plenty." Maledicta 2 (1978), 146-48.
        [MilT; Dryden]

671   BARTHEL, CAROL. "Prince Arthur and Bottom the Weaver: The
        Renaissance Dream of the Fairy Queen," in 778, pp. 72-83.
        [Th]

672   BASSIL, VERONICA. "The Faces of Griselda: Chaucer, Prior, and
        Richardson." TSLL 26 (1984), 157-82. [+Not-Browne Mayd]

673   BEIDLER, PETER G. "Conrad's 'Amy Foster' and Chaucer's
        Prioress." NCF 30 (1975), 111-15.

674   BENNETT, J. A. W. "Those Scotch Copies of Chaucer." RES 32
        (1981), 294-96. [John of Irelande, Meroure of Wysdome; TC,
        ParsT]

675   BENSON, C. DAVID. "A Chaucerian Allusion and the Date of the
       Alliterative 'Destruction of Troy'." N&Q 21 (1974), 206-07.

676   BENSON, C. DAVID. "Troilus and Cresseid in Henryson's
       'Testament'." ChauR 13 (1979), 263-71.

677   BERRY, REGINALD. "Chaucer and Absalom and Achitophel." N&Q 26,
       522-23. [Dryden]

678   BERRY, REGINALD. "Chaucer Transformed 1700-1721." DAI 40
       (1979), 231A. University of Toronto, 1978. [in Dryden,
       Kynaston, Pope]

679   BOSWELL, JACKSON C[AMPBELL]. "Chaucer Allusions: Addenda to
       Spurgeon." N&Q 24 (1977), 493-95. [eight unnoted allusions]

680   BOSWELL, JACKSON CAMPBELL. "Chaucer and Spenser Allusions not in
       Spurgeon and Wells." AEB 1 (1977) 30-32.

681   BOWDEN, BETSY. "The Artistic and Interpretive Context of Blake's
       'Canterbury Pilgrims'." Blake 13 (1980), 164-90.

682   BRADBROOK, M. C. "Marlowe's Hero and Leander," in Aspects of
       Dramatic Form in the English and the Irish Renaissance: The
       Collected Papers of Muriel Bradbrook. Sussex: Harvester
       Press, 1983, pp. 156-79. [TC, III]

683   BRADBROOK, M. C. "What Shakespeare Did to Chaucer's Troilus and
       Criseyde," in The Artist and Society in Shakepeare's England:
       The Collected Papers of Muriel Bradbrook. Sussex: Harvester
       Press, 1982, pp. 133-43.

684   BRASWELL, MARY FLOWERS. "Madness, Mayhem, and the Search for
       Gold: William Faulkner's Use of The Pardoner's Tale." ELN
       23:1 (1985), 55-70.

685   BURNET, R. A. L. "Some Chaucerian Echoes in The Merchant of
       Venice." N&Q, n. s., 29 (1982), 115-16. [TC, LGW, WBP]

686   BURROW, J. A. "Sir Thopas in the Sixteenth Century," in 59, pp.
       69-91. [Dunbar; ballads; Gamelyn; Skelton; Warton;
       Puttenham; "E. K."; Drayton; Spenser; Harvey; Lyly;
       Shakespeare; Speght]

687   CARETTA, VINCENT. "The Kingis Quair and The Consolation of
       Philosophy." SSL 16 (1981), 14-28.

688   CHAPMAN, ANTONY U. "The Influences of Shakespeare's Sources on

Influence and Allusions

the Dramaturgy of _Troilus and Cressida_." _DAI_ 36 (1975), 1520A. Kent State University.

689   CLOGAN, PAUL M. "Chaucer and Leigh Hunt." _M&H_, n. s., 9 (1979), 163-74. [Hunt's criticism of Chaucer]

690   CONLEE, JOHN W. "John Barth's Version of _The Reeve's Tale_." _AN&Q_ 12 (1974), 137-38.

691   CONROY, ANNE ROSEMARIE. "_The Isle of Ladies_: A Fifteenth Century English Chaucerian Poem." _DAI_ 38 (1977), 253-54A. Yale University, 1976.

692   COOPER, HELEN. "Wyatt and Chaucer: A Re-Appraisal." _LeedsSE_ 13 (1982), 104-23. [language; rhyme royal]

693   DANE, JOSEPH A. "Genre and Authority: The Eighteenth-Century Creation of Chaucerian Burlesque." _HLQ_ 48 (1985), 345-62. [_Th_, _SqT_]

694   DARJES, BRADLEY and THOMAS RENDALL. "A Fabliau in the _Prologue to the Tale of Beryn_." _MS_ 48 (1985), 416-31.

695   DAVIS, WALTER R. "Commentary on Carol Barthel's 'Prince Arthur and Bottom the Weaver'," in 778, pp. 84-91. [_Th_]

696   DOEDERLIN, SUE WARRICK. "_Ut Pictura Poesis_: Dryden's _Aeneïs_ and _Palamon and Arcite_." _CL_ 33 (1981), 156-66.

697   DOHERTY, MARY JANE MARGARET. "The Mistress-Knowledge: Literary Architectonics in the English Renaissance." _DAI_ 38 (1978), 4840A. University of Wisconsin-Madison, 1977. [poetic theory]

698   DONALDSON, E. TALBOT and JUDITH J. KOLLMANN, eds. _Chaucerian Shakespeare: Adaptation and Transformation_. Medieval and Renaissance Monograph Series, 2. Ann Arbor: Michigan Consortium for Medieval and Early Modern Studies, 1983. See nos. 707, 716, 740, 743, 763, 780, 797, 801.

699   DONALDSON, E. TALBOT. _The Swan at the Well: Shakespeare Reading Chaucer_. New Haven, CT: Yale University Press, 1985. [_TC_, _KnT_, _MerT_, _WBT_]
Reviews: Ann Thompson, _THES_ (27 September, 1985), 28.

700   DONNELLY, M. L. "A Commentary on _The Canterbury Tales_ in _The Faerie Queene_," in 777, pp. 237-48.

701   DOWNER, MABEL WILHELMINA. "Chaucer Among the Victorians." _DAI_

43 (1982), 1537A. City University of New York.

702 DRESSMAN, MICHAEL R. "Whitman, Chaucer, and French Words." WWR
    23 (1977), 77-82. [Whitman's study of Chaucer's language]

703 DYE, E. H. "Milton's Comus and Boethius' Consolation." MiltonQ
    19 (1985), 1-7. [+Chaucer's Boece]

704 EBIN, LOIS A. "Boethius, Chaucer, and The Kingis Quair." PQ 53
    (1974), 321-41.

705 EBIN, LOIS [A]. "Lydgate's Views on Poetry." AnM 18 (1977),
    76-105. [language]

706 EDWARDS, A. S. G. "Hardyng's Chronicle and Troilus and
    Criseyde." N&Q, n. s., 31 (1984), 156.

707 EDWARDS, A. S. G. "Lydgate's Use of Chaucer: Structure,
    Strategy, and Style." RCEI 10 (1985), 175-82. [GP, Siege of
    Thebes]

708 FINKE, LAURIE A. "Falstaff, the Wife of Bath, and the Sweet
    Smoke of Rhetoric," in 698, pp. 7-24.

709 FLAHIFF, F. T. "'The Great Gatsby': Scott Fitzgerald's
    Chaucerian Rag," in Figures in a Ground: Canadian Essays on
    Modern Literature Collected in Honor of Sheila Watson.
    Edited by Diane Bessai and David Jackel. Saskatoon: Western
    Producer Prarie Books, 1979, pp. 87-98.
    Reviews: Charles R. Steele, Ariel 9:4 (1979), 93-94

710 FLEMING, JOHN. "Chaucer and Erasmus on the Pilgrimage to
    Canterbury: An Iconographic Speculation," in 60, pp. 148-66.
    [KnT, PardT, SumT, GP]

711 FOX, ALISTAIR. "Thomas More's Dialogue and the Book of the Tales
    of Canterbury: 'Good Mother Wit' and Creative Imagination,"
    in Familiar Colloquy: Essays Presented to Arthur Edward
    Barker. Edited by Patricia Brückmann. Ontario: Oberon
    Press, 1978, pp. 15-24.
    Reviews: P. G. Stanwood, CanL 83 (1979), 196-97.

712 FRADENBURG, LOUISE OLGA. "Chaucer and the Middle Scots Poets:
    Studies in Fifteenth-Century Reception." DAI 43 (1983),
    3313A. University of Virginia, 1982. [The Kingis Quair;
    Henryson; Dunbar]

713 GOODALL, PETER. "An Outline of the English Fabliau After
    Chaucer." AUMLA 57 (1982), 5-23.

Influence and Allusions

714   GREENBERG, MARK. "The Canterbury Pilgrims by Stothard and Blake:
       An Account with Reproductions in 'The Architect'." N&Q 23
       (1976), 401–02.

715   GRENNEN, JOSEPH E. "Tudd, Tibbys Sonne, and Trowle the Trewe:
       Dramatic Complexities in the Chester Shepherds' Pageant." SN
       57 (1985), 165–73.

716   GUGELBERGER, GEORG. "Zum Mittelaltereinfluss in der modernen
       Dichtung: Ezra Pounds Chaucerbild." OL 35 (1980), 220–34.

717   GUSSENHOVEN, SR. FRANCIS, RSHM. "Shakespeare's Taming of the
       Shrew and Chaucer's Wife of Bath: The Struggle for Marital
       Mastery," in 698, pp. 69–79.

718   HALE, DAVID G. "Bottom's Dream and Chaucer." SQ 36 (1985),
       219–20. [BD]

719   HANNA, RALPH, III. "Cresseid's Dream and Henryson's Testament,"
       in 69, pp. 288–97.

720   HARDMAN, C. B. "Eloquence and Morality in the Old Poet and the
       New: Chaucer and Spenser." RMSt 6 (1980), 20–30.

721   HARRIS, NEIL SHETTRON. "Images of Chaucer in the Seventeenth
       Century." DAI 35 (1975), 4429A. University of Michigan,
       1974.

722   HASKELL, ANN S. "A Pirandellian Perspective of Chaucer." NM 76
       (1975), 236–46.

723   HATTON, THOMAS J. "Medieval Anticipations of Dryden's Stylistic
       Revolution: The Knight's Tale." Lang&S 7 (1974), 261–70.

724   HIEATT, A. KENT. "The Canterbury Tales in The Faerie Queene," in
       777, pp. 217–29.

725   HIEATT, A. KENT. Chaucer, Spenser, Milton: Mythopoeic
       Continuities and Transformations. Montreal: McGill-Queen's
       University Press, 1975. 292 pp.
          Reviews: MiltonQ 11 (1977), 23–24; John Buxton, RES 28
       (1977), 345–46; Elizabeth Dipple, MLQ 38 (1977), 304–06;
       Mario Praz, ES 58 (1977), 160–62; Judith M. Kennedy, ESC 4
       (1978), 468–77; Philip C. Kolin, SCN 37 (1979), 12–13.

726   HOLAHAN, MICHAEL. "Chaucer and Spenser: Poetic Influence and
       Literary History," in 777, pp. 230–36.

727 HOLLOWAY, JULIA BOLTON. "Medieval Liturgical Drama: The
Commedia, Piers Plowman, and the Canterbury Tales." ABR 32
(1981), 114-21.

728 HOWARD, DONALD R. "Flying Through Space: Chaucer and Milton,"
in Milton and The Line of Vision. Edited by Joseph Anthony
Wittreich, Jr. Madison: University of Wisconsin Press,
1975, pp. 3-23.

729 HUDSON, ANNE. "Lollardy: The English Heresy?" in Religion and
National Identity. Studies in Church History, 18. Edited by
Stuart Mews. Oxford: Blackwell, 1982, pp. 261-83.

730 HUNTER, MICHAEL. "Alexander Pope and Geoffrey Chaucer," in The
Warden's Meeting: A Tribute to John Sparrow. Oxford:
Oxford University Society of Bibliophiles, 1977, pp. 29-32.

731 IKEGAMI, TADAHIRO. "Chaucer's Influence," in Introduction to
English Literature—Society and Literature. Edited by Bishu
Saito. Tokyo: Shuppan Publishing Company, 1978, pp. 68-72.
In Japanese.

732 JEFFERY, C. D. "Anglo-Scots Poetry and The Kingis Quair," in 46,
pp. 207-21.

733 JESKE, JEFFERY M. "Clough's Mari Magno: A Reassessment." VP 20
(1982), 21-32.

734 KEHLER, JOEL R. "A Note on the Epigraph to Conrad's The Rescue."
ELN 12:2 (1975), 184-87.

735 KENDRICK, LAURA. "Rhetoric and the Rise of Public Poetry: The
Career of Eustache Deschamps." SP 80 (1983), 1-13.
[+Brunetto Latini]

736 KENNEDY, RICHARD F. "Another Chaucer Allusion." N&Q, n. s., 31
(1984), 156. [in Sir Richard Barckley]

737 KING, PAMELA M. "Dunbar's The Golden Targe: A Chaucerian
Masque." SSL 19 (1984), 115-31.

738 KOFF, LEONARD MICHAEL. "Wordsworth and the Manciple's Tale."
ChauR 19 (1985), 338-51.

739 KOHL, STEPHAN. "Chaucer's Pilgrims in Fifteenth-Century
Literature." FCS 7 (1982), 221-36. [Tale of Beryn; Lydgate]

740 KOLLMANN, JUDITH J. "'Ther is noon oother incubus but he': The
Canterbury Tales, Merry Wives of Windsor and Falstaff," in

Influence and Allusions

698, pp. 43-68.

741   LANHAM, RICHARD A. "Games and High Seriousness," Chapter 3 in
       The Motives of Eloquence: Literary Rhetoric in the
       Renaissance. New Haven: Yale University Press, 1976, Ch. 3.
       [CT; Host; rhetoric; Matthew Arnold]

742   LASATER, ALICE E.. "The Chaucerian Narrator in Spenser's
       Shepheardes Calender." SoQ 12 (1974), 189-201.

743   LESLIE, NANCY T. "The Worthy Wife and the Virtuous Knight:
       Survival of the Wittiest," in 698, pp. 25-41. [+Falstaff]

744   LESTER, G. A. "Chaucer's Knight and the Earl of Warwick." N&Q
       28 (1981), 200-02.

745   LEVY, ROBERT A. "Dryden's Translation of Chaucer: A Study of
       the Means of Re-Creating Literary Models." DAI 34 (1974),
       5108-09A. University of Tennessee.

746   LOFTIN, ALICE. "Landscapes of Love and Poetry: Chaucerian Dream
       Allegory in England through the Renaissance." Chaucer
       Newsletter 1:1 (1979), 17.

747   LONGO, JOSEPH A. "Apropos the Love Plot in Chaucer's Troilus and
       Criseyde and Shakespeare's Troilus and Cressida." CahiersE
       11 (1977), 1-15.

748   LYNCH, STEPHEN JOSEPH. "Shakespeare's Troilus and Cressida: A
       Study of the Characters, Themes, and Sources." DAI 43
       (1983), 2681A. Indiana University, 1982.

749   MACK, MAYNARD. "Pope's Copy of Chaucer," in Evidence in Literary
       Scholarship: Essays in Memory of Marshall Osborn. Edited by
       René Wellek and Alvaro Ribeiro. Oxford: Clarendon Press,
       1979, pp. 105-21.

750   MACLEAN, HUGH. "'Restlesse anguish and unquiet paine': Spenser
       and the Complaint, 1579-1590," in The Practical Vision:
       Essays in English Literature in Honor of Flora Roy. Edited
       by Jane Campbell and James Doyle. Waterloo: Wilfrid Laurier
       University Press, pp. 29-47.

751   MASON, T[OM] A. "Dryden's Chaucer." Ph.D. Thesis, University of
       Cambridge, 1978.

752   MASON, TOM [A]. "Dryden's Version of The Wife of Bath's Tale."
       CQ 6 (1975), 240-56.

753   MASUI, MICHIO. "Chusei kara Mita Renaissance to Hyogen--Chaucer
       no naka no Tenkaiteki na Mono." EigoS 119 (1974), 678-79.
       [evolution in Chaucer's work]

754   McCOBB, LILIAN M. "The English Partenope of Blois, Its French
       Source, and Chaucer's Knight's Tale." ChauR 11 (1977),
       369-72.

755   McCOLLY, WILLIAM. "The Book of Cupid as an Imitation of Chaucer:
       A Stylo-Statistical View." ChauR 18 (1984), 239-49.

756   MIESZKOWSKI, GRETCHEN. "'Pandras' in Deschamps' Ballade for
       Chaucer." ChauR 9 (1975), 327-36.

757   MILNE, FRED L. "Dryden's Palamon and Arcite: Its Merits and
       Flaws as a Translation of Chaucer's Knight's Tale. Meta 23
       (1978), 200-10.

758   MILOSH, JOSEPH. "John Gardner's Grendel: Sources and
       Analogues." ConL 19 (1978), 48-57. [cf. NPT]

759   MISKIMIN, ALICE S. "Counterfeiting Chaucer: The Case of 'Dido'
       Wyatt and the 'Retraction'." SMC 10 (1977), 133-45.
       [textual tradition]

760   MISKIMIN, ALICE. "The Design of Douglas's Palice of Honour," in
       46, pp. 396-408.

761   MISKIMIN, ALICÉ S. The Renaissance Chaucer. New York and New
       Haven, CT; London: Yale University Press, 1975. 315 pp.
       [TC, CT]
          Reviews: Priscilla Bawcutt, ELN 13:2 (1975), 140-42;
       Donald Cheney, SpenN 6 (1975), 26-29; John M. Steadman, JEGP
       74 (1975), 574-76; Gustaf Fredén, Samlaren 96 (1975), 292-93;
       N. F. Blake, MLR 71 (1976), 881-82; A. Kent Hieatt, MAE 45
       (1976), 338-42; J. A. W. Bennett, RenQ 29 (1976), 266-67;
       Alastair Fowler, TLS (2 January, 1976), 11; A. V. C. Schmidt,
       N&Q 23 (1976), 250-52; J. A. Burrow, RES 28 (1977), 68-70;
       André Crépin, EA 30 (1977), 477; Peter M. Vermeer, ES 59
       (1978), 261-65; Götz Schmitz, Anglia 96 (1978), 215-20; John
       King, MP 76 (1979), 285-87.

762   MOISAN, THOMAS. "Chaucer's Pandarus and the Sententious Friar
       Lawrence." PAPA 8 (1982), 38-48.

763   MOISAN, THOMAS. "Shakespeare's Chaucerian Allegory: The Quest
       for Death in Romeo and Juliet and the Pardoner's Tale," in
       698, pp. 131-49. [rhetoric]

Bibliography of Chaucer, 1974 - 1985

Influence and Allusions

764   NEWLYN, EVELYN S. "Of Sin and Courtliness: Henryson's Tale of
       the Cock and the Fox," in 46, pp. 268-77.

765   NORTON-SMITH, JOHN and I. PRAVADA, eds. The Quare of Jelusy.
       Middle English Texts 3. Heidelberg: C. Winter, 1976. 224
       pp.
         Reviews: Dorothea Siegmund-Schultze, ZAA 26 (1978), 91-92.

765a   OGOSHI, INZO, ed. Chosa to Sheikusupia [Chaucer and
       Shakespeare]. Tokyo: Nan'undo, 1983. 234 pp.

766   OLMERT, MICHAEL. "Troilus in Piers Plowman: A Contemporary View
       of Chaucer's Troilus and Criseyde." Chaucer Newsletter 2
       (1980), 13-14.

767   OLSEN, ALEXANDRA HENNESSEY. "Chaucer and the Eighteenth Century:
       The Wife of Bath and Moll Flanders." Chaucer Newsletter 1:2
       (1979), 13-15.

768   O'NEILL, WILLIAM. "'L'Allegro', 'Il Penseroso', and some
       Daybreak Scenes from 'The Canterbury Tales'." N&Q 29 (1982),
       494-95.

769   ORAM, WILLIAM A. "A Mirror for Arthur Gorges: Spenser's
       Daphnaida," in Spenser at Kalamazoo. Proceedings from a
       Special Session at the 13th Conference on Medieval Studies in
       Kalamazoo, Michigan, 5-6 May 1978. Edited by David A.
       Richardson. Cleveland: Cleveland State University, 1978,
       pp. 238-53. [+BD]

770   OSSELTON, N. E. "Bilderdijk and Chaucer," in Ten Studies in
       Anglo-Dutch Relations. Edited by Jan van Dorsten. London:
       Oxford University Press; Leyden: Leyden University Press for
       the Sir Thomas Browne Institute, 1974, pp. 231-45. [Dutch
       poet Bilderdijk (1813) refers to NPT, WBT, LGW, translates
       NPT]

771   PEARSALL, DEREK. "The English Romance in the Fifteenth Century."
       E&S, n. s., 29 (1976), 56-83.

772   PRIMEAU, RONALD. "Chaucer's Troilus and Criseyde and the Rhythm
       of Experience in Keats's 'What can I do to drive away'." KSJ
       23 (1974), 106-18.

773   RATELIFF, JOHN D. "J. R. R. Tolkien: 'Sir Thopas' Revisited."
       N&Q, n. s., 29 (1982), 348.

774   REGAN, CHARLES LIONEL. "Of Owls and Apes Again: CT, B^2 4282."
       ChauR 17 (1983), 278-80. [Chester Deluge; Burton's Anatomy

of Melancholy]

775   REISNER, M. E.   "Effigies of Power : Pitt and Fox as Canterbury
        Pilgrims."   ECS 12 (1979), 481-503. [GP Pardoner, Summoner;
        Blake]

776   REISS, EDMUND.   "Dunbar's Self-Revelation and Poetic Tradition,"
        in 46, pp. 326-38.

777   RICHARDSON, DAVID A., ed.   Spenser and the Middle Ages.
        Proceedings from a Special Session at the Eleventh Conference
        on Medieval Studies in Kalamazoo, Michigan, 2-5 May, 1976.
        Cleveland, OH: Department of English, Cleveland State
        University, 1976. See nos. 700, 724, 726.
            Reviews: Caroline D. Eckhardt, SCN 35 (1977), 82-83.

778   RICHARDSON, DAVID A., ed.   Spenser: Classical, Medieval,
        Renaissance, and Modern.   Proceedings from a Special Session
        at the Twelfth Conference on Medieval Studies in Kalamazoo,
        Michigan, 5-8 May, 1977. Cleveland, OH: Department of
        English, Cleveland State Univeristy, 1977. 322 pp. See nos.
        324, 391, 671, 695.

779   RICHER, CAROL F.   "The Fabliau: Chaucer to Barth and Back
        Again."   BSUF 23:2 (1982), 46-52. [RvT]

780   ROBERTS, VALERIE S.   "Ironic Reversal of Expectations in
        Chaucerian and Shakespearean Gardens," in 698, pp. 97-117.
        [KnT, MerT, Midsummer Night's Dream]

781   ROSS, GORDON N.   "The Franklin's Tale and The Tempest."   N&Q 25
        (1978), 156.

782   ROWLAND, BERYL.   "Dryden Refurbishes Chaucer's Barnyard."   Archiv
        217 (1980), 349-54.

783   RUDAT WOLFGANG E. H.   "Pope's Rape of the Lock and Chaucer's
        Parson's Tale."   AN&Q 21 (1982), 7-8.

784   RUDE, DONALD W.   "Two Additional Allusions to Chaucer in the Work
        of Stephen Hawes."   AN&Q 16 (1978), 82-83.

785   RUDE, DONALD W.   "An Unreported Allusion to Chaucer in The Female
        Tatler."   AN&Q 23 (1985), 129-30. [TC]

786   RUDE, DONALD W.   "Two Unreported Renaissance Allusions to
        Chaucer."   AN&Q 23 (1984), 4-5. [John Jones]

787   RUTHERFORD, CHARLES S.   "The Boke of Cupide Reopened."   NM 78

Influence and Allusions

(1977), 350-58. [Clanvowe]

788 SCATTERGOOD, V. J. "A Caxton Prologue and Chaucer." Chaucer
Newsletter 2:1 (1980), 14-15.

789 SCHÖWERLING, RAINER. "Chaucers Troilus and Criseyde in der
englischen Literatur von Henryson bis Dryden" [Chaucer's
Troilus and Criseyde in English Literature from Henryson to
Dryden]. Anglia 97 (1979), 326-49. [+Sidnam, Shakespeare]

790 SCHRICKER, GALE C. "The Case of Cress: Implications of Allusion
in Paterson." WCWR 11 (1985), 16-29. [TC, CT, GP]

791 SCHULER, ROBERT M. "The Renaissance Chaucer as Alchemist."
Viator 15 (1984), 305-333.

792 SCHUMAN, SAMUEL. "Man, Magician, Poet, God—An Image in
Medieval, Renaissance, and Modern Literature." Cithara 19:2
(1980), 40-54. [FranT; Shakespeare, Tempest]

793 SHASSERE, KATHY E. "Hawthorne's Chaucer Connection." TPB 21
(1984), 57. [GP]

794 SHAW, PRISCILLA D. "A Comparative Study of Troilus and Criseyde
and Romeo and Juliet." DAI 42 (1982), 3169A. University of
Kansas, 1981.

795 SHIGEO, HISASHI. "Chaucer ni okeru Humanism," in Renaissance ni
okeru Dokebungaku. Edited by Shonosuke Ishii and Peter
Mulward. Tokyo: Aratake, 1983, pp. 25-55. In Japanese.

796 SHIGEO, HISASHI. "Shakespeare to chusei" [Shakespeare and the
Middle Ages], in Shakespeare no shiki [Collected Essays on
Shakespeare]. Tokyo: Shinozaki Shorin, 1984, pp. 466-74.
In Japanese.

797 SHILKETT, CAROL L. "The Manipulations of Chaucer's Pandarus and
Shakespeare's Iago," in 698, pp. 119-30.

798 SIENNICKI, BARBARA LORRAINE. "No Harbour for the Shippe of
Travayle: A Study of Thomas Usk's Testament of Love." DAI
46 (1985), 1276A. Queen's University, Kingston, Canada.

799 SINGH, CATHERINE. "The Alliterative Ancestry of Dunbar's 'The
Tretis of the Tua Mariit Wemen and the Wedo'." LeedsSE 7
(1973-74), 22-54. [WBT]

800 SPEARING, A. C. "Lydgate's Canterbury Tale: The Siege of Thebes
and Fifteenth-Century Chaucerianism," in 821, pp. 333-64.

Influence and Allusions

801 SPISAK, JAMES W. "Pyramus and Thisbe in Chaucer and
     Shakespeare," in 698, pp. 81-95.

802 STEVENSON, WARREN. "Interpreting Blake's Canterbury Pilgrims."
     CLQ 13 (1977), 115-26.

803 STOUCK, MARY-ANN. "Chaucer and Capgrave's Life of St.
     Katherine." ABR 33 (1982), 276-91.

804 STRAUS, BARRIE RUTH. "The Role of the Reader in The Kingis
     Quair," in 46, pp. 198-206.

805 STROHM, PAUL. "Chaucer's Fifteenth-Century Audience and the
     Narrowing of the 'Chaucer Tradition'." SAC 4 (1982), 3-32.

806 SUNDWELL, McKAY. "The Destruction of Troy, Chaucer's Troilus and
     Criseyde, and Lydgate's Troy Book." RES 26 (1975), 313-17.
     [dating of Lydgate's work]

807 SWART, FELIX. "Chaucer and the English Reformation." Neophil 62
     (1978), 616-19. [Plowman's Tale, Pilgrim's Tale]

808 TANNER, JERI. "A 16th-Century Allusion to Chaucer." AN&Q 12
     (1973), 3-4. [John Jones]

809 THOMPSON, R. ANN. "The Irony of Chaucer's Legend of Good Women
     Perceived in 1576." Archiv 213 (1976), 342-43. [allusion in
     "Common Conditions"]

810 THOMPSON, R. ANN. "'Our revels now are ended': An Allusion to
     The Franklin's Tale?" Archiv 212 (1975), 317.

811 THOMPSON, [R.] ANN. Shakespeare's Chaucer: A Study in Literary
     Origins. Liverpool English Texts and Studies. Liverpool
     University Press; New York: Barnes & Noble, 1978. 239 pp.
     [TC, CT, LGW, PF]
         Reviews: G. C. Britton, N&Q 27 (1980), 184-86; E. Talbot
     Donaldson, RenQ 33 (1980), 284-86; Thomas McAlindon, JEGP 80
     (1981), 237-43; J. M. Maguin, CahiersE 19 (1981), 100-01.

812 THOMPSON, [R.] ANN. "Troilus and Criseyde and Romeo and Juliet."
     YES 6 (1976), 26-37.

813 THOMPSON, [R.] ANN. "The 'Two Buckets' Image in Richard II and
     The Isle of Gulls." Archiv 213 (1976), 108. [KnT]

814 TRIPP, RAYMOND P., JR. "The Loss of Suddenness in Lydgate's A
     Complaynt of a Loveres Lyfe." FCS 6 (1983), 253-69. [cf.

Influence and Allusions

BD]

815   TURNER, ROBERT K. "The Two Noble Kinsmen and Speght's Chaucer."
      N&Q 27 (1980), 175-76. [KnT]

816   TUSO, JOSEPH F. "Grendel, Chapter 1: John Gardner's Perverse
      Prologue." CollL 12 (1985), 184-86. [GP]

817   WALLER, MARTHA S. "A Comment on 'Tattle's Well's Faire'." CE 47
      (1985), 873-74. [ParsT; Aquinas' Summa Theologica]

818   WHITE, ROBERT B., JR. "Chaucer's Physician: An Uncollected
      Allusion 1611." N&Q 26 (1979), 102-03. [in Edmund Gardiner]

819   WILLIAMS, FRANKLIN B., JR. "Alsop's 'Fair Custance': Chaucer in
      Tudor Dress." ELR 6 (1976), 351-68. [includes text; MLT]

820   WINSTON, ROBERT P. "Chaucer's Influence on Barth's The Sot-Weed
      Factor." AL 56 (1985), 584-90. [RvT, MilT]

821   YEAGER, ROBERT F., ed. Fifteenth-Century Studies: Recent
      Essays. Hamden, CT: Archon Books, 1984. [essays on
      reviews of scholarship] See nos. 800, 943.

822   YORK, LORRAINE M. "'River Two Blind Jacks': Dave Godfrey's
      Chaucerian Allegory." SCL 9 (1984), 206-13. [+ PardT]

See also: 16, 78, 114a, 130, 143, 144, 148, 151, 173, 287, 307, 323,
           344, 387, 436, 490, 534, 562, 831, 836, 842, 843, 1213, 1369,
           1553, 1836, 2021, 2195, 2226, 2368, 2392, 2495, 2821, 2880.

STYLE INCLUDING VERSIFICATION AND PUNS

823   BEAVER, JOSEPH C. "Current Metrical Issues." CE 33 (1971),
       177-97. [Halle and Keyser] See also nos. 829, 839, 842,
       844, 845.

824   BIGGINS, DENNIS. "Chaucer's Metrical Lines: Some Internal
       Evidence." Parergon 17 (1977), 17-24. [iambic pentameter;
       CT; Ellesmere]

825   BLOOMFIELD, MORTON W. "Personification-Metaphors." ChauR 14
       (1980), 287-97.

826   BRODY, SAUL NATHANIEL. "Chaucer's Rhyme Royal Tales and the
       Secularization of the Saint." ChauR 20 (1985), 113-31.
       [SNT, PrT, MLT, ClT]

827   BROGAN, TERRY VANCE F. "Three Models for English Verse:
       Inquiries in Metatheory." DAI 43 (1983), 3917A. University
       of Texas at Austin, 1982.

828   BURNLEY, J. D. "Chaucer, Usk, and Geoffrey of Vinsauf." Neophil
       69 (1985), 286-91. [allusions to rhetoric]

829   CABLE, THOMAS. "A Garland of Pomposities: Comment on
       Halle-Keyser Prosody." CE 34 (1973), 593-95. See also nos.
       823, 839, 842, 844, 845.

830   CLARK, ROY PETER. "A Possible Pun on Chaucer's Name." Names 25
       (1977), 49-50.

831   CONNER, JACK. English Prosody from Chaucer to Wyatt. Janua
       Linguarum Studia Memoriae Nicolai VanWijk Dedicata, Series
       Practica 193. The Hague: Mouton, 1974. 104 pp.
          Reviews: Fitzroy Pyle, MAE 45 (1976), 332-36; Derek
       Attridge, MLR 72 (1977), 147-48.

832   CRÉPIN, ANDRÉ. "From 'Swutol Sang Scopes' to 'Rum Ram Ruf'--Or
       the Problems of Alliteration," in 46, pp. 113-24.

Style Including Versification and Puns

833   DIEKSTRA, FRANS. "The Language of Equivocation: Some Chaucerian
       Techniques." DQR 11 (1981), 267-77. [TC, CT, LGW]

834   EASTHOPE, ANTONY. "Problematizing the Pentameter." NLH 12
       (1981), 475-92.

835   ELIASON, NORMAN E. The Language of Chaucer's Poetry. An
       Appraisal of the Verse Style, and Structure. Anglistica, 17.
       Copenhagen: Rosenkilde and Bagger, 1972.
           Reviews: C. Schaar, SN 46 (1974), 547-51; Charles A Owen,
       Jr., Speculum 49 (1974), 727-30; T. F. Hoad, N&Q 21 (1974),
       230-32; Theodore A. Stroud, MP 72 (1974), 60-70; Dieter Mehl,
       Anglia 92 (1974), 451-54; R. W. V. Elliott, ES 56 (1975),
       153-54; Heiner Gillmeister, Archiv 212 (1975), 366-69.

836   FOX, ALLAN B. "Chaucer's Prosody and the Non-Pentameter Line in
       John Heywood's Comic Debates." Lang&S 10 (1977), 23-41.

837   GAYLORD, ALAN T. "Scanning the Prosodists: An Essay in
       Metacriticism." ChauR 11 (1976), 22-82.

838   GILBERT, DOROTHY. "The Rude Sweetness: A Study of Chaucer's
       Prosody and of Its Examiners." DAI 37 (1976), 288A.
       University of California, Davis, 1975.

839   HALLE, MORRIS and SAMUEL J. KEYSER. "Illustration and Defense of
       a Theory of the Iambic Pentameter." CE 33 (1971), 154-176.
       See also nos. 823, 829, 842, 844, 845.

840   KELLY, H. A. "'Occupatio' as a Negative Narration: A Mistake for
       'Occultatio/Praeteritio'." MP 74 (1977), 311-15.
       [preterition]

841   KNIGHT, STEPHEN. Rymyng Craftily: Meaning in Chaucer's Poetry.
       Sydney and London: Angus and Robertson, 1973. 247 pp.
       [Geoffrey of Vinsauf; CT, TC, A&A, PF]
           Reviews: Derek Brewer, RES 27 (1976), 55-57; Martin
       Lehnert, ZAA 24 (1976), 357-62; G. C. Britton, N&Q 222
       (1977), 82-86; F. Diekstra, ES 58 (1977), 58-61; Stephan
       Kohl, Anglia 95 (1977), 518-20.

842   LYNN, KAREN. "Chaucer's Decasyllabic Line: The Myth of the
       Hundred-Year Hibernation." ChauR 13 (1978), 116-27. [Halle
       and Keyser] See also nos. 823, 829, 839, 844, 845.

843   LYNN, KAREN. "Computational Prosodics: The Decasyllabic Line
       from Chaucer to Skelton." DAI 34 (1974), 4210A. University
       of Southern California, 1973.

Style Including Versification and Puns

844   MAGNUSON, KARL and FRANK G. RYDER. "Second Thoughts on English
       Prosody." CE 33 (1971), 198-216. See also nos. 823, 829,
       839, 842, 845.

845   MAGNUSON, KARL and FRANK G. RYDER. "The Study of English
       Prosody: An Alternative Proposal." CE 31 (1970), 789-820.
       [Halle and Keyser] See also nos. 823, 829, 839, 842, 844.

846   MANABE, KAZUMI. "Notes on Gramstylistic Analysis: With
       Reference to Articles in Chaucer." SELL 27 (1977), 95-107.
       In Japanese.

847   MORGAN, MARY VALENTINA. "The Shaping of Experience: A Study of
       Rhetorical Methods and Structure in Narrative Works by
       Chaucer, Fielding, and Dickens." DAI 41 (1980), 2126A.
       University of California, San Diego. [MLT, MkT]

848   MOSELEY, C. W. R. D. "Chaucer, Sir John Mandeville, and the
       Alliterative Revival: A Hypothesis Concerning
       Relationships." MP 72 (1974), 182-84.

849   MURPHY, JAMES J. Rhetoric in the Middle Ages: A History of
       Rhetorical Theory from St. Augustine to the Renaissance.
       Berkeley: University of California Press, 1974. 395 pp.
       [artes poetica, artes dictaminis, artes praedicandi]
       Reviews: VQR 51:2 (1975), lxvi.

850   MUSTANOJA, TAUNO F. "Chaucer's Prosody," in 70, pp. 65-94.

851   MUSTANOJA, TAUNO F. "Verbal Rhyming in Chaucer," in 69, pp.
       104-10.

852   NAGER, RAE ANN. "English II Bibliographical," in Versification:
       Major Types. Edited by W. K. Wimsatt. New York: Modern
       Language Association, 1972, pp. 212-13. [biblio. ME
       versification]

853   OSBERG, RICHARD H. "The Alliterative Lyric and
       Thirteenth-Century Devotional Prose." JEGP 76 (1977), 40-54.

854   PARR, ROGER P. "Chaucer's Art of Portraiture." SMC 4 (1974),
       428-36.

855   PAYNE, ROBERT O. "Chaucer and the Art of Rhetoric," in 70, pp.
       42-64.

856   PAYNE, ROBERT O. "Chaucer's Realization of Himself as Rhetor,"
       in 2625, pp. 270-87.

Style Including Versification and Puns

857   ROBINSON, IAN. Chaucer's Prosody: A Study of the Middle English
      Verse Tradition. London: Cambridge University Press, 1971.
      251 pp.
         Reviews: K. C. Phillipps, ES 54 (1973), 272-74; Donald K.
      Fry, ELN 11:2 (1973), 123-26; Mechthild Gretsch, Anglia 92
      (1974), 454-60; Charles A. Owen, Jr., Speculum 49 (1974),
      148-51.

858   ROSCOW, G[REGORY] H. "The Pattern of the Sentence in Chaucer's
      Poetry." Ph.D. thesis, University of Cambridge, 1976.

859   ROSCOW, GREGORY [H]. Syntax and Style in Chaucer's Poetry.
      Chaucer Studies, 6. Cambridge: D. S. Brewer, 1981. 158 pp.
      [word order; idiomatic usage; pleonasm; ellipsis; relative
      clauses; coordination and parataxis]
         Reviews: Valerie Adams, TLS (15 October, 1982), 1135;
      Charles A. Owen, Jr., SAC 5 (1983), 200-02; N. F. Blake, ES
      64 (1983), 75-77; Mark Lambert, Speculum 58 (1983), 811-13;
      Joyce Bazire, MAE 52 (1983), 131-32; David C. Fowler, MP 81
      (1984), 407-14; André Crépin, EA 37 (1984), 184.

860   ROWLAND, BERYL. "Earle Birney and Chaucer." ECW 21 (1981),
      73-84.

861   SASAGAWA, HISAAKI. "Chaucer ni okeru bunsaiteki hitei"
      [Figurative Negation in Chaucer]. Journal of General
      Education Department, Niigata University (1984), 1-11. In
      Japanese.

862   SHIGEO, HISASHI. "Chaucer no buntai o megutte" [Some
      Observations on Chaucer's Style]. Katahira 20 (1984), 1-22.
      In Japanese.

863   SMOOT, MAXINE BIXBY. "The Art of Chaucer's Verse." DAI 35
      (1975), 6735A. University of California, Berkeley, 1974.

864   STEVENS, MARTIN. "The Royal Stanza in Early English Literature."
      PMLA 94 (1979), 62-76. [TC, CT, MLT]

864a TARLINSKAJA, MARINA [G]. English Verse: Theory and History. De
      proprietatibus litterarum: Series practica, 117. The Hague:
      Mouton, 1976. 352 pp.
         Reviews: Ewald Standop, Anglia 97 (1979), 218-32.

865   TARLINSKAJA, M[ARINA] G. "Meter and Rhythm of Pre-Chaucerian
      Rhymed Verse." Linguistics 121 (1974), 65-87. [final-e]

866   TUGGLE, THOMAS TERRY. "Medieval Rhetoric and Chaucer's An A B C,
      Book of the Duchess, and Parliament of Fowls." DAI 35

Style Including Versification and Puns

(1975), 7882-83A. University of Iowa, 1974. [Rhetorica ad Herennium, Ars Poetica]

867 WOOD, CHAUNCEY. "Affective Stylistics and the Study of Chaucer." SAC 6 (1984), 21-40.

See also: 261, 292, 342, 348, 350, 403, 589, 631, 855, 1086, 1190, 1348, 1386, 1393, 1399, 1548, 1561, 1782, 1817, 1827, 1836, 1891, 1922, 1956, 1968, 1969, 1994, 2002, 2025, 2034, 2040, 2048, 2057, 2075, 2132, 2181, 2202, 2287, 2406, 2413, 2414, 2425, 2463, 2512, 2518, 2866.

LANGUAGE AND WORD STUDIES

868   ANDO, SHINSUKE. "Chaucer's Conception of Nature." Key-Words in
       Beowulf and Chaucer 1 (1980), 49–57. In English.
       [+Naturalism]

869   BALD, WOLF-DIETRICH. "On the Diachrony of English Linking
       Verbs," in 41, pp. 175–89.

870   BARNEY, STEPHEN A. "Suddenness and Process in Chaucer." ChauR
       16 (1981), 18–37. [sodeyn, proces]

871   BATESON, F. W. "Could Chaucer Spell?" EIC 25 (1975), 2–24.

872   BEECK, FRANS JOZEF VAN. "A Note on Ther in Curses and Blessings
       in Chaucer." Neophil 69 (1985), 276–83. [TC, CT]

873   BJELICA, NEVENKA. "Analitički i sintetički komparativ i
       superlativ: jedna analiza Čoserovog proznog korpusa" [The
       Analytic and Synthetic Comparative and Superlative in
       Chaucer's Prose Works]. FP 15 (1977), 95–113.

874   BLAKE, N. F. The English Language in Medieval Literature.
       London: J. M. Dent, 1977; Methuen: University Paperback,
       1979. 190 pp. [linguistic conditions within which writers
       worked]
          Reviews: Alan Bliss, N&Q 25 (1978), 353–56; Gillis
       Kristensson, ES 60 (1979), 321–23; G. S. Ivy, DUJ, n. s., 43
       (1981–82), 135–36.

875   BURNLEY, J. D[AVID]. "Chaucer Through His Language." Chaucer
       Newsletter 4:1 (1985), 1, 5.

876   BURNLEY, J. D[AVID]. "Chaucer's Termes." YES 7 (1977), 53–67.

877   BURNLEY, [J.] DAVID. A Guide to Chaucer's Language. Norman:
       University of Oklahoma Press, 1983. 264 pp. [text; grammar;
       syntax; use; style]
          Reviews: J. J. Brosamer, Choice 22 (1984), 92; Barry
       Windeatt, Encounter 63 (1984), 55–59; Bernard O'Donoghue, TLS

Bibliography of Chaucer, 1974 - 1985

Language and Word Studies

(18 May, 1984), 555; Norman Davis, RES 36 (1985), 554-555; M. L. Samuels, SAC 7 (1985), 172-75; R. A. Waldron, ES 66 (1985), 465-66.

878   BURNLEY, [J.] DAVID. "Inflexion in Chaucer's Adjectives." NM 83 (1982), 169-77. [final -e in Hengwrt, Ellesmere]

879   CALUWÉ-DOR, JULIETTE DE. "Chaucer's Contribution to the English Vocabulary: A Chronological Survey of French Loan-Words." NOWELE 2 (1983), 73-91.

880   CALUWÉ-DOR, JULIETTE DE. "Chaucer's Derivational Morphemes Revisited," in Linguistic and Stylistic Studies in Medieval English. Edited by André Crépin. Publications de l'Association des Medievistes de l'Enseignement Superieur, 10. Paris: 1984, pp. 63-79.

881   CALUWÉ-DOR, JULIETTE DE. "Chaucer's French Loan-Words and the Use of French in Fourteenth-Century England." Bulletin des Anglicistes Médiévistes 28 (1985), 435-38. [CT]

882   CHIAPPELLI, CAROLYN. "Chaucer's Use of solas." Comitatus 2 (1971), 91-92.

883   COSMOS, SPENCER. "Toward a Visual Stylistics: Assent and Denial in Chaucer." VLang 12 (1978), 406-27.

884   COSTIGAN, EDWARD. "'Privitee' in The Canterbury Tales." SELit 60 (1983), 217-30. [+cognates in CT]

885   DAVIS, NORMAN. "Chaucer and the English Language," in Geoffrey Chaucer: Conferenze origanizzate dall'Accademia Nazionale dei Lincei in Collaborazione con la British Academy. Problemi Attuali di Scienza e di Cultura, Quaderno 234. Roma: Accademia Nazionale dei Lincei, 1977, pp. 23-34.

886   DAVIS, NORMAN. "Chaucer and Fourteenth-Century English," in 49, pp. 58-84.

887   DE WEEVER, JACQUELINE. "Chaucerian Onomastics: The Formation and Use of Personal Names in Chaucer's Works." Names 28 (1980), 1-31.

888   DONALDSON, E. TALBOT. "Adventures with the Adversative Conjunction in the General Prologue to the Canterbury Tales; or, What's before the but?" in So Meny People, Longages and Tonges: Philological Essays in Scots and Mediaeval English Presented to Angus McIntosh. Edited by Michael Benskin and M. L. Samuels. Edinburgh: Authors, 1981, pp. 355-66.

Bibliography of Chaucer, 1974 - 1985

Language and Word Studies

889   DONALDSON, E. TALBOT. "Gallic Flies in Chaucer's English Word
       Web," in 68, pp. 193-202. [CT, TC]

890   DONNER, MORTON. "Derived Words in Chaucer's Language." ChauR 13
       (1978), 1-15. [+coinages]

891   ELLIOTT, RALPH W. V. Chaucer's English. Language Library
       Series. New York: Academic Press; London: Deutsch, 1974.
       447 pp. [comprehensive]
          Reviews: K. C. Phillipps, ES 57 (1976), 258-60; Cecily
       Clark, MAE 45 (1976), 336-38.

892   ELLIOTT, RALPH W. V. "'Faire Subtile Wordes': An Approach to
       Chaucer's Verbal Art." Parergon 13 (1975), 3-20. [+levels
       of style]

893   EMONDS, JOSEPH. "The Derived Nominals, Gerunds, and Participles
       in Chaucer's English," in Issues in Linguistics: Papers in
       Honor of Henry and Renee Kahane. Edited by Braj B. Kachru.
       Chicago: University of Illinois Press, 1973, pp. 185-98.

894   FINNIE, W. BRUCE. "On Chaucer's Stressed Vowel Phonemes." ChauR
       9 (1975), 337-41. [reply to Adams, JEGP 71 (1972), 527-39;
       PMLA 88 (1973), 8-18]

895   FISCHER, OLGA. "A Comparative Study of Philosophical Terms in
       the Alfredian and Chaucerian Boethius." Neophil 63 (1979),
       622-39.

896   FISHER, JOHN H., MALCOLM RICHARDSON, and JANE L. FISHER. An
       Anthology of Chancery English, 1417-1455. Knoxville:
       University of Tennessee Press, 1984.
          Reviews: Martin Camargo, SAC 7 (1985), 191-94.

897   FISHER, JOHN H. "Chaucer and the French Influence," in 68, pp.
       177-191. [prosody; style]

898   FISHER, JOHN H. and DIANE D. BORNSTEIN. In Forme of Speche is
       Chaunge. Lanham, MD: University Press of America, 1984.
       [history of English language; +GP]

899   FRIES, UDO. Einführung in die Sprache Chaucers: Phonologie,
       Metrik und Morphologie. Tübingen: Niemeyer, 1985.
          Reviews: J. D. Burnley, Speculum 62 (1987), 187-89.

900   GILBERT, A. J. Literary Language from Chaucer to Johnson. New
       York: Barnes & Noble; London: Macmillan, 1979. See esp.
       Chapter 1, "Chaucer and Skelton." [+GP, KnT]

BIBLIOGRAPHY OF CHAUCER, 1974 - 1985

Language and Word Studies

Reviews: Basil Cottle, <u>TLS</u> (14 March, 1980), 300.

901 GLOWKA, ARTHUR W. "Chaucer's Bird Sounds." <u>LangQ</u> 21 (1983), 15-17. [<u>CT</u>, <u>PF</u>, <u>TC</u>]

902 GÖRLACH, MANFRED. "Chaucer's English: What Remains to Be Done." <u>ArAA</u> 4 (1978), 61-79.

903 GRAHAM, PAUL TREES. "The Meaning of Structure in Chaucerian Narrative." <u>DAI</u> 40 (1980), 5045A. University of Missouri-Columbia, 1979. [sentence as model]

904 HÄCKEL, WILLI. <u>Das Sprichwort bei Chaucer</u>. Amsterdam: Rodopi, 1970. [enlargement of author's 1890 Leipzig thesis]

905 HART, PAXTON. "Chaucer's Regard for English." <u>Interpretations</u> 14 (1982), 1-10.

906 HEUER, HERMANN. <u>Studien zur syntaktischen und stilistischen Funktion des Adverbs bei Chaucer und im Rosenroman.</u> Anglistische Forschungen 75. Heidelberg: C. Winter, 1932. 168 pp.

907 HIGUCHI, MASAYUKI. "Chaucer ni okeru <u>drem</u> to <u>sweven</u>." <u>EigoS</u> 127 (1982), 632-34. In Japanese. [<u>PF</u>, <u>NPT</u>, <u>HF</u>, <u>TC</u>, <u>BD</u>]

908 HIGUCHI, MASAYUKI. "On the Counterfactual Force of <u>Wenen</u>--with Special Reference to Chaucer's Use." <u>SELit</u>, English no. (Tokyo, 1983), pp. 101-25.

909 HOLLEY, LINDA TARTE. "Chaucer and the Function of the Word." <u>DAI</u> 36 (1976), 8075A. Tulane University, 1975.

910 HOYA, KATSUZO. "Canterbury Monogatari Sojobun no nakade Chaucer ga hajimete shiyoshita Latin-go to France-go no kenkyu, I" [A Study of Latin and French Loan Words Which Chaucer First Used in the General Prologue of <u>The Canterbury Tales</u>, I]. <u>Bulletin of Yamanashi Medical College</u> 1 (1984), 51-57. In Japanese.

911 HUNTSMAN, JEFFREY F. "Caveat Editor: Chaucer and Medieval English Dictionaries." <u>MP</u> 73 (1976), 276-79. [<u>stot</u>, <u>nakers</u>, <u>astromye</u> in <u>CT</u>]

912 IKEGAMI, MASA T. <u>Rhyme and Pronunication: Some Studies of English Rhymes from 'Kyng Alisaunder' to Skelton.</u> Hogaku-Kenkyu-Kai, Keio University, Extra Series 5. Tokyo: Keio University, 1984.

913 IKEGAMI, TADAHIRO. "Chusei bungaku ni okeru yosei" [Fairies in

95

Language and Word Studies

Medieval European Literature], in Renaissance Bungaku no
nakano Yosei [Fairies in Renaissance Literature]. Edited by
Shounosuke Ishii and Peter Milward. Tokyo: Aratake Shuppan,
1984, pp. 33-58. In Japanese. [key-words: elf, dwarf,
fairy, fay]

914   IKEGAMI, YOSHIHIKO. "The Semological Structure of the English
        Verbs of Motion: Old and Middle English." Key-Word Studies
        in Beowulf and Chaucer 1 (1980), 67-104. In English.

915   ITO, EIKO. "Reflexive Verbs in Chaucer." SELit, English no.
        (Tokyo, 1978), 65-89.

916   IWASAKI, HARUO. "'Not worth a straw' and Similar Idioms."
        Key-Word Studies in Chaucer 1 (1984), 33-49. [in CT, TC]

917   IWASAKI, HARUO. "Some Notes on the gan-Periphrasis." Key-Word
        Studies in Chaucer 1 (1984), 15-32.

918   KACHRU, BRAJ. B., ROBERT B. LEES, YAKOV MALKIEL, ANGELINA
        PIETRANGELI, and SOL SAPORTA, eds. Issues in Linguistics:
        Papers in Honor Of Henry and Renee Kahane. Urbana; Chicago;
        London: Illinois University Press, 1974. 933 pp. See no.
        927.

919   KANNO, M[ASAHIKO]. "Another Word-Play in Chaucer?" MESN 5
        (1981), 2-3.

920   KANNO, MASAHIKO. "Glenyng Here and There," in Studies in English
        and Germanic Languages--Essays in Honour of Professor Niwa.
        Tokyo: 1983, pp. 28-46. In English.

921   KANNO, MASAHIKO. "Glenyng Here and There II." Bulletin of Aichi
        University of Education (Humanities) 33 (1984), 33-44.

922   KERKHOF, J. Studies in the Language of Geoffrey Chaucer. 2nd
        rev. enl. ed. Leidse Germanistische en Anglistische Reeks
        van de Rijksuniversiteit te Leiden. Brill: Leiden, 1982.
        Reviews: F. N. M. Diekstra, ES 65 (1984), 564-67.

923   LEANA, JOYCE F. "Chaucer the Word-Master: The House of Fame and
        The Canterbury Tales." DAI 35 (1974), 1049-50A. Columbia
        University.

924   MAČEK, DORA. "A Draft for the Analysis of Verbal Periphrases in
        the Canterbury Tales." SRAZ 33-36 (1972-73), 695-708.

925   MAGOUN, FRANCIS P., JR. "Two Chaucer Items." NM 78 (1977), 46.
        [at the townes ende; estres]

Language and Word Studies

926 MIZUTORI, YOSHITAKA. "Chaucer ni okeru Perfect ni tsuite: the
     Canterbury Tales o chushin ni" [Perfect in Chaucer: With
     Special Reference to The Canterbury Tales]. The Review of
     Inquiry and Research (The Kansai University of Foreign
     Studies, Japan) 40 (1984), 105-19. In Japanese.

927 MORGAN, J. L. "Sentence Fragments and the Notion 'Sentence'," in
     918 above, pp. 719-51.

928 MUSTANOJA, TAUNO F. "Chaucer's Use of gan: Some Recent
     Studies," in 59, pp. 59-64.

929 NACHISCHIONE, A. S. "Inversiia kak elementarnyi priem
     okkazional'nogo preobrazovaniia frazeologicheskikh edinits v
     rechi (na materiale proizvedenii Dzh. Chosera)," in
     Sintagmaticheskaia obuslovlennost' leksicheskoi semantiki
     [The Syntagmatic Conditionality of Lexical Semantics].
     Edited by V. I. Agamdzhanova. Riga: Latvian University,
     1980, pp. 128-44.

930 NACHISCHIONE, A. S. "K voprosu o slozhnykh okkazional'nykh
     probazovaniyakh frazeologicheskikh edinits: na materiale
     proizvedeniy Dzh. Chosera" [On the Question of Complex
     Occasional Transformations of Phraseological Units: On
     Material Taken from the Works of Chaucer]. Inostrannye
     yazyki v vysshev shkole (Riga) 2 (1975), 76-93.

931 NACHISCHIONE, A. S. "Nekotorye okkazional'nye izmeneniya
     frazeologicheskikh edinits v proizvedeniyakh Dzh. Chosera"
     [Occasional Changes of Phrase-Units in the Works of Chaucer].
     Latvivyskii gosudarstvennyi universitet (Riga) 197 (1973),
     23-48.

932 NESS, LYNN and CAROLINE DUNCAN-ROSE. "A Syntactic Correlate of
     Style Switching in the Canterbury Tales," in Papers from the
     3rd International Conference on Historical Linguistics.
     Edited by Peter J. Maher, Allan R. Bomhard, and E. F. Konrad
     Koerner. Current Issues in Linguistic Theory, 13. Amsterdam
     Studies in the Theory and History of Linguistic Science, 4th
     series. Amsterdam: Benjamins, 1982, pp. 292-322. [tense
     shifting]

933 NIXON, P. M. "Studies in Chaucer's Colour Vocabulary." M.Phil.
     thesis, University of York, 1978.

934 PETERS, ROBERT A. Chaucer's Language. Western Washington
     University (Bellingham) Journal of English Linguistics:
     Occasional Monographs, 1 (July, 1980). 125 pp.

BIBLIOGRAPHY OF CHAUCER, 1974 - 1985

Language and Word Studies

Reviews: Walter S. Phelan, <u>SAC</u> 4 (1982), 178–81.

935   PHELAN, WALTER S. "From Morpheme to Motif in Chaucer's <u>Canterbury</u>
<u>Tales</u>," in <u>Proceedings of the International Conference on</u>
<u>Literary and Linguistic Computing, Israel, Tel Aviv</u>
<u>University, 1979</u>. Edited by Zvi Malachi. Tel Aviv: Katz
Research Institute, 1980, pp. 291–316.
Reviews: L. D. Barnard, <u>CHum</u> 15 (1981), 119–20.

936   PHELAN, WALTER S. "The Study of Chaucer's Vocabulary." <u>CHum</u> 12
(1978), 61–69. [comparison with Gower, Dryden]

937   REX, RICHARD. "'Spiced Conscience' in the <u>Canterbury Tales</u>." <u>MP</u>
80 (1982), 53–54. [+<u>WBT</u>]

938   ROBERTSON, D. W., JR. "Some Disputed Chaucerian Terminology."
<u>Speculum</u> 52 (1977), 571–81. [in <u>CT</u>]

939   ROGERS, WILLIAM E. "Individualization of Language in the
Canterbury Frame Story." <u>AnM</u> 15 (1974), 74–108. [+Romance
and Latinate loans]

940   ROMANOVS'KA, IU. IU. "Semantychni osoblyvosti vstavnykh
predykatyvnykh odynyts': Na materiali seredn'oanhliĭs'koï
movy." <u>Mov</u> 2 (1985), 47–50. [parenthetical construction;
semantics]

941   ROSS, THOMAS W. and EDWARD BROOKS, eds. <u>English Glosses (A</u>
<u>Fifteenth Century Word-List) from British Library MS</u>
<u>Additional 37075</u>. Norman, OK: Pilgrim Books, 1984.
[+Latin-English instruction books]

942   ROSS, THOMAS W. "Me 'Meving'." <u>Chaucer Newsletter</u> 2:2 (1980), 11
(University of Oklahoma).

943   ROSS, THOMAS W. "Taboo-Words in Fifteenth-Century English," in
821, pp. 137–60. [+Scottish Chaucerians]

944   SAITO, ISAMU. "Chaucer bungaku no kadoguchi: Sono kōshosei."
<u>EigoS</u> 126 (1980), 66–68. [oral element]

945   SAITO, ISAMU. "A Gateway to Chaucer." <u>EigoS</u> 127 (1980), 66–68.
[oral cliches]

946   SAMUELS, M. L. "Chaucer's Spelling," in 59, pp. 17–37. [in
<u>Equat</u>, Hengwrt]

947   SANDVED, ARTHUR O. <u>Introduction to Chaucerian English</u>. Chaucer
Studies 11. Cambridge: D. S. Brewer, 1985.

Language and Word Studies

Reviews: J. D. Burnley, Speculum 62 (1987), 187–89.

948   SASAGAWA, HISAAKI. "The Historical Present and Perfect in
       Chaucer's Knight's Tale." Journal of the General Education
       Department, Niigata University 12 (1981), 179–91. In
       Japanese.

949   SCHMIDT, A. V. C. and F. W. BATESON. "Could Chaucer Spell?" EIC
       25 (1975), 391–93.

950   SHIMOGASA, TOKUJI. "Middle English Adverbs of Affirming." HSELL
       25 (1980), 13–28. [ywis, wytterly, sikerly, verayment]

951   SMITH, MERETE. "Literary Loanwords from Old French in The
       Romaunt of the Rose: A Note." ChauR 17 (1982), 89–93.

952   SMITH, SARAH STANBURY. "'Game in myn hood': The Traditions of a
       Comic Proverb." SIcon 9 (1983), 1–12. [CT, TC]

953   SMITHERS, G. V. "The Scansion of Havelok and the Use of ME –en
       and –e in Havelok and by Chaucer," in 59, pp. 195–233.

954   TAKAMIYA, TOSHIYUKI. "Chaucer's Sad and its Related Words."
       Key-Word Studies in "Beowulf" and Chaucer 1 (1980), 59–65.
       In English.

955   TERASAWA, YOSHIO. "'Daunger': Specimen of Chaucer Lexicon."
       Key-Word Studies in "Beowulf" and Chaucer 1 (1980), 17–22.
       In English. [+WBT]

See also: 258, 261, 276, 306, 307, 344, 367, 403, 493, 541, 542, 575,
           585a, 668a, 702, 825, 830, 833, 835, 854, 855, 996, 1050,
           1054, 1060, 1083, 1160, 1190, 1263, 1308, 1321, 1330, 1344,
           1347, 1354, 1371, 1374, 1379, 1380, 1382, 1385, 1390, 1414,
           1427, 1517, 1523, 1525, 1535, 1558, 1560, 1570, 1581, 1587,
           1591, 1596, 1601, 1606, 1656, 1704, 1767, 1773, 1775, 1779,
           1789, 1801, 1806, 1830, 1838, 1854, 1858, 1910, 1924, 1931,
           1942, 1958, 1968, 1990, 1993, 1995, 1996, 1997, 1998, 2005,
           2032, 2042, 2058, 2102, 2212, 2237, 2242, 2245, 2258, 2281,
           2292, 2317, 2318, 2319, 2344, 2392, 2395, 2399, 2400, 2417,
           2430, 2443, 2448, 2382.

THE CANTERBURY TALES

GENERAL

956   ALFORD, JOHN A. "Scriptural Testament in The Canterbury Tales,"
      in 63, pp. 197-203. [glosing in WBP, WBT, FrT, SumT]

957   ALLEN, JUDSON BOYCE and THERESA ANNE MORITZ. A Distinction of
      Stories: The Medieval Unity of Chaucer's Fair Chain of
      Narratives for Canterbury. Columbus: Ohio State University
      Press, 1981. 258 pp. [order of CT; Ovid; marriage;
      morality]
         Reviews: Theodore A. Stroud, MP 80 (1982), 177-80; Robert
      M. Jordan, DalR 62 (1982), 164-66; Dieter Mehl, N&Q, n. s.,
      29 (1982), 429-31; Thomas H. Bestul, Speculum 57 (1982),
      850-52; Derek Pearsall, SAC 4 (1982), 135-40; Emerson Brown,
      Jr., JEGP 81 (1982), 554-56; N. F. Blake, ES 64 (1983),
      569-70; Helen Cooper, RES 35 (1984), 219-21; John C. Hirsh,
      MAE 53 (1984), 123-25; Douglas J. McMillan, Anglia 103
      (1984), 194-96; Beryl Rowland, ESC 10 (1984), 221-26.

958   ALLINGHAM, ANTHONY. "The Song of Songs as Literary Influence in
      Selected Works of the English Renaissance." DAI 37 (1977),
      5840A. University of Oregon, 1976. [MilT]

959   ALLINSON, JANE FRANK. "The Fabliau in Medieval England." DAI 42
      (1981), 1140A. University of Connecticut.

960   AMES, RUTH M. "Prototype and Parody in Chaucerian Exegesis," in
      72a, pp. 87-105. [Bible; allegory; Mel, MLT, MilT, MerT]

961   ANDERSEN, WALLIS MAY. "Rhetoric and Poetics in the Canterbury
      Tales: The Knight, the Squire, and the Franklin." DAI 41
      (1980), 239A. University of Detroit, 1979.

962   ANDREAS, JAMES R. "Festive Liminality in Chaucerian Comedy."
      Chaucer Newsletter 1:1 (1979), 3-6. [+anthropological
      studies of Turner and van Gennep; GP]

963   BAKER, DONALD C. "The Evolution of Henry Bradshaw's Idea of the
          Order of the Canterbury Tales." Chaucer Newsletter 3:1
          (1981), 2-6.

964   BARBEITO, MANUEL. "Dos problemas formales en The Canterbury
          Tales." Atlantis 5 (1983), 39-53. [+allegory, didacticism]

964a   BARISONE, ERMANNO and ATTILIO BRILLI, eds. I racconti di
          Canterbury. Milan: Mondadori, 1983. 394 pp.

965   BARON, F. XAVIER. "Children and Violence in Chaucer's Canterbury
          Tales." Journal of Psychohistory 7 (1979), 77-103. [MLT,
          ClT, PhyT, PrT, Mel, MkT]

966   BENNETT, J. A. W. Chaucer at Oxford and at Cambridge. Oxford:
          Clarendon Press, 1974. 131 pp. [MilT, RvT]

967   BENSON, C. DAVID. "Their Telling Difference: Chaucer the
          Pilgrim and His Two Contrasting Tales." ChauR 18 (1983),
          61-76. [Th, Mel; narrative technique]

968   BENSON, LARRY D. "The Order of The Canterbury Tales." SAC 3
          (1981), 77-120. [Ellesmere; G-fragment] See also no. 974
          below.

969   BERGGREN, RUTH. "Who Really is the Advocate of Equality in the
          Marriage Group?" MSE 6:1-2 (1977), 25-36. [WBT, ClT, MerT,
          FrT]

970   BESSERMAN, LAWRENCE. "Glosing is a Glorious Thyng: Chaucer's
          Biblical Exegesis," in 63, pp. 65-73. [Glossa ordinaria;
          antifraternalism; WBT, MerT, ParsT]

971   BLACK, ROBERT RAY. "Sacral and Biblical Parody in Chaucer's
          Canterbury Tales." DAI 35 (1975), 6090A. Princeton
          University, 1974. [parody, Bible, Marriage Group]

972   BLAKE, N. F. "Aspects of Syntax and Lexis in the Canterbury
          Tales." RCEI 7 (1983), 1-20. [GP Prioress]

973   BLAKE, N. F. "Critics, Criticism and the Order of the Canterbury
          Tales." Archiv 218 (1981), 47-58.

974   BLAKE, N.F. "The Debate on the Order of The Canterbury Tales."
          RCEI 10 (1985), 31-42. Disagrees with Benson, no. 968,
          above.

975   BLODGETT, E. D. "Chaucerian Pryvetee and the Opposition to

Canterbury Tales

Time." Speculum 51 (1976), 477-93. [MilT, RvT, KnT]

976   BLOOMFIELD, MORTON W. "The Canterbury Tales as Framed
       Narratives." LeedsSE, n. s., 14 (1983), 44-56. [+Host] See
       no. 66.

977   BOOKIS, JUDITH MAY. "Chaucer's Creation of Universal
       Professional Stereotypes in Five of The Canterbury Tales."
       DAI 43 (1982), 1140A. Drew University. [the saint's life;
       PrT, MLT, ClT, SNT, PhT]

978   BOWERS, JOHN M. "The Tale of Beryn and The Siege of Thebes:
       Alternative Ideas of The Canterbury Tales." SAC 7 (1985),
       23-50. [+pilgrimage frame]

979   BOYD, HEATHER. "Fragment A of the Canterbury Tales: Character,
       Figure, and Trope." ESA 26:2 (1983), 77-97. [GP, KnT, MilT,
       RvT]

980   BRESLIN, CAROL ANN. "Justice and Law in Chaucer's Canterbury
       Tales." DAI 39 (1978), 2246A. Temple University. [KnT,
       FranT, MLT, SumT]

981   BREWER, D. S. "The Fabliaux," in 70, pp. 296-325.

982   BREWER, D. S. "Structures and Character-Types of Chaucer's
       Popular Comic Tales." Estudios sobre los géneros literarios
       1 (1975), 106-18.

983   BRODY, SAUL N. "The Comic Rejection of Courtly Love," in In
       Pursuit of Perfection: Courtly Love in Medieval Literature.
       Edited by Joan M. Terrante and George D. Economou. Port
       Washington, NY: Kennikat, 1975, pp. 221-61. [KnT, MerT, TC]

984   BUFFONI, FRANCO. Chaucer Testone Medievale. Università degli
       Studi di Trieste, Facoltà di Economia e Commercio, Istituto
       di Lingue Straniere Moderne, 10. Trieste: Nuova Del Bianco
       Industrie Grafiche, 1981. [Padua's Defensor Pacis and
       Wyclif; +Mel, MLT]

985   BUŞULENGA-DUMITRESCU, ZOË. "Chaucer." Secolul 20 (Bucharest,
       1974), 45-47. [CT; Dan Dutescu]

986   CAHN, KENNETH S. "Chaucer's Merchants and the Foreign Exchange:
       An Introduction to Medieval Finance." SAC 2, 81-119. [GP:
       Merchant; ShT]

987   CALUWÉ-DOR, JULIETTE DE. "Le Diable dans les Contes de
       Cantorbéry: Contribution à l'étude sémantique du terme

devil," in Le Diable au Moyen Age: Doctrine, problèmes
moraux, représentations. (Sénéfiance 6.) Aix-en-Provence:
Pubs. du CUER MA, Univ. de Provence, 1979, pp. 97–116.

988 CANNON, THOMAS F., JR. "Chaucer's Pilgrims as Artists." DAI 34
     (1974), 4190–91A. University of Virginia.

989 CHASKALSON, LORRAINE DIANNE. "'Or telle his tale untrewe': An
     Enquiry into a Narrative Strategy in The Canterbury Tales."
     Transvaal, South Africa: Ph.D. Thesis, University of the
     Witwatersrand, 1980.

990 CLARK, ROY PETER. "Chaucer and Medieval Scatology." DAI 35
     (1975), 6091A. State University of New York at Stony Brook,
     1974. [scatology; scholasticism; devil; Simia Dei; sodomy;
     MilT, SumT]

991 COHEN, EDWARD S. "The Sequence of the Canterbury Tales." ChauR
     9 (1974), 190–95.

992 CONDREN, EDWARD I. "Transcendent Metaphor or Banal Reality:
     Three Chaucerian Dilemmas." PLL 21 (1985), 233–57. [MilT,
     MerT, TC]

993 COOKE, THOMAS D. The Old French and Chaucerian Fabliaux: A
     Study of their Comic Climax. Columbia; London: Missouri
     University Press, 1978. 220 pp. [MerT, ShT, MilT]
       Reviews: Victoria Rothschild, TLS (21 July, 1978), 827;
     Glending Olson, SAC 1 (1979), 151–55; Enrico Giaccherini, MAE
     48 (1979), 300–02; Roy J. Pearcy, Speculum 55 (1980), 783–86;
     Patricia Harris Stäblein, RPh 34 (1981), 558–62.

994 COOPER, HELEN. "The Girl with Two Lovers: Four Canterbury
     Tales," in 62, pp. 65–80. [KnT, MilT, MerT, FranT]

995 COOPER, HELEN. The Structure of the 'Canterbury Tales'. London:
     Duckworth, 1983. [literary and social conventions; genre;
     themes; order of CT; undercutting]
       Reviews: Barry Windeatt, Encounter 63 (July/August, 1984),
     55–59; Bernard O'Donoghue, TLS (18 May, 1984), 5; N. F.
     Blake, ES 66 (1985), 170–71; A. J. Minnis, EIC 35 (1985),
     265–69; Paula Neuss, RES 36 (1985), 408–09; Charles A. Owen,
     Jr., SAC 7 (1985), 178–80; Paul G. Ruggiers, Speculum 60
     (1985), 958–59.

996 COSTIGAN, EDWARD. "'Privetee' in The Canterbury Tales." SELit
     60 (Tokyo, 1983), 217–30. [WBT, ShT, MilT, MerT]

997 COWGILL, BRUCE KENT. "'By corpus dominus': Harry Bailly as

Canterbury Tales

False Spiritual Guide." JMRS 15 (1985), 157-81. [+GP Monk]

998　CRÉPIN, ANDRÉ. "'Sustres and paramours': sexe et domination
dans les Contes de Cantorbéry" ["Sustres and paramours" Sex
and Domination in the Canterbury Tales]. Caliban 17 (1980),
3-21. [NPT, WBT, Mel]

999　CRISP, DELMAS SWINFIELD, JR. "Internal Evidence of Formulaic
Diction in The Canterbury Tales." DAI 40 (1980), 5450A.
University of Southern Mississippi, 1979.

1000　CURTZ, THADDEUS BANKSON, JR. "Chaucer and His Churls." DAI 39
(1978), 893A. University of California, Santa Cruz, 1977.
[ManT, SumT, MilT, GP: Miller, Summoner, Manciple]

1001　DAUBY, HÉLÈNE TAURINYA. Le rôle social de la femme d'après The
Canterbury Tales de Chaucer et Le Ménagier de Paris. Paris:
Publications de l'Association des Médiévistes Anglicistes de
l'Enseignement Supérieur, 1985.

1002　DAVENANT, JOHN. "Chaucer's View of the Proper Treatment of
Women." Maledicta 5 (1981), 153-61. [ShT, MLT, MilT, Mel,
WBT, MkP]

1003　DAWOOD, IBRAHIM. Letter. PMLA 99 (1984), 109. [frame of CT]
Reply to Gittes, nos. 1032-35, below. See also 1016, 1091,
1105.

1004　DEAN, JAMES. "Dismantling the Canterbury Book." PMLA 100
(1984), 746-62. [SNT, CYT, ManT, ParsT, Ret; Ellesmere,
Hengwrt]

1005　DEAN, JAMES. "Spiritual Allegory and Chaucer's Narrative Style:
Three Test Cases." ChauR 18 (1984), 273-287. [FrT, PardT,
CYT]

1006　DELANY, SHEILA. Writing Woman: Women Writers and Women in
Literature Medieval to Modern. New York: Schocken Books,
1983. 218 pp. [Marxist treatment] See nos. 1400, 1448,
1935.
Reviews: Carolyn Emerson, LJ 108 (1 December, 1983), 2251;
Barbara F. Williamson, NYTBR (17 June, 1984), 21; Lorrayne Y.
Baird-Lange, SAC 8 (1986), 175-77.

1007　DELASANTA, RODNEY. "Pilgrims in the Blean." Chaucer Newsletter
6:1 (1984), 1-2. [Harbledown]

1008　DELIGIORGIS, STAVROS. "Poetics of Anagogy for Chaucer: The
Canterbury Tales," in 58, pp. 129-41.

1009   DIAMOND, ARLYN. "Chaucer's Women and Women's Chaucer," in 56,
        pp. 60–83. [ClT, WBT]

1010   DONALDSON, E. TALBOT. "Some Readings in the Canterbury Tales,"
        in 45, pp. 99–110. [GP, WBT]

1011   DUDER, CLYBURN. "Thematic Relationships Between Hagiographical
        References and the Canterbury Tales." DAI 41 (1981), 4707A.
        University of North Dakota, 1980. [+medieval art; WBT,
        PardT, GP, FrT, SumT, CYT]

1012   DUNĂREANU, LUCIAN. "Realistic Elements and Narrative Technique
        in the Canterbury Tales and Ion Creangă's Works." Doctoral
        diss., Cluj-Napoca University, Romania, 1979. 159 pp.

1013   DUNN, E. CATHERINE. "The Saint's Legend as History and as
        Poetry: An Appeal to Chaucer." ABR 27 (1976), 357–78.
        [SNT, ClT, MLT]

1014   EAST, W. G. "'By Preeve Which That Is Demonstratif'." ChauR 12
        (1977), 78–82. [D-Group; marriage; debate]

1015   EBIN, LOIS. "Chaucer, Lydgate, and the Myrie Tale." ChauR 13
        (1979), 316–36. [GP, ParsT]

1016   ECKHARDT, CAROLINE D. Letter. PMLA 98 (1983), 902–03. Reply
        to Gittes, no. 1032, below. See also 1003, 1016, 1091, 1105.

1017   ECONOMOU, GEORGE D. "Chaucer's Use of the Bird in the Cage Image
        in the Canterbury Tales." PQ 54 (1975), 679–84. [MilT, SqT,
        ManT]

1018   EDSALL, DONNA MARIE. "Chaucer and the Chivalric Tradition." DAI
        42 (1981), 2663A. Ohio University. [KnT, Th]

1019   EISNER, SIGMUND. "Chaucer's Use of Nicholas of Lynn's Calendar."
        E&S 29 (1976), 1–22. [MLT, NPT, ParsT, GP, Astr]

1020   ENGELHARDT, GEORGE J. "The Lay Pilgrims of the Canterbury Tales:
        A Study in Ethology." MS 36 (1974), 278–330. [contemptus
        mundi]

1021   FARRELL, THOMAS JAMES. "The Sentence and Solaas of Chaucer's
        Canterbury Tales." DAI 44 (1983), 1785A. The University of
        Michigan.

1022   FINEMAN, JOEL. "The Structure of Allegorical Desire," in
        Allegory and Representation. Edited by Stephen J.

Canterbury Tales

Greenblatt. Selected Papers from the English Institute, 1979-80, n. s., 5. Baltimore, MD: Johns Hopkins University Press, 1981, pp. 26-60. [+pilgrimage]

1023   FISHER, SHEILA MARIE. "Chaucer's Poetic Alchemy: A Study of Value and Its Transformation in The Canterbury Tales." DAI 43 (1982), 1977A. Yale University. [Listed without abstract.]

1024   FISHER, WILLIAM NOBLES. "Play and Perspective in The Canterbury Tales." DAI 36 (1976), 7435A. University of California, Santa Barbara, 1975. [+Host]

1025   FLEMING, JOHN V. "Chaucer's Ascetical Images." C&L 28:4 (1979), 19-26. [GP, SumT]

1026   FOWLER, ALASTAIR. "Patterns of Pilgrimage." TLS (12 November, 1976), 1410-12. [review article] See no. 1052 for Angus Easson's reply and review in TLS.

1027   FREED, E. R. "'Whoso shal telle a tale'—Narrative Voices and Personae in Chaucer's Canterbury Tales and Sir Gawain and the Green Knight." UMS 2 (Pretoria, 1985), 80-94.

1028   GALLICK, SUSAN. "A Look at Chaucer and His Preachers." Speculum 50 (1975), 456-76. [RvP, WBP, PardP, PardT, NPT]

1029   GIACCHERINI, ENRICO. I "Fabliaux" di Chaucer: Tradizione e innovazione nella narrativa comica chauceriana. Pisa: ETS Universita 12, 1980. [MilT, RvT, FrT, SumT, ShT, MerT]

1030   GILLMEISTER, HEINER. Chaucer's Conversion: Allegorical Thought in Medieval Literature. Aspekt der englischen Geistes- und Kulturgeschichte 2. New York: Peter Lang, 1984. 281 pp. [onomastics] See also no. 2525.

1031   GINSBERG, WARREN. "The Lineaments of Desire: Wish-Fulfillment in Chaucer's Marriage Group." Criticism 25 (1983), 197-210. [WBT, KnT, FrankT]

1032   GITTES, KATHERINE SLATER. "The Canterbury Tales and the Arabic Frame Tradition." PMLA 98 (1983), 237-51. [Petrus Alfonsi's Disciplina clericalis] See also nos. 1003, 1016, 1034, 1035, 1091, 1105.

1033   GITTES, KATHERINE SLATER. "The Frame Narrative: History and Theory." DAI 44 (1983), 1444A. University of California, San Diego.

1034 GITTES, KATHERINE SLATER. Letter. PMLA 98 (1983), 903–04.
      Reply to Owen, no. 1105, and Eckhardt, no. 1016.

1035 GITTES, KATHERINE SLATER. Letter. PMLA 99 (1984), 111–12.
      [frame tale] Reply to Dawood, no. 1003, and Meisami, no.
      1091.

1036 GREEN, DONALD C. "Chaucer as Nuditarian: The Erotic as a
      Critical Problem." PCP 18:1–2 (1983), 59–69.

1037 HALLISSY, MARGARET, M[ARY] D[UGGAN]. "Poison: Imagery and Theme
      in Chaucer's Canterbury Tales." DAI 35 (1974), 1623–24A.
      Fordham University. [PardT, PrT, KnT, NPT, MKT, MerT, CYT]

1038 HANNING, ROBERT W. "Chaucer and the Dangers of Poetry." CEA 46
      (1984), 17–25. [BD, PF, CT, MilT, WBP, WBT, ManT, Ret]

1039 HANNING, R[OBERT] W. "Roasting a Friar, Mis-taking a Wife, and
      Other Acts of Textual Harassment in Chaucer's Canterbury
      Tales." SAC 7 (1985), 3–21. [SumT, WBP]

1040 HARRINGTON, NORMAN T. "Experience, Art, and the Framing of the
      Canterbury Tales." ChauR 10 (1976), 187–200. [CYT, Host]

1041 HASKELL, ANN SULLIVAN. Essays on Chaucer's Saints. (Studies in
      English Literature, 107.) The Hague: Mouton, 1976. 83 pp.
      [PardT, CYT, GP: Prioress, MLT, PrT, SumT, WBT, MKT]
      Reviews: Thomas R. Liszka, SAC 2 (1980), 165–67.

1042 HASKELL, ANN S. "St. Nicholas and Saintly Allusion," in 67, pp.
      105–24. [MilT, PrT]

1043 HEFFERNAN, CAROL FALVO. "The Use of Simile in Dante's Divine
      Comedy and Chaucer's Canterbury Tales." CJItS 3 (1980),
      72–80.

1044 HIGGS, ELTON D. "'What Man Artow?' Harry Bailly and the
      'Elvyssh' Chaucer." MHLS 2 (1979), 28–43.

1045 HILL, GRANVILLE SYDNOR. "The Hagiographic Narrators of Geoffrey
      Chaucer's Canterbury Tales: The Second Nun, the Man of Law,
      the Prioress." DAI 38 (1977), 1409A. Rice University.

1046 HILL, JOHN M. "Chaucer's Canterbury Tales: The Idea!" in
      Proceedings of the Illinois Medieval Association, 2. Edited
      by Mark D. Johnston and Samuel M. Riley. Normal: Graduate
      School, Illinois State University, 1985, pp. 40–50. [reviews
      approaches to CT, esp. Howard's] See no. 1052 below.

Canterbury Tales

1047   HINTON, NORMAN D. "The Canterbury Tales as Compilatio," in
        Proceedings of the Illinois Medieval Association, 1. Edited
        by Roberta Bosse, et al. Macomb: Western Illinois
        University, 1984, pp. 28-48.

1048   HIRSHBERG, JEFFREY ALAN. "'Cosyn to the Dede': The Canterbury
        Tales and the Platonic Tradition in Medieval Rhetoric." DAI
        38 (1978), 6741-42A. University of Wisconsin--Madison, 1977.
        [Boethius; Plato; Augustine; paradise; hell; CT]

1049   HOLLEY, LINDA TARTE. "Chaucer, T. S. Eliot, and the Regenerative
        Pilgrimage." SiM 2 (1982), 19-33. [a comparison]

1050   HOLLEY, LINDA TARTE. "The Function of Language in Three
        Canterbury Churchmen." Parergon 28 (1980), 36-44. [PardT,
        FrT, SumT]

1051   HOLLOWAY, JULIA B. "The Figure of the Pilgrim in Medieval
        Poetry." DAI 35 (1974), 2225-26A. University of California,
        Berkeley. [iconography]

1052   HOWARD, DONALD R. The Idea of the 'Canterbury Tales'. Berkeley:
        University of California Press, 1976. 403 pp. See also nos.
        1046, 1904.
            Reviews: Donald K. Fry, LJ 101 (1976), 1423; Angus Easson,
        TLS (10 December, 1976), 1560; Paul G. Ruggiers, CEA 39
        (1976), 38-41; Robert Edwards, WHR 30 (1976), 260-63;
        Alastair Fowler, TLS (12 November, 1976), 1410-12; Jerome
        Mitchell, GaR 30 (1976), 1015-19; Lee C. Ramsey, Cithara 16
        (1977), 133-35; Gabriel Josipovici, NYRB (28 April, 1977),
        18-22; Charles Blyth, EIC 27 (1977), 162-70; Derek S. Brewer,
        ELN 15:2 (1977), 123-25; Marvin Mudrick, HudR 30 (1977),
        426-36; Florence Ridley, Speculum 52 (1977), 994-97; D. W.
        Robertson, M&H 8 (1977), 252-55; Beryl Rowland, MLQ 38
        (1977), 390-95; Ellen Spolsky, ES 58 (1977), 56-58; A. V. C.
        Schmidt, RES 29 (1978), 466-69; Robert Cook, JEGP 77 (1978),
        419-23; Jill Mann, MAE 47 (1978), 356-60; Thomas L. Wright,
        SHR 12 (1978), 160-61; Stanley B. Greenfield, CL 30 (1978),
        72-77; Lee W. Patterson, UTQ 48 (1979), 263-82; Derek
        Pearsall, MLR 74 (1979), 154-57; Dieter Mehl, Anglia 97
        (1979), 241-46.

1053   HOWARD, DONALD. R. Writers and Pilgrims: Medieval Pilgrimage
        Narratives and Their Posterity. Berkeley: University of
        California Press, 1980. 133 pp.
            Reviews: Valerie Adams, TLS (13 March, 1981), 290; TLS (10
        April, 1981), 409; Paul Strohm, Criticism 23 (1981), 180-81;
        Donald W. Rowe, Speculum 57 (1982), 135-37; Edmund Reiss, SAQ
        81 (1982), 126-27; Penn R. Szittya, SAC 4 (1982), 161-65.

1054   HOYT, DOUGLAS H. "Thematic Word-Play in Chaucer's Canterbury
        Tales." DAI 35 (1974), 2941A. St. Louis University.

1055   HUSSEY, MAURICE, comp. Chaucer's World: A Pictorial Companion.
        With Introduction, Photographs, and Maps. London: Cambridge
        University Press, 1967. [astrology; architecture; medicine;
        mythology; art; alchemy]

1056   HUSSEY, STANLEY S. "Chaucer and Character," in 42, pp. 121-30.
        [FranT; MilT; TC; GP: Host, Merchant; MerT; RvT]

1057   HYMAN, ERIC J. "'Thy Verray Lewednesse': From the Canterbury
        Tales Toward a Theory of Comedy." DAI 45 (1985), 2111A.
        Rutgers University, New Brunswick. [NPT, Th, MilP, MilT,
        WBP]

1058   JAMESON, HUNTER THOMAS. "Moral Seriousness in The Canterbury
        Tales: Human Conduct and Providential Order in the Knight's
        Tale, Franklin's Tale, and Parson's Tale." DAI 36 (1976),
        7437A. Indiana University, 1975. [Boethius, Christianity,
        gentilesse, trouthe, fredom]

1059   JAUNZEMS, JOHN. "Unifying Patterns in the Canterbury Tales."
        DAI 34 (1974), 5105-06A. University of Toronto, 1972.

1060   JOHNSON, JUDITH A. "Ye and Thou Among the Canterbury Pilgrims."
        MichA 10 (1977), 71-76. [Host]

1061   JONES, ALEX I. "MS Harley 7334 and the Construction of the
        Canterbury Tales." ELN 23:2 (1985), 9-15. [Lombard
        mathematician Fibonacci, number symbolism]

1062   JOSEPH, GERHARD [J]. "The Gifts of Nature, Fortune, and Grace in
        the Physician's, Pardoner's, and Parson's Tales." ChauR 9
        (1975), 237-45.

1063   JUSTMAN, STEWART. "Literal and Symbolic in the Canterbury
        Tales." ChauR 14 (1980), 199-214. [Chaucer's parody of
        analogic thought]

1064   JUSTMAN, STEWART. "Medieval Monism and Abuse of Authority in
        Chaucer." ChauR 11 (1976), 95-111.

1065   KAHLERT, SHIRLEY ANN. "The Breton Lay and Generic Drift: A
        Study of Texts and Contexts." DAI 42 (1981), 1629A.
        University of California, Los Angeles.

1066   KEENAN, HUGH T. "A Curious Correspondence: Canterbury Tales A

Canterbury Tales

24-25, Mirk's Festial and Becket's Martyrdom." AN&Q 16
(1977-78), 66-67.

1067   KEISER, GEORGE R. "The Middle English Planctus Mariae and the
        Rhetoric of Pathos," in 60, pp. 167-93. [MLT, PrT, ClT,
        PhyT]

1068   KEMPTON, DANIEL ROBERT. "The Social Determination of Narrative
        Performance in Three Canterbury Tales." DAI 39 (1978),
        273-74A. University of California, Santa Cruz, 1977. [ClT,
        ManT, PhyT]

1069   KERN, EDITH. The Absolute Comic. Bloomington: Indiana
        University Press; New York: Columbia University Press, 1980.
        219 pp. [Mikhail Bakhtin's carnivalesque spirit; MilT, ShT,
        MerT]
        Reviews: Gilbert H. Muller, SR 89:3 (1981),
        lxxxvi-lxxxviii; Robert M. Torrance, CL 33 (1981), 380-82;
        Richard Keller Simon, SNNTS 13:3 (1981), 322-29.

1070   KLEINHANS, CLANCY. "Chaucer's Role as Observer/Pilgrim."
        Cresset 41 (1977), 13-15.

1071   KNAPP, JANET SCHLAUCH. "A Grammar of Narrative." DAI 38 (1978),
        6690A. University of Michigan, 1977. [+Marriage Group]

1072   KNIGHT, STEPHEN THOMAS. The Poetry of the 'Canterbury Tales'.
        Sydney: Angus & Robertson, 1973. 200 pp.
        Reviews: Derek Brewer, RES 27 (1976), 55-57; Martin
        Lehnert, ZAA 24 (1976), 357-62; F. C. de Vries, AUMLA 45
        (1976), 105-07; Barbara C. Raw, N&Q 23 (1976), 25; F.
        Diekstra, ES 58 (1977), 58-61; Alan Gaylord, Speculum 52
        (1977), 148-50.

1073   KOLVE, V. A. Chaucer and the Imagery of Narrative: The First
        Five Canterbury Tales. Stanford: Stanford University Press,
        1984. 551 pp. [+visual arts]
        Reviews: A. J. Minnis, TLS (3 August, 1984), 865; Paula
        Neuss, English 33 (1984), 247-51; Barry Windeatt, Encounter
        63 (July/August, 1984), 55-59; Martin Stevens, MLQ 45 (1984),
        287-91; J. A. Burrow, EIC 35 (1985), 76-82; Richard K.
        Emmerson and Ronald B. Herzman, SAC 7 (1985), 212-18; Hugh T.
        Keenan, C&L 34 (1985), 83-86; Buck McMullen, ELN 23:2 (1985),
        69-71; Derek Pearsall, ES 66 (1985), 80-81; Charles
        Muscatine, Speculum 61 (1986), 674-76.

1074   KOSSICK, SHIRLEY. "Love, Sex, and Marriage in the Merchant's and
        Franklin's Tales." Communique 7 (1982), 25-38. [satire,
        parody]

1075   KUROKAWA, KUSUE. "Chaucer to Tenmongaku" [Chaucer and
        Astronomy], in Igirisu Bungaku ni okeru Kagau Shiso
        [Scientific Ideas in English Literature]. Edited by Masao
        Watanabe. Tokyo: Kenkyusha, 1983, pp. 5-29. In Japanese.
        [astronomy; astrology]

1076   LANHAM, RICHARD A. "Games and High Seriousness," Chapter 3 in
        The Motives of Eloquence: Literary Rhetoric in the
        Renaissance. New Haven: Yale University Press, 1976. 234
        pp. [KnT, WBP, WBT, ClT, TC, Host]

1077   LAWLER, TRAUGOTT. The One and the Many in the 'Canterbury
        Tales'. Hamden, CT: Archon, 1980. 209 pp. [+closure]
        Reviews: Choice (1981), 797; R. B. Burlin, Speculum 56
        (1981), 630-31; Valerie Adams, TLS (29 May, 1981), 651; John
        Norton-Smith, SAC 4 (1982), 175-78; Dieter Mehl, Anglia 100
        (1982), 497-98; David Staines, SN 55 (1983), 206-09; S. S.
        Hussey, YES 13 (1983), 297-98; Cecily Clark, ES 64 (1983),
        92-93; Paula Neuss, RES 34 (1983), 483-85.

1078   LEICESTER, H. MARSHALL, JR. "The Art of Impersonation: A
        General Prologue to the Canterbury Tales." PMLA 95 (1980),
        8-22. [deconstructionist]

1079   LEITCH, L. M. "Sentence and Solaas: The Function of the Hosts
        in the Canterbury Tales." ChauR 17 (1982), 5-20.

1080   LEYERLE, JOHN. "Thematic Interlace in The Canterbury Tales."
        E&S 29 (1976), 107-21. [sexuality, food, money, death]

1081   LINDAHL, CARL. "Chaucer the Storyteller: Folkloric Patterns in
        the Canterbury Tales." DAI 41 (1981), 5204A. Indiana
        University, 1980. [historical authenticity]

1082   LINDAHL, CARL. "The Festive Form of the Canterbury Tales." ELH
        52 (1985), 531-74. [+Host]

1083   MANDEL, JEROME. "'Boy' as Devil in Chaucer." PLL 11 (1975),
        407-11. [PrT, PardT, FrT]

1084   MANDEL, JEROME. "Courtly Love in the Canterbury Tales." ChauR
        19 (1985), 277-89. [+TC]

1085   MANDEL, JEROME. "Other Voices in the Canterbury Tales."
        Criticism 19 (1977), 338-49. [indirect discourse in GP,
        MerT]

1085a   MANN, JILL. "Parents and Children in the Canterbury Tales," in

Canterbury Tales

2064, pp. 165–83. [MkT, MLT, PhyT, PrT, ClT]

1086   MANNING, STEPHEN. "Rhetoric, Game, Morality, and Geoffrey
        Chaucer." SAC 1 (1979), 105–18. [Marriage Group]

1087   MARSHALL, CAROL A. "Love, Salvation, and Order in the Libro de
        buen amor and the Canterbury Tales." DAI 35 (1974),
        2946–47A. St Louis University, 1973.

1088   McGRADY, DONALD. "Were Sercambi's Novelle Known from the Middle
        Ages On? (Notes on Chaucer, Sacchetti, Cent Nouvelles
        nouvelles. Pauli, Timoneda, Zayas)." Italica 57 (1980),
        3–18.

1089   McKEE, JOHN. "Chaucer's Canterbury Tales." Expl 32 (1974), 54.

1090   McQUAIN, JEFFREY HUNTER. "'The Authority of Her Merit': Virtue
        and Women in Chaucer and Shakespeare." DAI 44 (1983), 761A.
        The American University. [+BD]

1091   MEISAMI, JULIE SCOTT. Letter. PMLA 99 (1984), 109–11.
        [response to Gittes, no. 1032, above] See also nos. 1003,
        1016, 1105.

1092   MIDDLETON, ANNE. "Chaucer's 'New Men' and the Good of Literature
        in the Canterbury Tales," in Literature and Society. Edited
        by Edward W. Said. Selected Papers from the English
        Institute, n. s., 3 (1978). Baltimore: Johns Hopkins, 1980,
        pp. 15–56. [Chaucer as precursor of Renaissance]

1093   MIDDLETON, ANNE. "War by Other Means: Marriage and Chivalry in
        Chaucer," in 72, pp. 119–33. [KnT, SqT, FranT]

1094   MILLER, ROBERT P. "Allegory in the Canterbury Tales," in 70, pp.
        326–51. [KnT, ClT]

1095   MORGAN, GERALD. "Rhetorical Perspectives in the General Prologue
        to the Canterbury Tales." ES 62 (1981), 411–22.

1096   MORITZ, THERESA ANNE. "Married Love and Incarnational Imagery:
        Bernard of Clairvaux's Sermones super Cantica Canticorum
        within Medieval Spirituality and as a Model for Love Allegory
        in Chaucer's Canterbury Tales." DAI 42 (1982), 4445A.
        University of Toronto, 1981. [+Guillaume de Saint-Thierry]

1097   MORSE, CHARLOTTE C. "The Politics of Marriage: Power in
        Paradise?" BForum 5 (1980), 265–69. [Song of Songs;
        marriage; ClT, WBT, FranT]

1098   NIMS, MARGARET F., I. B. V. M. "Translatio: 'Difficult
        Statement' in Medieval Poetic Theory." UTQ 43 (1974),
        215-30. [+BD]

1099   OLSON, CLAIR C. "The Interludes of the Marriage Group in the
        Canterbury Tales," in 69, pp. 164-72.

1100   OLSON, GLENDING. "Chaucer, Dante, and the Structure of Fragment
        VIII (G) of the Canterbury Tales." ChauR 18 (1982), 222-36.
        [Paradiso in SNT; Inferno in CYT]

1101   OLSON, GLENDING. "Rhetorical Circumstances and the Canterbury
        Storytelling," in 72, pp. 211-18. [game and play, Aristotle,
        Aquinas, Albertano of Brescia]

1102   OLSON, GLENDING. "The Terrain of Chaucer's Sittingbourne." SAC
        6 (1984), 103-19.

1103   OTAL, JOSÉ LUIS. "Aspectos de la estructura diagonal en The
        Canterbury Tales," in Actas del IV Congreso de AEDEAN.
        Salamanca: Ed. de la Universidad de Salamanca, 1984.

1104   OWEN, CHARLES A., JR. "The Design of the Canterbury Tales," in
        70, pp. 221-42. [reviews of scholarship]

1105   OWEN, CHARLES A., JR. Letter. PMLA 98 (1983), 902. [response
        to Gittes, no. 1032, above] See also nos. 1003, 1016, 1091.

1106   OWEN, CHARLES A., JR. Pilgrimage and Storytelling in the
        'Canterbury Tales': The Dialectic of "Ernest" and "Game".
        Norman: University of Oklahoma Press, 1977. 253 pp.
        [+speculations about various plans for CT]
           Reviews: Choice 14 (1977), 1215; M. L. del Mastro, LJ 102
        (1977), 1650; Earl F. Guy, Ariel 9:2 (1978), 94-97; J. H.
        Fisher, Speculum 53 (1978), 835-36; Robert L. Kindrick, RMRLL
        32 (1978), 64-66; Robert P. Miller, ELN 17:1 (1979), 48-51;
        Theodore A. Stroud, MP 77 (1979), 193-96; A. C. Spearing, MAE
        48 (1979), 142-46; Gerald Morgan, ES 61 (1980), 462-65;
        Thomas J. Garbáty, SAC 2 (1980), 196-202.

1107   OWEN, CHARLES A, JR. "The Transformation of a Frame Story: The
        Dynamics of Fiction," in 67, pp. 125-46.

1108   PALMER, DAVID ANDREW. "Chaucer and the Nature of Chivalric
        Ideas." DAI 37 (1977), 6507-08A. McMasters University,
        Canada, 1976. [KnT, SqT]

1109   PAŹDZIORA, MARIAN. "The Sapiential Aspect of The Canterbury
        Tales." KN 27 (1980), 413-26. [proverbs]

Canterbury Tales

1110   PEARSALL, DEREK. The 'Canterbury Tales'. Unwin Critical
        Library. London; Boston; Sydney: George Allen and Unwin,
        1985. 380 pp. [unfinished nature of CT; subversion of
        convention]
           Reviews: N. F. BLake, THES (20 December, 1985), 17.

1111   PEARSALL, DEREK. "Epidemic Irony in Modern Approaches to
        Chaucer's Canterbury Tales," in 48, pp. 79-89.

1112   PECK, RUSSELL A. "Biblical Interpretation: St. Paul and The
        Canterbury Tales," in 63, pp. 143-70. [fables; fruit-chaff
        metaphor]

1113   PERRY, SIGRID POHL. "Trewe Wedded Libbynge Folk: Metaphors of
        Marriage in Piers Plowman and the Canterbury Tales. DAI 42
        (1981), 2125A. Northwestern University. [+sexual politics]

1114   PICHASKE, DAVID R. and LAURA SWEETLAND. "Chaucer on the Medieval
        Monarchy: Harry Bailly in the Canterbury Tales. ChauR 11
        (1977), 179-200.

1115   PISON, THOMAS. "Liminality in The Canterbury Tales." Genre 10
        (1977), 157-71. [Host, Mel, ParsT]

1116   PONOVA, M. K. "Problemy realizma v rannem anglijskom Vozroždenii
        i Kenterberijskie rasskazy Čosera" [The Problems of Realism
        in the Early English Renaissance and Chaucer's Canterbury
        Tales]. VLU 14:3 (1980), 50-55. With English abstract.
        [Realism]

1117   PRINS, A. A. "The Dating in the Canterbury Tales," in 69, pp.
        342-47.

1118   QUINN, ESTHER C. "Religion in Chaucer's Canterbury Tales: A
        Study in Language and Structure," in 58, pp. 55-73.
        [+pilgrimage]

1119   RAMSEY, VANCE. "Modes of Irony in the Canterbury Tales," in 70,
        pp. 352-79.

1120   REISS, EDMUND. "Biblical Parody: Chaucer's 'Distortions' of
        Scripture," in 63

1121   REISS, EDMUND. "Chaucer and Medieval Irony." SAC 1 (1979),
        67-82. [+TC, +Ret]

1122   REISS, EDMUND. "Chaucer's 'deerne love' and the Medieval View of
        Secrecy in Love," in 73, pp. 164-79.

1123   REX, RICHARD. "In Search of Chaucer's Bawdy." MSE 8 (1982),
        20-32. [+KnT]

1124   RHODES, JAMES F. "Pilgrimage: Chaucer's Ernest Game." DAI 35
        (1974), 1669A. Fordham University.

1125   ROBBINS, PAUL CAREY. "The Telling Difference: Chaucer's
        Canterbury Tales and Patristic Textual Theory." DAI 44
        (1983), 1446A. University of Colorado at Boulder.

1126   RONEY, LOIS. "The Theme of Protagonist's Intention Versus Actual
        Outcome in the Canterbury Tales." ES 64 (1983), 193-200.
        [+Host]

1127   ROWLAND, BERYL. "What Chaucer Did to the Fabliau." SN 51
        (1979), 205-13.

1128   RUDAT, WOLFGANG E. H. "The Canterbury Tales: Anxiety Release
        and Wish Fulfillment." AI 35 (1978), 407-18.
        [psychoanalytical]

1129   RUDAT, WOLFGANG E. H. and PATRICIA LEE YOUNGUE. "From Chaucer to
        Whitman and Eliot: Cosmic Union and the Classical/Christian
        Tradition." DVLG 55 (1981), 19-43. [Virgilian Iuppiter
        descendens in CT]

1130   RUDAT, WOLFGANG E. H. "Heresy and Springtime Ritual: Biblical
        and Classical Allusions in the Canterbury Tales." RBPH 54
        (1976), 823-36. [+Virgil; Horace]

1131   RUGGIERS, PAUL G. "A Vocabulary for Chaucerian Comedy: A
        Preliminary Sketch," in 45, pp. 193-225.

1132   RUTLEDGE, SHERYL P. "Chaucer's Zodiac of Tales." Costerus 9
        (1973), 117-43.

1133   SAITO, ISAMU. Canterbury Monogatari: Chuseijin no Kokkei Hizoku
        Kaishun [The Canterbury Tales: Humor, Vulgarity and
        Penitential Mind of Medieval People]. Tokyo: Chuokoron,
        1984. In Japanese. [ernest, game, ParsT]

1134   SALMON, VIVIAN. "The Representation of Colloquial Speech in The
        Canterbury Tales," in Style and Text: Studies Presented to
        Nils Erik Enkvist. Edited by Håkan Ringbom, Alfhild Ingberg,
        Ralf Norrman, Kurt Nyholm, Rolf Westman, and Kay Wikberg.
        Stockholm: Språkförlaget Skriptor, 1975, pp. 263-77.

1135   SATO, TSUTOMU. Sentence and Solaas: Thematic Development and
        Narrative Technique in 'The Canterbury Tales'. Tokyo:

Canterbury Tales

Kobundo Publishing Company, 1979. 400 pp. [Th, PhyT, PardT, WBT, CYT]
Reviews: Thomas W. Ross, SAC 3 (1981), 176–79.

1136 SCHEPS, WALTER. "Chaucer's Use of Nonce Words, Primarily in the Canterbury Tales." NM 80 (1979), 69–77. [as method of dating] [+LGW]

1137 SCHEPS, WALTER. "'Up roos oure Hoost, and was oure aller cok': Harry Bailly's Tale-Telling Competition." ChauR 10 (1975), 113–28.

1138 SCHULENBURG, JANE TIBBETTS. "Clio's European Daughters: Myopic Modes of Perception," in The Prism of Sex: Essays in the Sociology of Knowledge. Edited by Julia A. Sherman and Evelyn Torton Beck. Madison: University of Wisconsin Press, 1979, pp. 33–53. [mistreatment of women by clerical historians, WBT]

1139 SEVERS, J. BURKE. "Chaucer's Clerks," in 69, pp. 140–52.

1140 SEVERS, J. BURKE. "The Tales of Romance," in 70, pp. 271–95.

1141 SHAW, JUDITH. "Wrath in the Canterbury Pilgrims." ELN 21:3 (1984), 7–10. [sources in Augustine]

1142 SHIKII, KUMIKO. "A Religious Approach to The Canterbury Tales." SELLA (10 March, 1980), 28–32.

1143 SIEGEL, MARSHA. "What the Debate Is and Why It Founders in Fragment A of the Canterbury Tales." SP 82 (1985), 1–24. [Boethius, KnT, MilT, RvT, CkT]

1144 SMALLWOOD, T. M. "Chaucer's Distinctive Digressions." SP 82 (1985), 437–49. [PardT, WBT, MerT, FranT, PhyT, ManT]

1145 SMITH, WALTER R. "Geoffrey Chaucer, Dramatist." Interpretations 1 (1968), 1–10.

1146 SOLA BUIL, RICARDO. Dinámina social en 'The Canterbury Tales'. Serie/Critica 5. Zaragoza: Publicaciones de la Universidad de Zaragoza, 1981.
Reviews: Manuel Górriz Villaroya, RCEI 4 (1982), 177.

1147 STARK, MARILYNN DIANNE. "Chaucer as Literary Critic: The Medieval Romance Genre in The Canterbury Tales." DAI 39 (1978), 2925A. University of Illinois at Urbana–Champaign.

1148 STOUCK, MARY-ANN. "Studies in English Verse Hagiography,

1300–1500." <u>DAI</u> 36 (1975) 1538–39A. University of Toronto, 1974. [+<u>Legenda Aurea</u>, Lydgate, Capgrave]

1149 STROHM, PAUL. "Form and Social Statement in <u>Confessio Amantis</u> and <u>The Canterbury Tales</u>." <u>SAC</u> 1 (1979), 17–40. [+<u>PF</u>, Host]

1150 STUGRIN, MICHAEL. "Ricardian Poetics and Late Medieval Cultural Pluriformity: The Significance of Pathos in the <u>Canterbury Tales</u>." <u>ChauR</u> 15 (1980), 155–67.

1151 STURGES, ROBERT S. "<u>The Canterbury Tales</u>' Women Narrators: Three Traditions of Female Authority." <u>MLS</u> 13:2 (1983), 41–51.

1152 TAITT, PETER S. <u>Incubus and Ideal: Ecclesiastical Figures in Chaucer and Langland</u>. Elizabethan & Renaissance Studies, 44. Salzburg: Inst. für eng. Sprache & Lit., Univ. Salzburg, 1975. 228 pp.

1153 TAYLOR, P. B. "Chaucer's <u>Cosyn to the Dede</u>." <u>Speculum</u> 57 (1982), 315–27. [<u>GP</u>, <u>PardT</u>, <u>ParsT</u>, Christian Platonism]

1154 THOMPSON, CHARLOTTE. "Cosmic Allegory and Cosmic Error in the Frame of <u>The Canterbury Tales</u>." <u>PCP</u> 18:1–2 (1983), 77–83. [+zodiac; astrology]

1155 THUNDY, ZACHARIAS [P]. "Chaucer's Quest for Wisdom in <u>The Canterbury Tales</u>." <u>NM</u> 77 (1976), 582–98.

1156 THUNDY, ZACHARIAS P. "Significance of Pilgrimage in Chaucer's <u>Canterbury Tales</u>." <u>LHY</u> 20:2 (1979), 64–77. [+allegory]

1157 TRAVERSI, DEREK. <u>The 'Canterbury Tales': A Reading</u>. Newark: University of Delaware Press, 1983. 251 pp.
      Reviews: Avril Bruten, <u>TLS</u> (6 January, 1984), 20; <u>Choice</u> (March, 1984), 981–82; Phillipa Hardman, <u>RES</u> 36 (1985), 556; C. A. Owen, Jr., <u>SAC</u> 7 (1985), 254–57.

1158 UHLIG, CLAUS. <u>Chaucer und die Armut: Zum Prinzip der kontextuellen Wahrheit in den 'Canterbury Tales'</u>. Akad. der Wissenschaft und der Literatur, Abh. der Geistes- und Sozialwissenschaftliche Klasse 1973, 14. Mainz: Steiner, for the Akademie der Wissenschaften und der Literatur, 1974. 51 pp.
      Reviews: Derek Pearsall, <u>YES</u> 6 (1976), 216–17; Martin Lehnert, <u>ZAA</u> 24 (1976), 357–62.

1159 ULLMANN, INGEBORG MARIA. <u>Der Erzähler der 'Canterbury Tales': das literarische Werk in seiner kommunikativen Funktion</u>.

BIBLIOGRAPHY OF CHAUCER, 1974 - 1985

Canterbury Tales

(Europäische Hochschulschriften, Reihe XIV: Angelsächsische
Sprache und Literatur, 15.) Berne: Herbert Lang;
Frankfurt-am-Main: Peter Lang, 1973. 232 pp. [semiotics;
pilgrimage; allegory; symbolism]
Reviews: Hans Käsmann, Anglia 93 (1975), 512-17; Willi
Erzgräber, Erasmus 29 (1977), 611-13.

1160 VOSS, A. E. "Thematic Unity and Parallel Structure in Fragment
III of The Canterbury Tales." UMS 2 (Pretoria, 1985), 11-17.

1161 WASS, ROSEMARY T. A., O. P. "Chaucer and Late Medieval
Scholasticism: A Preliminary Study of Individuality and
Experience." DAI 34 (1974), 5128A. University of
Cincinnati. [allegory; Augustine; Aristotle; scholasticism;
patristic criticism]

1162 WASSERMAN, J. N. "The Ideal and the Actual: The Philosophical
Unity of Canterbury Tales, MS. Group III." Allegorica 7
(1982), 65-99. [sources in Nicholas of Clairvaux]

1163 WATANABE, IKUO. "An Aspect of Love in The Canterbury Tales."
Tenri University Journal (Nara, 1983), 16-34. In Japanese.

1164 WEISSMAN, HOPE PHYLLIS. "Antifeminism and Chaucer's
Characterization of Women," in 58, pp. 93-110.

1165 WELCH, JANE TOOMEY. "Chaucer's Low Seriousness: A Study of
Ironic Structure in the Canterbury Tales." DAI 39 (1978),
3569-70A. Syracuse University.

1166 WENTERSDORF, KARL P. Chaucer's Worthless Butterfly." ELN 14:3
(1977), 167-72. [MerT, MkT, ShT]

1167 WENTERSDORF, KARL P. "The Symbolic Significance of figurae
scatologicae in Gothic Manuscripts," in Word, Picture, and
Spectacle: Papers by Karl P. Wentersdorf, Roger Ellis,
Clifford Davidson, and R. W. Hanning. Edited by Clifford
Davidson. Early Drama, Art, and Music Monograph Series 5.
Kalamazoo: Western Michigan University Medieval Institute
Publications, 1984, pp. 1-19. [MilT, SumT]

1168 WENZEL, SIEGFRIED. "Chaucer and the Language of Contemporary
Preaching." SP 73 (1976), 138-61. [+HF, TC]

1169 WHITBREAD, L. "Six Chaucer Notes." NM 79 (1978), 41-43.
[+Catullus; Pynchbeck; Alexander the Great]

1170 WILDERMUTH, M. CATHERINE TURMAN. "Innocence, Suffering, and
Sensibility: The Narrative Function of the Pathetic in

118

General

Chaucer's Tales of the Clerk, Prioress, and Physician." DAI 45 (1984), 1112A. Rice University.

1171   WOO, CONSTANCE and WILLIAM MATTHEWS. "The Spiritual Purpose of the Canterbury Tales." Comitatus 1 (1970), 85-109.

1172   WOOD, CHAUNCEY. "Artistic Intention and Chaucer's Use of Scriptural Allusion," in 63, pp. 35-46 (also in RUO 53 [1983], 297-308). [ParsT, GP, RvP, MerT, MilT, SumT]

1173   WOOLF, ROSEMARY. "Moral Chaucer and Kindly Gower," in 71, pp. 221-45.

See also: 11, 94, 96, 97, 99, 124, 126, 128, 129, 133, 134, 135, 139, 140, 145, 146, 149, 150, 153, 154, 158, 159, 165, 168, 169, 170, 171, 174, 182, 183, 189, 190, 194, 206, 208, 217, 218, 221, 222, 223, 224, 229, 233, 234, 235, 241, 242, 243, 246, 247, 254, 258, 263, 265, 271, 280, 281, 285, 286, 288, 293, 295, 296, 299, 300, 301, 303, 305, 306, 311, 321, 326, 330, 333, 334, 340, 341, 344, 346, 349, 350, 357, 362, 363, 366, 367, 368, 373, 377, 382, 385, 394, 396, 404, 405, 407, 412, 416, 417, 423, 425, 427, 429, 430, 442, 443, 444, 458, 460, 474, 475, 476, 483, 484, 497, 501, 505, 525, 532, 536, 540, 542, 543, 544, 552, 555, 567, 572, 576, 577, 580, 586, 678, 681, 711, 724, 726, 727, 729, 733, 740, 741, 745, 761, 768, 790, 800, 811, 824, 833, 841, 851, 864, 872, 909, 911, 923, 924, 925, 937, 938, 1767, 1960, 2102, 2145, 2376, 2552, 2566, 2611, 2648, 2649, 2651, 2660, 2691, 2735, 2755, 2781, 2788, 2792, 2839, 2845, 2846, 2847, 2848, 2849, 2851, 2852, 2853, 2854, 2855, 2856, 2857, 2863, 2869, 2872, 2874, 2880, 2884, 2885, 2888, 2892.

>>> Canterbury Tales: Source Studies <<<

1174   ANDREAS, JAMES R. "The Rhetoric of Chaucerian Comedy: The Aristotelian Legacy." Comparatist 8 (1984), 56-66. [+HF, TC]

1175   FLEMING, JOHN V. "Gospel Asceticism: Some Chaucerian Images of Perfection," in 63, pp. 183-95. [scriptural exegesis, asceticism, Peter Damian, Dante, St. Jerome]

1176   GINSBERG, WARREN STUART. "'Le grant translateur': Chaucer and His Sources." DAI 36 (1975), 2843-44A. Yale University. [Petrarch; Boccaccio; Teseida]

Canterbury Tales

1177   GUERIN, RICHARD S. "The Canterbury Tales and Il Decamerone."
        DAI 28 (1967), 1396A. University of Colorado.

1178   HAVELY, NICHOLAS. "Chaucer, Boccaccio and the Friars," in 47,
        pp. 249-68. [Decameron]

1179   KIRKPATRICK, ROBIN. "The Wake of the Commedia: Chaucer's
        Canterbury Tales and Boccaccio's Decameron," in 47, pp.
        201-29.

1180   McGRADY, DONALD. "Chaucer and the Decameron Reconsidered."
        ChauR 12 (1977), 1-26.

1181   TEDESCHI, SVETKO. "Some Recent Opinions about the Possible
        Influence of Boccaccio's Decameron on Chaucer's Canterbury
        Tales." SRAZ 33-36 (1972-73), 849-72.

1182   WURTELE, DOUGLAS. "Chaucer's Canterbury Tales and Nicholas of
        Lyre's Postillae litteralis et moralis super totam Bibliam,"
        in 63, pp. 89-108 (also in RUO 53 (1983), 351-69).

See also Source Studies for individual tales of the Canterbury Tales
listed at the end of each tale.

See also: 595, 611, 622, 629, 633, 641, 644, 645, 649, 654, 656, 657,
           1173.

GENERAL PROLOGUE

1183   ANDREW, MALCOLM. "Chaucer's General Prologue to the Canterbury
        Tales." Expl 43 (1984), 5-6. [language; Lent; OT Genesis;
        sources]

1184   DiMARCO, VINCENT J. "Chaucer, Walter Sibile and the Composition
        of the General Prologue." RBPH 56 (1978), 650-62. [date;
        historical background]

1185   EBERLE, PATRICIA J. "Commercial Language and the Commercial
        Outlook in the General Prologue." ChauR 18 (1983), 161-74.

1186   ECKHARDT, CAROLINE D. "The Number of Chaucer's Pilgrims: A
        Review and Reappraisal." YES 5 (1975), 1-18. Reprinted in
        Essays in the Numerical Criticism of Medieval Literature.

Lewisburg: Bucknell University Press; London: Associated
University Presses, 1980, pp. 156–84.

1187   ENGELHARDT, GEORGE J.   "The Ecclesiastical Pilgrims of the
        Canterbury Tales: A Study in Ethology." MS 37 (1975),
        287–315.

1188   ENGELHARDT, GEORGE J.   "The Lay Pilgrims of the Canterbury Tales:
        A Study in Ethology." MS 36 (1974), 278–330.

1189   GELLRICH, J. M.   "Interpreting the 'Naked Text' in the 'General
        Prologue' to The Canterbury Tales," Chapter 7 in no. 365, pp.
        224–47. [structure, voice, persona, irony, order, closure]

1190   GREEN, EUGENE.   "The Voices of the Pilgrims in the General
        Prologue to the Canterbury Tales." Style 9 (1975), 55–81.
        [cf. RR, place names, narrator]

1191   HIGGS, ELTON D.   "The Old Order and the 'Newe World' in the
        General Prologue to the Canterbury Tales." HLQ 45 (1982),
        155–73.

1192   HUGHES, GEOFFREY.   "Gold and Iron: Semantic Change and Social
        Change in Chaucer's Prologue." Standpunte 137 (1978), 1–11.

1193   KEENAN, HUGH T.   "A Curious Correspondence: Canterbury Tales A
        24–25, Mirk's Festial, and Becket's Martyrdom." AN&Q 16
        (1978), 66–67. [numerology]

1194   KIRBY, THOMAS A.   "The General Prologue," in 70, pp. 243–70.

1195   MANDEL, JEROME.   "Other Voices in the Canterbury Tales."
        Criticism 19 (1977), 338–49. [style; personae]

1196   MANN, JILL.   Chaucer and Medieval Estates Satire: The Literature
        of Social Classes and the General Prologue to the 'Canterbury
        Tales'. New York and London: Cambridge University Press,
        1973. 330 pp.
        Reviews: Choice 10 (1973), 1551; Hugh T. Keenan, LJ 98
        (1973), 2443; R. M. Wilson, ELN 12:2 (1974), 128–29; P. M.
        Kean, MAE 43 (1974), 296–99; Stephan Kohl, Anglia 93 (1975),
        243–47; Joseph E. Milosh, Cithara 15 (1975), 91–93; S. S.
        Hussey, MLR 70 (1975), 387–89; A. S. Haskell, Speculum 51
        (1976), 336–38; Peter M. Vermeer, ES 59 (1978), 261–65.

1197   MARTIN, LOY D.   "History and Form in the General Prologue to the
        Canterbury Tales." ELH 45 (1978), 1–17. [rhetoric;
        catalogue of types]

Canterbury Tales

1198   MORGAN, GERALD. "The Design of the General Prologue to the
        Canterbury Tales." ES 59 (1978), 481-98. [as spiritual
        vision; Christian doctrine]

1199   MORGAN, GERALD. "Rhetorical Perspectives in the General Prologue
        to the Canterbury Tales." ES 62 (1981), 411-22. [satire,
        irony]

1200   MORGAN, GERALD. "The Universality of the Portraits in the
        General Prologue to the Canterbury Tales." ES 58 (1977),
        481-93.

1201   NITZSCHE, J. C. "Creation in Genesis and Nature in Chaucer's
        General Prologue 1-18." PLL 14 (1978), 459-64.

1202   OWEN, CHARLES A., JR. "Development of the Art of Portraiture in
        Chaucer's General Prologue." LeedsSE, n. s., 14 (1983),
        116-33. See no. 66.

1203   ROBERTSON, D. W., JR. "Chaucer and the 'Commune Profit': The
        Manor." Mediaevalia 6 (1980), 239-59. [characterization]

1204   SAITO, ISAMU. "Chaucer's Realism and His Character Portrayal."
        Main Current: Extra Number in Memory of Professor Toichiro
        Ohta (Kyoto, 1982), 220-36. In Japanese.

1205   SKLUTE, LARRY. "Catalogue Form and Catalogue Style in the
        General Prologue of the Canterbury Tales." SN 52 (1980),
        35-46.

1206   SPECHT, HENRIK. "The Beautiful, the Handsome, and the Ugly:
        Some Aspects of the Art of Character Portrayal in Medieval
        Literature." SN 56 (1984), 129-46. [Summoner; Cicero,
        Priscian, Matthew of Vendôme]

1207   TAYLOR, PAUL B. "The Alchemy of Spring in Chaucer's General
        Prologue." ChauR 17 (1982), 1-4. [Zephirus, licour]

1208   WURTELE, DOUGLAS. "Some Uses of Physiognomical Lore in Chaucer's
        Canterbury Tales." ChauR 17 (1982), 130-41. [Miller, Reeve,
        Pardoner, Secreta Secretorum]

See also: 82, 94, 128, 129, 130, 176, 208, 218, 222, 256, 264, 271, 284,
            285, 286, 293, 302, 321, 356, 379, 392, 430, 437, 478, 481,
            501, 514, 572, 583, 587, 688a, 706, 710, 714, 724, 739, 740,
            790, 793, 802, 816, 859, 891, 898, 910, 916, 932, 937, 962,
            979, 988, 996, 1010, 1011, 1015, 1019, 1025, 1051, 1072, 1077,
            1085, 1088, 1100, 1117, 1120, 1121, 1130, 1141, 1149, 1152,

General Prologue

1153, 1159, 1165, 1172, 1174, 1695, 1926, 1965, 2102, 2542,
2549, 2550, 2560, 2566, 2567, 2591, 2659, 2691, 2781, 2785,
2788, 2792, 2841a, 2847, 2848, 2852, 2853, 2857a, 2859, 2866,
2892.

>>> General Prologue: Source Studies <<<

1209   SPRAYCAR, RUDY S. "The Prologue to the General Prologue:
        Chaucer's Statement about Nature in the Opening Lines of the
        Canterbury Tales." NM 81 (1980), 142–49. [Alain de Lille's
        De Planctu Naturae]

See also: 641, 642, 645, 1260.

>>> Knight, Lines 43-78 <<<

1210   JONES, TERRY. Chaucer's Knight: The Portrait of a Medieval
        Mercenary. Baton Rouge: Louisiana State University Press,
        1980. 319pp. [Chaucer's Knight as venal mercenary] See
        also no. 1293.
        Reviews: J. A. Burrow, TLS (15 February, 1980), 163;
        Choice 18 (1980), 248; Economist (26 January, 1980), 103;
        Jill Mann, Encounter (July, 1980), 60–64; Jill Mann, Listener
        103 (1980), 157; Tom Shippey, Quarto 3 (1980), 19; Observer
        (10 February, 1980), 38; Spectator (19 January, 1980), 21;
        TES (1 February, 1980), 23; Wall Street Journal (2 April,
        1980), 28; John M. Fyler, YES 12 (1982), 235–36; Phillipa
        Hardman, RES, n. s., 33 (1982), 311–13; G. C. Britton, N&Q,
        n. s., 29 (1982), 431; David Aers, SAC 4 (1982), 169–75; G.
        A. Lester, MAE 52 (1983), 122–25; Emerson Brown, Jr. and Eren
        Hostetter Branch, Anglia 102 (1984), 525–32.

1211   KEENE, MAURICE. "Chaucer's Knight, the English Aristocracy and
        the Crusade," in 2716, pp. 45–61.

1212   KUHN, SHERMAN M. "Chaucer's ARMEE: Its French Ancestors and Its
        English Posterity," in 42, pp. 85–102.

1213   LESTER, G. A. "Chaucer's Knight and the Earl of Warwick." N&Q
        28 (1981), 200–02. [+Warwick Pageant]

1214   McCOLLY, WILLIAM. "Why Chaucer's Knight Has No Coat of Arms."
        ELN 21:3 (1984), 1–6.

Canterbury Tales

1215   URBAN, WILLIAM. "When was Chaucer's Knight in 'Ruce'?" ChauR 18
        (1984), 347-53. [Ruce as Lithuania]

See also: 284, 367, 392, 744, 1010, 1066, 1188, 1191, 1193, 1217, 1278,
            1293, 1298, 1624, 2540, 2553, 2704.

>>> Squire, Lines 79-100 <<<

1216   FEHRENBACH, ROBERT J. "The Chivalric Tradition and the Red and
        White Gown of Chaucer's Squire." ELN 15:1 (1977), 4-7.

See also: 264, 550, 1188, 1202.

>>> Yeoman, Lines 101-17 <<<

1217   McCOLLY, WILLIAM B. "Chaucer's Yeoman and the Rank of His
        Knight." ChauR 20 (1985), 14-27.

See also: 336, 938, 1188, 1624.

>>> Prioress, Nun, and Three Priests, Lines 118-64 <<<

1218   BLAKE, N. F. "Aspects of Syntax and Lexis in The Canterbury
        Tales." RCEI 7 (1983), 1-19.

1219   BOWLES, PATRICK. "Chaucer's General Prologue, 133-136." Expl
        35:3 (1977), 5-6. [Prioress's table manners]

1220   BROSNAHAN, LEGER. "The Authenticity of 'And Preestes Thre'."
        ChauR 16 (1982), 293-310. [textual study]

1221   BRUMBLE, H. DAVID, III. "Chaucer's General Prologue: Canterbury
        Tales." Expl 37:1 (1978), 45. [St. Augustine; mousetrap]

1222   CUTTS, JOHN P. "Madame Eglentyne's Saint Loy." StHum 7:2
        (1979), 34-38. [+St. Louis; roi de France]

1223   DAICHMAN, GRACIELA SUSANA. "The Figure of the Wayward Nun in
        Late Medieval Literature: The Ambiguous Portraits of the
        Archpriest of Hita's Doña Garoza and Chaucer's Madame

Eglentyne." DAI 44 (1983), 485A. Rice University.

1224 FLEISSNER, ROBERT F. "That Oath of the Prioress." NM 86 (1985), 197-98. [Seinte Loy]

1225 HODGES, LAURA F. "Chaucer's Costume Rhetoric in His Portrait of the Prioress." DAI 46 (1985), 1620A. Rice University.

1226 JUNGMAN, ROBERT E. "'Amor vincit omnia' and the Prioress's Brooch." Lore&L 9:3 (1983), 1-7.

1227 MOORMAN, CHARLES. "The Prioress as Pearly Queen." ChauR 13 (1978), 25-33.

1228 ROTHWELL, W. "Stratford atte Bowe and Paris." MLR 80 (1985), 39-54.

1229 SALVIATI, YVETTE. "Geoffrey Chaucer: Les Contes de Cantorbery: 'Charitas' ou 'Cupiditas'? Madame Eglentyne devant la critique," in MCRel 2 (Université d'Avignon, 1984), 9-29.

1230 SHIKII, KUMIKO. "Chaucer's Anti-Clericalism as Seen in the Prioresse." SELLA 11 (1982), 22-33. In Japanese.

1231 WATANABE, IKUO. "Two of the Canterbury Pilgrims—the Prioress and the Wife of Bath." Tenri University Journal (Nara, 1983), 176-96. In Japanese.

1232 WITTE, STEPHEN P. "Muscipula Diaboli and Chaucer's Portrait of the Prioress." PLL 13 (1977), 227-37. [St. Augustine; mice; devil]

1233 WOOD, CHAUNCEY. "Chaucer's Use of Signs in His Portrait of the Prioress," in 61, pp. 81-101.

See also: 325, 378, 673, 937, 972, 1041, 1130, 1152, 1164, 1187, 1234, 1438, 1797, 1798, 1804, 1805, 1858, 1879, 1908, 2838.

>>> Prioress, Nun, and Three Priests: Source Studies <<<

1234 JACOBS, EDWARD CRANEY. "Further Biblical Allusions for Chaucer's Prioress." ChauR 15 (1980), 151-54. [caritas, amor]

1235 JUNGMAN, ROBERT E. "Amor Vincit Omnia and the Prioress's Brooch." Lore&L 3:9 (1983), 1-7. [Virgil]

Canterbury Tales

>>> <u>Monk</u>, Lines 165–207 <<<

1236   DELASANTA, RODNEY. "Chaucer's <u>General Prologue</u>." <u>Expl</u> 38:3
        (1980), 39–40.

See also: 367, 997, 1152, <u>1175</u>, 1187, 1195, 1202, 1879.

>>> <u>Monk</u>: Source Studies <<<

1237   FLEMING, JOHN V. "Daun Piers and dom Pier: Waterless Fish and
        Unholy Hunters." <u>ChauR</u> 15 (1981), 287–94. [Dante, <u>Paradiso</u>,
        Peter Damian]

>>> <u>Friar</u>, Lines 208–69 <<<

1238   BESSERMAN, LAWRENCE. "Chaucer and the Pope of Double Worstede."
        <u>Chaucer Newsletter</u> 1:1 (1979), 15–16. [proverbs]

1239   HAVELY, NICHOLAS [R]. "Chaucer, Boccaccio, and the Friars," in
        47, pp. 249–68. [<u>Decameron</u>]

1240   HAVELY, N[ICHOLAS] R. "Chaucer's Friar and Merchant." <u>ChauR</u> 13
        (1979), 337–45.

1241   KANNO, MASAHIKO. "Subtlety in Chaucer's Expression: The Dual
        View." <u>HSELL</u> 24 (1979), 54–66. In Japanese, English
        abstract. [physiognomy; symbolism]

1242   SHIKII, KUMIKO. "Consideration on Chaucer's 'Frere'." <u>The</u>
        <u>Fleur-de-lis Review</u> 18 (Tokyo, 1982), 112–37. In Japanese.
        [Cf. Saint Francis of Assisi]

See also: 1010, 1152, <u>1175</u>, 1178, 1187, 1195, 1202, 1521, 1522, 2782.

>>> <u>Friar</u>: Source Studies <<<

1243   BRASWELL, LAUREL. "Chaucer and the Legendaries: New Sources for
        Anti-Mendicant Satire." <u>ESC</u> 2 (1976), 373–80.

>>> Merchant, Lines 270–84 <<<

1244   CAHN, KENNETH S. "Chaucer's Merchants and the Foreign Exchange:
        An Introduction to Medieval Finance." SAC 2 (1980), 81–119.

See also: 402, 587, 986, 1056, 1240, 1657.

>>> Clerk, Lines 285–308 <<<

1245   LONG, CHARLES. "The Clerk's Secret Shame: He Is Jankyn."
        Interpretations 9 (1977), 22–33.

See also: 392, 1139, 1152, 1187, 1550, 1559.

>>> Clerk: Source Studies <<<

1246   BEALL, CHANDLER B. "And Gladly Teche." ELN 13:2 (1975), 85–86.
        [Seneca's epistle to Lucilius]

>>> Sergeant of the Law, Lines 309–30 <<<

1247   McKENNA, ISOBEL. "The Making of a Fourteenth Century Sergeant of
        the Lawe." RUO 45 (1975), 244–62.

1248   SLEETH, CHARLES. "Astrology as a Bone of Contention Between the
        Man of Law and the Franklin." Chaucer Newsletter 1:1 (1979),
        20–21.

1249   WENTERSDORF, KARL P. "The Termes of Chaucer's Sergeant of the
        Law." SN 53 (1981), 269–74.

See also: 393, 1169, 1188, 1401, 1402, 1403, 1405, 1413.

>>> Franklin, Lines 331–60 <<<

1250   KEENAN, HUGH T. "The General Prologue to the Canterbury Tales,

Canterbury Tales

> Lines 345-346: The Franklin's Feast and Eucharistic
> Shadows." <u>NM</u> 79 (1978), 36-40.

1251 MILLER, ROBERT P. "'It snewed in his hous'." <u>ELN</u> 23:4 (1985),
      71-72.

1252 SAUL, NIGEL. "The Social Status of Chaucer's Franklin: A
      Reconsideration." <u>MAE</u> 52 (1983), 10-26. [satire]

1253 SPECHT, HENRIK. <u>Chaucer's Franklin in 'The Canterbury Tales':</u>
      <u>The Social and Literary Background of a Chaucerian Character.</u>
      Publications of the Department of English, University of
      Copenhagen, 10. Copenhagen: Akademisk Forlag, 1981. 206
      pp. [legal status, contemporary evidence]
      Reviews: M. Teresa Tavormina, <u>Speculum</u> 58 (1983), 825-27;
      George D. Gopen, <u>JEGP</u> 82 (1983), 436-39; Gerald Morgan, <u>MAE</u>
      52 (1983), 125-26; Marianne Powell, <u>OL</u> 38 (1983), 280-81;
      David C. Fowler, <u>MP</u> 81 (1984), 407-14; Phillipa Hardman, <u>RES</u>
      35 (1984), 528-29; Jason T. Reakes, <u>Anglia</u> 102 (1984),
      218-22.

1254 TURVILLE-PETRE, THORLAC. "The Lament for Sir John Berkeley."
      <u>Speculum</u> 57 (1982), 332-39. [Franklin as straightforward
      portrait]

See also: 402, 600, 1188, 1203, 1248, 1636, 1657.

>>> <u>Tradesman</u>, Lines 361-78 <<<

1255 GOODALL, PETER. "Chaucer's 'Burgesses' and the Aldermen of
      London." <u>MAE</u> 50 (1981), 284-91. [guild feud in London,
      1370-1390]

1256 McKEE, JOHN. "Chaucer's <u>Canterbury Tales</u>, 'General Prologue'."
      <u>Expl</u> 32:7 (1974), 54.

>>> <u>Cook</u>, Lines 379-87 <<<

1257 HIEATT, CONSTANCE B. "'To boille the chiknes with the
      marybones': Hodge's Kitchen Revisited," in 73, pp. 149-63.

See also: 1938, 1940, 1945.

>>> Shipman, Lines 338-410 <<<

See nos. 402, 1763.

>>> Physician, Lines 411-44 <<<

1258   BENSON, C. DAVID. "The Astrological Medicine of Chaucer's
            Physician and Nicholas of Lynn's Kalendardium." AN&Q 22:5-6
            (1984), 62-66.

1259   USSERY, HULING E. Chaucer's Physician: Medicine and Literature
            in Fourteenth-Century England. TSE Monographs, 19. New
            Orleans, LA: Tulane University Press, 1971. 158 pp.
                Reviews: R. Balfour Daniels, SCB 33 (1973), 159; R. T.
            Davies, N&Q, n. s., 20 (1973), 30-32; Edward D. Kennedy, SAB
            38 (1973), 108-09; Phillip D. Thomas, Isis 64 (1973), 550-51;
            Jill Mann, MAE 43 (1974), 195-97; Joseph E. Grennen, Speculum
            49 (1974), 158-59; G. Storms, Neophil 58 (1974), 144-45;
            Malcolm Andrew, ES 56 (1975), 154-56; Wolfgang Weiss, Anglia
            94 (1976), 505-07.

See also: 430, 818, 1188, 1675, 1676, 1677.

>>> Wife of Bath, Lines 445-76 <<<

1259a   HARRIS, JOCELYN. "Anne Elliot, the Wife of Bath, and Other
            Friends." W&L, n. s., 3 (1983), 273-93.

1260   HOFFMAN, RICHARD L. "The Wife of Bath's Uncharitable Offerings."
            ELN 11:3 (1974), 165-67. [Seven Deadly Sins: anger;
            +sources]

1261   PLUMMER, JOHN F. "The Wife of Bath's Hat as Sexual Metaphor."
            ELN 18:2 (1980), 89-90.

1262   WEISSMAN, HOPE PHYLLIS. "Why Chaucer's Wife is from Bath."
            ChauR 15 (1980), 11-36. [iconography; baths; prostitution]

See also: 381, 1077, 1164, 1169, 1188, 1203, 1231, 1270, 1434, 1437,
            1438, 1472, 1481, 1488, 1492, 1499, 1502.

Canterbury Tales

>>> Parson, Lines 477–528 <<<

1263   GRENNAN, EAMON. "Dual Characterization: A Note on Chaucer's Use
        of 'But' in the Portrait of the Parson." ChauR 16 (1982),
        195–200.

See also: 392, 937, 1077, 1152, 1191, 1195, 1965.

>>> Plowman, Lines 529–41 <<<

See nos. 938, 1191, 1203.

>>> Miller, Lines 542–66 <<<

See nos. 264, 325, 402, 1000, 1169, 1202, 1203, 1208, 1367.

>>> Manciple, Lines 567–86 <<<

See nos. 1000, 1202, 1945.

>>> Reeve, Lines 587–622 <<<

1264   FLETCHER, ALAN J. "Chaucer's Norfolk Reeve." MAE 52 (1983),
        100–03.

See also: 402, 938, 1203, 1208.

>>> Summoner, Lines 623–68 <<<

1265   RENN, GEORGE A., III. "Chaucer's Canterbury Tales." Expl 43:2
        (1985), 8–9. ["bokeleer" of cake; parody of Host]

See also: 264, 352, 402, 550, 775, 1000, 1010, 1169, 1175, 1187, 1202,
           1206, 1238, 1267, 1521, 1522, 2702.

>>> Pardoner, Lines 669-714 <<<

1266   McALPINE, MONICA E. "The Pardoner's Homosexuality and How It
        Matters." PMLA 95 (1980), 8-22.

1267   McVEIGH, TERRENCE A. "Chaucer's Portraits of the Pardoner and
        Summoner and Wycliff's Tractatus de Simonia." CF 29 (1975),
        54-58. [simony, leprosy, sodomy]

1268   ORTON, P. R. "Chaucer's General Prologue, A 673 Burdoun and Some
        Sixteenth-Century Puns." ELN 23:1 (1985), 3-4. [ribaldry]

1269   RHODES, JAMES F. "The Pardoner's Vernycle and His Vera Icon."
        MLS 13:2 (1983), 34-40. [St. Veronica]

1270   WEISSMAN, HOPE PHYLLIS. "The Pardoner's Vernicle, the Wife's
        Coverchiefs, and Saint Paul." Chaucer Newsletter 1:2 (1979),
        10-12.

See also: 333, 402, 775, 937, 1152, 1175, 1187, 1202, 1208, 1720, 1752,
           2702.

>>> Chaucer the Pilgrim <<<

See nos. 402, 584, 586, 1044, 1070, 1179, 1263, 1811, 1981.

>>> The Host <<<

See nos. 346, 425, 586, 741, 891, 975, 997, 1024, 1040, 1044, 1056, 1060,
         1076, 1079, 1082, 1114, 1115, 1126, 1137, 1676, 1683, 1707,
         1712, 1731, 1736, 1748, 1925, 1952, 1954.

THE KNIGHT'S TALE

1271   ANDERSEN, WALLIS MAY. "Canterbury Tales 'Rethors': The Knight."
        FCS 10 (1984), 1-14. [occupatio; brevitas; digressio;
        descriptio]

Canterbury Tales

1272   BOHEEMEN, CHRISTEL VAN.   "Chaucer's Knight's Tale and the
       Structure of Myth."   DQR 9 (1979), 176–90.

1273   BURROW, JOHN.   "Chaucer's Knight's Tale and the Three Ages of
       Man," in 51, pp. 27–48; also in 48, pp. 91–108.   [+Boccaccio,
       Teseida]

1274   CHASKALSON, L.   "'What is this world? What asketh men to have?':
       Examined Life in the Knight's Tale."   UMS 1 (Pretoria, 1983),
       90–118.   [Boethius; pagan/Christian philosophy]

1275   CHERCHI, PAOLO.   "The Knight's Tale: Lines 1774–81."   MP 76
       (1978), 46–48.   [Aeneid 6]

1276   CIAVOLELLA, M.   "Mediaeval Medicine and Arcite's Love Sickness."
       Florilegium 1 (1979), 222–41.   [+Boccaccio, Teseida]

1277   CLASBY, EUGENE.   "Medieval Ideas of Order: Selections from Four
       Basic Texts," in 2881, pp. 230–31.

1278   COWGILL, BRUCE KENT.   "The Knight's Tale and the Hundred Years'
       War."   PQ 54 (1975), 670–79.

1279   DONALDSON, E. TALBOT.   "Arcite's Injury," in 59, pp. 65–67.

1280   ENGLE, LARS DAVID.   "Character in Poetic Narrative: Action and
       Individual in Chaucer and Milton."   DAI 45 (1984), 525A.
       Yale University, 1983.   [+Paradise Lost]

1281   FICHTE, JOERG O.   "Man's Free Will and the Poet's Choice: The
       Creation of Artistic Order in Chaucer's Knight's Tale."
       Anglia 93 (1975), 335–60.   [+closure]

1282   GAYLORD, ALAN T.   "The Role of Saturn in the Knight's Tale."
       ChauR 8 (1974), 172–90.   [+Boethius, Statius, Boccaccio]

1283   GREEN, JOHN MARTIN.   "World Views and Human Power: The Four
       Phases of Chaucer's Knight's Tale."   DAI 35 (1975), 5403A.
       University of California, Santa Cruz, 1974.

1284   GREEN, RICHARD FIRTH.   "Arcite at Court."   ELN 18:4 (1981),
       251–57.   [+Havelock the Dane]

1285   HALLISSY, MARGARET.   "Poison and Infection in Chaucer's Knight's
       and Canon's Yeoman's Tales."   EAS 10 (1981), 31–39.

1286   HARDER, BERNARD D.   "Fortune's Chain of Love: Chaucer's Irony in
       Theseus' Marriage Counselling."   UWR 18:1 (1984), 47–52.

The Knight's Tale

[+Boethius: De Consolatione Philosophiae]

1287 HARRISON, JOSEPH. "'Tears for Passing Things': The Temple of Diana in the Knight's Tale." PQ 63 (1984), 108–116. [+Boccaccio's Teseida]

1288 HERZMAN, RONALD B. "The Paradox of Form: The Knight's Tale and Chaucerian Aesthetics." PLL 10 (1974), 339–52.

1289 HOEBER, DANIEL R. "Chaucer's Friday Knight." Chaucer Newsletter 2:1 (1980), 8–10.

1290 HOLTZ, NANCY ANN. "The Triumph of Saturn in the Knight's Tale: A Clue to Chaucer's Stance Against the Stars." in Literature and the Occult: Essays in Comparative Literature. Edited by Luanne Frank. University of Texas at Arlington Publications in Literature. Arlington: University of Texas at Arlington, 1977, pp. 159–73.

1291 INFUSINO, MARK H. and YNEZ VIOLÉ O'NEILL. "Arcite's Death and the New Surgery in The Knight's Tale," in 72, pp. 221–30. [Ancients/Modern controversy; +Boccaccio]

1292 JUSTMAN, STEWART. "'Auctoritee' and the Knight's Tale." MLQ 39 (1978), 3–14. [+Boethius]

1293 LESTER, G. A. "Chaucer's Knight and the Medieval Tournament." Neophil 66 (1982), 460–68. [+Terry Jones]

1294 NELSON, JOSEPH EDWARD. "Chaucer's Knight's Tale: A Vision of a Secular Ideal of Chivalry." DAI 41 (1980), 242A. University of Kansas, 1979.

1295 NEUMANN, FRITZ-WILHELM. "Zeremonie, Gestalt und Wirklichkeit: Anmerkungen zur Phänomenologie der Knight's Tale," in Literarische Ansichten der Wirklichkeit: Studien zur Wirklichkeitskonstitution in englischsprachiger Literatur (to Honour Johannes Kleinstück). Edited by Hans-Heinrich Freitag and Peter Hühn. (AAF 12.) Frankfurt: Lang, 1980, pp. 41–57.

1296 OLSON, PAUL A. "Chaucer's Epic Statement and the Political Milieu of the Late Fourteenth Century." Mediaevalia 5 (1979), 61–87.

1297 PORTER, ELIZABETH. "Chaucer's Knight, the Alliterative Morte Arthure, and the Medieval Laws of War: A Reconsideration." NMS 27 (1983), 56–78.

Canterbury Tales

1298   RAFFEL, BURTON. "Chaucer's Knight as Don Quijote." NDEJ 10
        (1976), 1-11.

1299   REIDY, JOHN. "The Education of Chaucer's Duke Theseus," in The
        Epic in Medieval Society: Aesthethic and Moral Values.
        Edited by Harald Scholler. Tübingen: Niemeyer, 1977, pp.
        391-408.

1300   RONEY, LOIS YVONNE. "Scholastic Philosophies in Chaucer's
        Knight's Tale." DAI 39 (1979), 5498A. University of
        Wisconsin-Madison, 1978.

1301   SCHWEITZER, EDWARD C. "Fate and Freedom in The Knight's Tale."
        SAC 3 (1981), 13-45. [astrology; medicine; Boethius,
        Consolation]

1302   SHIBATA, TAKEO. "Kishi no monogatari ni okeru kunshuzo" [The
        Image of Lord Theseus in Chaucer's Knight's Tale]. Shuru 44
        (Doshisha University, 1983), 1-22. In Japanese.

1303   SPIEGEL, HARRIET. "Characterization and Decision Making in the
        Romances of Chrétien de Troyes and Geoffrey Chaucer." DAI 37
        (1976), 2855A. Brandeis University. [male/female]

1304   TAYLOR, ANN M. "Epic Descent in the Knight's Tale." CF 30
        (1976), 40-56.

1305   TURNER, FREDERICK. "A Structuralist Analysis of the Knight's
        Tale." ChauR 8 (1974), 279-96. [+Levi-Strauss]

1306   WATSON, CHRISTOPHER. "Chaucer's Knight and His Tale." CR 22
        (1980), 56-64.

1307   WRIGHT, M. J. "Comic Perspective in Two Middle English Poems."
        Parergon 18 (1977), 3-15. [+TC, Pearl]

1308   YAMANAKA, TOSHIO. "Theseus in The Knight's Tale." SES 4 (1979),
        11-22. In Japanese. [+word study]

See also: 94, 128, 129, 130, 218, 256, 267, 269, 276, 277, 285, 286,
           293, 302, 306, 318, 323, 342, 346, 348, 355, 358, 367, 369,
           370, 379, 381, 402, 405, 429, 430, 441, 442, 444, 447, 449,
           459, 462, 488, 503, 524, 525, 532, 548, 563, 566, 577, 580,
           581, 584, 590, 696, 699, 710, 721, 723, 725, 745, 754, 757,
           780, 813, 815, 840, 841, 859, 891, 903, 925, 957, 961, 975,
           979, 980, 983, 994, 996, 1007, 1018, 1031, 1037, 1058, 1072,
           1073, 1076, 1093, 1094, 1098, 1108, 1112, 1122, 1123, 1126,
           1139, 1143, 1147, 1157, 1164, 1168, 1188, 1210, 1211, 1214,

The Knight's Tale

1319, 1348, 1367, 1624, 1770, 1775, 2005, 2173, 2247, 2330, 2416, 2620, 2675, 2680, 2792, 2859.

>>> The Knight's Tale: Source Studies <<<

1309   ANDERSON, DAVID. "The Legendary History of Thebes in Boccaccio's
        Teseida and Chaucer's Knight's Tale." DAI 40 (1980), 4585A.
        Princeton University. [+Statius' Thebaid]

1310   BACHMAN, W. BRYANT, JR. "Mercury, Virgil, and Arcite:
        Canterbury Tales, A 1384-1397." ELN 13:3 (1976), 168-73.
        [+Aeneid 4]

1311   BOITANI, PIERO. "Style, Iconography, and Narrative: The Lesson
        of the Teseida," in 47, pp. 185-99. [+A&A, PF, TC]

1312   BOITANI, PIERO. "A Translation of Boccaccio's Teseida and a
        Study of Its Relation to Chaucer's Knight's Tale." Ph.D.
        thesis, University of Cambridge, 1975.

1313   BRANCH, EREN HOSTETTER. "Man Alone and Man in Society:
        Chaucer's Knight's Tale and Boccaccio's Teseida." DAI 35
        (1975), 7861A. Stanford University.

1314   HANNING, ROBERT W. "'The Struggle between Noble Design and
        Chaos': The Literary Tradition of Chaucer's Knight's Tale."
        LitR 23 (1980), 519-41.

1315   PERRYMAN, JUDITH C. "The 'False Arcite' of Chaucer's Knight's
        Tale." Neophil 68 (1984), 121-133. [Boccaccio, Teseida]

1316   RUDAT, WOLFGANG H. "Chaucer's Mercury and Arcite: The Aeneid
        and the World of the Knight's Tale." Neophil 64 (1980),
        307-19.

1317   SCHEPS, WALTER. "Chaucer's Theseus and the Knight's Tale."
        LeedsSE 9 (1976-77), 19-34. [+Statius, Ovid, Plutarch]

1318   THOMPSON, CHARLOTTE BARCLAY. "The Old Testament of Babylon: A
        Rereading of Chaucer's Knight's Tale." DAI 40 (1980),
        4612-13A. Princeton University, 1979.

See also: 530, 1176, 1275, 1282, 1284, 1285, 1286, 1287, 1291, 1292,
           1300, 1301, 1307, 2416.

Canterbury Tales

THE MILLER'S TALE

1319   BEIDLER, PETER G. "Art and Scatology in the Miller's Tale."
         ChauR 12 (1977), 90-102.

1320   BLACK, ROBERT. "Chaucer's Allusion to the Sermon on the Mount in
         the Miller's Tale." RUO 55 (1985), 23-32. [ParsT, lechery]

1321   BLAKE, N. F. "'Astromye' in The Miller's Tale." N&Q 26 (1979),
         110-11. Cf. nos. 1343 and 1360.

1322   BLECHNER, MICHAEL HARRY. "Chaucer's Nicholas and Saint
         Nicholas." NM 79 (1978), 367-71. [+Jacobus de Voragine, The
         Golden Legend]

1323   BOENIG, ROBERT. "The Miller's Bagpipe: A Note on the Canterbury
         Tales A 565-566." ELN 21:1 (1983), 1-6.

1324   BOWKER, ALVIN W. "Comic Illusion and Dark Reality in The
         Miller's Tale." MLS 4:2 (1974), 27-34.

1325   BRATCHER, JAMES T. and NICOLAI VON KREISLER. "The Popularity of
         the Miller's Tale." SFQ 35 (1971), 325-55.

1326   CLARK, ROY PETER. "Chaucer and Medieval Scatology." DAI 35
         (1975), 6091A. SUNY, Stonybrook, 1974. [+SumT]

1327   CLARK, ROY PETER. "Christmas Games in Chaucer's The Miller's
         Tale." SSF 13 (1976), 277-87.

1328   CLARK, ROY P[ETER]. "Squeamishness and Exorcism in Chaucer's
         Miller's Tale." Thoth 14:1 (1974), 37-43.

1329   COCKELREAS, JOANNE. "'Hende' Nicholas in The Miller's Tale:
         Epithet, Structure and Theme." CCTE 41 (1976), 40-45.

1330   COOPER, GEOFFREY. "'Sely John' in the 'Legende' of the Miller's
         Tale." JEGP 79 (1980), 1-12. [word study]

1331   DANE, JOSEPH A. "The Mechanics of Comedy in Chaucer's Miller's
         Tale." ChauR 14 (1980), 215-24.

1332   DiGANGI, JOHN J. "Chaucer's 'Hende Nicholas': A Possible
         Identification." AN&Q 13 (1974), 50-51. [+Nicholas of
         Lynne]

1333 FRESE, DOLORES WARWICK. "The Homoerotic Underside in Chaucer's
      Miller's Tale and Reeve's Tale." MichA 10 (1977), 143-50.

1334 GALLACHER, PATRICK J. "Perception and Reality in the Miller's
      Tale." ChauR 18 (1983), 38-48. [perception theories of
      Maurice Merleau-Ponty]

1335 GELLRICH, JESSE [M]. "'Lemman, thy grace, and sweete byrd, thyn
      oore!' Miller's Tale, 3726." AN&Q, supp. 1, (1978), 15-19.

1336 GELLRICH, JESSE M. "The Parody of Medieval Music in The Miller's
      Tale." JEGP 73 (1974), 176-88. [comic irony]

1337 GOODALL, PETER. "The Figure of Absolon in the Miller's Tale:
      Chaucer's Most Original Contribution to the Development of a
      Story." Parergon 29 (1981), 33-36.

1338 GRAYBILL, ROBERT V. "Chaucer's The Miller's Tale: Exemplum of
      Caritas," in Proceedings of the Illinois Medieval Association
      2. Edited by Mark D. Johnston and Samuel M. Riley. Normal:
      Graduate School, Illinois State University, 1985, pp. 51-65.
      [+Neoplatonism, patristic exegesis]

1339 HANKS, D. THOMAS, JR. "'Goddes Pryvetee' and Chaucer's Miller's
      Tale." C&L 33:2 (1984), 7-12. [comic irony]

1340 HARWOOD, BRITTON J. "The 'Nether Ye' and Its Antitheses: A
      Structuralist Reading of The Miller's Tale." AnM 21 (1981),
      5-30.

1341 HERZMAN, RONALD B. "Millstones: An Approach to the Miller's
      Tale and the Reeve's Tale." EngR 28:2 (1977), 18-21, 26.
      [+St. Paul; Augustine]

1342 HIRSH, JOHN C. "Why Does the Miller's Tale Take Place on
      Monday?" ELN 13:2 (1975), 86-90.

1343 HUNTSMAN, JEFFREY F. "Astromye in the Miller's Tale Yet Again."
      N&Q, n. s., 29 (1982), 237. [+Piers Plowman] Cf. nos. 1321
      and 1360.

1344 JAMBECK, THOMAS J. "Characterization and Syntax in the Miller's
      Tale." JNT 5 (1975), 73-85.

1345 JENNINGS, MARGARET, C. S. J. "Ironic Dancing Absolon in the
      Miller's Tale." Florilegium 5 (1983), 178-88. [+Morris
      troupes; Fool]

1346 JORDAN, TRACEY. "Fairy Tale and Fabliau: Chaucer's The Miller's

Canterbury Tales

Tale." SSF 21:2 (1984), 87-93. [+sources in the Old
Testament; +anti-feminist themes]

1347   KANNO, MASAHIKO. "Difference in Diction Between The Miller's
        Tale and The Reeve's Tale." The Bulletin of Aichi University
        of Education 7 (Aichi, 1983), 17-23. In Japanese. [word
        study]

1348   KIERNAN, KEVIN S. "The Art of the Descending Catalogue, and a
        Fresh Look at Alisoun." ChauR 10 (1975), 1-16.

1349   LEWIS, ROBERT E. "The English Fabliau Tradition and Chaucer's
        The Miller's Tale." MP 79 (1982), 241-55. [+Dame Sirith]

1350   LEYLAND, A. "Miller's Tale [I (A) 3449]." N&Q 21 (1974),
        126-27. [St. Frideswide]

1351   LONG, CHARLES. "The Miller's True Story." Interpretations 6
        (1974), 7-13.

1352   MARTIN, B. K. "The Miller's Tale as Critical Problem and Dirty
        Joke," in 74, pp. 86-120.

1353   MILOSH, JOSEPH E., JR. "Reason and Mysticism in Fantasy and
        Science Fiction," in Young Adult Literature: Background and
        Criticism. Edited by Millicent Lenz and Ramona M. Mahood.
        Chicago: American Library Association, 1980, pp. 433-40.

1354   NEUSS, PAULA. "Double Meanings: I. Double Entendre in The
        Miller's Tale." EIC 24 (1974), 325-40.

1355   NICHOLSON, LEWIS E. "Chaucer's 'Com pa me': A Famous Crux
        Reexamined." ELN 19:2 (1981), 98-102.

1356   NITZSCHE, JANE CHANCE. "'As swete as is the roote of lycorys, or
        any cetewale': Herbal Imagery in Chaucer's Miller's Tale."
        Chaucer Newsletter 2:1 (1980), 6-8.

1357   PLUMMER, JOHN F. "The Woman's Song in Middle English and Its
        European Backgrounds," in Vox Feminae: Studies in Medieval
        Woman's Songs. Edited by John F. Plummer. Studies in
        Medieval Culture, 15. Kalamazoo: Medieval Institute,
        Western Michigan University, 1981, pp. 135-54.

1358   REVARD, CARTER. "The Tow on Absalom's Distaff and the Punishment
        of Lechers in Medieval London." ELN 17:3 (1980), 168-70.

1359   RICHARDS, MARY P. "The Miller's Tale: 'By Seinte Note'." ChauR
        9 (1975), 212-15.

The Miller's Tale

1360   ROSS, THOMAS W. "'Astromye' in the Miller's Tale Again." N&Q 28 (1981), 202. Cf. nos. 1321 and 1343.

1361   ROSS, THOMAS W. "Notes on Chaucer's Miller's Tale, A 3216 and 3320." ELN 13:4 (1976), 256-58. [+Jerome]

1362   ROWLAND, BERYL. "Chaucer's Blasphemous Churl: A New Interpretation of the Miller's Tale," in 69, pp. 43-55.

1363   RUDAT, WOLFGANG H. "The Misdirected Kisses in the Miller's Tale." JEP 3 (1982), 103-108.

1364   SELL, ROGER D. "Politeness in Chaucer: Suggestions Towards a Methodology for Pragmatic Stylistics." SN 57 (1985), 175-85.

1365   SELL, ROGER D. "Tellability and Politeness in The Miller's Tale: First Steps in Literary Pragmatics." ES 66 (1985), 446-512.

1366   STEVENS, JOHN. "Angelus ad virginem: The History of a Medieval Song," in 62, pp. 297-328. [+MS British Library Arundel 248]

1367   STORMS, G. "Chaucers Verhaal van de Molenaar," in Handelingen van het drieendertigste Nederlands Filologencongres: Gehouden te Nijmegen op woensdag 17, donderdag 18 en vrijdag 19 april 1974. Amsterdam: Holland University Press, pp. 1-12. [upper class audience, satire]

1368   VAUGHAN, M. F. "Chaucer's Imaginative One-Day Flood." PQ 60 (1981), 117-23.

1369   WILLIAMS, DAVID. "Radical Therapy in the Miller's Tale." ChauR 15 (1981), 227-35. [+John of Ardenne's Fistula in ano; Book of Quinte Essence]

See also: 94, 128, 176, 207, 213, 218, 246, 256, 258, 264, 286, 340, 364, 370, 377, 379, 382, 402, 423, 430, 447, 504, 550, 560, 577, 583, 587, 589, 670, 820, 859, 884, 891, 952, 957, 958, 959, 960, 966, 975, 979, 981, 982, 990, 992, 993, 994, 996, 1000, 1002, 1017, 1029, 1038, 1042, 1056, 1057, 1069, 1072, 1073, 1096, 1098, 1120, 1122, 1123, 1130, 1131, 1140, 1143, 1155, 1157, 1164, 1165, 1167, 1172, 1174, 1175, 1188, 1296, 1298, 1376, 1466, 1764, 1770, 1945, 2614, 2785, 2841, 2849, 2850, 2853a, 2858, 2883.

Canterbury Tales

>>> The Miller's Tale: Source Studies <<<

See nos. 595, 604, 641, 645, 1180, 1322, 1332, 1337, 1349, 1357, 1366, 1368.

THE REEVE'S PROLOGUE AND TALE

1370   BERKHOUT, CARL T. "A Sixteenth-Century Allusion to Chaucer's 'Soler Halle'." AN&Q 23 (1984), 33-34. [Parker's De Antiquitate Britannicae Ecclesiae (1572); Clare, not King's Hall]

1371   BLAKE, N. F. "Another Northernism in The Reeve's Tale?" N&Q 24 (1977), 400-01. [MSS: scribal additions]

1372   BLAKE, N. F. "The Northernisms in The Reeve's Tale." Lore&L 3:1 (1979), 1-8.

1373   BROWN, PETER. "The Containment of Symkyn: The Function of Space in the Reeve's Tale." ChauR 14 (1980), 225-36.

1374   CLARK, CECILY. "Another Late-Fourteenth-Century Case of Dialect-Awareness." ES 62 (1981), 504-05. [+Towneley Secunda Pastorum]

1375   GIACCHERINI, ENRICO. "The Reeve's Tale e 'Decameron' IX, 6." RLM 29 (1976), 99-121.

1376   GOODALL, PETER. "The Reeve's Tale, Le Meunier et les ii Clers and the Miller's Tale." Parergon 27 (1980), 13-16.

1377   GRENNEN, JOSEPH E. "The Calculating Reeve and His Camera obscura." JMRS 14 (1984), 254-59. [+optics]

1378   HEFFERNAN, CAROL FALVO. "A Reconsideration of the Cask Figure in the Reeve's Prologue." ChauR 15 (1980), 37-43.

1379   HERZMAN, RONALD B. "The Reeve's Tale, Symkyn, and Simon the Magician." ABR 33 (1982), 325-33.

1380   HIGUCHI, MASAYUKI. "Verbal Exploitation in the Reeve's Tale." HSELL 25 (1980), 1-12.

1381   MURPHY, MICHAEL. "North: The Significance of a Compass Point in

The Reeve's Prologue and Tale

Some Medieval English Literature." Lore&L 3 (1983), 65-76.
[+FrT]

1382   O'KEEFE, TIMOTHY J. "Meanings of 'Malyne' in The Reeve's Tale."
        AN&Q 12 (1973), 5-7.

1383   OLSON, GLENDING. "The Reeve's Tale as a Fabliau." MLQ 35
        (1974), 219-30.

1384   PLUMMER, JOHN F. "'Hooly Chirches Blood': Simony and Patrimony
        in Chaucer's Reeve's Tale." ChauR 18 (1983), 49-60.

1385   REGAN, CHARLES LIONEL. "Chaucer's Reeve's Tale, I, 4096 and
        4127: More Word-Play." AN&Q 22 (1984), 97-99.

1386   TKACZ, CATHERINE BROWN. "Chaucer's Beard-Making." ChauR 18
        (1983), 127-36.

1387   VASTA, EDWARD. "The Devil in Chaucer's Reeve." AN&Q 22 (1984),
        126-28. [+beard]

1388   VASTA, EDWARD. "How Chaucer's Reeve Succeeds." Criticism 25
        (1983), 1-12.

See also: 82, 94, 121, 128, 176, 209, 256, 258, 286, 325, 340, 352, 514,
          583, 690, 715, 779, 820, 830, 859, 891, 925, 938, 957, 959,
          966, 975, 979, 981, 982, 1028, 1029, 1056, 1073, 1123, 1139,
          1143, 1157, 1168, 1172, 1188, 1333, 1341, 1347, 1351, 1770,
          2850, 2852, 2858.

>>> The Reeve's Tale: Source Studies <<<

1389   PEARCY, ROY J. "The Reeve's Tale and Gombert Again." AN&Q 23
        (1985), 64-68. [+CkT, Jean Bodel]

See also: 595, 604, 632, 645, 1375, 1376.

THE COOK'S PROLOGUE AND TALE

1390   HORNSTEIN, LILLIAN. "Mutual Clawing." Chaucer Newsletter 1:2
        (1975), 7.

Canterbury Tales

1391   MAGOUN, F[RANCIS] P., JR. "The Cook's 'Jakke of Dovere': CT A
        4347-48." NM 77 (1976), 79.

1392   SCATTERGOOD, V. J. "Perkyn Revelour and the Cook's Tale." ChauR
        19 (1984), 14-23.

See also: 981, 982, 1073, 1131, 1143, 1389.

INTRODUCTION, PROLOGUE AND THE MAN OF LAW'S TALE

1393   BESTUL, THOMAS H. "The Man of Law's Tale and the Rhetorical
        Foundations of Chaucerian Pathos." ChauR 9 (1975), 216-26.

1394   BLOOMFIELD, MORTON W. Reply. PMLA 88 (1973), 142. [to Hughes,
        no. 1407, below]

1395   CLARK, SUSAN L. and JULIAN N. WASSERMAN. "Constance as Romance
        and Folk Heroine in Chaucer's Man of Law's Tale." RUS 64
        (1978), 13-24.

1396   CLARK, S[USAN] L. and JULIAN N. WASSERMAN. "Echoes of Leviathan
        and the Harrowing of Hell in Chaucer's Man of Law's Tale."
        SCB 38 (1978), 140-42.

1397   CLARK, S[USAN] L. and JULIAN N. WASSERMAN. "Exempla in The Man
        of Law's Tale: The Recasting of a Romance." PAPA 4:3
        (1978), 11-17.

1398   CLASBY, EUGENE. "Chaucer's Constance: Womanly Virtue and the
        Heroic Life." ChauR 13 (1979), 221-33. Cf. no. 1400 below.

1399   CLOGAN, PAUL M. "The Narrative Style of the Man of Law's Tale."
        M&H, n. s., 8 (1977), 217-33.

1400   DELANY, SHEILA. "Womanliness in the Man of Law's Tale." ChauR
        9 (1974), 63-72, rpt. in Writing Woman, no. 1006, Chapter 3,
        pp. 36-46. See no. 1398 for rebuttal.

1401   FARRELL, ROBERT T. "Chaucer's Man of Law and His Tale: The
        Eccentric Design," in 71, pp. 159-72.

1402   FINNEGAN, ROBERT EMMETT. "The Man of Law, His Tale, and the
        Pilgrims." NM 77 (1976), 227-40.

Introduction, Prologue and the Man of Law's Tale

1403 GRENNEN, JOSEPH E. "Chaucer's Man of Law and the Constancy of Justice." JEGP 84 (1985), 489-514.

1404 HARTY, KEVIN J. "Chaucer's Man of Law and the 'Muses that men clepe Pierides'." SSF 18 (1981), 75-77. [Ovid; Metamorphosis 5]

1405 HARTY, KEVIN J. "The Tale and Its Teller: The Case of Chaucer's Man of Law." ABR 34 (1983), 361-71.

1406 HIRSH, JOHN C. "Chaucer's Man of Law's Tale 847: A Conjectural Emendation." ChauR 21 (1985), 68-69. [Ellesmere, Hengwrt]

1407 HUGHES, K. J. "The Man of Law's Tale." PMLA 88 (1973), 140-42. See no. 1394 above.

1408 JOHNSON, WILLIAM C., JR. "The Man of Law's Tale: Aesthetics and Christianity in Chaucer." ChauR 16 (1982), 201-21.

1409 JOHNSON, WILLIAM C., JR. "Miracles in The Man of Law's Tale." BRMMLA 28:2 (1974), 57-65.

1410 LEFFINGWELL, WILLIAM. "Saints' Lives and the Sultaness: A Note on a Perplexing Episode in Chaucer's Man of Law's Tale." Thoth 12:1 (1971), 29-32.

1411 LOOMIS, DOROTHY BETHURUM. "Constance and the Stars," in 73, pp. 207-20.

1412 MANNING, STEPHEN. "Chaucer's Constance, Pale and Passive," in 73, pp. 13-23.

1413 MILLER, ROBERT P. "Constancy Humanized: Trivet's Constance and the Man of Law's Custance." Costerus, n. s., 3 (1975), 49-71. [+irony]

1414 ORTEGO, PHILIP D. "Chaucer's 'Phislyas': A Problem in Paleography and Linguistics." ChauR 9 (1974), 182-89.

1415 RODDY, KEVIN. "Mythic Sequence in the Man of Law's Tale." JMRS 10 (1980), 1-22.

1416 SCHEPS, WALTER. "Chaucer's Man of Law and the Tale of Constance." PMLA 89 (1974), 285-95. [+rhetoric]

1417 THEINER, PAUL. "The Man of Law Tells His Tale." SMC 5 (1975), 173-79.

143

Canterbury Tales

1418   WEISS, MERLE MADELYN. "The Man of Law's Tale: A Spatial Form in the Canterbury Tales." DAI 36 (1975), 2861A. State University of New York, Buffalo.

1419   WEISSMAN, HOPE PHYLLIS. "Late Gothic Pathos in The Man of Law's Tale." JMRS 9 (1979), 133-53. [+parody]

1420   WURTELE, DOUGLAS. "'Proprietas' in Chaucer's Man of Law's Tale." Neophil 60 (1976), 577-93. [rhetoric, Quintilian, Cicero]

See also: 109, 128, 130, 134, 256, 286, 296, 339, 368, 370, 374, 393, 442, 567, 581, 584, 674, 819, 826, 847, 859, 864, 891, 955, 960, 965, 977, 980, 984, 1002, 1013, 1019, 1041, 1045, 1067, 1072, 1073, 1085a, 1112, 1117, 1120, 1121, 1148, 1150, 1165, 1168, 1176, 1188, 1248, 1566, 1618, 1689, 1865, 2135, 2650, 2792, 2852, 2890.

>>> The Man of Law's Tale: Source Studies <<<

1421   BENSON, C. DAVID. "Incest and Moral Poetry in Gower's Confessio Amantis." ChauR 19 (1984), 100-09. [MLT]

1422   BURCH, BETH. "Chaucer's Man of Law's Tale and The Handless Maiden." LangQ 17:3-4 (1979), 50-51. [Emaré]

1423   HANKS, D. THOMAS, JR. "Emaré: An Influence on the Man of Law's Tale." ChauR 18 (1983), 182-86. [Emaré]

1424   HINTON, NORMAN D. "Lucan and the Man of Law's Tale." PLL 17 (1981), 339-46. [Pharsalia]

1425   PEED, MICHAEL R. "An Analogue of the Man of Law's Tale." AN&Q 12 (1974), 94-96. [Charlemagne's mother, Berta aus Grans Pies]

1425a   WYNN, PHILLIP. "The Conversion Story in Nicholas Trevet's Tale of Constance." Viator 13 (1982), 259-74.

See also: 616, 617, 624, 636, 645, 653, 1176, 1396, 1404, 1408, 1409, 1413, 1416, 1417, 1689.

THE WIFE OF BATH'S PROLOGUE AND TALE

1426   ADAMS, ROBERTA E. "Chaucer's Wife of Bath and Marriage in
        Fourteenth-Century England." DAI 44 (1984), 3069A. Indiana
        University, 1983.

1427   ANDŌ, SHINSUKE. "A Note on Line 1196 of The Wife of Bath's
        Tale." PoetT 15/16 (1983), 154-59. In English.

1428   ARTHUR, ROSS G. "A Head for a Head: A Testamental Template for
        Sir Gawain and the Green Knight and The Wife of Bath's Tale."
        Florilegium 6 (1984), 178-94.

1429   ATKINSON, MICHAEL. "Soul's Time and Transformations: The Wife
        of Bath's Tale." SoRA 13:2 (1980), 72-78.

1430   AXELROD, STEVEN. "The Wife of Bath and the Clerk." AnM 15
        (1974), 109-24.

1431   BAIRD-LANGE, LORRAYNE Y. "Trotula's Fourteenth-Century
        Reputation, Jankyn's Book, and Chaucer's Trot," in 72, pp.
        245-66.

1432   BIGGINS, DENNIS. "Chaucer's Wife of Bath's Prologue, D.608."
        Expl 32:6 (1974), 44. [quoniam]

1433   BIGGINS, DENNIS. "'O Jankyn, Be Ye There?'," in 69, pp. 249-54.

1434   BLAKE, N. F. "The Wife of Bath and Her Tale." LeedsSE 13
        (1982), 42-55.

1435   BLANCH, ROBERT J. "'Al was this land fulfild of fayerye': The
        Thematic Employment of Force, Willfulness, and Legal
        Conventions in Chaucer's Wife of Bath's Tale." SN 57 (1985),
        41-51.

1436   BOLTON, W. F. "The Wife of Bath: Narrator as Victim," in Gender
        and Literary Voice. Edited by Janet Todd. Women and
        Literature, n. s., 1. New York and London: Holmes and
        Meier, 1980, pp. 54-65.

1437   BOREN, JAMES L. "Alysoun of Bath and the Vulgate 'Perfect
        Wife'." NM 76 (1975), 247-56. [Book of Proverbs]

1438   BOSSE, ROBERTA BUX. "Female Sexual Behavior in the Late Middle
        Ages." FCS 10 (1984), 15-37.

Canterbury Tales

1439   BROWN, ERIC D. "Symbols of Transformation: A Specific
        Archetypal Examination of the Wife of Bath's Tale." ChauR 12
        (1978), 202-17.

1440   BROWN, ERIC D. "Transformation and the Wife of Bath's Tale: A
        Jungian Discussion." ChauR 10 (1976), 303-15.

1441   BURTON, T. L. "The Wife of Bath's Fourth and Fifth Husbands and
        Her Ideal Sixth: The Growth of a Marital Philosophy." ChauR
        13 (1978), 34-50.

1442   CAIE, GRAHAM D. "The Significance of the Early Chaucer
        Manuscript Glosses (with Special Reference to the Wife of
        Bath's Prologue)." ChauR 10 (1976), 350-60. [Ellesmere,
        Jerome]

1443   CARRUTHERS, MARY. "Clerk Jankyn: 'At hom to bord / With my
        gossib'." ELN 22:3 (1985), 11-20.

1444   CARRUTHERS, MARY. "The Wife of Bath." PMLA 94 (1979), 952-53.
        See also nos. 1445, 1461, 1510.

1445   CARRUTHERS, MARY. "The Wife of Bath and the Painting of Lions."
        PMLA 94 (1979), 209-22. [+parody, St. Jerome] See nos. 1461
        and 1510.

1446   COOK, JAMES W. "'That She Was Out of Alle Charitee': Point-
        Counterpoint in the Wife of Bath's Prologue and Tale." ChauR
        13 (1978), 51-65.

1447   COOK, ROBERT. "Another Biblical Echo in the Wife of Bath's
        Prologue?" ES 59 (1978), 390-94.

1448   DELANY, SHEILA. "Sexual Economics, Chaucer's Wife of Bath, and
        The Book of Margery Kempe." MinnR, n. s., 5 (1975), 104-15;
        rpt. in Writing Woman, no. 1006, Chapter 5, pp. 76-92.

1449   DELASANTA, RODNEY. "Alisoun and the Saved Harlots: A Cozening
        of Our Expectations." ChauR 12 (1978), 218-35.
        [iconography; iconology]

1450   FISCHER, OLGA C. M. "Gower's Tale of Florent and Chaucer's Wife
        of Bath's Tale: A Stylistic Comparison." ES 66 (1985),
        205-25.

1451   FLEISSNER, R[OBERT] [F]. "Innocent as a Bird." AN&Q 11 (1973),
        90. [proverb, irony]

1452   FLEISSNER, ROBERT F. "The Wife of Bath's Five." ChauR 8 (1973),

The Wife of Bath's Prologue and Tale

128–32.

1453   GALLACHER, PATRICK J. "Dame Alice and the Nobility of Pleasure."
       Viator 13 (1982), 275–93.

1454   GLASSER, MARC. "'He Nedes Moste Hire Wedde': The Forced
       Marriage in the Wife of Bath's Tale and Its Middle English
       Analogues." NM 85 (1984), 239–41. [comparisons: The
       Marriage of Sir Gawaine; The Weddynge of Sir Gawen and Dame
       Ragnell; John Gower: "The Tale of Florent"]

1455   GOTTFRIED, BARBARA. "Conflict and Relationship, Sovereignty and
       Survival: Parables of Power in the Wife of Bath's Prologue."
       ChauR 19 (1985), 202–24.

1456   HAGEN, SUSAN K. "The Wife of Bath, the Lion, and the Critics,"
       in 2725, pp. 130–38. [opposes Kittredge on Marriage Group]

1457   HAMEL, MARY. "The Wife of Bath and a Contemporary Murder."
       ChauR 14 (1979), 132–39.

1458   HAMLIN, B. F. "Astrology and the Wife of Bath: A
       Reinterpretation." ChauR 9 (1974), 153–65.

1459   HOFFMAN, RICHARD L. "The Wife of Bath's Uncharitable Offerings."
       ELN 11:3 (1974), 165–67.

1460   IKEGAMI, TADAHIRO. "The Wife of Bath's Discussion of Marriage,"
       in 1479, pp. 101–22. In Japanese. [irony, antifeminism,
       wife as comic character]

1461   JORDAN, ROBERT M. "The Wife of Bath." PMLA 94 (1979), 950–51.
       Refers to no. 1445. See also nos. 1444, 1510.

1462   KAWASAKI, MASATOSHI. "From Conflict to Harmony––in the Case of
       the Wife of Bath," in 1497, pp. 123–42. In Japanese.

1463   KERNAN, ANNE. "The Archwife and the Eunuch." ELH 41 (1974),
       1–25.

1464   KNIGHT, STEPHEN. "The Poetry of the Wife of Bath's Prologue and
       Tale." Teaching of English 25 (August, 1973), 3–17.

1465   LEICESTER, H. MARSHALL, JR. "The Wife of Bath as Chaucerian
       Subject," in 72, pp. 201–10. [astrology, antifeminism]

1466   LINDSKOOG, VERNA DE JONG. "Chaucer's Wife of Bath: Critical
       Approaches in the Twentieth Century." DAI 45 (1985), 2520A.
       University of Arkansas, 1983.

Canterbury Tales

1467   LONG, CHARLES. "The Wife of Bath's Confessions and the Miller's
       True Story." Interpretations 8 (1976), 54-66.

1468   MAGOUN, FRANCIS P., JR. "The Dumdow Flitch: An Addendum and
       Adieu." NM 77 (1976), 253. [refers to WBP, 11. 217-18]

1469   MALVERN, MARJORIE M. "'Who peyntede the leon, tel me who?':
       Rhetorical and Didactic Roles Played by an Aesopic Fable in
       the Wife of Bath's Prologue." SP 80 (1983), 238-52.

1470   MATTHEWS, WILLIAM. "The Wife of Bath and All Her Sect." Viator
       5 (1974), 413-43.

1471   MENDELSON, ANNE. "Some Uses of the Bible and Biblical Authority
       in the Wife of Bath's Prologue and Tale." DAI 39 (1978),
       2295A. Bryn Mawr College, 1972.

1472   MEYER, ROBERT J. "Chaucer's Tandem Romances: A Generic Approach
       to the Wife of Bath's Tale as Palinode." ChauR 18 (1984),
       221-38.

1473   MILWARD, PETER. "The Orthodoxy of the Wife of Bath," in 1497,
       pp. 48-62. In Japanese.

1474   MIYOSHI, YOKO. "Why Is It the Tale of 'The Wife of Bath'?" in
       1497, pp. 30-47. In Japanese.

1475   MOODY, HELEN FLETCHER. "The Debate of the Rose: The querelle
       des femmes as Court Poetry." DAI 42 (1982), 3153A.
       University of California, Berkeley, 1981. [RR, Jean Le
       Fevre, Lamentations de Matheolus; WBP]

1476   MURPHY, ANN B. "The Process of Personality in Chaucer's Wife of
       Bath's Tale." CentR 28 (1984), 204-22.

1477   OBEREMBT, KENNETH J. "Chaucer's Anti-Misogynist Wife of Bath."
       ChauR 10 (1976), 287-302.

1478   PALMER, BARBARA D. "'To Speke of Wo that Is in Mariage': The
       Marital Arts in Medieval Literature," in Human Sexuality in
       the Middle Ages and Renaissance. Edited by Douglas
       Radcliffe-Umstead. University of Pittsburgh: Center for
       Medieval and Renaissance Studies, 1978, pp. 3-14.

1479   PALOMO, DOLORES. "The Fate of the Wife Bath's 'Bad Husbands'."
       ChauR 9 (1975), 303-19.

1480   PATTERSON, LEE. "'For the Wyves Love of Bathe': Feminine

The Wife of Bath's Prologue and Tale

Rhetoric and Poetic Resolution in the Roman de la Rose and the Canterbury Tales." Speculum 58 (1983), 656-95. [satire, antifeminism]

1481   PUHVEL, MARTIN. "The Wyf of Bath and Alice Kyteler--A Web of Parallelism." SN 53 (1981), 101-06.

1482   QUINN, ESTHER C. "Chaucer's Arthurian Romance." ChauR 18 (1984), 211-20. [+Marie de France; Lanval; Sir Gawain and the Green Knight]

1483   REISNER, M. E. "New Light on Judoc the Obscure." Chaucer Newsletter 1:1 (1979), 19-20. [St. Joce]

1484   REISNER, THOMAS A. "The Wife of Bath's Dower: A Legal Interpretation." MP 71 (1974), 301-02.

1485   RENOIR, ALAIN. "The Impossible Dream: An Underside to the Wife of Bath." MS 70 (1976), 311-22.

1486   REX, RICHARD. "Old French Bacon and the Wife of Bath." MSE 10 (1985), 132-37. [WBP 418; obscenity]

1487   RHODES, JEWELL PARKER. "Female Stereotypes in Medieval Literature: Androgyny and the Wife of Bath." JWSL 1 (1979), 348-52.

1488   ROBERTSON, D. W., JR. "'And for My Land Thus Hastow Mordred Me?': Land Tenure, the Cloth Industry, and the Wife of Bath." ChauR 14 (1980), 403-20.

1489   ROBERTSON, D. W., JR. "The Wife of Bath and Midas." SAC 6 (1984), 1-20. [Ovid; Roman de la Rose]

1490   ROTH, ELIZABETH. "On the Wife of Bath's 'Embarrassing Question'." AN&Q 17 (1978-79), 54-55.

1491   SANDERS, BARRY. "Chaucer's Dependence on Sermon Structure in the Wife of Bath's Prologue and Tale." SMC 4 (1974), 437-45. [+satire on antifeminism]

1492   SANDS, DONALD B. "The Non-Comic, Non-Tragic Wife: Chaucer's Dame Alys as Sociopath." ChauR 12 (1977), 171-82.

1493   SCHAUBER, ELLEN and ELLEN SPOLSKY. "The Consolation of Alison: The Speech Acts of the Wife of Bath." Centrum 5 (1977), 20-34.

1494   SCHULENBURG, JANE TIBBETTS. "Clio's European Daughters: Myopic

Canterbury Tales

Modes of Perception," in The Prism of Sex: Essays in the
Sociology of Knowledge. Edited by Julia A. Sherman and
Evelyn Torton Beck. Madison: University of Wisconsin Press,
1979, pp. 33-53. [WBT, III, 688-96, on sexist distortion of
history; +Christine de Pisan]

1495 SEKIMOTO, EIICHI. "Women Portraits in Dunbar," in 1497, pp.
      79-100. In Japanese. [WBP]

1496 SHEEHAN, MICHAEL M. "The Wife of Bath and Her Four Sisters:
      Reflections on a Woman's Life in the Age of Chaucer." M&H 13
      (1985), 23-42. [social classes]

1497 SHIGEO, HISASHI, HISAO TSURU, ISAMU SAITO, and TADAHIRO IKEGAMI,
      eds. The Wife of Bath. Medieval English Literature Symposia
      2. Tokyo: Gaku Shobo, 1985. In Japanese. See nos. 1460,
      1462, 1473, 1474, 1495, 1498, 1503, 1504.

1498 SHIGEO, HISASHI. "The Wife of Bath," in 1497, pp. 1-29. In
      Japanese.

1499 SINGER, MARGARET. "The Wife of Bath's Prologue and Tale," in 74,
      pp. 28-37.

1500 SPISAK, JAMES. "Anti-Feminism Bridled: Two Rhetorical
      Contexts." NM 81 (1980), 150-60. [St. Jerome's Adversus
      Jovinianum]

1501 STORM, MELVIN. "Alisoun's Ear." MLQ 42 (1981), 219-26.
      [characterization]

1502 TAKAMIYA, TOSHIYUKI. "Margery Kempe and the Wife of Bath."
      Reports of the Keio Institute of Cultural and Linguistic
      Studies 15 (Tokyo, 1983), 199-212. In Japanese.

1503 TAKAMIYA, TOSHIYUKI. "Margery Kempe and the Wife of Bath," in
      1497, pp. 63-78. In Japanese.

1504 TSURU, HISAO. "Alison's Sorrow—Her Old Age and Marriages," in
      1497, pp. 143-65. In Japanese.

1505 VERDONK, P. "'Sire Knyght, heer forth ne lith no wey?': A
      Reading of Chaucer's The Wife of Bath's Tale." Neophil 60
      (1976), 297-308.

1506 WEST, PHILIP. "The Perils of Pauline Theology: The Wife of
      Bath's Prologue and Tale." EAS 8 (1979), 7-16. [Pauline
      parodies]

The Wife of Bath's Prologue and Tale

1507 WILLIAMS, MICHAEL E. "Three Metaphors of Criticism and the Wife
      of Bath's Tale." ChauR 20 (1985), 144-57.

1508 WILSON, KATHARINA M. "Chaucer and St. Jerome: The Use of
      'Barley' in the Wife of Bath's Prologue." ChauR 19 (1985),
      245-51. [source in St. Jerome's letter to Pammachius]

1509 WILSON, KATHARINA M. "Figmenta vs. Veritas: Dame Alice and the
      Medieval Literary Depiction of Women by Women." TSWL 4
      (1985), 17-32. [+Hrotsvita, Christine de Pizan]

1510 WIMSATT, JAMES I. "The Wife of Bath." PMLA 94 (1979), 951-52.
      See nos. 1444, 1445, 1461.

1511 WURTELE, DOUGLAS. "The Predicament of Chaucer's Wife of Bath:
      St. Jerome on Virginity." Florilegium 5 (1983), 208-36.
      [Saint Jerome: Epistola Adversus Jovinianum]

See also: 128, 130, 195, 228, 239, 243, 256, 267, 271, 304, 306, 346,
           349, 364, 377, 378, 381, 388, 405, 410, 423, 453, 479, 481,
           503, 514, 527, 532, 548, 560, 574, 579, 678, 685, 699, 708,
           717, 725, 740, 743, 745, 752, 767, 770, 799, 859, 884, 891,
           916, 937, 955, 957, 969, 970, 996, 998, 1002, 1010, 1011,
           1014, 1028, 1031, 1038, 1039, 1041, 1057, 1064, 1065, 1069,
           1072, 1076, 1077, 1086, 1097, 1099, 1106, 1112, 1120, 1126,
           1131, 1135, 1139, 1140, 1144, 1151, 1157, 1161, 1164, 1165,
           1168, 1169, 1173, 1178, 1188, 1245, 1259a, 1515, 1524, 1525,
           1547, 1558, 1567, 1609, 1649, 1733, 1736, 1904, 1906, 1909,
           2144, 2173, 2257, 2477, 2620, 2680, 2785, 2792, 2838, 2849,
           2856, 2860, 2890.

           >>> The Wife of Bath's Tale: Source Studies <<<

1512 BRASWELL, LAUREL. "Chaucer and the Legendaries: New Sources for
      Anti-Mendicant Satire." ESC 2 (1976), 373-80. [Legenda
      aurea]

1513 THUNDY, ZACHARIAS P. "Matheolus, Chaucer, and the Wife of Bath,"
      in 73, pp. 24-58.

See also: 601, 638, 645, 649, 1065, 1437, 1447, 1450, 1453, 1454, 1469,
           1471, 1475, 1481, 1489, 1500, 1506, 1508, 1511.

Canterbury Tales

THE FRIAR'S PROLOGUE AND TALE

1514   BLOOMFIELD, MORTON W. "The Friar's Tale as a Liminal Tale."
        ChauR 17 (1983), 286–91. [anthropological approach]

1515   BROWN, CAROLE K. and MARION F. EGGE. "The Friar's Tale and the
        Wife of Bath's Tale." PMLA 91 (1976), 291–92. [morality]
        For response, see no. 1524. See also no. 1525.

1516   BUGGE, JOHN. "Tell-Tale Context: Two Notes on Biblical
        Quotation in The Canterbury Tales." AN&Q 14 (1976), 82–85.
        [+PrT]

1517   HAHN, THOMAS. "The Devil and His Panne: Friar's Tale D 1614."
        NM 86 (1985), 348–52.

1518   HAHN, THOMAS and RICHARD W. KAEUPER. "Text and Context:
        Chaucer's Friar's Tale." SAC 5 (1983), 67–101. [+historical
        background; corruption of archdeacons, summoners]

1519   HASSAN-YUSUFF, Z. DOLLY. "'Wynne thy cost': Commercial and
        Feudal Imagery in the Friar's Tale." Chaucer Newsletter 1:1
        (1979), 15–18. [+devil]

1520   JACOBS, EDWARD C. and ROBERT E. JUNGMAN. "His Mother's Curse:
        Kinship in The Friar's Tale." PQ 64 (1985), 256–59.
        [ironies]

1521   LEICESTER, H. MARSHALL, JR. "'No Vileyns Word': Social Context
        and Performance in Chaucer's Friar's Tale." ChauR 17 (1982),
        21–39.

1522   RICHARDSON, JANETTE. "Friar and Summoner, The Art of Balance."
        ChauR 9 (1975), 227–36.

1523   ROSS, THOMAS W. "Chaucer's Friar's Tale, D.1377 and 1573." Expl
        34:2 (1975), 17. [rebec]

1524   SZITTYA, PENN R. "The Friar's Tale and the Wife of Bath's Tale."
        PMLA 91 (1976), 292–93. [parody] Response to no. 1515. See
        also no. 1525.

1525   SZITTYA, PENN R. "The Green Yeoman as Loathly Lady: The Friar's
        Parody of the Wife of Bath's Tale." PMLA 90 (1975), 386–94.
        [+maistrie]

1526   ZELLEFROW, W. KEN. "Chaucer's View of Robin Hood." Chaucer

The Friar's Prologue and Tale

Newsletter 1:1 (1979), 12-15. [comic use of ballads]

See also: 128, 199, 256, 321, 352, 358, 392, 584, 859, 891, 925, 957,
959, 969, 981, 982, 1005, 1007, 1011, 1014, 1029, 1050, 1083,
1112, 1131, 1174, 1175, 1178, 1238, 1239, 1381, 1729.

>>> The Friar's Tale: Source Studies <<<

1527   BALLARD, LINDA-MAY. "Chaucer and the Bailiff in the Hills Above
Pomeroy," in Studies in English Language and Early Literature
in Honour of Paul Christophersen. Edited by P. M. Tilling.
Coleraine: New University of Ulster, 1981. OPLiLL 8 (1981),
1-12. [folktale analogue]

1528   NICHOLSON, PETER. "The Analogues of Chaucer's Friar's Tale."
ELN 17:2 (1979), 93-98.

1529   NICHOLSON, PETER. "The Rypon Analogue of the Friar's Tale."
Chaucer Newsletter 3:1 (1981), 1-2. [translation of the
Latin exemplum]

See also: 622, 645, 648, 1239, 1526, 1540, 1808.

THE SUMMONER'S PROLOGUE AND TALE

1530   CLARK, ROY PETER. "Doubting Thomas in Chaucer's Summoner's
Tale." ChauR 11 (1976), 164-78. [parody]

1531   CLARK, ROY PETER. "Wit and Witsunday [sic] in Chaucer's
Summoner's Tale." AnM 17 (1976), 48-57. [Pentecostal
parody; controversy on Wycliffite translation of Bible]

1532   CROWTHER, J. D. W. "The Summoner's Tale: 1955-69." Chaucer
Newsletter 2:1 (1980), 12-13. [on division of confession]

1533   FLEMING, JOHN V. "Anticlerical Satire as Theological Essay:
Chaucer's Summoner's Tale." Thalia 6:1 (1983), 5-22.
[+iconography]

Canterbury Tales

1534   FLEMING, MARTHA H. "'Glosynge Is a Glorious Thing, Certyn': A Reconsideration of The Summoner's Tale," in 53, pp. 89–101. [irony; anger]

1535   JUNGMAN, ROBERT E. "'Covent' in the Summoner's Tale." MissFR 14:1 (1980), 20–23. [pun on "coven"]

1536   LANCASHIRE, IAN. "Moses, Elijah and the Back Parts of God: Satiric Scatology in Chaucer's Summoner's Tale." Mosaic 14:3 (1981), 17–30. [typological exegesis; Pentecostal parody]

1537   SZITTYA, PENN R. "The Friar as False Apostle: Antifraternal Exegesis and the Summoner's Tale." SP 71 (1974), 19–46. [pseudo-Pentecostal parody; knights of the Round Table]

1538   WENTERSDORF, KARL P. "The Motif of Exorcism in the Summoner's Tale." SSF 17 (1980), 249–54. [scatalogical tradition; Pentecostal parody; iconography]

See also: 128, 153, 199, 286, 392, 430, 437, 481, 589, 710, 859, 891, 957, 959, 980, 981, 982, 987, 990, 1000, 1011, 1014, 1025, 1029, 1039, 1041, 1050, 1112, 1120, 1131, 1165, 1167, 1168, 1172, 1175, 1178, 1239, 1326, 1521, 1522, 1525, 2634.

>>> The Summoner's Tale: Source Studies <<<

1539   PEARCY, ROY J. "Structural Models for the Fabliaux and the Summoner's Tale Analogues." Fabula 15 (1974), 103–13.

1540   PRATT, ROBERT A. "Albertus Magnus and the Problem of Sound and Odor in the Summoner's Tale." PQ 57 (1978), 267–68. [Albertus Magnus, Liber de sensu et sensato]

See also: 595, 645, 1239, 1531, 1536, 1537, 1539, 1540.

THE CLERK'S PROLOGUE, TALE, ENVOY AND WORDS OF THE HOST

1541   BESTUL, THOMAS H. "True and False Cheere in Chaucer's Clerk's Tale." JEGP 82 (1983), 500–14. [facial expression; dissimulation]

The Clerk's Prologue, Tale, Envoy and Words of the Host

1542   BRONFMAN, JUDITH. "The Griselda Legend in English Literature."
       DAI 38 (1977), 2105-06A. New York University.

1543   CARRUTHERS, MARY J. "The Lady, the Swineherd, and Chaucer's
       Clerk." ChauR 17 (1983), 221-34. [medieval audience;
       gentilesse]

1544   CONDREN, EDWARD I. "The Clerk's Tale of Man Tempting God."
       Criticism 26 (1984), 99-114. [Griselda as Christ; sources in
       Petrarch]

1545   DAVIDSON, H. R. ELLIS. "Folklore and Literature." Folklore 86
       (1975), 73-93.

1546   DEAN, JAMES. "Time Past and Time Present in Chaucer's Clerk's
       Tale and Gower's Confessio Amantis." ELH 44 (1977), 401-18.

1547   GERKE, ROBERT S. "Fortitude and Sloth in the Wife of Bath's Tale
       and the Clerk's Tale." PPMRC 5 (1980), 119-35.

1548   GILLAM, D. "Three References to High Style in the Clerk's
       Prolgoue and Tale." SGG 19 (1978), 63-73.

1549   GILMARTIN, KRISTINE. "Array in the Clerk's Tale." ChauR 13
       (1979), 234-46.

1550   GINSBERG, WARREN. "'And Speketh so Pleyn': The Clerk's Tale and
       Its Teller." Criticism 20 (1978), 307-23. [+sources in
       Petrarch]

1551   HARDMAN, PHILLIPA. "Chaucer's Tyrants of Lombardy." RES 31
       (1980), 172-78. [+LGW, MerT]

1552   HAWKINS, HARRIETT. Poetic Freedom and Poetic Truth: Chaucer,
       Shakespeare, Marlowe, and Milton. Oxford: Clarendon, 1976.
       135 pp. [anti-Robertsonian] See no. 1553 below.
       Reviews: W. W. Robson, RES 28 (1977), 342-44.

1553   HAWKINS, HARRIETT. "The Victim's Side: Chaucer's Clerk's Tale
       and Webster's Duchess of Malfi." Signs 1 (1975), 339-61;
       rpt. as Chapter 2 of no. 1552 above, pp. 26-54.

1554   HEFFERNAN, CAROL FALVO. "Tyranny and 'Commune Profit' in the
       Clerk's Tale." ChauR 17 (1983), 332-40.

1555   JOHNSON, LYNN STALEY. "The Prince and His People: A Study of
       the Two Covenants in the Clerk's Tale." ChauR 10 (1975),
       17-29. [+Old and New Testament covenants]

Canterbury Tales

1556   KNAPP, PEGGY A. "Knowing the Tropes: Literary Exegesis and
        Chaucer's Clerk." Criticism 27 (1985), 331-45. [exemplum,
        trope irony]

1557   KRIEGER, ELLIOT. "Re-Reading Allegory: The Clerk's Tale."
        Paunch 40-41 (1975), 116-35.

1558   LEVY, BERNARD S. "Gentilesse in Chaucer's Clerk's and Merchant's
        Tales." ChauR 11 (1977), 306-18.

1559   LONGSWORTH, ROBERT. "Chaucer's Clerk as Teacher," in 43, pp.
        61-66.

1560   MANN, JILL. "Satisfaction and Payment in Middle English
        Literature." SAC 5 (1983), 17-48. [word study; +Pearl]

1561   MANNING, STEPHEN. "The Paradox of the Narrator's Styles in
        Chaucer's Clerk Tale." JNT 15 (1985), 29-42. [folktale
        style vs. literary]

1562   MORSE, CHARLOTTE C. "The Exemplary Griselda." SAC 7 (1985),
        51-86. [Petrarch, Philippe de Mézières, Ménagier de Paris]

1563   PEARLMAN, E. "The Psychological Basis of the Clerk's Tale."
        ChauR 11 (1977), 248-57. [Freudian principles; +medieval
        psychology]

1564   RAMSEY, ROGER. "Clothing Makes a Queen in The Clerk's Tale."
        JNT 7 (1977), 104-15.

1565   STEINMETZ, DAVID C. "Late Medieval Nominalism and the Clerk's
        Tale." ChauR 12 (1977), 38-54. [+Occamist philosophy]

1566   STEPSIS, ROBERT. "Potentia Absoluta and the Clerk's Tale."
        ChauR 10 (1975), 129-46. [+Bradwardine, ockham]

1567   TAYLOR, JEROME. "Fraunceys Petrak and the Logyk of Chaucer's
        Clerk," in Francis Petrarch, Six Centuries Later: A
        Symposium. Edited by Aldo Scaglione. North Carolina Studies
        in the Romance Languages and Literatures, Symposia, 3.
        Chapel Hill: Department of Romance Languages, University of
        North Carolina, 1975, pp. 364-83. [+Aristotelian logic]

1568   WALL, JOHN. "The Clerk's Tale as Parable." Parergon 8 (1974),
        12-19.

1569   WALLACE, KRISTINE GILMARTIN. "Array as Motif in the Clerk's
        Tale." RUS 62 (1976), 99-110.

The Merchant's Prologue, Tale, and Epilogue

1570   WILCOCKSON, COLIN. "'Thou' and 'Ye' in Chaucer's <u>Clerk's Tale</u>."
    <u>Use of English</u> 31:3 (Edinburgh, 1980), 37-43.

1571   WIMSATT, JAMES I. "The Blessed Virgin and the Two Coronations of
    Griselda." <u>Mediaevalia</u> 6 (1980), 187-207.

See also: 94, 126, 128, 130, 195, 256, 296, 306, 346, 351, 368, 382,
    481, 584, 672, 725, 826, 859, 891, 937, 938, 957, 965, 969,
    977, 996, 1013, 1067, 1068, 1072, 1076, 1085a, 1086, 1094,
    1097, 1099, 1112, 1139, 1148, 1150, 1157, 1165, 1170, 1418,
    1430, 1434, 1618, 1904, 1906, 2578, <u>2633, 2821,</u> 2860, 2890.

>>> <u>The Clerk's Tale</u>: Source Studies <<<

1572   BORNSTEIN, DIANE. "An Analogue to Chaucer's <u>Clerk's Tale</u>."
    <u>ChauR</u> 15 (1981), 322-31. [Christine de Pizan, <u>Livre de la
    Cité des Dames</u>]

1573   KADISH, EMILIE P. "Petrarch's <u>Griselda</u>: An English
    Translation." <u>Mediaevalia</u> 3 (1977), 1-24. [+introduction]

1574   KIRKPATRICK, ROBIN. "The Griselda Story in Boccaccio, Petrarch
    and Chaucer," in 47, pp. 231-48.

1575   LEMOS, BRUNILDA REICHMANN. "Some Differences Between Boccaccio's
    and Chaucer's Tales of Griselda." <u>RLet</u> 30 (1981), 7-16.
    [+Petrarch; Philippe de Mézières]

1576   MIDDLETON, ANNE. "The Clerk and His Tale: Some Literary
    Contexts." <u>SAC</u> 2 (1980), 121-50. [Boccaccio; Petrarch]

See also: 640, 641, <u>645,</u> 1542, 1544, 1545, 1546, 1550, 1552, 1555, 1562,
    1566, 1567, 1571.

THE MERCHANT'S PROLOGUE, TALE, AND EPILOGUE

1577   ACKER, PAUL. "'Wades boot' (Chaucer's <u>MerchT</u> E 1424): A
    Different Tack." <u>AN&Q</u> 21 (1982), 2-4.

1578   ADAMS, JOHN F. "The Janus Symbolism in <u>The Merchant's Tale</u>."
    <u>SMC</u> 4 (1974), 446-51. [+Zodiacal signs]

Canterbury Tales

1579   ANDREW, MALCOLM. "January's Knife: Sexual Morality and
        Proverbial Wisdom in the Merchant's Tale." ELN 16:4 (1979),
        273-77.

1580   ANNUNZIATA, ANTHONY. "Tree Paradigms in the Merchant's Tale," in
        72a, pp. 125-35.

1581   ARRATHOON, LEIGH A. "Antinomic Cluster Analysis and the
        Boethian Verbal Structure of Chaucer's Merchant's Tale."
        Lang&S 17 (1984), 92-120.

1582   BENSON, DONALD R. "The Marriage 'Encomium' in the Merchant's
        Tale: A Chaucerian Crux." ChauR 14 (1979), 48-60.

1583   BESSERMAN, L. L. "Chaucer and the Bible: The Case of the
        Merchant's Tale." HUSL 6 (1978), 10-31.

1584   BLEETH, KENNETH A. "The Image of Paradise in the Merchant's
        Tale," in 43, pp. 45-60.

1585   BLOOMFIELD, MORTON W. "The Merchant's Tale: A Tragicomedy of
        the Neglect of Counsel--The Limits of Art," in Medieval and
        Renaissance Studies. Proceedings of the Southeastern
        Institute of Medieval & Renaissance Studies, Summer 1975.
        Edited by Siegfried Wenzel. Medieval & Renaissance Series 7.
        Chapel Hill: University of North Carolina Press, pp. 37-50.
        [+parody, irony]

1586   BROWN, EMERSON, JR. "Biblical Women in the Merchant's Tale:
        Feminism, Antifeminism, and Beyond." Viator 5 (1974),
        387-412.

1587   BROWN, EMERSON, JR. "Chaucer and a Proper Name: January in The
        Merchant's Tale." Names 31 (1983), 79-87. [Janus; St.
        Peter; god of passageways]

1588   BROWN, EMERSON, JR. "Chaucer, the Merchant, and Their Tale:
        Getting Beyond Old Controversies: Part I." ChauR 13 (1978),
        141-56; Part II: ChauR 13 (1979), 247-62. [narrative voice]

1589   BROWN, PETER. "An Optical Theme in The Merchant's Tale," in 72,
        pp. 231-43. [Alhazen, Witelo, Bartholomew]

1590   BUGGE, JOHN. "Damyan's Wanton Clyket and an Ironic New Twiste to
        the Merchant's Tale." AnM 14 (1973), 53-62.

1591   BURGER, DOUGLAS A. "Deluding Words in the Merchant's Tale."
        ChauR 12 (1977), 103-10. [+glossing]

The Merchant's Prologue, Tale, and Epilogue

1592   BURNLEY, J. D. "The Morality of The Merchant's Tale." YES 6 (1976), 16–25. [+marriage services]

1593   DALBEY, MARCIA A. "The Devil in the Garden: Pluto and Proserpine in Chaucer's Merchant's Tale." NM 75 (1974), 408–15.

1594   EWALD, WILLIAM B., III. "A Correction to the Robinson Edition of Chaucer." ELN 15:4 (1978), 267–68. [1.1662 as reference to January's funeral]

1595   FROST, CHERYL. "Illusion and Reality: Psychological Truth in Chaucer's Portrait of January." LiNQ 5:1 (James Cook University, North Queensland, 1976), 37–45.

1596   GATES, BARBARA T. "'A Temple of False Goddis': Cupidity and Mercantile Values in Chaucer's Fruit-Tree Episode." NM 77 (1976), 369–75.

1597   GROVE, ROBIN. "The Merchant's Tale: Seeing, Knowing and Believing." CR 18 (1976), 23–38.

1598   HAMAGUCHI, KEIKO. "January's Marriage in The Merchant's Tale." Tokushima Bunri Daigaku Kiyo 30 (1985), 99–112. In Japanese. [pear tree motif]

1599   HAMAN, MARK STEFAN. "The Introspective and Egocentric Quests of Character and Audience: Modes of Self-Definition in the York Corpus Christi Cycle and in Chaucer's Merchant's Tale." DAI 42 (1982), 4444A. University of Rochester. [+Gower; Langland; CYT]

1600   HARTY, KEVIN J. "The Reputation of Queen Esther in the Middle Ages: The Merchant's Tale, IV (E). 1742–45." BSUF 19:3 (1978), 65–68.

1601   KANNO, MASAHIKO. "Another Word-Play in Chaucer?" MESN 5 (1981), 2–3. [syde as a pun]

1602   KEISER, GEORGE R. "Chaucer's Merchant's Tale, E 2412–16." SSF 15 (1978), 191–92.

1603   KLOSS, ROBERT J. "Chaucer's The Merchant's Tale: Tender Youth and Stooping Age." AI 31 (1974), 65–79.

1604   KOSSICK, S[HIRLEY] G. "Geoffrey Chaucer: The Merchant's Tale." Communiqué 6:3 (1982), 6–26; UES 18:2 (1980), 3–14. [a reading]

Canterbury Tales

1605   KOSSICK, SHIRLEY [G.]. "Love, Sex and Marriage in the Merchant's
        and Franklin's Tales." Communiqué 7:1 (1982), 25–38.

1606   MATSUO, MASATSUGU and YOSHIYUKI NAKAO. "Lexical Proximity and
        Its Application to a Literary Text: A Case Study on The
        Merchant's Tale." HSELL 29 (1984), 49–57. In Japanese with
        English abstract. [+irony]

1607   ROGERS, H. L. "The Tales of the Merchant and the Franklin: Text
        and Interpretation," in 74, pp. 3–27. [Hengwrt manuscript
        order]

1608   RUDAT, WOLFGANG E. H. "Chaucer's Merchant's Tale, E 1263, 1854,
        and 2360–65." Expl 35:4 (1977), 25–26.

1609   RUDAT, WOLFGANG E. H. "Chaucer's Spring of Comedy: The
        Merchant's Tale and Other 'Games' with Augustinian Theology."
        AnM 21 (1981), 111–20. [+WBT, bawdry]

1610   SCHLEUSENER, JAY. "The Conduct of the Merchant's Tale." ChauR
        14 (1980), 237–50. [mores, audience]

1611   SCHMIDT, GARY D. "The Marriage Irony in the Tales of the
        Merchant and Franklin," in Portraits of Marriage in
        Literature. Edited by Anne C. Hargrove and Maurine
        Magliocco. Essays in Literature. Macomb: Western Illinois
        University, 1984, pp. 97–105. [+courtly love; adultery]

1612   SCHWARTZ, ROBERT B. "The Social Character of May Games: A
        Popular Background for Chaucer's Merchant's Tale." ZAA 27
        (1979), 43–51.

1613   SUZUKI, EIICHI. "A Note on the Meaning of Wombe: The Merchant's
        Tale, 1. 2414." ESELL 71 (1980), 101–12. In Japanese.

1614   TUCKER, EDWARD F. J. "'Parfite Blisses Two': January's Dilemma
        and the Themes of Temptation and Doublemindedness in MerT."
        ABR 33 (1982), 172–81. [Epistle of James; Bede;
        caritas/cupiditas]

1615   WALL, JOHN. "The Figure of Solomon in Chaucer's Merchant's
        Tale." RUO 47 (1977), 478–87.

1616   WURTELE, DOUGLAS. "The Blasphemy of Chaucer's Merchant." AnM 21
        (1981), 91–110. [May/Virgin Mary; irony, parody; Canticum
        Canticorum]

1617   WURTELE, DOUGLAS. "Ironical Resonance in the Merchant's Tale."

ChauR 13 (1978), 66–79. [parody; <u>Canticum Canticorum</u>; May/Virgin Mary]

1618   WURTELE, DOUGLAS. "Marian Overtones in Chaucer's <u>Merchant's</u> <u>Tale</u>." <u>Proceedings of the Third Annual Symposium of</u> <u>Ottawa-Carleton Medieval-Renaissance Club</u> 1 (1976), 56–74. [<u>Canticum Canticorum</u>; parody; May/Virgin Mary]

See also: 128, 130, 237, 256, 304, 339, 383, 423, 501, 560, 581, 587, 699, 725, 780, 859, 891, 901, 957, 960, 969, 970, <u>981</u>, 982, 983, 992, <u>993</u>, 994, 996, 1029, 1037, 1048, 1056, 1069, 1072, 1074, 1085, 1086, 1099, 1120, 1126, 1130, 1131, 1144, 1166, 1168, 1172, 1173, 1188, 1195, 1244, 1434, 1551, <u>1558</u>, 1665, 1904, 1906, 1945, 2477, 2790, 2792, 2812, 2838, 2841, 2860, 2890.

>>> The Merchant's Tale: Source Studies <<<

1619   ALTMAN, LESLIE J. "January's Decision: An Example of Chaucer's Use of the <u>Miroir de Mariage</u> in the <u>Merchant's Tale</u>." <u>RPh</u> 29 (1976), 514–18.

1620   DiMARCO, VINCENT. "Richard Hole and the <u>Merchant's</u> and <u>Squire's</u> <u>Tales</u>:   An Unrecognized Eighteenth-Century (1797) Contribution to Source and Analogue Study." <u>ChauR</u> 16 (1981), 171–80.

1621   DONOVAN, MORTIMER J. "Chaucer's January and May: Counterparts in Claudian," in 73, pp. 59–69.

1622   HIRA, TOSHINORI. "Chaucer to Lydia Monogatari" [Chaucer and the Comedy of Lydia], 1 & 2. <u>Bulletin of the Faculty of Liberal</u> <u>Arts, Humanities</u> 23 (1982), 29–41; 24 (Nagasaki, 1983), 97–111.   In Japanese.

See also: 595, 608, 612, 628, 630, <u>645</u>, 663, 1581, 1589, 1609, 1612, 1614.

THE SQUIRE'S PROLOGUE AND TALE

1623   GOODMAN, JENNIFER R. "Chaucer's <u>Squire's Tale</u> and the Rise of

Canterbury Tales

Chivalry." <u>SAC</u> 5 (1983), 127–36.

1624   HATTON, THOMAS J. "Thematic Relationships Between Chaucer's
        Squire's Portrait and Tale and the Knight's Portrait and
        Tale." <u>SMC</u> 4 (1974), 452–58.

1625   LARSON, CHARLES. "<u>The Squire's Tale</u>: Chaucer's Evolution from
        the Dream Vision." <u>RLV</u> 43 (1977), 598–607.

1626   MEINDL, ROBERT J. "'For Drye as Whit as Chalk': Allegory in
        Chaucer and Malory." <u>Studia Mystica</u> 6:1 (1983), 45–58.

1627   MOSELEY, C. W. R. D. "Some Suggestions about the Writing of <u>The
        Squire's Tale</u>." <u>Archiv</u> 212 (1975), 124–27. [audience]

1628   STORM, MELVIN. "The Tercelet as Tiger: Bestiary Hypocrisy in
        the <u>Squire's Tale</u>." <u>ELN</u> 14:3 (1977), 172–74. [+Satan]

See also: 128, 130, 374, 405, 444, 459, 479, 548, 555, 589, 693, 725,
           859, 891, 957, 961, 1017, 1093, 1108, 1117, 1140, 1147, 1649,
           2650, <u>2792</u>.

>>> <u>The Squire's Tale</u>: Source Studies <<<

1629   CORNELIA, MARIE. "Chaucer's Tartarye." <u>DalR</u> 57 (1977), 81–89.

1630   DiMARCO, VINCENT. "A Note on Canacee's Magic Ring." <u>Anglia</u> 99
        (1981), 399–405. [Roger Bacon's <u>Opus maius</u>]

1631   MOSELEY, C. W. R. D. "Chaucer, Sir John Mandeville, and the
        Alliterative Revival: A Hypothesis Concerning
        Relationships." <u>MP</u> 72 (1974), 182–84.

See also: 595, 608, 612, 628, 630, <u>645</u>, 663, <u>1620</u>, 1626.

THE WORDS OF THE FRANKLIN,

THE FRANKLIN'S PROLOGUE AND TALE

1632   BACHMAN, W. BRYANT, JR. "'To Maken Illusioun': The Philosophy
        of Magic and the Magic of Philosophy in the <u>Franklin's Tale</u>."

The Words of the Franklin, The Franklin's Prologue and Tale

ChauR 12 (1977), 55–67. [+Boethius]

1633   BERGNER, HEINZ. "Der gelöste Konflikt: Zu Chaucers Franklin's
        Tale," in Liebe—Ehe—Ehebruch in der Literatur des
        Mittelalters. Edited by Xenja von Ertzdorff and Marianne
        Wynn. Vorträge des Symposiums vom 13. bis 16. Juni 1983 am
        Institut für deutsche Sprache und mittelalterliche Literatur
        der Justus Liebig-Universität Giessen. Beiträge zur
        deutschen Philologie 58. Giessen: Wilhelm Schmitz, 1984,
        pp. 140–47. [marriage]

1634   BLOOMFIELD, MORTON W. "The Franklin's Tale: A Story of
        Unanswered Questions," in 52, pp. 189–98.

1635   BRASWELL, MARY FLOWERS. "The Magic of Machinery: A Context for
        Chaucer's Franklin's Tale." Mosaic 18:2 (1985), 101–10.

1636   CARRUTHERS, MARY J. "The Gentilesse of Chaucer's Franklin."
        Criticism 23 (1981), 283–300. [social classes; historical
        approach]

1637   COLMER, DOROTHY. "The Franklin's Tale: A Palimpsest Reading."
        EIC 20 (1970), 375–80.

1638   FRAZIER, J. TERRY. "The Digression on Marriage in The Franklin's
        Tale." SAB 43 (1978), 75–85.

1639   FUJIMOTO, MASASHI. "A Reading of Chaucer's The Franklin's Tale."
        The Bulletin of Faculty of Literature of Tokai University 32
        (1980), 123–42. [gentilesse]

1640   HEFFERNAN, CAROL FALVO. "The Two Gardens of The Franklin's
        Tale," in 50, pp. 177–88.

1641   JACOBS, KATHRYN. "The Marriage Contract of the Franklin's Tale:
        The Remaking of Society." ChauR 20 (1985), 132–43.

1642   KANNO, MASAHIKO. "The Franklin's Tale—Aurelius's
        'gentillesse'." Studies in Foreign Languages and Literature
        19 (Aichi, 1983), 85–98. In Japanese.

1643   KEE, KENNETH. "Illusion and Reality in Chaucer's Franklin's
        Tale." ESC 1 (1975), 1–12.

1644   KNIGHT, STEPHEN. "Ideology in The Franklin's Tale." Parergon 28
        (1980), 3–35. [sources; onomastics]

1645   LANE, ROBERT. "The Franklin's Tale: Of Marriage and Meaning,"
        in Portraits of Marriage in Literature. Edited by Anne C.

Canterbury Tales

Hargrove and Maurine Magliocco. Essays in Literature.
Macomb: Western Illinois University, 1984, pp. 107-24.
[+narrative structure]

1646   LEE, ANNE THOMPSON. "'A Woman True and Fair': Chaucer's
        Portrayal of Dorigen in the Franklin's Tale." ChauR 19
        (1984), 169-78.

1647   LUCAS, ANGELA. "Astronomy, Astrology and Magic in Chaucer's
        Franklin's Tale." MayR 8 (Co. Kildare, Ireland, 1983), 5-16.
        [Chaucer's knowledge and ambivalence]

1648   LUECKE, JANEMARIE. "Dorigen: Marriage Model or Male Fantasy."
        JWSL 1 (1979), 107-21. [+Margaret Paston and Christine de
        Pizan]

1649   LUENGO, ANTHONY E. "Magic and Illusion in The Franklin's Tale."
        JEGP 77 (1978), 1-16.

1650   MAGNUS, LAURY. "The Hem of Philosophy: Free and Bound Motifs in
        the Franklin's Tale." Assays 2 (1983), 3-18. [+formalist
        criticism]

1651   MATHEWSON, EFFIE JEAN. "The Illusion of Morality in The
        Franklin's Tale." MAE 52 (1983), 27-37.

1652   MILLER, ROBERT P. "Augustinian Wisdom and Eloquence in the
        F-Fragment of the Canterbury Tales." Mediaevalia 4 (1978),
        245-75. [+Cicero]

1653   MILLER, ROBERT P. "The Epicurean Homily on Marriage by Chaucer's
        Franklin." Mediaevalia 6 (1980), 151-86. [Boethius; John of
        Salisbury; Jean de Meun, RR]

1654   MITCHELL, SUSAN. "Deception and Self-Deception in The Franklin's
        Tale." PPMRC 1 (Villanova, PA, 1976), 67-72.

1655   MORGAN, GERALD. "A Defence of Dorigen's Complaint." MAE 46
        (1977), 77-97. [+Jerome's Adversus Jovinianum]

1656   PEARCY, ROY J. "A Pun in the Franklin's Tale 942: 'Withouten
        coppe he drank al his penaunce'." N&Q 22 (1975), 198. [+L.
        culpa]

1657   ROBERTSON, D. W., JR. "Chaucer's Franklin and His Tale."
        Costerus, n. s., 1 (1974), 1-26.

1658   RUDAT, WOLFGANG E. H. "Aurelius' Quest for Grace: Sexuality and
        the Marriage Debate in the Franklin's Tale." CEA 45:1

The Words of the Franklin, The Franklin's Prologue and Tale

(1982), 16–22.

1659 RUDAT, WOLFGANG E. H. "Gentillesse and the Marriage Debate in the Franklin's Tale: Chaucer's Squires and the Question of Nobility." Neophil 68 (1984), 451–70.

1660 SCHUMAN, SAMUEL. "Man, Magician, Poet, God—An Image in Medieval, Renaissance, and Modern Literature." Cithara 19:2 (1980), 40–54. [+Shakespeare's The Tempest]

1661 SIMONS, JOHN. "Chaucer's Franklin's Tale and The Tempest." N&Q 32 (1985), 56.

1662 STORM, MELVIN. "Chaucer's Franklin and Distraint of Knighthood." ChauR 19 (1984), 162–68.

1663 TRAVERSI, DEREK. "The Franklin's Tale," in 562, pp. 87–119.

1664 WATANABE, IKUO. "The Franklin's Tale: A Narrative." Journal of Tenri University 132 (1981), 91–109. In Japanese.

1665 WHITE, GERTRUDE M. "The Franklin's Tale: Chaucer or the Critics." PMLA 89 (1974), 454–62. [+MerT]

See also: 128, 130, 201, 256, 267, 339, 370, 379, 383, 429, 430, 444, 449, 450, 481, 499, 501, 532, 548, 581, 584, 589, 725, 734, 740, 781, 792, 810, 841, 859, 891, 916, 957, 961, 980, 994, 1031, 1056, 1058, 1065, 1074, 1086, 1093, 1097, 1098, 1099, 1139, 1140, 1144, 1147, 1157, 1165, 1173, 1188, 1248, 1250, 1252, 1253, 1607, 1611, 1677, 1904, 1906, 2034, 2144, 2173, 2510, 2651, 2680, 2792, 2812, 2841, 2860.

>>> The Franklin's Tale: Source Studies <<<

1666 BESTON, JOHN B. "How Much was Known of the Breton Lai in Fourteenth Century England?" in 43, pp. 319–42.

1667 BLEETH, KENNETH A. "The Rocks in the Franklin's Tale and Ovid's Medea." AN&Q 20 (1982), 130–31. [+Boccaccio's Filocolo]

1668 HAMEL, MARY. "The Franklin's Tale and Chrétien de Troyes." ChauR 17 (1983), 316–331. [Cligès, +Boccaccio, Il Filocolo]

1669 REISNER, THOMAS A. and MARY ELLEN REISNER. "A British Analogue for the Rock-Motif in the Franklin's Tale." SP 76 (1979), 1–12. [legend of St. Balred]

Canterbury Tales

1670   ROSENBERG, BRUCE A.   "The Bari Widow and the Franklin's Tale."
       ChauR 14 (1980), 344–52.

1671   WILSON, EDWARD.   "An Aristotelian Commonplace in Chaucer's
       Franklin's Tale."   N&Q 32 (1985), 303–05.

1672   WRIGHT, CONSTANCE S.   "On the Franklin's Prologue, 716–721,
       Persius, and the Continuity of the Mannerist Style."   PQ 52
       (1973), 739–46.   [Modesty Topos in FranP]

1673   YODER, EMILY K.   "Chaucer and the 'Breton' Lay."   ChauR 12
       (1977), 74–77.

See also: 605, 624, 625, 637, 641, 645, 1065, 1652, 1653, 1655.

THE PHYSICIAN'S TALE

1674   AMOILS, E. R.   "Fruitfulness and Sterility in the Physician's and
       Pardoner's Tales."   ESA 17:1 (1974), 17–37.

1675   ARNOLD, RICHARD A.   "Chaucer's Physician: The Teller and the
       Tale."   RUO 51 (1981), 172–79.

1676   BAIRD, LORRAYNE Y.   "The Physician's 'urynals and jurdones'."
       FCS 2 (1979), 1–8.   [irony]

1677   BROWN, EMERSON, JR.   "What is Chaucer Doing with the Physician
       and His Tale?"   PQ 60 (1981), 129–49.   [Titus Livius; Jean de
       Meun's RR; +FranT, PardT]

1678   CROWTHER, J. D. W.   "Chaucer's Physician's Tale and Its Saint."
       ESC 8 (1982), 125–37.

1679   DELANY, SHEILA.   "Politics and the Paralysis of the Poetic
       Imagination in the Physician's Tale."   SAC 3 (1981), 47–60.
       [PhyT as sadistic sensationalism]

1680   FICHTE, JOERG O.   "Incident—History Exemplum—Novella: The
       Transformation of History in Chaucer's Physician's Tale."
       Florilegium 5 (1983), 189–207.   [narrative form]

1681   HAINES, R. MICHAEL.   "Fortune, Nature, and Grace in Fragment C."
       ChauR 10 (1976), 220–35.   [+PardT, ParsT]

1682   JOSEPH, GERHARD [J]. "The Gifts of Nature, Fortune, and Grace in the Physician's, Pardoner's, and Parson's Tales." ChauR 9 (1975), 237-45.

1683   KEMPTON, DANIEL. "The Physician's Tale: The Doctor of Physic's Diplomatic 'Cure'." ChauR 19 (1984), 24-38. [+Host]

1684   KINNEY, THOMAS L. "The Popular Meaning of Chaucer's Physician's Tale." L&P 28 (1978), 76-84. [psychological analysis]

1685   MANDEL, JEROME H. "Governance in the Physician's Tale." ChauR 10 (1976), 316-25.

1686   MATHEWSON, JEANNE T. "For Love and Not for Hate: The Value of Virginity in Chaucer's Physician's Tale." AnM 14 (1973), 35-42.

1687   TROWER, KATHERINE B. "Spiritual Sickness in the Physician's and Pardoner's Tales: Thematic Unity in Fragment VI of the Canterbury Tales." ABR 29 (1978), 67-86.

See also: 256, 264, 374, 375, 430, 481, 584, 818, 859, 957, 965, 977, 1062, 1067, 1068, 1085a, 1135, 1144, 1148, 1150, 1165, 1170, 1188, 1258, 1414, 1708, 1935, 2135, 2162, 2643.

>>> The Physician's Tale: Source Studies <<<

1688   KANNO, MASAHIKO. "Chaucer no The Physician's Tale—Ruiwa tono Hikaku" [The Physician's Tale—Comparison with Its Analogue]. Studies in Foreign Languages and Literatures 21 (Aichi University of Education, 1985), 47-58. In Japanese. [Gower]

1689   LANCASHIRE, ANNE. "Chaucer and the Sacrifice of Isaac." ChauR 9 (1975), 320-26. [+MLT]

1690   WALLER, MARTHA S. "The Physician's Tale: Geoffrey Chaucer and Fray Juan García de Castrojeriz." Speculum 51 (1976), 292-306.

See also: 638, 645, 1677, 1680, 2162.

Canterbury Tales

WORDS OF THE HOST

(OR INTRODUCTION TO THE PARDONER'S TALE),

THE PARDONER'S PROLOGUE AND TALE

1691   ANDERSEN, DAVID M. "The Pardoner's True Profession." NM 75
        (1974), 630–39.

1692   BAUSCHATZ, PAUL C. "Chaucer's Pardoner's Beneficent Lie."
        Assays 2 (1983), 19–43. [Augustine, De mendacio; St. Anselm]

1693   BEIDLER, PETER G. "Noah and the Old Man in the Pardoner's Tale."
        ChauR 15 (1981), 250–54.

1694   BEIDLER, PETER G. "The Plague and Chaucer's Pardoner." ChauR 16
        (1982), 257–69.

1695   BESSERMAN, LAWRENCE. "Chaucer and the Bible: Parody and
        Authority in the Pardoner's Tale," in Biblical Patterns in
        Modern Literature. Edited by David H. Hirsch and Nehama
        Aschkenasy. Brown Judaic Studies 77. Chico, CA: Scholars,
        1984, pp. 43–50. [glosing, parody; +TC, GP, CT, PardP]

1696   BESSERMAN, LAWRENCE. Letter. PMLA 98 (1983), 405–06. [false
        relics] See Storm, no. 1748, below. See also nos. 1711,
        1730, 1746, 1747, 1749.

1697   BOLTON, W. F. "Structural Meaning in The Pardoner's Tale and The
        Nun's Priest's Tale." Lang&S 11 (1978), 201–11.

1698   CESPEDES, FRANK V. "Chaucer's Pardoner and Preaching." ELH 44
        (1977), 1–18. [cf. ParsT]

1699   COLETTI, THERESA. "The Pardoner's Vernicle and the Image of Man
        in the Pardoner's Tale." Chaucer Newsletter 1:1 (1979),
        10–12.

1700   COLLETTE, CAROLYN P. "'Ubi Peccaverant, Ibi Punirentur': The
        Oak Tree and the Pardoner's Tale." ChauR 19 (1984), 39–45.

1701   CONDREN, EDWARD I. "The Pardoner's Bid for Existence." Viator 4
        (1973), 177–205. [Christian symbolism]

1702   DANE, JOSEPH A. "The Pardoner's Baskettes (Canterbury Tales VI,
        Lines 444–6)." N&Q 32 (1985), 155–56. [antecedents in
        Virgil's Eclogue 10]

Words of the Host, The Pardoner's Prologue and Tale

1703   DELASANTA, RODNEY. "Sacrament and Sacrifice in the Pardoner's Tale." AnM 14 (1973), 43–52.

1704   DÜRMÜLLER, URS. "Sociolinguistics and the Study of Medieval English," in Linguistic and Stylistic Studies in Medieval English. Edited by André Crépin. Publications de l'Association des Médievistes de l'Enseignement Supérieur, 10. Paris, 1984, pp. 5–22. [verbal behavior of the Pardoner]

1704a ERICKSON, JON. "Chaucer's Pardoner's Tale as Anti-Märchen." Folklore 94 (1983), 235–39.

1705   GILL, RICHARD. "Jung's Archetype of the Wise Old Man in Poems by Chaucer, Wordsworth, and Browning." JEP 2:1-2 (1981), 18–32.

1706   GINSBERG, WARREN. "Preaching and Avarice in the Pardoner's Tale." Mediaevalia 2 (1976), 77–99. [medieval treatises; exegetical tradition; Pardoner's literalism]

1707   GLASSER, MARC. "The Pardoner and the Host: Chaucer's Analysis of the Canterbury Game." CEA 46 (1983–84), 37–45.

1708   HAINES, R. MICHAEL. "Fortune, Nature, and Grace in Fragment C." ChauR 10 (1976), 220–35.

1709   HARROW, KENNETH. "The Money Order: False Treasure or True Benefice," in Interdisciplinary Dimensions of African Literature. Edited by Kofi Anyidoho, Abioseh M. Porter, Daniel Racine, and Janice Spleth. Washington, D. C.: Three Continents Press, 1985, pp. 75–87.

1710   HATCHER, ELIZABETH R. "Life Without Death: The Old Man in Chaucer's Pardoner's Tale." ChauR 9 (1975), 246–52.

1711   HYDE, WILLIAM J. Reply. PMLA 98 (1983), 253. Response to Melvin Storm, no. 1748, below. See also nos. 1696, 1711, 1730, 1746, 1747, 1749.

1712   JUNGMAN, ROBERT E. "The Pardoner's Quarrel with the Host." PQ 55 (1976), 279–81.

1713   KANNO, MASAHIKO. "'Purs' and 'relikes' in The Pardoner's Tale." Bulletin of Aichi University of Education 32 (Aichi, 1983), 31–38. In Japanese.

1714   KAWASAKI, MASATOSHI. "The Character and Meaning of Chaucer's Pardoner," in Literature and Man—the Papers for the Late

Canterbury Tales

Professor Kanji Nakajima." Tokyo: Kinseido, 1981, pp. 21–40. In Japanese. [+irony]

1715   KNIGHT, STEPHEN. "Chaucer's Pardoner in Performance." SSEng 9 (1983–84), 21–36.

1716   KUNTZ, ROBERT ALDEN. "The Pardoning of the Pardoner: Critical Approaches to the Morality of Chaucer's Pardoner." DAI 42 (1981), 1141A. University of California, Irvine.

1717   LAWTON, D. A. "The Pardoner's Tale: Morality and Its Context," in 74, pp. 38–63.

1718   LEICESTER, H. MARSHALL, JR. "'Synne Horrible': The Pardoner's Exegesis of His Tale, and Chaucer's," in 52, pp. 25–50.

1719   LUENGO, A. "Audience and Exempla in the Pardoner's Prologue and Tale." ChauR 11 (1976), 1–10.

1720   MANNING, STEPHEN. "Chaucer's Pardoner: Sex and Non-Sex." SAB 39 (1974), 17–26. [oral imagery]

1721   MERRIX, ROBERT P. "Sermon Structure in the Pardoner's Tale." ChauR 17 (1983), 235–49.

1722   MILLICHAP, JOSEPH R. "Transubstantiation in the Pardoner's Tale." BRMMLA 28 (1974), 102–08.

1723   MOORE, BRUCE. "'I Wol No Lenger Pleye with Thee': Chaucer's Rejection of the Pardoner." Parergon 14 (1976), 52–62.

1724   MORGAN, GERALD. "The Self-Revealing Tendencies of Chaucer's Pardoner." MLR 71 (1976), 241–55. [cf. RR]

1725   MOVSHOVITZ, HOWARD PAUL. "The Trickster Myth and Chaucer's Pardoner." DAI 38 (1977), 2768A. University of Colorado at Boulder.

1726   NAKAGAWA, TOKIO. "Chaucer no Menzaifu Uri no Seikaku Byosha to Kare no Hanashi no Geifutsu sei," in Eibungaku to no Deai. Edited by Naomi Matsuura. Kyoto: Showado, 1983, pp. 251–59.

1727   NITECKI, ALICIA K. "The Convention of the Old Man's Lament in the Pardoner's Tale." ChauR 16 (1981), 76–84. [+sources: Maximianus, Innocent III]

1728   NOLL, DOLORES L. "The Serpent and the Sting in the Pardoner's Prologue and Tale." ChauR 17 (1982), 159–62. [+St. Paul]

Words of the Host, The Pardoner's Prologue and Tale

1729   OLSEN, ALEXANDRA HENNESSEY. "'They shul desiren to dye, and
        deeth shal flee fro hem': A Reconsideration of the
        Pardoner's Old Man." NM 84 (1983), 367-71. [cf. FrT]

1730   OWEN, CHARLES A., JR. Reply. PMLA 98 (1983), 254. Response to
        Melvin Storm, no. 1748, below. See also nos. 1696, 1711,
        1746, 1747, 1749.

1731   PARSIGIAN, ELISE K. "A Note on the Conclusion of The Pardoner's
        Tale." RLSt 6 (1975), 51-54. [+Host]

1732   PATTERSON, LEE W. "Chaucerian Confession: Penitential
        Literature and the Pardoner." M&H 7 (1976), 153-73.

1733   PEARSALL, DEREK. "Chaucer's Pardoner: The Death of a Salesman."
        ChauR 17 (1983), 358-65. [cf. WBT]

1734   PETERSON, JOYCE E. "With Feigned Flattery: The Pardoner as
        Vice." ChauR 10 (1976), 326-36. [cf. Shakespeare's Iago,
        Richard III]

1735   PITTOCK, MALCOLM. "The Pardoner's Tale and the Quest for Death."
        EIC 24 (1974), 107-23.

1736   RHODES, JAMES F. "Motivation in Chaucer's Pardoner's Tale:
        Winner Take Nothing." ChauR 17 (1982), 40-61. [+Host, WBT]

1737   RHODES, JAMES F. "The Pardoner's Vernycle and His Vera Icon."
        MLS 13:2 (1983), 34-40. [+St. Veronica]

1738   ROWLAND, BERYL. "Chaucer's Idea of the Pardoner." ChauR 14
        (1979), 140-54. [hermaphrodites]

1739   RUDAT, WOLFGANG H. "Sexuality and Self-Recognition in The
        Pardoner's Tale." JEP 3 (1982), 124-29. [homosexuality]

1740   SATO, NORIKO. "The Old Man in The Pardoner's Tale." TCEL 54
        (1981), 11-36.

1741   SCHAUBER, ELLEN and ELLEN SPOLSKY. "Conversational
        Noncooperation: The Case of Chaucer's Pardoner." Lang&S 16
        (1983), 249-61.

1742   SCHEPS, WALTER. "Chaucer's Numismatic Pardoner and the
        Personification of Avarice," in 72a, pp. 107-23. [coins;
        money; sex]

1743   STANDOP, EWALD. "Chaucers Pardoner: das Charakterproblem und
        die Kritiker," in Geschichtlichkeit und Neuanfang im

Canterbury Tales

sprachlichen Kunstwerk. Studien zur englischen Philologie zu
Ehren von Fritz W. Schulze. Edited by Peter Erlebach,
Wolfgang G. Müller, and Klaus Reuter. Tübingen: Gunter Narr
Verlag, 1981, pp. 59-69. [sexual deviance]

1744   STEVENS, MARTIN and KATHLEEN FAHEY. "Substance, Accident, and
        Transformations: A Reading of the Pardoner's Tale." ChauR
        17 (1982), 142-58.

1745   STORM, MELVIN. "'A Culpa et a Poena': Christ's Pardon and the
        Pardoner's Tale." NM 83 (1982), 439-42.

1746   STORM, MELVIN. Reply. PMLA 98 (1983), 255-56. Response to
        William J. Hyde, no. 1711, Charles A. Owen, Jr., no. 1730,
        and Claude J. Summers, no. 1749, below. See also nos. 1696,
        1746, 1747.

1747   STORM, MELVIN. Letter. PMLA 98 (1983), 406. [false relics,
        Lollards] Reply to Besserman, no. 1696, above. See also no.
        1746.

1748   STORM, MELVIN. "The Pardoner's Invitation: Quaestor's Bag or
        Becket's Shrine?" PMLA 97 (1982), 810-18. [+Host] See also
        nos. 1696, 1711, 1730, 1746, 1747, 1749.

1749   SUMMERS, CLAUDE J. Reply. PMLA 98 (1983), 254-55. Response to
        Melvin Storm, no. 1748. See also nos. 1696, 1711, 1730,
        1746, 1747.

1750   TAYLOR, DENNIS. "The Confidence Man from the Pardoner's Tale to
        'The Fall'." ArQ 31 (1975), 73-85.

1751   TRISTRAM, PHILIPPA. "Strange Images of Death." LeedsSE, n. s.,
        14 (1983), 196-209. See no. 66.

1752   YAMANAKA, TOSHIO. "Chaucer's Pardoner." SES 2 (1977), 1-9.

1753   YEAGER, R. F. "Aspects of Gluttony in Chaucer and Gower." SP 81
        (1984), 42-55. [cf. Gower, Confessio Amantis; penitentials]

See also: 192, 199, 238, 246, 256, 321, 333, 392, 437, 442, 534, 560,
            684, 709, 763, 822, 859, 891, 952, 957, 1005, 1011, 1028,
            1037, 1041, 1050, 1062, 1069, 1077, 1083, 1086, 1087, 1112,
            1120, 1131, 1135, 1144, 1152, 1153, 1157, 1161, 1168, 1174,
            1266, 1414, 1677, 1681, 1682, 1687, 1757, 1962, 1965, 2263,
            2592, 2594, 2681, 2699, 2838, 2843, 2849, 2850, 2852, 2853,
            2853a, 2854, 2866, 2874, 2877, 2890.

The Shipman's Prologue and Tale

>>> The Pardoner's Tale: Source Studies <<<

1754 HALLISSY, MARGARET. "Poison Lore and Chaucer's Pardoner." MSE 9 (1983), 54–63. [Ibn Sīnā, Abū 'Alī al-Hasan b. 'Abdallāh: Canon Medicinae]

1755 JUNGMAN, ROBERT E. "The Pardoner's 'Confession' and St. Augustine's De Doctrina Christiana." Chaucer Newsletter 1:1 (1979), 16–17.

1756 McKENNA, CONAN. "The Irish Analogues to Chaucer's Pardoner's Tale." Béaloideas 45–47 (1977–79), 63–77.

1757 TAYLOR, PAUL BECKMAN. "Peynted Confessiouns: Boccaccio and Chaucer." CL 34 (1982), 116–29. [St. Augustine, De Mendacio; Boccaccio, Decameron]

See also: 604, 610, 622, 645, 1176, 1692, 1702, 1712, 1727, 1753.

THE SHIPMAN'S PROLOGUE OR THE EPILOGUE
OF THE MAN OF LAW'S TALE (II [B^1] 1163-1190)
AND THE SHIPMAN'S TALE

1758 ABRAHAM, DAVID H. "Cosyn and Cosynage: Pun and Structure in the Shipman's Tale." ChauR 11 (1977), 319–27.

1759 ADAMS, ROBERT. "The Concept of Debt in The Shipman's Tale." SAC 6 (1984), 85–102.

1760 COLETTI, THERESA. "Biblical Wisdom: Chaucer's Shipman's Tale and the Mulier Fortis," in 63, pp. 171–82. Rpt. from no. 1762 below. [parody; Proverbs 31:10–31; cf. WBP]

1761 COLETTI, THERESA. "The Meeting at the Gate: Comic Hagiography and Symbol in The Shipman's Tale." SIcon 3 (1977), 47–56. [Biblical iconography]

1762 COLETTI, THERESA. "The Mulier Fortis and Chaucer's Shipman's Tale." ChauR 15 (1981), 236–49. Rpt. in no. 1760.

Canterbury Tales

1763   FERRIS, SUMNER. "'His barge ycleped was the Maudelayne':
        Canterbury Tales A 410." Names 31 (1983), 207-10.

1764   GIBSON, GAIL McMURRAY. "Resurrection as Dramatic Icon in the
        Shipman's Tale," in 61, pp. 102-12.

1765   HERMANN, JOHN P. "Dismemberment, Dissemination, Discourse: Sign
        and Symbol in the Shipman's Tale." ChauR 19 (1985), 302-37.

1766   JOSEPH, GERHARD. "Chaucer's Coinage: Foreign Exchange and the
        Puns of the Shipman's Tale." ChauR 17 (1983), 341-57.

1767   KEISER, GEORGE R. "Language and Meaning in Chaucer's Shipman's
        Tale." ChauR 12 (1977), 147-61. [+Bradshaw Shift]

1768   MARTIN, WALLACE and NICK CONRAD. "Formal Analysis of Traditional
        Fictions." PLL 17 (1981), 3-22. [theories of Lévi-Strauss,
        Claude; Barthes, Roland]

1769   McGALLIARD, JOHN C. "Characterization in Chaucer's Shipman's
        Tale." PQ 54 (1975), 1-18.

1770   NICHOLSON, PETER. "The Shipman's Tale and the Fabliaux." ELH 45
        (1978), 583-96.

1771   SCATTERGOOD, V. J. "The Originality of the Shipman's Tale."
        ChauR 11 (1977), 210-31.

1772   SCHNEIDER, PAUL STEPHEN. "'Taillynge Ynough': The Function of
        Money in the Shipman's Tale." ChauR 11 (1977), 201-09.

1773   STOCK, LORRAINE KOCHANSKE. "The Meaning of 'Chevyssaunce':
        Complicated Word Play in Chaucer's Shipman's Tale." SSF 18
        (1981), 245-49.

1774   STOCK, LORRAINE KOCHANSKE. "The Reenacted Fall in Chaucer's
        Shipman's Tale." SIcon 7-8 (1981-82), 135-45.

1775   YOTS, MICHAEL. "Chaucer's Shipman's Tale." Expl 36:4 (1978),
        23-24. [use of proverb]

See also: 94, 286, 423, 448, 560, 587, 725, 859, 891, 954, 957, 959,
            981, 982, 986, 993, 996, 1002, 1029, 1069, 1088, 1112, 1120,
            1131, 1157, 1161, 1166, 1175, 2397.

>>> The Shipman's Tale: Source Studies <<<

1776   MILLICHAP, JOSEPH R. "Source and Theme in the Shipman's Tale."
        UDR 10:3 (1974), 3-6. [Boccaccio's Decameron; Sercambi's
        Novelle]

1777   NICHOLSON, PETER C. "The Literary Relations of Chaucer's
        Shipman's Tale." DAI 34 (1974), 5114A. University of
        Pennsylvania, 1973.

1778   NICHOLSON, PETER [C]. "The Medieval Tales of the Lover's Gift
        Regained." Fabula 21 (1979), 200-22.

1779   PEARCY, ROY L. "Punning on 'Cosyn' and 'Cosynge' in Chaucer's
        Shipman's Tale." AN&Q 17 (1978-79), 70-71.

1780   STOCK, LORRAINE KOCHANSKE. "La Vieille and the Merchant's Wife
        in Chaucer's Shipman's Tale." SHR 16 (1982), 333-39. [RR]

See also: 595, 641, 1180, 1763.

THE PRIORESS'S HEADLINK, PROLOGUE, AND TALE

1781   ARCHER, JOHN. "The Structure of Anti-Semitism in the Prioress's
        Tale." ChauR 19 (1984), 46-54.

1782   BURNLEY, DAVID. "Stylistic Reconstruction and Chaucer's
        Prioress." Indian Journal of Applied Linguistics 10 (1984),
        77-90.

1783   BURROW, J. A. "'Young Saint, Old Devil': Reflections on a
        Medieval Proverb." RES 30 (1979), 385-96. [+Dunbar; ages of
        man]

1784   COLLETTE, CAROLYN P. "Sense and Sensibility in the Prioress's
        Tale." ChauR 15 (1980), 138-50.

1785   COLLINS, TERENCE GEORGE. "A Psychoanalytic Introduction to
        Reader Response to Racial Literature." DAI 37 (1976), 3611A.
        University of Minnesota.

1786   DACHSLAGER, EARL L. "'Hateful to Crist and to His Compaignye':
        Theological Murder in 'The Prioress's Tale' and The Fixer."

Canterbury Tales

LJHum 11 (1985), 43–50.

1787 DAVIDSON, AUDREY. "Alma Redemptoris Mater: The Little
      Clergeon's Song." SMC 4 (1974), 459–66. [Hermannus
      Contractus; use of Sarum]

1788 FERRIS, SUMNER. "Chaucer at Lincoln (1387): The Prioress's Tale
      as a Political Poem." ChauR 15 (1981), 295–321. [+Richard
      II, John Buckingham]

1789 FERRIS, SUMNER. "A Hissing Stanza in Chaucer's Prioress's Tale."
      NM 80 (1979), 164–68.

1790 FERRIS, SUMNER. "The Mariology of the Prioress's Tale." ABR 32
      (1981), 232–54. [Biblical sources]

1791 FRANK, HARDY LONG. "Chaucer's Prioress and the Blessed Virgin."
      ChauR 13 (1979), 346–62.

1792 FRANK, ROBERT WORTH, JR. "Miracles of the Virgin, Medieval
      Anti-Semitism, and Prioress's Tale," in 44, pp. 177–88.
      [apocryphal Transitus]

1793 FRIEDMAN, ALBERT B. "The Mysterious 'Greyn' in the Prioress's
      Tale." ChauR 11 (1977), 328–33.

1794 FRIEDMAN, ALBERT B. "The Prioress's Tale and Chaucer's
      Anti-Semitism." ChauR 9 (1974), 118–29.

1795 FRITZ, DONALD W. "The Prioress's Avowal of Ineptitude." ChauR 9
      (1974), 166–81. [topos]

1796 HAMEL, MARY. "And Now for Something Completely Different: The
      Relationship Between the Prioress's Tale and the Rime of Sir
      Thopas." ChauR 14 (1980), 251–59.

1797 HIRSH, JOHN C. "Reopening the Prioress's Tale." ChauR 10
      (1975), 30–45. [anti-Semitism; Jews; gem imagery; Mass of
      the Holy Innocent]

1798 JACOBS, EDWARD CRANEY. "Further Biblical Allusions for Chaucer's
      Prioress." ChauR 15 (1980), 151–54. [Amor vincit omnia]

1799 JEMBER, GREGORY K. "Cum Grano Salis: A Note on the Prioress's
      Tale." AN&Q 15 (1976–77), 82–86. [grain of salt]

1800 MALTMAN, SISTER NICHOLAS, O. P. "The Divine Granary, or the End
      of the Prioress's 'Greyn'." ChauR 17 (1982), 163–70. [Feast
      of the Holy Innocents]

The Prioress's Headlink, Prologue and Tale

1801 MASUI, MICHIO. "The Prioress's Prologue and Tale: A Structural and Semantic Approach," in Gengo to Buntai: Higashida Chiaki Kyoju Kanreki Kinen Rombunshu [Language and Style: Essays Commemorating the 60th Birthday of Professor C. Higashida]. Edited by Chiaka Higashida. Osaka: Osaka Kyoiku Tosho, 1975, pp. 9-18.

1802 REX, RICHARD. "Chaucer and the Jews." MLQ 45 (1984), 107-22.

1803 RICE, NANCY HALL. "Beauty and the Beast and the Little Boy: Clues About the Origins of Sexism and Racism from Folklore and Literature: Chaucer's The Prioress's Tale, Sir Gawain and the Green Knight, the Alliterative Morte Arthure, Webster's The Duchess of Malfi, Shakespeare's Othello, Hawthorne's 'Rapaccini's Daughter', Melville's 'Benito Cereno'." DAI 36 (1975), 875A. University of Massachusetts.

1804 SAITO, TOMOKO. "Chaucer's Women 2—The Prioress." Konan Daigaku Kiyo 53 (1985), 61-77. In Japanese.

1805 SHIKII, KUMIKO. "Chaucer's Prioresse Re-Considered." Soundings 7 (Tokyo, 1981), 11-24. In Japanese.

1806 TRIPP, RAYMOND P., JR. "Ignorance, System, and Sacrifice: A Literary Reading of the Prioress's Tale." PoetT 15-16 (1983), 136-53. [thematic, semantic analysis]

nnnn WURTELE, DOUGLAS. "Prejudice and Chaucer's Prioress." RUO 55 (1985), 33-43.

See also: 124, 130, 214, 289, 481, 560, 584, 826, 859, 957, 965, 977, 1037, 1041, 1042, 1045, 1054, 1067, 1083, 1085a, 1112, 1120, 1148, 1150, 1151, 1157, 1165, 1168, 1170, 1227, 1516, 1818, 1821, 1858, 2075, 2135, 2501, 2758, 2785.

>>> The Prioress's Tale: Source Studies <<<

1808 BUGGE, JOHN. "Tell-Tale Context: Two Notes on Biblical Quotation in The Canterbury Tales." AN&Q 14 (1975-76), 82-85. [+FrT source]

1809 GABRIELI, VITTORIO. "Magia e miracolo in due favole medievali." La Cultura 17 (1980), 90-104. [Petrarch, Familiares]

Canterbury Tales

1810   JUNGMAN, ROBERT E. "Amor Vincit Omnia and the Prioress's
        Brooch." Lore&L 9:3 (1983), 1-7. [Virgil]

See also: 1790, 1792, 1800.

SIR THOPAS: PROLOGUE AND TALE

1811   BENSON, C. DAVID. "Their Telling Difference: Chaucer the
        Pilgrim and His Two Contrasting Tales." ChauR 18 (1983),
        61-75. [+Mel]

1812   BREWER, DEREK. "The Arming of the Warrior in European Literature
        and Chaucer," in 73, pp. 221-43.

1813   BURROW, J. A. "Chaucer's Sir Thopas and La Prise de Nuevile," in
        English Satire and the Satiric Tradition. Edited by Claude
        Rawson. Oxford: Blackwell, 1984, pp. 44-55. Also in YES 14
        (1984), 44-55. [burlesque; parody]

1814   BURTON, T. L. "Chaucer's Tale of Sir Thopas." Expl 40:4 (1982),
        6. [parody, arming]

1815   CONLEY, JOHN. "The Peculiar Name Thopas." SP 73 (1976), 42-61.
        [gem symbolism]

1816   CULLEN, DOLORES L. "Chaucer's The Tale of Sir Thopas." Expl
        32:5 (1974), 35. [Olifaunt/Elephantiasis]

1817   GAYLORD, ALAN T. "Chaucer's Dainty 'Dogerel': The 'Elvyssh'
        Prosody of Sir Thopas." SAC 1 (1979), 83-104. [ME
        tail-rhyme romances]

1818   GAYLORD, ALAN T. "The 'Miracle' of Sir Thopas." SAC 6 (1984),
        65-84. [+CT, PrT]

1819   GAYLORD, ALAN T. "The Moment of Sir Thopas: Towards a New Look
        at Chaucer's Language." ChauR 16 (1982), 311-29.

1820   HASKELL, ANN S. "Sir Thopas: The Puppet's Puppet." ChauR 9
        (1975), 253-61.

1821   KOOPER, E. S. "Inverted Images in Chaucer's Tale of Sir Thopas."
        SN 56 (1984), 147-54. [parody; gem symbolism; PrT, Mel]

1822   MURPHY, MICHAEL. "Vows, Boasts and Taunts, and the Role of Women
in Some Medieval Literature." ES 66 (1985), 105-12.
[+Tournament of Tottenham, burlesques]

1823   OLSON, GLENDING. "A Reading of the Thopas-Melibee Link." ChauR
10 (1975), 147-53.

1824   SCATTERGOOD, V. J. "Chaucer and the French War: Sir Thopas and
Melibee," in 50, pp. 287-96. [satire]

1825   TRIPP, RAYMOND P., JR. "The Arming Topos and the Comparative
Modernity of Chaucer, the Gawain Poet, and Malory." Bulletin
of Hirosaki College 3 (Japan, 1981), 179-87.

1826   VAN ARSDALE, RUTH. "The Chaste Sir Thopas." AN&Q 13 (1974-75),
146-48. [tale as burlesque of love]

See also: 124, 172, 256, 268, 269, 284, 362, 367, 392, 405, 459, 542,
548, 555, 568, 667, 671, 686, 693, 773, 859, 957, 967, 1018,
1057, 1112, 1135, 1140, 1147, 1157, 1188, 1695, 1796, 2620,
2650, 2883.

>>> Sir Thopas: Source Studies <<<

See nos. 600, 1815.

MELIBEUS: HEADLINK AND TALE

1827   BORNSTEIN, DIANE. "Chaucer's Tale of Melibee as an Example of
the Style clergial." ChauR 12 (1978), 236-54. [Chaucer's
trans. from Renaud de Louens]

1828   BRINTON, LAUREL J. "Chaucer's Tale of Meilbee: A Reassessment."
ESC 10 (1984), 251-64. [+allegory]

1829   Item cancelled.

1830   FARRELL, THOMAS J. "Chaucer's Little Treatise, the Melibee."
ChauR 20 (1985), 61-67. [B[2] 2143-54]

1831   HOFFMAN, RICHARD L. "Chaucer's Melibee and Tales of Sondry
Folk." C&M 30 (1969), 552-77.

Canterbury Tales

1832   LUNZ, ELISABETH. "Chaucer's Prudence as the Ideal of the
        Virtuous Woman." ELWIU 4 (1977), 3-10.

1833   MARKS, HERBERT. "Poetic Purpose in the Tale of Melibee." MSE
        8:3 (1982), 50-55.

1834   MYERS, DE E. "Justesse rationnelle: Le 'Myrie Tale in Prose' de
        Chaucer." MA 78 (1972), 267-86.

1835   RUGGIERS, PAUL G. "Serious Chaucer: The Tale of Melibeus and
        the Parson's Tale," in 73, pp. 83-94.

See also: 124, 141, 187, 256, 269, 306, 316, 349, 392, 393, 410, 463,
           542, 891, 957, 960, 965, 967, 984, 998, 1002, 1112, 1115,
           1121, 1155, 1157, 1188, 1695, 1811, 1821, 1823, 1824, 2574,
           2608, 2889.

                >>> Melibeus: Source Studies <<<

1836   BORNSTEIN, DIANE. "French Influence on Fifteenth-Century English
        Prose as Exemplified by the Translation of Christine de
        Pisan's 'Livre du Corps de Policie'." MS 39 (1977), 369-86.
        See pp. 371-73.

1837   PALOMO, DOLORES. "What Chaucer Really Did to Le Livre de
        Mellibee." PQ 53 (1974), 304-20.

See also: 629, 630, 1827.

                THE MONK'S PROLOGUE AND TALE

1838   BAIRD, LORRAYNE Y. "O. E. D. Cock 20: The Limits of
        Lexicography of Slang." Maledicta 5 (1981), 213-26.
        [tredefowel]

1839   BORNSTEIN, DIANE. "Chaucer's Monk's Tale, 2095-2142." Expl 33:9
        (1975), 77. [+Boethius, Consolatione Philosophiae]

1840   FLEMING, JOHN V. "Daun Piers and Dom Pier: Waterless Fish and
        Unholy Hunters." ChauR 15 (1981), 287-94. [Dante, Paradiso,

The Monk's Prologue and Tale

Peter Damian]

1841   HAAS, RENATE. "Chaucers Tragödienkonzept im europäischen
        Rahmen," in Zusammenhänge, Einflüsse, Wirkungen. Edited by
        Joerg O. Fichte, Karl Heinz Göller, and Bernhard
        Schimmelpfennig. Berlin and New York: de Gruyter, 1986, pp.
        451-65. [+Petrarch, Boccaccio]

1842   LEPLEY, DOUGLAS L[EE]. "The Monk's Boethian Tale." ChauR 12
        (1978), 162-70. [Fortune; Boethius, Consolatione
        Philosophiae]

1843   LEPLEY, DOUGLAS LEE. "The Philosophic and Artistic Purposes of
        Chaucer's Monk's Tale." DAI 39 (1978), 1539A. Lehigh
        University. [tragedy; comedy; Boethius, Consolatione
        Philosophiae]

1844   LOCK, F. P. "Chaucer's Monk's Use of Lucan, Suetonius, and
        'Valerie'." ELN 12:4 (1975), 251-55.

1845   OLSSON, KURT. "Grammar, Manhood, and Tears: The Curiosity of
        Chaucer's Monk." MP 76 (1978), 1-17.

1846   SHIKII, KUMIKO. "Chaucer's Anti-Clericalism as Seen in the
        Monk." The Fleur-de-lis Review (25 December, 1980), 25-54.

1847   TAGGIE, BENJAMIN F. "John of Gaunt, Geoffrey Chaucer and 'O
        Noble, O Worthy Petro, Glorie of Spayne'." FCS 10 (1984),
        195-228. [+Pedro I, King of Castille]

1848   WALLER, MARTHA S. "The Monk's Tale: Nero's Nets and Caesar's
        Father—An Inquiry into the Transformations of Classical
        Roman History in Medieval Tradition." ISSQ 31 (1978), 46-55.

See also: 124, 256, 268, 305, 364, 463, 481, 555, 560, 847, 859, 957,
           965, 1002, 1037, 1041, 1085a, 1120, 1150, 1157, 1166, 1169,
           1609, 1865, 1886.

>>> The Monk's Tale: Source Studies <<<

1849   BOITANI, PIÉRO. "The Monk's Tale: Dante and Boccaccio." MAE 45
        (1976), 50-69.

See also: 645, 646, 1839, 1840, 1841, 1842, 1843, 1844, 1848, 1894.

Canterbury Tales

THE NUN'S PRIEST'S PROLOGUE, TALE, AND EPILOGUE

1850   ANDERSON, J. J. "The Climax of Chaucer's Nun's Priest's Tale."
        CritS 6 (1973), 3-7.

1851   ANJUM, A. R. "'The Nonnes Preestes Tale': A 'Framework' Story."
        Explorations 5:1 (1978), 40-48. [structure NPT/CT]

1852   BAIRD, LORRAYNE Y. "Christus Gallinaceus: A Chaucerian Enigma;
        or the Cock as Symbol of Christ." SIcon 9 (1983), 19-30.
        [background study, Jerome, Prudentius, hymnody; iconography;
        folklore]

1853   BAIRD, LORRAYNE Y. "Priapus Gallinaceus: The Role of the Cock
        in Fertility and Eroticism in Classical Antiquity and the
        Middle Ages." SIcon 7-8 (1981-82), 81-111. [background
        study]

1854   BESSERMAN, LAWRENCE L. "Chaucerian Wordplay: The Nun's Priest
        and His Womman Divyne." ChauR 12 (1977), 68-73.

1855   BISHOP, IAN. "The Nun's Priest's Tale and the Liberal Arts."
        RES 30 (1979), 257-67.

1856   BLOOMFIELD, MORTON W. "The Wisdom of the Nun's Priest's Tale,"
        in 73, pp. 70-82.

1857   BOULGER, JAMES D. "Chaucer's Nun's Priest's Tale," in Literary
        Studies: Essays in Memory of Francis A. Drumm. Edited by
        John H. Dorenkamp. Worcester, MA: College of the Holy
        Cross, 1973, pp. 13-32.

1858   BOYD, HEATHER. "Chauntecleer and the Eagle." ESA 21:2 (1978),
        65-69. [rhetoric; language]

1859   BREWER, DEREK. "On the Nun's Priest's Tale." BAM 11 (1977),
        115. [summary of text published in Limoges]

1860   BRODY, SAUL NATHANIEL. "Truth and Fiction in the Nun's Priest's
        Tale." ChauR 14 (1979), 33-47.

1861   CORREALE, ROBERT M. "Nun's Priest's Tale, VII, 3444-46." Expl
        39:1 (1980), 43-45. [St. Paul; Mirk's Festial]

1862   CRÉPIN, ANDRÉ. "Module de douze vers dans le Conte du Prêtre des

The Nun's Priest's Prologue, Tale, and Epilogue

Nonnains." BAM 11 (1977), 116–21. Also published in
Linguistique, civilisation, litterature. (EA 76.) Preface
by Andre Bordeaux. Paris: Didier, 1980, pp. 180–84.
[function of groups of twelve lines; +structure]

1863 CRÉPIN, ANDRÉ. "'Sustres and paramours': Sexe et domination
dans les Contes de Cantorbéry." Caliban 17 (1980), 3–21.

1864 CULLEN, DOLORES L. "Chaucer's The Nun's Priest's Tale." Expl
38:1 (1979), 11. [Pertelote, confuser of fate]

1865 DEAN, NANCY. "Chaucerian Attitudes Towards Joy with Particular
Consideration of the Nun's Priest's Tale." MAE 44 (1975),
1–13. [+Boethius]

1866 DELANY, SHEILA. "'Mulier est hominis confusio': Chaucer's
Anti-Popular Nun's Priest's Tale." Mosaic 17:1 (1984), 1–8.
[Pauline/Augustinian ideology; sex roles]

1867 DuVAL, JOHN. "'Si coume Renart prist Chantecler le coc' and 'The
Nonnes Preestes Tale': A Comparison." PAPA 1:3 (1975),
15–24. [comparison]

1868 FOX, ALISTAIR. "Chaucer's Revision of the Nun's Priest's
Character and Its Consequences," in The Interpretative Power:
Essays on Literature in Honour of Margaret Dalziel. Edited
by C. A. Gibson. Punedia: Department of English, University
of Otago, 1980, pp. 25–34.

1869 FRESE, DOLORES WARWICK. "The Nun's Priest's Tale: Chaucer's
Identified Masterpiece?" ChauR 16 (1982), 330–43. [hidden
names in NPT; anagrams]

1870 GALLACHER, PATRICK. "Food, Laxatives, and the Catharsis in
Chaucer's Nun's Priest's Tale." Speculum 51 (1976), 49–68.
[+moral, metaphysical meanings]

1871 GALLICK, SUSAN. "Styles of Usage in the Nun's Priest's Tale."
ChauR 11 (1977), 232–47.

1872 GALVÁN-REULA, J. F. "The Modernity of the Nun's Priest's Tale:
Narrator, Theme and Ending." Lore&L 10:3 (1984), 63–69.

1873 HENDERSON, ARNOLD CLAYTON. "Medieval Beasts and Modern Cages:
The Making of Meaning in Fables and Bestiaries." PMLA 97
(1982), 40–49. [+allegory]

1874 JOHNSON, LYNN STALEY. "'To Make in Som Comedye': Chaunticleer,
Son of Troy." ChauR 19 (1985), 225–44. [+TC]

Canterbury Tales

1875   KEALY, J. KIERAN. "Chaucer's Nun's Priest's Tale, VII.3160-71."
        Expl 33:2 (1974), 12. [dreams]

1876   KNIGHT, STEPHEN. "Form, Content and Context in The Nun's
        Priest's Tale," in 74, pp. 64-85.

1877   LALL, RAMA RANI. Satiric Fable in English: A Critical Study of
        the Animal Tales of Chaucer, Spenser, Dryden, and Orwell.
        New Delhi: New Statesman, 1979. 155 pp. See Chapter 3.

1878   MANN, JILL. "The Speculum Stultorum and the Nun's Priest's
        Tale." ChauR 9 (1975), 262-82. [Nigel]

1879   McGINNIS, WAYNE D. "The Dramatic Fitness of the Nun's Priest's
        Tale." CEA 37:2 (1975), 24-26. [cf. GP Monk, Prioress]

1880   PAYNE, F. ANNE. "Foreknowledge and Free Will: Three Theories in
        the Nun's Priest's Tale." ChauR 10 (1976), 201-19.
        [Boethius; Augustine; Bradwardine]

1881   PEARSALL, DEREK. "Chaucer, the Nun's Priest's Tale, and the
        Modern Reader." DQR 10 (1980), 164-74. [on modern
        criticism]

1882   REX, RICHARD. "Chauntecleer's 'Sisters'." StHum 7:2 (1979),
        39-42.

1883   SCHAUBER, ELLEN and ELLEN SPOLSKY. "Stalking a Generative
        Poetics." NLH 12 (1981), 397-413. [beast fable/epic]

1884   SCHUMAN, SAMUEL. "The Widow's Garden: The Nun's Priest's Tale
        and the Great Chain of Being." StHum 6:2 (1978), 12-14.

1885   SHALLERS, A. PAUL. "The Nun's Priest's Tale: An Ironic
        Exemplum." ELH 42 (1975), 319-37. [+Roman de Renard]

1886   SIMMS, NORMAN. "Nero and Jack Straw in Chaucer's Nun's Priest's
        Tale." Parergon 8 (1974), 2-12. [+MkT]

1887   THOMAS, PAUL R. "An Ironic Monkish Allusion: Chaucer's Learned
        Audience in 'The Nun's Priest's Tale'." Encyclia 59 (1985,
        for 1982), 45-52. [comparison: Nigel de Longchamps'
        Speculum Stultorum]

1888   TRAVIS, PETER W. "The Nun's Priest's Tale as Grammar-School
        Primer," in 72, pp. 81-91.

1889   TRÜTER, W. "Geoffrey Chaucer: Die Erzählung des Nonnenpriesters

The Nun's Priest's Prologue, Tale, and Epilogue

Zeilenkommentar." DAI 39 (1979), 4698C. Universität
Hamburg, 1978. [line-by-line commentary]

1890   WENTERSDORF, KARL P. "Heigh Ymaginacioun in Chaucer's Nun's
       Priest's Tale." SN 52 (1980), 31-34.

1891   WENTERSDORF, KARL P. "Symbol and Meaning in Chaucer's Nun's
       Priest's Tale." NMS 26 (1982), 29-46. [eroticism]

1892   WINNY, JAMES. "'Owles and Apes' in Chaucer's Nun's Priest's Tale
       3082." MS 27 (1965), 322-25.

1893   ZACHARIAS, RICHARD. "Chaucer's Nun's Priest's Tale, B^2.4552-63."
       Expl 32:8 (1974), 60.

See also: 94, 204, 218, 256, 264, 271, 286, 288, 294, 318, 321, 330,
           340, 341, 342, 358, 367, 369, 374, 375, 378, 429, 430, 450,
           463, 488, 545, 567, 572, 590, 668, 736, 745, 758, 764, 770,
           774, 841, 859, 891, 901, 903, 907, 938, 957, 998, 1007, 1019,
           1021, 1028, 1037, 1057, 1087, 1112, 1117, 1120, 1131, 1137,
           1157, 1165, 1168, 1174, 1178, 1187, 1289, 1348, 1566, 1697,
           1900a, 1908, 2034, 2075, 2247, 2602, 2672, 2792, 2838, 2843,
           2850, 2854.

           >>> The Nun's Priest's Tale: Source Studies <<<

1894   BAIRD-LANGE, LORRAYNE Y. "Symbolic Ambivalence in 'I have a
       gentil cock'." FCS 11 (1985), 1-5. [analogue to images in
       NPT and MkT]

1895   BLAKE, N. F. "Reynard the Fox in England," in Aspects of the
       Medieval Animal Epic. Edited by E. Rombauts and A.
       Welkenhuysen. Mediaevalia Lovaniensia, Ser. I, Studia 3.
       Louvain: Louvain University Press; The Hague: Nijhoff,
       1975, pp. 53-65.

1896   CRIDER, RICHARD. "Daniel in the Nun's Priest's Tale." AN&Q 18
       (1979-80), 18-19. [Bible]

1897   GUERIN, RICHARD. "The Nun's Priest and Canto V of the Inferno."
       ES 54 (1973), 13-15.

1898   PRATT, R[OBERT] A. "Chaucer's Adaptation of Three Old French
       Narratives of the Cock and the Fox to Form the 'Nonnes
       Preestes Tale'," in Expression, Communication and Experience
       in Literature and Language. Edited by Ronald G. Popperwell.

185

Canterbury Tales

Proceedings of the XII Congress of the International
Federation for Modern Languages and Literatures. London:
Modern Humanities Research Association, 1973, pp. 290-92.

1899   PRATT, ROBERT A. "Some Latin Sources of the Nonnes Preest on
        Dreams." Speculum 52 (1977), 538-70. [Holcot, Vincent of
        Beauvais, Albertus Magnus, Cicero]

1900   TERRY, PATRICIA, trans. Renard the Fox: The Misadventures of an
        Epic Hero. Boston: Northeastern University Press, 1983.
        [trans. from Old French]

1900a   THOMAS P. R. "The Literary Contexts of the Nun's Priest's Tale:
        Studies in Chaucer's Narrative Art." Doct. diss, University
        of York, 1983.

1901   YATES, DONALD. "Chanticleer's Latin Ancestors." ChauR 18
        (1983), 116-26. [Isengrimus]

See also: 600, 603, 604, 616, 617, 618, 645, 650, 1878, 1885, 1887.

THE SECOND NUN'S PROLOGUE AND TALE

1902   COLLETTE, CAROLYN P. "A Closer Look at Seinte Cecile's Special
        Vision." ChauR 10 (1976), 337-49. [+Plato, Augustine,
        Prudentius]

1903   EGGEBROTEN, ANNE. "Laughter in the Second Nun's Tale: A
        Redefinition of the Genre." ChauR 19 (1984), 55-61.
        [Legenda Aurea]

1904   GLASSER, MARC D. "Marriage and the Second Nun's Tale." TSL 23
        (1978), 1-14. [Marriage Group; argument against D. Howard]

1905   HIRSH, JOHN C. "The Politics of Spirituality: The Second Nun
        and the Manciple." ChauR 12 (1977), 129-46. [Great Schism]

1906   JOHNSTON, MARK E. "The Resonance of the Second Nun's Tale."
        MHLS 3 (1980), 25-38. [Marriage Group]

1907   KOLVE, V. A. "Chaucer's Second Nun's Tale and the Iconography of
        Saint Cecilia," in 68, pp. 137-74.

1908   LANDRUM, GRAHAM. "The Convent Crowd and the Feminist Nun." TPB

186

The Canon's Yeoman's Prologue and Tale

13:1 (1976), 5-12.

1909   LUECKE, JANEMARIE, O. S. B. "Three Faces of Cecilia: Chaucer's Second Nun's Tale." ABR 33 (1982), 335-48.

1910   MALINA, MARILYN. "Chaucer's The Second Nun's Prologue and Tale." Expl 43:1 (1984), 3-4. [idleness; idolatry, pagan images]

1911   OLSON, GLENDING. "Chaucer, Dante, and the Structure of Fragment VIII(G) of the Canterbury Tales." ChauR 16 (1982), 222-37.

See also: 256, 306, 364, 501, 826, 859, 891, 957, 977, 1004, 1013, 1045, 1100, 1148, 1151, 1165, 1187, 1928, 2504.

>>> The Second Nun's Tale: Source Studies <<<

1912   BEICHNER, PAUL E., C. S. C. "Confrontation, Contempt of Court, and Chaucer's Cecilia." ChauR 8 (1974), 198-204. [Jacobus de Voragine's Legenda Aurea and B. Mombritius's Sanctuarium seu vitae sanctorum]

1913   REAMES, SHERRY L. "The Cecilia Legend as Chaucer Inherited It and Retold It: The Disappearance of an Augustinian Idea." Speculum 55 (1980), 38-57. [Passio S. Caeciliae; Jacobus de Voragine, Legenda aurea]

1914   REAMES, SHERRY L. "The Sources of Chaucer's Second Nun's Tale." MP 76 (1978), 111-35. [Passio S. Caeciliae; Lipomanus-Metaphrastes; Middle English analogues]

1915   WATERHOUSE, RUTH. "'A Rose by Any Other Name': Two Versions of the Legend of Saint Cecilia." NM 79 (1978), 126-36. [Aelfric; Mombritius' Passio]

See also: 645, 1902, 1903, 1905, 1908, 1909, 1911.

THE CANON'S YEOMAN'S PROLOGUE AND TALE

1916   BROWN, DOROTHY H. "The Unreliable Narrator: The Canon's Yeoman." NLauR 12:1-2 (1982), 6-16.

1917   BROWN, PETER. "Is the Canon's Yeoman's Tale Apocryphal?" ES 64

Canterbury Tales

(1983), 481-90. [Hengwrt manuscript]

1918   CAMPBELL, JACKSON J.   "The Canon's Yeoman as Imperfect Paradigm."
       ChauR 17 (1982), 171-81.   [cf. ParsT]

1919   DICKSON, DONALD R.   "The 'Slidynge' Yeoman: The Real Drama in
       the Canon's Yeoman's Tale."   SCRev 2 (1985), 10-22.

1920   DUNCAN, EDGAR HILL.   "Chaucer and 'Arnald of the Newe Town':   A
       Reprise."   Interpretations 9 (1977), 7-11.   [De secretis
       naturae]

1921   ENGELHARDT, GEORGE J.   "The Lay Pilgrims of the Canterbury Tales:
       A Study in Ethology."   MS 36 (1974), 278-330.
       [ancient/medieval ethics]

1922   FELSEN, KARL E.   "Chaucer's Canon's Yeoman's Tale."   Expl 41:1
       (1982), 2.   [alchemy; rhetoric]

1923   HARTUNG, ALBERT E.   "'Pars Secunda' and the Development of the
       Canon's Yeoman's Tale."   ChauR 12 (1977), 111-28.   [Edward
       III; alchemy]

1924   KANNO, MASAHIKO.   "The Canon's Yeoman's Tale ni okeru 'craft' no
       Imi" [Implications of the Word "Craft" in The Canon's
       Yoeman's Tale].   Studies in Foreign Languages and Literatures
       18 (Aichi University of Education, 1982), 99-112.   In
       Japanese.

1925   RYAN, LAWRENCE V.   "The Canon's Yeoman's Desperate Confession."
       ChauR 8 (1974), 297-310.   [alchemy; Host]

1926   SCHMIDT, A. V. C., ed. and "Introduction," The General Prologue
       to the 'Canterbury Tales' and the Canon's Yeoman's Prologue
       and Tale.   New York: Holmes & Meier, 1976.   [+review of
       scholarship; commentary; alchemy, Holmyard, Rhazes, Jabir]
       See no. 208.

1927   SHIBATA, TAKEO.   "Chaucer's The Canon's Yeoman's Tale."   Shuru 48
       (1985), 1-16.   In Japanese.

1928   TAYLOR, PAUL B.   "The Canon's Yeoman's Breath: Emanations of a
       Metaphor."   ES 60 (1979), 380-88.   [parody of Divine
       creation; +SNT]

1929   WATANABE, IKUO.   "Three English Poetical Works and Alchemy: A
       Study."   Tenri Daigaku Gakuho 136 (Nara, 1982), 52-70.   In
       Japanese.   [+Donne; Jonson]

See also: 176, 208, 256, 271, 286, 364, 379, 430, 459, 561, 583, 587,
791, 859, 891, 957, 1004, 1005, 1007, 1011, 1037, 1040, 1041,
1077, 1100, 1131, 1135, 1174, 1285, 1599, 1775, 1943, 1954,
1980, 2106, 2662, 2759, 2787.

>>> The Canon's Yeoman's Tale: Source Studies <<<

See nos. 645, 1920, 1926.

THE MANCIPLE'S TALE

1930   ASKINS, WILLIAM. "The Historical Setting of The Manciple's
Tale." SAC 7 (1985), 87–105. [+Gaston Phoebus, Count of
Foix]

1931   BROWN, EMERSON, JR. "Word Play in the Prologue to the Manciple's
Tale, 98: 'T'acord and love and many a wrong apese'."
Chaucer Newsletter 2:2 (1980), 11–12.

1932   CROOK, E. J. and T. LAMBERT. "The Manciple: Typology of the
Traitor." LangQ 11:3–4 (1973), 15–16.

1933   DAVIDSON, ARNOLD E. "The Logic of Confusion in Chaucer's
Manciple's Tales." AnM 19 (1979), 5–12.

1934   DEAN, JAMES. "The Ending of the Canterbury Tales, 1952–1976."
TSLL 21 (1979), 17–33.

1935   DELANY, SHEILA. "Slaying Python: Marriage and Misogyny in a
Chaucerian Text," in 1006, pp. 47–75. [+PhyT; sources in
Ovid]

1936   DIEKSTRA, F. N. M. "Chaucer's Digressive Mode and the Moral of
the Manciple's Tale." Neophil 67 (1983), 131–48. [+analogue
in Machaut's Voir dit]

1937   FRADENBURG, LOUISE. "The Manciple's Servant Tongue: Politics
and Poetry in The Canterbury Tales." ELH 52 (1985), 85–118.

1938   FULK, R. D. "Reinterpreting the Manciple's Tale." JEGP 78

Canterbury Tales

(1979), 485–93. [+Cook]

1939 JEFFREY, DAVID L. "The Manciple's Tale: The Form of
Conclusion." ESC 2 (1976), 249–61.

1940 JONES, DONNA. "The Manciple's Diplomatic Immunity." TPB 21
(1984), 68.

1941 KANNO, MASAHIKO. "Manciple no Ito" [Manciple's Intention].
Studies in Foreign Languages and Literatures 20 (Aichi
University of Education, 1984), 1–13. In Japanese.

1942 KEARNEY, MARTIN. "Much Ado in a 'Litel Toun'." Innisfree
(1978), 30–41. [on "wyn ape" = fool's wine]

1943 MARSHALL, DAVID F. "A Note on Chaucer's Manciple's Tale 105–10."
Chaucer Newsletter 1:1 (1979), 17–18. [alchemy; CYT]

1944 PEARCY, ROY J. "Does the Manciple's Prologue Contain a Reference
to Hell's Mouth?" ELN 11:3 (1974), 167–75.

1945 SCATTERGOOD, V. J. "The Manciple's Manner of Speaking." EIC 24
(1974), 124–46. [Seven Deadly Sins]

1946 TRASK, RICHARD M. "The Manciple's Problem." SSF 14 (1977),
109–16. [satire on lawyers]

1947 TRAVERSI, DEREK. "The Manciple's Tale," in 562, pp. 120–44.

1948 WESTERVELT, L. A. "The Medieval Notion of Janglery and Chaucer's
Manciple's Tale." SoRA 14 (1981), 107–15. [+Ovid]

1949 WOOD, CHAUNCEY. "Speech, the Principle of Contraries, and
Chaucer's Tales of the Manciple and the Parson." Mediaevalia
6 (1980), 209–29.

See also: 189, 256, 330, 374, 375, 377, 407, 429, 481, 738, 841, 859,
891, 901, 957, 1000, 1004, 1017, 1038, 1048, 1068, 1072, 1112,
1121, 1144, 1159, 1165, 1188, 1905.

>>> The Manciple's Tale: Source Studies <<<

1950 DELANY, SHEILA. "Doer of the Word: The Epistle of St. James as
a Source for Chaucer's Manciple's Tale." ChauR 17 (1983),
250–54.

The Parson's Prologue and Tale

1951   WOOD, CHAUNCEY. "Speech, the Principle of Contraries, and
        Chaucer's Tales of the Manciple and the Parson." Mediaevalia
        6 (1980), 209-22. [Augustine, De Doctrina Christiana;
        Boethius, De Consolatione Philosophiae; RR; Martianus
        Capella, De Nuptiis Philologiae et Mercurii]

See also: 622, 1905, 1936, 1945, 1948.

THE PARSON'S PROLOGUE AND TALE

1952   BRASWELL, MARY FLOWERS. "Poet and Sinner: Literary
        Characterization and the Mentality of the Late Middle Ages."
        FCS 10 (1984), 39-56. [penitential motifs; irony; Host]

1953   BROWN, EMERSON, JR. "The Poet's Last Words: Text and Meaning at
        the End of the Parson's Prologue." ChauR 10 (1976), 236-42.
        [manuscript study]

1954   DELASANTA, RODNEY. "Penance and Poetry in the Canterbury Tales."
        PMLA 93 (1978), 240-47. [Last Supper; eschatology] See also
        nos. 1955, 1961.

1955   DELASANTA, RODNEY. Reply to William A. Kretzschmar. PMLA 93
        (1978), 1008. See also nos. 1954, 1961.

1956   FINKE, LAURIE A. "'To Knytte up al this Feeste': The Parson's
        Rhetoric and the Ending of the Canterbury Tales." LeedsSE,
        n. s., 15 (1984), 95-107. [closure; rhetoric]

1957   GLOWKA, ARTHUR W. "Chaucer's Parson and the Devil's Other Hand."
        Interpretations 14:2 (1983), 15-19. [Peraldus's Summa de
        Vitiis; Ovid's Metamorphoses]

1958   GRENNAN, EAMON. "Dual Characterization: A Note on Chaucer's Use
        of 'But' in the Portrait of the Parson." ChauR 16 (1982),
        195-201.

1959   HALLISSY, MARGARET M. "The She-Ape in Chaucer's Parson's Tale."
        ELWIU 9 (1982), 127-31. [symbolism]

1960   KASKE, CAROL V. "Getting Around the Parson's Tale: An
        Alternative to Allegory and Irony," in 67, pp. 147-78.

1961   KRETZSCHMAR, WILLIAM A., JR. "Chaucer Criticism." PMLA 93

Canterbury Tales

(1978), 1007–08. See also nos 1954, 1955.

1962   LUENGO, ANTHONY E. "Synthesis and Orthodoxy in Chaucer's
       Parson's Tale: An Analysis of the Concordance of Different
       Authoritative sententiae According to the Principles of the
       Medieval artes praedicandi." RUO 50 (1980), 223–32.
       [+Thomas Walleys, De modo componendi sermones]

1963   OLMERT, MICHAEL. "The Parson's Ludic Formula for Winning on the
       Road to Canterbury." ChauR 20 (1985), 158–68.

1964   PATTERSON, LEE W. "The Parson's Tale and the Quitting of the
       Canterbury Tales." Traditio 34 (1978) 331–80.

1965   PECK, RUSSELL A. "St. Paul and the Canterbury Tales."
       Mediaevalia 7 (1981), 91–131. [pilgrimage; +St. Paul]

1966   RUDAT, WOLFGANG H. "Chaucer's The Parson's Tale." Expl 42:1
       (1983), 6–8. [Augustine's The City of God]

1967   SHAW, JUDITH. "Corporal and Spiritual Homocide, the Sin of
       Wrath, and the Parson's Tale." Traditio 38 (1982), 281–300.
       [+canon-law tradition]

1968   SHIMOGASA, TOKUJI. "Chaucer's Colloquial Style in The Parson's
       Tale." Era, n. s., 2 (Hiroshima, 1981), 41–61. In English.

1969   SHIMOGASA, TOKUJI. "Chaucer's Parallelism in The Parson's Tale."
       Bulletin of Yamaguchi Women's University (Yamaguchi, 1982),
       11–27. In English.

1970   TAYLOR, PAUL BECKMAN. "The Parson's Amyable Tongue." ES 64
       (1983), 401–09.

1971   WENZEL, SIEGFRIED. "Chaucer's Parson's Tale: 'Every Tales
       Strengthe'," in Europäische Lehrdichtung. Festschrift für
       Walter Naumann zum 70. Geburtstag. Edited by Hans Gerd
       Rötzer and Herbert Walz. Darmstadt: Wissenschaftliche
       Buchgesellschaft, 1981, pp. 86–98.

1972   WURTELE, DOUGLAS. "The Penitence of Geoffrey Chaucer." Viator
       11 (1980), 335–61. [+Gascoigne]

See also: 94, 256, 271, 306, 316, 339, 440, 580, 581, 674, 783, 786,
           808, 817, 832, 891, 957, 970, 987, 1004, 1015, 1019, 1048,
           1054, 1058, 1062, 1077, 1079, 1106, 1107, 1112, 1115, 1120,
           1133, 1137, 1141, 1152, 1153, 1155, 1159, 1168, 1172, 1207,
           1223, 1320, 1681, 1682, 1698, 1835, 1918, 1949, 1955, 1961,

Chaucer's Retraction

1962, 1980, 1982, 2322, 2643, 2792, 2855, 2889.

>>> The Parson's Tale: Source Studies <<<

1973   CORREALE, ROBERT M. "Nicholas of Clairvaux and the Quotation
from 'Seint Bernard' in Chaucer's The Parson's Tale,
130–132." AN&Q 20 (1981), 2–3. [+San Ramon de Penyafort,
Summa de Casibus Poenitentiae; Saint Bernard de Clarivaux, De
Septem Gradibus Confessionis; Nicolas de Clairvaux, Sermo in
Festo Sancti Andreae]

1974   CORREALE, ROBERT M. "The Source of the Quotation from
'Crisostom' in The Parson's Tale." N&Q 27 (1980), 101–02.
[+St. Raymund of Pennaforte; "Sancti Iohannis Os Aureum"]

1975   CORREALE, ROBERT M. "The Sources of Some Patristic Quotations in
Chaucer's The Parson's Tale." ELN 19:2 (1981), 95–98.
[Pseudo-Augustine; Isidore of Seville; St. Jerome; St.
Gregory]

1976   WENZEL, SIEGFRIED. "Notes on the Parson's Tale." ChauR 16
(1982), 237–56. [treatises on the Seven Deadly Sins by
Pennaforte and Peraldus]

1977   WENZEL, SIEGFRIED. "The Source of Chaucer's Seven Deadly Sins."
Traditio 30 (1974), 351–78. [Peraldus, Summa de vitiis and
Quoniam]

1978   WENZEL, SIEGFRIED, ed. Summa Virtutum de Remediis Anime. The
Chaucer Library. Athens: The University of Georgia Press,
1984. 373 pp.
Reviews: Martha H. Fleming, CH 54 (1985), 397.

See also: 616, 617, 629, 645, 656, 1951, 1957, 1965, 1966, 1967.

CHAUCER'S RETRACTION

1979   KNAPP, ROBERT S. "Penance, Irony, and Chaucer's Retraction."
Assays 2 (1983), 45–67.

1980   KNIGHTEN, MERRELL A. "Yeoman, Parson, Poet: A Validation."
PAPA 8:1 (1982), 27–32. [+CYT, ParsT]

Canterbury Tales

1981   MARSHALL, DAVID F. "Unmasking the Last Pilgrim: How and Why
        Chaucer Used the Retraction to Close The Tales of
        Canterbury." C&L 31:4 (1982), 55-74. [+ParsT]

1982   McGERR, ROSEMARIE POTZ. "Retraction and Memory: Retrospective
        Structure in the Canterbury Tales." CL 37 (1985), 97-113.

1983   SCHRICKER, GALE C. "On the Relation of Fact and Fiction in
        Chaucer's Poetic Endings." PQ 60 (1981), 13-27. [+closure;
        persona]

See also: 130, 187, 224, 286, 377, 407, 759, 1004, 1038, 1112, 1121,
           1954, 1964, 1972, 2755.

LONGER WORKS OTHER THAN THE CANTERBURY TALES

ANELIDA AND ARCITE

1984   GILLAM, DOREEN M. E. "Lovers and Riders in Chaucer's Anelida and
        Arcite." ES 63 (1982), 394–401.

1985   NORTON-SMITH, JOHN. "Chaucer's Anelida and Arcite," in 62, pp.
        81–99.

See also: 22, 180, 181, 187, 188, 224, 256, 263, 281, 285, 364, 417,
           425, 429, 459, 555, 841, 859, 891, 1625.

>>> Anelida and Arcite: Source Studies <<<

See nos. 597, 605, 608, 654, 841, 859, 891, 1311, 1625, 2498.

ASTROLABE

1986   CARTER, TOM. "Geoffrey Chaucer: Amateur Astronomer?" Sky and
        Telescope 63 (1982), 246–47. [+Equat]

1987   EISNER, SIGMUND. "Chaucer as a Technical Writer." ChauR 19
        (1985), 179–201. [Astr, Equat]

1988   JAMBECK, THOMAS J. and KAREN K. JAMBECK. "Chaucer's Treatise on
        the Astrolabe: A Handbook for the Medieval Child," in
        Children's Literature: The Great Excluded. Vol. III.
        Edited by Francelia Butler and Bennett A. Brockman. Storrs,
        CT: Children's Literature Association, pp. 117–22.

1989   LIPSON, CAROL. "'I n'am but a lewd compilator': Chaucer's

Longer Works other than The Canterbury Tales

>Treatise on the Astrolabe< as Translation." NM 84 (1983), 192-200.

1990　NAGUCKA, RUTA. The Syntactic Component of Chaucer's 'Astrolabe'. Zeszyty Naukowe Uniwersytetu Jagiellońskiego, 199 (Kraków), Prace Językoznawcze Zeszyt, 23. Cracow: University Jagielloniensis, 1968. 123 pp.
Reviews: Horst Weinstock, Anglia 92 (1974), 201-03.

1991　OVITT, GEORGE, JR. "A Late Medieval Technical Directive: Chaucer's Treatise on the Astrolabe," in Proceedings: 28th International Technical Communication Conference, May 20-23, 1981. Pittsburgh, PA: Society for Technical Communication, 1981, pp. E/78-81.

See also:　130, 224, 286, 316, 440, 481, 555, 831, 891, 1019, 1332, 2650, 2841a.

>>> Astrolabe: Source Studies <<<

1992　MASI, MICHAEL. "Chaucer, Massahala, and Bodleian Selden Supra 78." Manuscripta 19 (1975), 36-47.

See also:　616, 617, 1989.

BOETHIUS

1993　DONNER, MORTON. "Derived Words in Chaucer's Boece: The Translator as Wordsmith." ChauR 18 (1984), 187-203. [+English translation of Boethius: De Consolatione Philosophiae]

1994　ECKHARDT, CAROLINE D. "The Medieval Prosimetrum Genre from Boethius to Boece." Genre 16:1 (1983), 21-38.

1995　FISCHER, OLGA. "A Comparative Study of Philosophical Terms in the Alfredian and Chaucerian Boethius." Neophil 63 (1979), 622-39.

1996　MACHAN, TIM WILLIAM. "Chaucer as Philologist: The Boece." DAI 45 (1984), 1393A. University of Wisconsin-Madison.

[Chaucer's translation of Boethius]

1997   MACHAN, TIM WILLIAM. "Forlynen: A Ghost Word Rematerializes."
        N&Q, n. s., 31 (1984), 22-24. [Jean de Meun's forlignier]

1998   MACHAN, TIM WILLIAM. Techniques of Translation: Chaucer's
        'Boece'. Norman, OK: Pilgrim Books, 1985. 163 pp.

1999   MINNIS, ALASTAIR. "Aspects of the Medieval French and English
        Tradition of the De Consolatione Philosophiae," in Boethius:
        His Life, Thought and Influence. Edited by Margaret Gibson.
        Oxford: Blackwell, 1981, pp. 312-61.

2000   OIZUMI, AKIO. "Chaucer and Jean de Meun: Their Translations of
        Boethius's De Consolatione Philosophiae." EigoS 131 (1985),
        294-96. In Japanese.

2001   SHIRLEY, PEGGY FAYE. "'Fals Felicite and Verray Blisfulnesse':
        Alfred and Chaucer Translate Boethius's Consolation of
        Philosophy." DAI 38 (1977), 1417-18A. University of
        Mississippi.

See also: 100, 103, 130, 152, 285, 293, 311, 316, 425, 440, 687, 703,
           891, 895, 2518.

>>> Boethius: Source Studies <<<

See nos. 619, 630, 646, 663.

BOOK OF THE DUCHESS

2002   AERS, DAVID R. "Chaucer's Book of the Duchess: An Art to
        Consume Art." DUJ 38 (1977), 201-05. [+rhetoric]

2003   BARTLETT, LEE A. "Sometimes a Cigar is Just a Cigar: The
        Dreamer in Chaucer's Book of the Duchess." Thoth 15:1
        (1974-75), 3-11.

2004   BEER, FRANCES. "The Pearl and the Book of the Duchess: Two
        Studies in Coming to Terms with Death." BForum 5 (1980),
        260-64. [+Kübler-Ross]

Longer Works other than The Canterbury Tales

2005   BOARDMAN, PHILLIP C. "Courtly Language and the Strategy of
        Consolation in the Book of the Duchess." ELH 44 (1977),
        567-79.

2006   BROSNAHAN, LEGER. "Now (This), Now (That) and BD 646," in 43,
        pp. 11-18.

2007   CHERNISS, MICHAEL D. "The Narrator Asleep and Awake in Chaucer's
        Book of the Duchess." PLL 8 (1972), 115-26. See also JEGP
        68 (1969), 655-65.

2008   CLARK, JOHN FRANK. "The Hunt as Metaphor: A Study of the Theme
        of Death in Four Middle English Poems." DAI 43 (1983),
        3490A. University of Wisconsin-Madison, 1982. [+The
        Parlement of the Thre Ages, Sir Gawain and the Green Knight,
        The Awntyrs off Arthure at the Terne Wathelyn]

2009   CONDREN, EDWARD I. "Of Deaths and Duchesses and Scholars
        Coughing in Ink." ChauR 10 (1975), 87-95. Reply to Palmer,
        no. 2039, below.

2010   DiLORENZO, RAYMOND DOUGLAS. "The Therapy of Epideictic Discourse
        in Chaucer's Book of the Duchess: Study of a Rhetorical
        Event." DAI 36 (1975), 1521-22A. University of Toronto,
        1974.

2011   DiLORENZO, RAYMOND D[OUGLAS]. "'Wonder and Words': Paganism,
        Christianity, and Consolation in Chaucer's Book of the
        Duchess." UTQ 52 (1982), 20-39.

2012   DINZELBACHER, PETER. Vision und Visionsliteratur im Mittelalter.
        Monographien zur Geschichte des Mittelalters, 23. Stuttgart:
        Hiersemann, 1981. [+Langland; BD, HF, LGW, PF]
            Reviews: F. Wagner, Fabula 23:3-4 (Berlin, 1981-82), 313.

2013   EBI, HISATO. "Light and Darkness in The Book of the Duchess--The
        'Aesthetics of Light' of Gothic Art." The Journal of The
        Liberal Arts Department, Kansai Medical University (December,
        1980), 15-126. [+Pseudo Dionysius Areopagita]

2014   EDWARDS, ROBERT. "The Book of the Duchess and the Beginnings of
        Chaucer's Narrative." NLH 13 (1982), 189-204. [+Dante's
        Vita Nuova]

2015   ELLMANN, MAUD. "Blanche," in Criticism and Critical Theory.
        Edited by Jeremy Hawthorn. Stratford-Upon-Avon Studies, 2nd
        Series. London: Arnold, 1984, pp. 98-110. [Freud, Lacan]

2016   FERRIS, SUMNER. "John Stow and the Tomb of Blanche the Duchess."

ChauR 18 (1983), 92-93. See Palmer, no. 2039, below.

2017 FERSTER, JUDITH ILANA. "Chaucer and l'art veritable: The
      Epistemology of Art in Two Early Dream Visions and Two of
      their French Sources. DAI 35 (1975), 7253-54A. Brown
      University, 1974. [RR; De planctu naturae]

2018 FERSTER, JUDITH [ILANA]. "Intention and Interpretation in the
      Book of the Duchess." Criticism 22 (1980), 1-24.

2019 FICHTE, JOERG O. "The Book of the Duchess--A Consolation?" SN
      45 (1973), 53-67.

2020 FYLER, JOHN M. "Irony and the Age of Gold in the Book of the
      Duchess." Speculum 52 (1977), 314-28.

2021 HARRIS, DUNCAN and NANCY L. STEFFEN. "The Other Side of the
      Garden: An Interpretive Comparison of Chaucer's Book of the
      Duchess and Spenser's Daphnaida." JMRS 8 (1978), 17-36.

2022 HILL, JOHN M. "The Book of the Duchess, Melancholy, and That
      Eight-Year Sickness." ChauR 9 (1974), 35-50.

2023 HOLLIS, STEPHANIE. "The Ceyx and Alceone Story in The Book of
      the Duchess." Parergon 19 (1977), 3-9.

2024 JOHNSON, WILLIAM C., JR. "Art as Discovery: The Aesthetics of
      Consolation in Chaucer's Book of the Duchess." SAB 40:2
      (1975), 53-62.

2025 JORDAN, ROBERT M. "The Compositional Structure of the Book of
      the Duchess." ChauR 9 (1974), 99-117. [+rhetoric]

2026 JULIUS, PATRICIA WARD. "Appearance and Reality in Chaucer's
      Early Dream-Visions." DAI 37 (1976), 3606-07A. Michigan
      State University. [+HF]

2027 KAISER, ULRIKE. "Die 'Schwurszene' in Chaucers Book of the
      Duchess." Euphorion 75 (1981), 110-17. [+source, Machaut's
      Judgement dou Roy de Behaingne]

2028 KISER, LISA J. "Sleep, Dreams, and Poetry in Chaucer's Book of
      the Duchess." PLL 19 (1983), 3-12.

2029 KNEDLIK, WILL ROGER. "Chaucer's Book of the Duchess: A
      Bibliographical Compendium of the First 600 Years." DAI 39
      (1978), 1538-39A. University of Washington.

2030 KRONLINS, IEVA. "The Still Point: Artifice in Chaucer's Book of

Longer Works other than The Canterbury Tales

the Duchess." Centerpoint 1:1 (1974), 73–81.

2031   LACKEY, ALLEN D. "Chaucer's Book of the Duchess, 330." Expl 32:9 (1974), 74. [Jason/Medea]

2032   LOGAN, HARRY M. and BARRY W. MILLER. "A Case for The Book of the Duchess: A Semantic Analysis of Sentence Structure," in Sixth International Conference on Computers and the Humanities. Edited by Sarah K. Burton and Douglas D. Short. Rockville, MD: Computer Science Press, 1983, pp. 384–90. [concordance]

2033   LOSCHIAVO, LINDA ANN. "The Birth of 'Blanche the Duchesse': 1340 versus 1347." ChauR 13 (1978), 128–32.

2034   MANNING, STEPHEN. "Rhetoric as Therapy: The Man in Black, Dorigen, and Chauntecleer." KPAB (1978), 19–25.

2035   MARTIN, ELLEN ELIZABETH. "'Be Processe of Tyme': Chaucer's Invention of Poetry in the Book of the Duchess." DAI 44 (1984), 3073A. City University of New York, 1983.

2036   MARTIN, ELLEN E[LIZABETH]. "The Interpretation of Chaucer's Alcyone." ChauR 18 (1983), 18–22. [+Ovid's Ceyx and Alcyone; Petrarch; Boccaccio]

2037   MORSE, RUTH. "Understanding the Man in Black." ChauR 15 (1981), 204–08.

2038   NEAMAN, JUDITH S. "Brain Physiology and Poetics in The Book of the Duchess." RPLit 3 (1980), 101–13. [melancholy]

2039   PALMER, JOHN N. "The Historical Context of the Book of the Duchess: A Revision." ChauR 8 (1974), 253–61. [+date of poem] See no. 2009.

2040   PAUL, JAMES ALLEN. "Aporia and Pearl: Medieval Narrative Irony." DAI 38 (1977), 3476A. University of Michigan. [+irony in BD]

2041   PELEN, MARC M. "Machaut's Court of Love Narratives and Chaucer's Book of the Duchess." ChauR 11 (1976), 128–55. [+Froissart]

2042   PERRYMAN, JUDTH C. "How They Talk: Speech and Meaning in The Book of the Duchess." NM 85 (1984), 227–38.

2043   PHILIPS, HELEN. "Structure and Consolation in the Book of the Duchess." ChauR 16 (1981), 107–18. [+Boethius]

2044   PIGOTT, MARGARET B. "The Dialectic of The Book of the Duchess
        and The Parliament of Fowls: A Movement Toward the Fifteenth
        Century." FCS 5 (1982), 167-90.

2045   PIGOTT, MARGARET B. "Progressive Skepticism in Chaucer: A
        Comparative Study of The Book of the Duchess and The
        Parliament of Fowls." DAI 35 (1975), 7266A. University of
        Detroit, 1974.

2046   RICHMOND, VELMA BOURGEOIS. "Chaucer's The Book of the Duchess
        and Guy of Warwick." PLL 11 (1975), 404-07.

2047   ROBERTSON, D. W., JR. "The Book of the Duchess," in 70, pp.
        403-13.

2048   ROSCOW, G. H. "From Sentence to 'Sentence' in a Medieval Poem."
        EiP 9:1 (1984), 78-94.

2049   ROSS, DIANE M. "The Play of Genres in the Book of the Duchess."
        ChauR 19 (1984), 1-13.

2050   SALTER, ELIZABETH. "Chaucer and Internationalism." SAC 2
        (1980), 71-79.

2051   SCHLESS, HOWARD. "A Dating for the Book of the Duchess: Line
        1314." ChauR 19 (1985), 273-76.

2052   SHOAF, R[ICHARD] A[LLEN]. "'Mutatio Amoris': 'Penitentia' and
        the Form of The Book of the Duchess." Genre 14 (1981),
        163-89. [+RR; Robert Mannyng, Handlyng Synne, penitential
        imagery]

2053   SHOAF, RICHARD ALLEN. "'Mutatio Amoris': Revision and Penitence
        in Chaucer's The Book of the Duchess." DAI 38 (1978), 4812A.
        Cornell University, 1977. [+Boethius; Ovid]

2054   SHOAF, R[ICHARD] A[LLEN]. "Stalking the Sorrowful H(e)art:
        Penitential Lore and the Hunt Scene in Chaucer's The Book of
        the Duchess." JEGP 78 (1979), 313-24.

2055   SPEARING, A. C. "Literal and Figurative in The Book of the
        Duchess," in 72, pp. 165-71.

2056   STEINLE, ERIC MARTIN. "The Medieval Lyric Romance." DAI 45
        (1985), 2869A. University of California at Berkeley, 1984.
        [comparison with sources]

2057   SUZUKI, TETSUYA. "The Art of Restatement in the Book of the
        Duchess." Shiron 23 (1984), 1-21. [elegy]

Longer Works other than The Canterbury Tales

2058   THIEBAUX, MARCELLE. The Stag of Love: The Chase in Medieval
Literature. Ithaca and London: Cornell University Press,
1974. 249 pp. [hunt in literature; allegory; symbolism;
amatory chase; hart/heart pun in BD; hunt in TC]
  Reviews: Derek Pearsall, RES 27 (1976), 200–03; Anne
Kernan, JEGP 75 (1976), 407–09; Kenneth Varty, MLR 71 (1976),
117–18; J. H. Fisher, Speculum 52 (1977), 437–39; P. B.
Taylor, ES 58 (1977), 242–45; Howard Helsinger, MP 76 (1978),
66–69.

2059   THOMS, JOHN CLIFTON. "Looking at Death: A Study in the Literary
and Historical Background of Chaucer's Book of the Duchess."
DAI 42 (1981), 208A. Columbia University, 1979. [+Henry,
Duke of Lancaster]

2060   TRIPP, RAYMOND P., JR. "The Dialectics of Debate and the
Continuity of English Poetry." MSE 7:1 (1978–80), 41–51.
[+conversion of Dreamer]

2061   UTLEY, FRANCES MAE. "The Hunt as Structural Paradigm in The Book
of the Duchess." DAI 35 (1975), 6684A. Columbia University,
1974.

2062   WALKER, DENIS. "Narrative Inconclusiveness and Consolatory
Dialectic in the Book of the Duchess." ChauR 18 (1983),
1–17. [closure]

2063   WIMSATT, JAMES I. "The Book of the Duchess: Secular Elegy or
Religious Vision?" in 61, pp. 113–29.

2064   ZIMBARDO, ROSE A. "The Book of the Duchess and the Dream of
Folly." ChauR 18 (1984), 329–46. [archetypal Fool]

See also: 98, 130, 180, 181, 188, 205, 224, 240, 242, 255, 256, 263,
264, 265, 267, 275, 280, 286, 293, 294, 299, 311, 346, 348,
349, 355, 359, 362, 363, 368, 369, 374, 375, 377, 379, 402,
407, 409, 425, 427, 430, 432, 433, 437, 447, 450, 451, 458,
474, 475, 478, 510, 517, 532, 547, 550, 563, 574, 581, 584,
586, 587, 718, 769, 814, 830, 851, 859, 866, 891, 903, 907,
1007, 1038, 1090, 1098, 2068a, 2147, 2197, 2273, 2523, 2621,
2631, 2665, 2667, 2866.

>>> The Book of the Duchess: Source Studies <<<

2065   MINNIS, A. J. "A Note on Chaucer and the Ovide moralisé." MAE

48 (1979), 254-58. [Ceyx and Alcione]

2066   NOLAN, BARBARA. "The Art of Expropriation: Chaucer's Narrator
        in The Book of the Duchess," in 68, pp. 203-22. [Jean
        Froissart, Paradys d'amour; Guillaume de Machaut, Dit de la
        fonteinne amoureuse]

2067   PALMER, R. BARTON. "The Book of the Duchess and Fonteinne
        amoureuse: Chaucer and Machaut Reconsidered." CRCL 7
        (1981), 380-93. [Machaut]

2068   PALMER, R. BARTON, ed. and trans. The Judgement of the King of
        Bohemia [Le Jugement dou roy de Behaingne by Guillaume de
        Machaut]. Garland Library of Medieval Literature, A/9. New
        York and London: Garland, 1984. 104 pp.
        Reviews: Howard B. Garey, Speculum 61 (1986), 153-55.

2068a   RICHARDS, M. J. B. "Translation, Borrowing and Original
        Composition in Medieval Poetry: Studies in the
        Metamorphoses, the Ovide Moralisé and in the Book of the
        Duchess." Doct. diss., University of Cambridge, 1982.

2069   WIMSATT, JAMES. "Machaut's Lay de Comfort and Chaucer's Book of
        the Duchess," in 67, pp. 11-26.

See also: 432, 611, 613, 618, 630, 637, 645, 650, 658, 663, 2001, 2014,
           2017, 2027, 2035, 2036, 2041, 2043, 2046, 2052, 2053, 2054,
           2056, 2059, 2063.

HOUSE OF FAME

2070   BENNETT, J. A. W. Chaucer's 'Book of Fame': An Exposition of
        'The House of Fame'. Oxford: Clarendon Press, 1968. 205
        pp.
        Reviews: Juliette De Caluwé-Dor, RBPH 52 (1974), 266-67.

2071   BERRY, REGINALD. "Chaucer's Eagle and the Element Air." UTQ 43
        (1974), 285-97. [sources; iconography]

2072   BILLINGTON, SANDRA. "'Suffer Fools Gladly': The Fool in
        Medieval England and the Play Mankind," in The Fool and the
        Trickster: Studies in Honour of Enid Welsford. Edited by
        Paul V. A. Williams. Cambridge: Brewer; Totowa, NJ: Rowman
        & Littlefield, pp. 36-54.

Longer Works other than The Canterbury Tales

2073   BOITANI, PIERO. Chaucer and the Imaginary World of Fame.
        Cambridge: D. S. Brewer; Totowa, NJ: Barnes & Noble, 1984.
        [Homer; Scholastics; Italian trecento; linguistic theory;
        archetypal imagery; closure]
        Reviews: Nicholas R. Havely, SAC 7 (1985), 167-70.

2074   BOITANI, PIERO. "Chaucer's Labyrinth: Fourteenth-Century
        Literature and Language." ChauR 17 (1983), 197-220.
        [+Dante; Boccaccio]

2074a   BOITANI, PIERO. "An Idea of Fourteenth-Century Literature," in
        2064, pp. 11-31. [HF, BD]

2075   BOYD, HEATHER. "Chauntecleer and the Eagle." ESA 21 (1978),
        65-69.

2076   BRASWELL, MARY FLOWERS. "Architectural Portraiture in Chaucer's
        House of Fame." JMRS 11 (1981), 101-12. [Temple of Venus;
        House of Fame and Rumor; Henry Yevele]

2077   BRIDGES, MARGARET. "The Sense of an Ending: The Case of the
        Dream-Vision." DQR 14 (1984), 81-96. [closure]

2078   CHIAPPELLI, CAROLYN PACE. "Chaucer's Anti-Scholasticism:
        Opposition and Composition in the House of Fame." DAI 38
        (1978), 4839A. University of California, Los Angeles, 1977.
        [pilgrimage, tidings, and false appearances; Satan]

2079   CHIAPPELLI, CAROLYN [PACE]. "Fals Apparences: Satan and
        Chaucer's House of Fame." PPMRC 4 (1979), 107-14.

2080   DANE, JOSEPH A. "Chaucer's Eagle's Ovid's Phaethon: A Study in
        Literary Reception." JMRS 11 (1981), 71-82.

2081   DANE, JOSEPH A. "Chaucer's House of Fame and the Rota Virgilii."
        CML 1 (1980), 57-75. [Aeneid; Georgics; Bucolics]

2082   DANE, JOSEPH A. "Yif I 'Arma Virumque' Kan: Note on Chaucer's
        House of Fame Line 143." AN&Q 19 (1981), 134-36. [Aeneid]

2083   DAVID, ALFRED. "How Marcia Lost Her Skin: A Note on Chaucer's
        Mythology," in 43, pp. 19-29.

2084   DELANY, SHEILA. Chaucer's 'House of Fame': The Poetics of
        Skeptical Fideism. Chicago and London: University of
        Chicago Press, 1972. 143 pp.
        Reviews: Laurence Eldredge, HAR 24 (1973), 325-27; Beryl
        Rowland, UTQ 44 (1974), 79-80; John M. Steadman, MAE 43

(1974), 289–91; P. G. Ruggiers, Speculum 50 (1975), 717–20; Lee Ramsey, Cithara 14 (1975), 118–22; Laurence K. Shook, MP 72 (1975), 290–92.

2085 DICKERSON, A. INSKIP. "Chaucer's House of Fame: A Skeptical Epistemology of Love." TSLL 18 (1976), 171–83.

2086 EAST, W. G. "'Lollius'." ES 58 (1977), 396–98. [Boccaccio]

2087 ERZGRÄBER, WILLI. "Problems of Oral and Written Transmission as Reflected in Chaucer's House of Fame," in 41, pp. 113–28.

2088 FRY, DONALD K. "The Ending of the House of Fame," in 67, pp. 27–40.

2089 GELLRICH, J. M. "The Origin of Language Reconsidered: Chaucer's House of Fame," Chapter 5 in 365, pp. 167–201. [indetermina cy]

2090 GIACCHERINI, ENRICO. "Una 'crux' chauceriana: I sogni nella House of Fame." RLM 27 (1974), 165–76. [dreams; Macrobius]

2091 HOWARD, DONALD R. "Chaucer's Idea of an Idea." E&S 29 (1976), 39–55.

2092 IKEGAMI, TADAHIRO. "The Gothic Structure of Chaucer's House of Fame." SeijoB 105 (1983), 185–96. In English.

2093 IKEGAMI, TADAHIRO. "The Structure of Chaucer's House of Fame." SeijoB 105 (Tokyo, 1983), 27–38. In English.

2094 IRVINE, MARTIN. "Medieval Grammatical Theory and Chaucer's House of Fame." Speculum 60 (1985), 850–66. [artes grammaticae]

2095 ISENOR, NEIL and KEN WOOLNER. "Chaucer's Theory of Sound." Physics Today 3 (1980), 114–16.

2096 JEFFREY, DAVID LYLE. "Sacred and Secular Scripture: Authority and Interpretation in The House of Fame," in 63, pp. 207–28. [Aeneas; Biblical language]

2097 JORDAN, ROBERT M. "Lost in the Funhouse of Fame: Chaucer and Postmodernism." ChauR 18 (1983), 100–15. [+Nabokov, solipsism; Barth; Joyce; Postmodernism; +HF]

2098 JOYNER, WILLIAM. "Parallel Journeys in Chaucer's House of Fame." PLL 12 (1976), 3–19. [+Aeneas]

2099 KANNO, MASAHIKO. "The Meaning of The House of Fame," in Essays

Longer Works other than The Canterbury Tales

in Honour of Professor Hiroshige Yoshida. Shinozaki Shorin
Press, 1980, pp. 47-57. [everyday speech]

2100   KELLEY, MICHAEL R. "Chaucer's House of Fame: England's Earliest
Science Fiction." Extrapolation 16:1 (1974), 7-16.

2101   KENDRICK, LAURA. "Fame's Fabrication," in 72, pp. 135-48.
[Froissart, Christine de Pisan]

2102   LEANA, JOYCE F. "Chaucer the Word-Master: The House of Fame and
the Canterbury Tales." DAI 35 (1974), 1049-50A. Columbia
University.

2103   LORRAH, JEAN. "The Shamanistic Vision in Fantastic Poetry," in
The Scope of the Fantastic--Culture, Biography, Themes,
Children's Literature: Selected Essays from the First
International Conference on the Fantastic in Literature and
Film. Edited by Robert A. Collins and Howard D. Pearce, III.
Westport, CT, and London: Greenwood Press, 1985, pp.
199-204. [eagle as guide]

2104   MAGOUN, FRANCIS P., JR. and TAUNO F. MUSTANOJA. "Chaucer's
Chimera: His Proto-Surrealist Portrait of Fame." Speculum
50 (1975), 48-54.

2105   MEADE, BR. ROBERT. "The Saints and the Problem of Fame in the
House of Fame." NM 84 (1983), 201-05.

2106   MERLO, CAROLYN. "Chaucer's Phaethon: 'The Sonnes Sone, the
Rede', House of Fame, II, 941." ELN 17:2 (1979), 88-90.

2107   MILLER, JACQUELINE T. "The Writing on the Wall: Authority and
Authorship in Chaucer's House of Fame." ChauR 17 (1982),
95-115.

2108   NEWMAN, FRANCIS X. "'Partriches Wynges': A Note on House of
Fame, 1391-92." Mediaevalia 6 (1980), 231-38. [Ovid:
Metamorphoses]

2109   PAYNE, ROBERT O. "Late Medieval Images and Self-Images of the
Poet: Chaucer, Gower, Lydgate, Henryson, Dunbar," in 57, pp.
249-61.

2110   RIEHLE, WOLFGANG. "Chaucer's House of Fame and the Dream-Journey
of Thomas Mann's Joseph." ArAA 10 (1985), 11-20.
[comparison]

2111   ROWLAND, BERYL. "The Art of Memory and the Art of Poetry in the
House of Fame." RUO 51 (1981), 162-71.

2112   ROWLAND, BERYL. "Bishop Bradwardine, the Artificial Memory, and
        the House of Fame," in 67, pp. 41-62. [Cicero, Ad Herennium
        and Bradwardine]

2113   SHEPHERD, GEOFFREY T. "Make Believe: Chaucer's Rationale of
        Storytelling in The House of Fame," in 71, pp. 204-20.

2114   SHOOK, LAURENCE K. "The House of Fame," in 70, pp. 414-27.

2115   STEVENSON, KAY. "The Endings of Chaucer's House of Fame." ES 59
        (1978), 10-26.

2116   TERESA, SISTER MARGARET, S. S. J. "Chaucer's High Rise: Aldgate
        and The House of Fame." ABR 33 (1982), 162-71.

2117   VANCE, EUGENE. "Chaucer's House of Fame and the Poetics of
        Inflation." Boundary 7:2 (1979), 17-37.

2118   WATTS, ANN C. "'Amor gloriae' in Chaucer's House of Fame." JMRS
        3 (1973), 87-113.

See also: 130, 180, 181, 187, 224, 232, 240, 242, 255, 256, 263, 265,
             268, 271, 275, 277, 280, 281, 285, 286, 293, 294, 299, 302,
             308, 311, 331, 348, 359, 362, 363, 364, 378, 379, 394, 407,
             409, 410, 417, 427, 430, 451, 458, 460, 474, 485, 497, 517,
             534, 540, 545, 547, 548, 555, 566, 577, 580, 581, 586, 589,
             678, 697, 728, 830, 851, 859, 891, 907, 923, 1168, 1174, 1858,
             2012, 2026, 2074a, 2147, 2197, 2273, 2621, 2665, 2667, 2669,
             2866.

>>> House of Fame: Source Studies <<<

2119   CARR, JOHN. "A Borrowing from Tibullus in Chaucer's House of
        Fame." ChauR 8 (1974), 191-97.

2120   GRENNEN, JOSEPH E. "Chaucer and Chalcidius: The Platonic
        Origins of the Hous of Fame." Viator 15 (1984), 237-62.
        [Timaeus]

2121   KENDRICK, LAURA. "Chaucer's House of Fame and the French Palais
        de Justice." SAC 6 (1984), 121-33.

2122   OVERBECK, PAT TREFZGER. "The 'Man of Gret Auctorite' in
        Chaucer's House of Fame." MP 73 (1975), 157-61. [RR;
        Panthère d'amours; La dance aux aveugles; Trionfo d'amore]

Longer Works other than The Canterbury Tales

See also: 592, 598, 618, 629, <u>645</u>, 650, <u>654</u>, 658, 659, <u>664</u>, 2071, 2073, 2074, 2080, 2081, 2082, 2090, <u>2093</u>, 2096, 2101, 2104, 2108, 2112, 2113, 2116.

LEGEND OF GOOD WOMEN

2123   ALLEN, PETER LEWIS. "Love Oft Expressed: Conventions and Irony in Ovid's <u>Amores, Aucassin et Nicolette,</u> and Chaucer's <u>Legend of Good Women.</u>" <u>DAI</u> 45 (1985), 2516-17A. University of Chicago, 1984.

2124   BREWER, DEREK. <u>Towards a Chaucerian Poetic.</u> London: Oxford University Press, 1974. 36 pp. [rpt. from <u>PBA</u> 60 (1974)]

2125   COWEN, JANET M. "Chaucer's <u>Legend of Good Women:</u> Structure and Tone." <u>SP</u> 82 (1985), 416-36.

2126   DESMOND, MARILYNN. "Chaucer's <u>Aeneid:</u> 'The Naked Text in English'." <u>PCP</u> 19 (1984), 62-67. [Virgil and Ovid]

2127   FEIMER, JOEL NICHOLAS. "The Figure of Medea in Medieval Literature: A Thematic Metamorphosis." <u>DAI</u> 44 (1984), 3057A. City University of New York, 1983. [+Gower, <u>Confessio Amantis;</u> Guido delle Colonne, <u>Historia Destructionis Troiae;</u> Boccaccio, <u>De Mulieribus Claris;</u> Benoît de Sainte-Maure, <u>Roman de Troie</u>]

2128   FISHER, JOHN H. "The <u>Legend of Good Women,</u>" in 70, pp. 464-76.

2129   FISHER, JOHN H. "The Revision of the Prologue to the <u>Legend of Good Women:</u> An Occasional Explanation." <u>SAB</u> 43:4 (1978), 75-84. [marriage of Richard II to Isabel in 1396]

2130   FRANK, ROBERT W[ORTH], JR. <u>Chaucer and 'The Legend of Good Women'.</u> Cambridge, MA: Harvard University Press, 1972; London: Oxford University Press, 1973. 229 pp.
Reviews: G. C. Britton, <u>N&Q</u> 21 (1974), 303-04; Janet M. Cowen, <u>MAE</u> 43 (1974), 291-93; Dieter Mehl, <u>Anglia</u> 93 (1975), 237-40; C. R. Blyth, <u>Speculum</u> 50 (1975), 305-07; S. S. Hussey, <u>MLR</u> 70 (1975), 387-89; J. H. Fisher, <u>MP</u> 72 (1975), 292-94; Peter J. Lucas, <u>Studies</u> 71 (1982), 309-10.

2131   FRANK, ROBERT WORTH, JR. "The <u>Legend of Good Women:</u> Some

Implications," in 67, pp. 63–76.

2132   GAYLORD, ALAN. "Dido at Hunt, Chaucer at Work." ChauR 17
        (1983), 300–15.

2133   GELLRICH, J. M. "Problems of Misreading: The 'Prologue' to The
        Legend of Good Women," Chapter 6 in 365, pp. 202–23.

2134   GUERIN, DOROTHY JANE. "The Art of Variation in Chaucer's Legend
        of Good Women." DAI 38 (1978), 4149A. University of
        Colorado at Boulder, 1977.

2135   GUERIN, DOROTHY [JANE]. "Chaucer's Pathos: Three Variations."
        ChauR 20 (1985), 90–112. [+PrT, MLT, PhyT]

2136   HAHN, THOMAS. "Natural Supernaturalism in the Prologue to the
        Legend of Good Women." Chaucer Newsletter 1:1 (1979), 7–8.

2137   HANNING, ROBERT W. "Poetic Emblems in Medieval Narrative Texts,"
        in 57, pp. 1–32, esp. 24–28. [Alceste as Chrisitan
        transformation]

2138   HANSEN, ELAINE TUTTLE. "Irony and the Antifeminist Narrator in
        Chaucer's Legend of Good Women." JEGP 82 (1983), 11–31.
        [+closure]

2139   KANE, GEORGE. "The Text of The Legend of Good Women in CUL MS
        Gg.4.27," in 59, pp. 39–58. [textual criticism]

2140   KISER, LISA JEAN. "In Service of the Flower: Chaucer and the
        Legend of Good Women." DAI 39 (1979), 4275A. University of
        Virginia, 1977. [+TC, Rom]

2141   KISER, LISA J[EAN]. Telling Classical Tales: Chaucer and 'The
        Legend of Good Women'. Ithaca, NY: Cornell University
        Press, 1983. [as defense of Chaucer's poetry]
            Reviews: VQR 60:3 (1984), 82; Mary Shaner, Speculum 60
        (1985), 691–93.

2142   KOLVE, V. A. "From Cleopatra to Alceste: An Iconographic Study
        of The Legend of Good Women," in 61, pp. 130–78.

2143   LANIER, SIDNEY. "The Flower of the Imagination: French
        Marguerite Poetry and Chaucer's Prologue to The Legend of
        Good Women." DAI 37 (1977), 5800A. University of
        California, Santa Barbara, 1976. [+Deschamps; Froissart;
        Machaut]

2144   McMILLAN, ANN HUNTER. "'Evere an Hundred Goode ageyn Oon Badde':

Longer Works other than The Canterbury Tales

Catalogues of Good Women in Medieval Literature." DAI 40 (1980), 5437A. Indiana University, 1979. [medieval stereotypes of women; Vergil, Ovid]

2145 McMILLAN, ANN [HUNTER]. "Heaven, Hell and The Legend of Good Women," in 2725, pp. 122-29.

2146 OVERBECK, PAT TREFZGER. "Chaucer's Good Woman." ChauR 2 (1967), 75-94.

2147 PAYNE, ROBERT O. "Making His Own Myth: The Prologue to Chaucer's Legend of Good Women." ChauR 9 (1975), 197-211. [+TC, PF, HF, BD]

2148 PEAVLER, JAMES M. "'The First Hevene': A Note on The Legend of Good Women, ll. 2234-2237." AN&Q, supp. I, (1978), 20-22.

2149 REISS, EDMUND. "Chaucer's 'fyn lovynge' and the Late Medieval Sense of fin amor," in 45, pp. 181-91.

2150 SHIGEO, HISASHI. "Chaucer's Idea of 'Love' and 'Goodness' in The Legend of Good Women." MeiGR (October, 1980), 37-54. [Hypsipyle; Medea; Lucrece; Ariadne]

2151 SHIGEO, HISASHI. "Chaucer's Idea of 'Love' and 'Goodness' in The Legend of Good Women (4)." MeiGR 323 (Tokyo, 1981), 29-45. In Japanese. [legends of Philomene, Phyllis, Hypermnestra; poet's ambivalence]

2152 SMITH, SARAH STANBURY. "Cupid's Sight in the Prologue to the Legend of Good Women." Centerpoint 4 (1981), 95-102.

See also: 88, 90, 112, 130, 132, 142, 167, 181, 182, 187, 188, 224, 240, 246, 255, 256, 263, 271, 280, 281, 285, 293, 294, 308, 311, 326, 331, 349, 355, 359, 362, 363, 364, 368, 374, 375, 378, 412, 441, 474, 542, 547, 555, 576, 582, 584, 685, 770, 801, 809, 811, 833, 851, 859, 891, 925, 1114, 1137, 1551, 1985, 2012, 2273, 2322, 2621, 2665, 2667, 2862.

>>> Legend of Good Women: Source Studies <<<

2153 COWEN, J. M. "Chaucer's Legend of Good Women, Lines 2501-03." N&Q, n. s., 31 (1984), 298-99. [Ovid, Heroides; Boccaccio, Genealogia Deorum Gentilium]

2154 GODMAN, PETER. "Chaucer and Boccaccio's Latin Works," in 47, pp.

269-95.

2155 HARDER, HENRY L. "Livy in Gower's and Chaucer's Lucrece
      Stories." PMPA 2 (1977), 1-7.

2156 KNOPP, SHERRON. "Chaucer and Jean de Meun as Self-Conscious
      Narrators: The Prologue to the Legend of Good Women and the
      Roman de la Rose 10307-680." Comitatus 4 (1973; pub. 1974),
      25-39.

2157 SHANER, MARY. "A Possible Source of Chaucer's Error in 'Legend
      of Hypermnestra'." N&Q 22 (1975), 341. [Lactantius
      Placidus' commentary on the Thebaid]

2158 SPISAK, JAMES W. "Chaucer's Pyramus and Thisbe." ChauR 18
      (1984), 204-10. [Ovid]

2159 SUTTON, JONATHAN WAYNE. "A Reading of Chaucer's Legend of Good
      Women Based on Its Ovidian Sources." DAI 40 (1979), 2052A.
      Indiana University.

2160 TAYLOR, BEVERLY. "The Medieval Cleopatra: The Classical and
      Medieval Tradition of Chaucer's Legend of Cleopatra." JMRS 7
      (1977), 249-69.

2161 WALLER, MARTHA S. "The Conclusion of Chaucer's Legend of
      Lucrece: Robert Holcot and the Great Faith of Women."
      Chaucer Newsletter 2:1 (1980), 10-12. [In Librum Sapientie]

2162 WEIHER, CAROL. "Chaucer's and Gower's Stories of Lucretia and
      Virginia." ELN 14:1 (1976), 7-9.

See also: 592, 598, 605, 608, 618, 633, 636, 637, 638, 645, 654, 664,
           2141, 2143, 2144.

PARLIAMENT OF FOWLS

2163 AERS, DAVID. "The Parliament of Fowls: Authority, the Knower
      and the Known." ChauR 16 (1981), 1-17. [reflexivity;
      open-mindedness]

2164 BAKER, DONALD C. "The Parliament of Fowls," in 70, pp. 428-45.
      [polarities]

Longer Works other than The Canterbury Tales

2165   BENNETT, J. A. W. "Some Second Thoughts on The Parlement of
        Foules," in 73, pp. 132–46. [Somnium Scipionis; structure]

2166   BENSON, LARRY D. "The Occasion of The Parliament of Fowls," in
        44, pp. 123–44. [cf. Somnium Scipionis]

2167   BROWN, EMERSON, JR. "Priapus and the Parlement of Foulys." SP
        72 (1975), 258–74. [figure of frustration]

2168   CLEARY, BARBARA A. "The Narrator and the Comic Framework in
        Chaucer's Parlement of Foules." Delta Epsilon Sigma Bull. 24
        (1979), 108–12. [incongruous juxtapositions]

2169   COWGILL, BRUCE KENT. "The Parlement of Foules and the Body
        Politic." JEGP 74 (1975), 315–35. [order vs. chaos]

2170   DUBBS, KATHLEEN E. and STODDARD MALARKEY. "The Frame of
        Chaucer's Parlement." ChauR 13 (1978), 16–24.

2171   ECONOMOU, GEORGE D. The Goddess Natura in Medieval Literature.
        Cambridge, MA: Harvard University Press, 1972. 222 pp.
        Reviews: TLS (21 September, 1973), 1093; D. W. Robertson,
        CL 26 (1974), 263–65; P. M. Kean, RES 25 (1974), 190–92; P.
        G. Walsh, MAE 44 (1975), 75–76; Chauncey Wood, JEGP 74
        (1975), 223–25; Paul L. Nyhus, Speculum 51 (1976), 132–35.

2172   ENTZMINGER, ROBERT L. "The Pattern of Time in The Parlement of
        Foules." JMRS 5 (1975), 1–11.

2173   FEIL, PATRICIA ANN. "Chaucer's Parlement of Fowles Considered in
        Relation to the Medieval Demande d'Amour and the Debate
        Genre." DAI 46 (1985), 1620A. Lehigh University. [Andreas
        Capellanus, Machaut]

2174   FERSTER, JUDITH. "Reading Nature: The Phenomenology of Reading
        in the Parliament of Fowls." Mediaevalia 3 (1977), 189–213.
        [world as text]

2175   FOWLER, DAVID C. "Chaucer's Parliament of Fowls and the
        Hexameral Tradition," Chapter 3 in 2761, pp. 128–70.
        [+Ambrose's Hexameron]

2176   FUJIKI, TAKAYOSHI. "Chaucer's 'love' in The Parliament of
        Fouls." Shukugawa Studies in Linguistics and Literature 4
        (1980), 1–13.

2177   GILBERT, A. J. "The Influence of Boethius on the Parlement of
        Foulys." MAE 47 (1978), 292–303.

2178 HUTCHINSON, JUDITH. "The Parliament of Fowls: A Literary
      Entertainment." Neophil 61 (1977), 143–51. [Valentine's
      Day]

2179 JORDAN, ROBERT M. "The Question of Unity and the Parlement of
      Foules." ESC 3 (1977), 373–85.

2180 KEARNEY, J[OHN] A. "The Parliament of Fowls: The Narrator, the
      'Certyn Thyng', and the 'Commune Profyt'." Theoria 45
      (1975), 55–71.

2181 KELLEY, MICHAEL R. "Antithesis as a Principle of Design in the
      Parlement of Foules." ChauR 14 (1979), 61–73.

2182 KELLY, HENRY ANSGAR. "The Genoese Saint Valentine and Chaucer's
      Third of May." Chaucer Newsletter 1:2 (1979), 6–10. [May 2
      date; Genoese St. Valentine]

2183 KITA, RUME. "The Parlement of Foules ni okeru ai no tankyu:
      'ernest' to 'game' no hazama" [In Quest of Love in The
      Parlement of Foules: Between 'ernest' and 'game']. Core
      (Doshisha University, Japan, 1984), 42–59. In Japanese.

2184 KREISLER, NICOLAI VON. "Bird Lore and the Valentine's Day
      Tradition in Chaucer's Parlement of Foules." ChauR 3 (1968),
      60–64.

2185 KREISLER, NICOLAI VON. "The 'Locus Amoenus' and Eschatological
      Lore in the Parliament of Fowls 204–10. PQ 50 (1971), 16–22.

2186 LAZARUS, ALAN J. "Venus in the 'North-North-West'? Chaucer's
      Parliament of Fowls, 117," in 44, pp. 145–49. [visibility of
      Venus, 1374–1382]

2187 LEICESTER, H. M., JR. "The Harmony of Chaucer's Parlement: A
      Dissonant Voice." ChauR 9 (1974), 15–34.

2188 LOGANBILL, DEAN. "Chaucer as Social Critic." PMPA 3 (1978),
      1–9. [PF as complicated art form]

2189 MUCCHETTI, EMIL A. "The Structural Importance of the Proem and
      the Somnium Scipionis to the Unity of The Parliament of
      Fowls." PAPA 4:3 (1978), 1–10.

2190 MUCCHETTI, EMIL A. "The Tragic Lovers in Chaucer's The
      Parliament of Fowls." PAPA 3:2 (1977), 40–46.

2191 NORRMAN, RALF. "Valsituationen i konsten: två exempel: I." [Two

Longer Works other than The Canterbury Tales

Instances of Representation in Art of the Situation of Choice: I.]. Horisont 25:5 (1978), 1-6. [stanzas 18-22]

2192   OIJI, TAKERO. "Chaucer no 'Tori no Gikai'--Sono Rinriteki Shukyoteki Seikaku ni tsuite" [Chaucer's Parliament of Fowls--Its Ethical and Religious Quality]. ELLS 10 (1973), 9-22.

2193   OLSON, PAUL A. "The Parlement of Foules: Aristotle's Politics and the Foundations of Human Society." SAC 2 (1980), 53-69.

2194   ORUCH, JACK B. "Nature's Limitations and the Demande d'Amour of Chaucer's Parlement." ChauR 18 (1983), 23-37.

2195   ORUCH, JACK B. "St. Valentine, Chaucer, and Spring in February." Speculum 56 (1981), 534-65. [Charles d'Orleans; Gower; Clanvowe; Oton de Graunson]

2196   PELEN, MARC M. "Form and Meaning of the Old French Love Vision: The Fableau dou Dieu d'Amors and Chaucer's Parliament of Fowls." JMRS 9 (1979), 277-305. [+RR]

2197   PFANNKUCHE, ANTHONY VOSS. "Dreams and Fictions: Essays on Medieval Dream Visions." DAI 35 (1975), 4449-50A. University of Iowa, 1974.

2198   REED, THOMAS L. "Chaucer's Parlement of Foules: The Debate Tradition and the Aesthetics of Irresolution." RUO 50 (1980), 215-22.

2199   ROTHSCHILD, VICTORIA. "The Parliament of Fowls: Chaucer's Mirror up to Nature?" RES 35 (1984), 164-84. [calendar; number symbolism]

2200   SEAH, VICTORIA LEES. "Marriage and the Love Vision: The Concept of Marriage in Three Medieval Love Visions as Relating to Courtship and Marriage Conventions of the Period." DAI 38 (1978) 4151A. McGill University, 1977. [+Temple of Glas; Kingis Quair]

2201   SKLUTE, LARRY M. "The Inconclusive Form of the Parliament of Fowls." ChauR 16 (1981), 119-28.

2202   TENEBRUSO, MARIE YRSA. "Chaucer's Parlement of Foules: An Interpretation Based Upon a Structural Analysis of Rhetorical Usage." DAI 40 (1980), 5856A. New York University, 1979.

2203   WALKER, D. B. "'Hic herde a strif bitweies two': A Study of the Principal Middle English Debate Poems, with Particular

Attention to the Bird Debates and the Devotional Debates,
Their Sources and Analogues." Doct. Diss., University of
Canterbury, N. Z., 1975.

2204   WALKER, DENIS. "Contentio: The Structural Paradigm of The
       Parliament of Fowls," in 72, pp. 173–80.

2205   WHITMAN, F. H. "'Olde feldes' and 'olde bokes' in Chaucer's
       Parliament of Fowls." AN&Q supp. I (1978), 9–11.

2206   YAMAMOTO, TOSHIKI. "Chaucer and The Parliament of Fowls."
       Essays on Classical Studies (March, 1980), 40–50. [nature in
       PF]

See also: 118, 130, 176, 180, 181, 182, 187, 188, 210, 224, 240, 242,
            255, 256, 263, 265, 275, 276, 277, 280, 285, 286, 288, 293,
            294, 299, 311, 330, 341, 346, 348, 359, 362, 363, 370, 377,
            383, 407, 409, 427, 429, 430, 432, 433, 442, 447, 451, 460,
            517, 532, 534, 542, 543, 545, 547, 553, 560, 568, 572, 579,
            580, 582, 583, 586, 725, 804, 811, 841, 859, 866, 901, 907,
            1038, 1149, 1174, 1197, 1311, 2012, 2017, 2044, 2045, 2147,
            2208, 2273, 2516, 2577, 2621, 2665, 2667, 2812, 2858a, 2866,
            2868.

>>> Parlement of Foules: Source Studies <<<

2207   DONALDSON, E. TALBOT. "Venus and the Mother of Romulus: The
       Parliament of Fowls and the Pervigilium Veneris." ChauR 14
       (1980), 313–18.

2208   QUILLIGAN, MAUREEN. "Allegory, Allegoresis, and the
       Deallegorization of Language: The Roman de la Rose, the De
       planctu naturae, and the Parlement of Foules," in Allegory,
       Myth, and Symbol. Edited by Morton W. Bloomfield. Harvard
       English Studies, 9. Cambridge, MA: Harvard University
       Press, 1981, pp. 163–86.

2209   WALLS, KATHRYN. "Patience and Her 'Hil of Sond' in the
       Parliament of Fowles." AN&Q 16 (1977–78), 34.
       [Deguileville's Pèlerinage de la Vie humaine]

See also: 432, 597, 605, 608, 613, 618, 626, 645, 650, 654, 664, 1311,
            2017, 2165, 2175, 2177, 2203.

Longer Works other than The Canterbury Tales

TROILUS AND CRISEYDE

2210   ABSHEAR-SEALS, LISA. "Boccaccio's Criseida and Chaucer's
        Criseyde." Spectrum 27:1-2 (1985), 25-32. [a comparison]

2211   AERS, DAVID. "Criseyde: Woman in Medieval Society." ChauR 13
        (1979), 177-200.

2212   ALEXANDER, JAMES. "Chaucer's Troilus and Criseyde." Expl 41:3
        (1983), 6-7. [sexual puns]

2213   ANDERSON, DAVID. "Cassandra's Analogy: Troilus V.1450-1521."
        HUSL 13 (1985), 1-17.

2214   ANDERSON, DAVID. "Theban History in Chaucer's Troilus." SAC 4
        (1982), 109-33.

2215   ANDREWS, BARBARA HAKKEN. "Value in Love: A Materialist Analysis
        of Chaucer's Troilus and Criseyde." DAI 40 (1980), 5855A.
        Brown University, 1979.

2216   apROBERTS, ROBERT. "The Growth of Criseyde's Love," in 42, pp.
        131-41.

2217   ARBUCKLE, NAN. "Categories of the Self-Conscious Narrator in
        Wolfram, Dante, and Chaucer." DAI 45 (1984), 2519A.
        University of Oklahoma.

2218   ARN, MARY-JO. "Three Ovidian Women in Chaucer's Troilus: Medea,
        Helen, Oënone." ChauR 15 (1980), 1-10.

2219   ASAKAWA, JUNKO. "Chaucer's Narrator and Criseyde." Bulletin of
        Tsuru University 21 (1984), 51-57.

2220   BAILEY, SUSAN E. "Controlled Partial Confusion: Concentrated
        Imagery in Troilus and Criseyde." ChauR 20 (1985), 83-89.

2221   BALOTĂ, NICOLAE. "Intoarcerea la Troia" [Return to Troy].
        RomLit 11 (Bucharest, 1978), 20. In Romanian.

2222   BARNEY, STEPHEN, ed. Chaucer's 'Troilus': Essays in Criticism.
        Hamden, CT: Archon Books, 1980. 323 pp. [17 articles, some
        classics] See also nos. 2361, 2426, 2428, 2452.
        Reviews: S. S. Hussey, SAC 4 (1982), 140-43; David
        Staines, Speculum 57 (1982), 351-53; R. T. Davies, N&Q 29
        (1982), 290-91.

2223 BARON, F. XAVIER. "Chaucer's Troilus and Self-Renunciation in
      Love." PLL 10 (1974), 5-14.

2224 BAUMGAERTNER, MARCIA ANNE. "An Approach to Characterization in
      Chaucer's Troilus and Criseyde." DAI 38 (1977), 2105A.
      University of North Carolina at Greensboro.

2225 BECKMAN, SABINA. "Color Symbolism in Troilus and Criseyde."
      CLAJ 20 (1976), 68-74.

2226 BENSON, C. DAVID. "A Chaucerian Allusion and the Date of the
      Alliterative Destruction of Troy." N&Q 21 (1974), 206-07.
      [+Guido delle Colonne's Historia Destructionis Troiae]

2227 BENSON, C. DAVID. "King Thoas and the Ominous Letter in
      Chaucer's Troilus." PQ 58 (1979), 264-67.

2228 BENSON, C. DAVID. "'O Nyce World': What Chaucer Really Found in
      Guido delle Colonne's History of Troy." ChauR 13 (1979),
      308-15.

2229 BERRY, GREGORY L. "Chaucer's Mnemonic Verses and the Siege of
      Thebes in Troilus and Criseyde." ELN 17:2 (1979), 90-93.

2230 BESTUL, THOMAS H. "Chaucer's Troilus and Criseyde: The
      Passionate Epic and Its Narrator." ChauR 14 (1980), 366-78.
      [tradition of pity]

2231 BIE, WENDY A. "Dramatic Chronology in Troilus and Criseyde."
      ELN 14:1 (1976), 9-13.

2232 BISCEGLIA, JULIE JEANNE. "Paradigms of Personality: Chaucer's
      Troilus and Criseyde and the Traditions of Ovid and Dante."
      DAI 41 (1980), 258A. University of California, Los Angeles.

2233 BISHOP, IAN. Chaucer's 'Troilus and Criseyde': A
      Critical Study. Bristol: University of Bristol, 1981. 116
      pp. [dialectical process; cupiditas/caritas]
         Reviews: Stephen A. Barney, Speculum 58 (1983), 843; Barry
      Windeatt, MAE 52 (1983), 132-34; J. D. Burnley, RES 35
      (1984), 218-19.

2234 BJÖRK, LENNART A. "Courtly Love or Christian Love: Animal
      Imagery in Book I of Chaucer's Troilus and Criseyde," in
      Studies in English Philology, Linguistics, and Literature
      Presented to Alarik Rynell 7 March 1978. Edited by Mats
      Rydén and Lennart A. Björk. Stockholm Studies in English,
      46. Stockholm: Almqvist & Wiksell International, 1978, pp.
      1-20. [TC as burlesque of courtly love]

Longer Works other than The Canterbury Tales

2235   BOWERS, JOHN M. "How Criseyde Falls in Love," in 2678, pp.
        141-55. [horse image]

2236   BOYD, JESSIE MARY HEATHER. "Figurative Patterns in the Poetry of
        Chaucer with Special Reference to Troilus and Criseyde and
        Selected Canterbury Tales." DAI 40 (1980), 4585A.
        University of South Africa, 1978. [spiral structure]

2237   BRENNAN, JOHN P. "Troilus and Criseyde, IV, 209-210." ELN 17:2
        (1979), 15-18.

2238   BREWER, D. S. "Observations on the Text of Troilus," in 62, pp.
        121-38.

2239   BRONSON, LARRY. "Chaucer's Pandarus: 'Jolly Good Fellow' or
        'Reverend Vice'?" BSUF 24:4 (1983), 34-41.

2240   BRONSON, LARRY. "The 'Sodeyn Diomede'—Chaucer's Composite
        Portrait." BSUF 25:2 (1984), 14-19.

2241   BRÜCKMANN, PATRICIA. "Troilus and Criseyde, III, 1226-1232: A
        Clandestine Topos." ELN 18:3 (1981), 166-70. [tree-vine
        topos]

2242   BURNLEY, J. D. "Criseyde's Heart and the Weakness of Women: An
        Essay in Lexical Interpretation." SN 54 (1982), 25-38.

2243   BURNLEY, J. D. "Proude Bayard: Troilus and Criseyde, I.218."
        N&Q 23 (1976), 148-52.

2244   BYRD, DAVID G. "Blanche Fever: The Grene Sekeness." BSUF 19:3
        (1978), 56-64. [TC lovers; +Confessio Amantis; Cuckoo and
        the Nightingale; Caxton's History of Jason]

2245   BYRD, FORREST M. "Conditional Statements in Troilus and
        Criseyde." PAPA 10:1 (1984), 29-43.

2246   CARTON, EVAN. "Complicity and Responsibility in Pandarus' Bed
        and Chaucer's Art." PMLA 94 (1979), 47-61. See no. 2403.

2247   CHRISTMAS, PETER. "Troilus and Criseyde: The Problems of Love
        and Necessity." ChauR 9 (1975), 285-96.

2248   CLARK, S. L. and JULIAN N. WASSERMAN. "The Heart in Troilus and
        Criseyde: The Eye of the Breast, the Mirror of the Mind, the
        Jewel and Its Setting." ChauR 18 (1984), 316-28.

2249   CLOETE, NETTIE. "The Reconciliation of Superstition and

Christian Ideas in <u>Troilus and Criseyde</u>." <u>Communiqué</u> 5:1 (Pietersburg, 1980), 48-57.

2250   CLOGAN, PAUL M. "Criseyde's Book of the Romance of Thebes." <u>HUSL</u> 13 (1985), 18-28. A shorter version of no. 2251.

2251   CLOGAN, PAUL M. "The Theban Scene in Chaucer's <u>Troilus</u>." <u>M&H</u>, n. s., 12 (1984), 167-85. [+<u>Roman de Thèbes</u>] See no. 2250.

2252   CLOUGH, ANDREA. "Medieval Tragedy and the Genre of <u>Troilus and Criseyde</u>." <u>M&H</u> 11 (1982), 211-27.

2253   CORMICAN, JOHN D. "Motivation of Pandarus in <u>Troilus and Criseyde</u>." <u>LangQ</u> 18:3-4 (1980), 43-48.

2254   COTTON, M. E. "Some Aspects of Contrast and Change in Chaucer's <u>Troilus and Cressida</u>." M.Phil. thesis, University of Leicester, England, 1976.

2255   CRAMPTON, GEORGIA R. "Action and Passion in Chaucer's <u>Troilus</u>." <u>MAE</u> 43 (1974), 22-36.

2256   DAHLBERG, CHARLES. "The Narrator's Frame for <u>Troilus</u>." <u>ChauR</u> 15 (1980), 85-100. [+St. Augustine; <u>RR</u>]

2257   DAVID, ALFRED. "Chaucerian Comedy and Criseyde," in 2390, pp. 90-104. [+Wife of Bath]

2258   DEAN, CHRISTOPHER. "Chaucer's Play on the Word <u>Beere</u> in <u>Troilus and Criseyde</u>." <u>ChauR</u> 15 (1981), 224-26.

2259   DEAN, JAMES. "Chaucer's <u>Troilus</u>, Boccaccio's <u>Filostrato</u>, and the Poetics of Closure." <u>PQ</u> 64 (1985), 175-84.

2260   DELANY, SHEILA. "Techniques of Alienation in <u>Troilus and Criseyde</u>," in <u>The Uses of Criticism</u>. Edited by A. P. Foulkes. Literaturwissenschaftliche Texte, Theorie und Kritik, 3. Frankfurt: Peter Lang; Bern: Herbert Lang, 1976, pp. 77-95.

2261   DE VRIES, F. C. "Notes of Trolius's Song to Love." <u>Parergon</u> 3 (1972), 17-19.

2262   DOBBS, ELIZABETH ANN. "Space in Chaucer's <u>Troilus and Criseyde</u>." <u>DAI</u> 37 (1976), 960A. State University of New York at Buffalo.

2263   DONALDSON, E. TALBOT. "Chaucer's Three Ps: Pandarus, Pardoner, and Poet." <u>MQR</u> 14 (1975), 282-301. [+Chaucer the poet]

Longer Works other than the Canterbury Tales

2264   DRAKE, GERTRUDE C. "The Moon and Venus: Troilus's Havens in
        Eternity." PLL 11 (1975), 3-17.

2265   DROST, JERRY. "Chaucer's Troilus and Criseyde." AN&Q 12 (1974),
        121.

2266   DULICK, MICHAEL GEORGE. "La Celestina and Chaucer's Troilus: A
        Comparative Study." DAI 40 (1980), 5852A. Saint Louis
        University, 1979.

2267   EBEL, JULIA. "Troilus and Oedipus: The Genealogy of an Image."
        ES 55 (1974), 15-21. [+Statius, Thebiad]

2268   ELDREDGE, LAURENCE. "Boethian Epistemology and Chaucer's Troilus
        in the Light of Fourteenth-Century Thought." Mediaevalia 2
        (1976), 50-75.

2269   ELLIS, DEBORAH. "'Calle It Gentilesse': A Comparative Study of
        Two Medieval Go-Betweens." Comitatus 8 (1977), 1-13.

2270   ERZGRÄBER, WILLI. "Zu Chaucers Troilus and Criseyde, Buch IV,"
        in Philologica Romanica: Erhard Lommatzsch gewidmet. Edited
        by Manfred Bambeck and Hans Helmut Christmann. Munich:
        Fink, 1975, pp. 97-117. [+Boethius]

2271   'ESPINASSE, MARGARET. "Chaucer's 'Fare-Carte'." N&Q 23 (1976),
        295-96.

2272   FALKE, ANNE. "The Comic Function of the Narrator in Troilus and
        Criseyde." Neophil 68 (1984), 131-41.

2273   FERGUSON, LINDA CAROL. "Music in Chaucer: Troilus and the Dream
        Poems." DMA diss., University of Missouri-Kansas City, 1977.
        Abstr. in MoJoResMusEd 4 (1978), 107-09; RILM 12 (1978), 119.
        [+LGW, BD, HF, PF]

2274   FISH, VARDA. "From 'Benigne Love' to the 'Blynde and Wynged
        Sone': Troilus and Criseyde as a Literary Critique of the
        Filostrato and the Tradition of Courtly Love Poetry." DAI 42
        (1981), 1628-29A. Cornell University.

2275   FISH, VARDA. "The Origin and Original Object of Troilus and
        Criseyde." ChauR 18 (1984), 304-15. [+Boccaccio, Il
        filostrato; Boethius, De Consolatione Philosophiae]

2276   FRANKIS, JOHN. "Paganism and Pagan Love in Troilus and
        Criseyde," in 2390, pp. 57-72.

2277   FRANKLIN, MICHAEL J. "The Fieldfare and the Nightingale: A Note
        on The Thrush and the Nightingale." MAE 47 (1978), 308-11.
        [TC III, 1.861; +Rom]

2278   FRIEDMAN, JOHN B. "Pandarus' Cushion and the 'pluma
        Sardanapalli'." JEGP 75 (1976), 41-55. [iconography;
        Luxuria, Fortuna]

2279   FRIES, MAUREEN. "'Slydynge of Corage': Chaucer's Criseyde as
        Feminist and Victim," in 56, pp. 45-59.

2280   FROST, MICHAEL H. "Narrative Devices in Chaucer's Troilus and
        Criseyde." Thoth 14:2-3 (1974), 29-38.

2281   FROST, WILLIAM. "A Chaucerian Crux." YR 66 (1977), 551-61.
        [sexual puns in 5.543]

2282   FYLER, JOHN M. "Auctoritee and Allusion in Troilus and
        Criseyde." RPLit 7 (1984), 73-92. [+Dante; Petrarch]

2283   FYLER, JOHN M. "The Fabrications of Pandarus." MLQ 41 (1980),
        115-30.

2284   GALLAGHER, JOSEPH E. "Criseyde's Dream of the Eagle: Love and
        War in Troilus and Criseyde." MLQ 36 (1975), 115-32.

2285   GALLAGHER, JOSEPH E. "The Double Sorrow of Troilus." MAE 41
        (1972), 27-31.

2286   GANIM, JOHN M. "Mutable Imagination: Time, Space and Audience
        in Medieval English Narrative." DAI 35 (1974), 2221A.
        Indiana University. [readings of TC]

2287   GANIM, JOHN M. Style and Consciousness in Middle English
        Narrative. Princeton, NJ: Princeton University Press, 1983.
        177pp. [+TC; Sir Gawain and the Green Knight; Lydgate's
        Siege of Thebes; Henryson's Testament of Cresseid]
            Reviews: R. W. Hanning, MLQ 45 (1984), 395-403; Alexandra
        Hennessey Olsen, Speculum 60 (1985), 401-04; Wolfgang Riehle,
        SAC 7 (1985), 197-99.

2288   GANIM, JOHN M. "Tone and Time in Chaucer's Troilus." ELH 43
        (1976), 141-53.

2289   GARBÁTY, THOMAS J. "Troilus V, 1786-92 and V, 1807-27: An
        Example of Poetic Process." ChauR 11 (1977), 299-305.
        [+Dante, Paradiso]

2290   GAYLORD, ALAN T. "The Lesson of the Troilus: Chastisement and

Longer Works other than the Canterbury Tales

Correction," in 2390, pp. 23–42.

2291 GEHLE, QUENTIN L. "A Study of Character Motivation in Chrétien's Cligès, Chaucer's Troilus and Criseyde, and Malory's Morte D'Arthur." DAI 35 (1974), 1622A. University of Kentucky, 1973.

2292 GILLMEISTER, HEINER. "Chaucer's Kan Ke Dort (Troilus II, 1752), and the 'Sleeping Dogs' of the Trouvères." ES 59 (1978), 310–23. [word study]

2293 GÓMEZ LARA, MANUEL J. "El proceso amoroso de Criseyde: aproximación a una heroina con voz propia," in Actas del V Congreso de AEDEAN. Oviedo: Alhambra, 1983, pp. 189–201.

2294 GORDON, IDA. The Double Sorrow of Troilus: A Study of Ambiguities in 'Troilus and Criseyde'. Oxford: Clarendon Press, 1970. 163 pp.
       Reviews: Martin Lehnert, ZAA 23 (1975), 64–67.

2295 GRANSDEN, K. W. "Lente Currite, Noctis Equi: Chaucer, Troilus and Criseyde 3.1422–70, Donne, 'The Sun Rising' and Ovid, Amores 1.13," in Creative Imitation and Latin Literature. Edited by David West and Tony Woodman. Cambridge: Cambridge University Press, 1979, pp. 157–71. [aubade of Troilus, Ovid]

2296 GREEN, D. H. Irony in the Medieval Romance. New York: Cambridge University Press, 1979. 441 pp. [irony in TC]
       Reviews: Paul G. Ruggiers, SAC 3 (1981), 138–42; M. W. Bloomfield, Speculum 57 (1982), 377–78; John Stevens, CL 34 (1982), 65–67.

2297 GREEN, RICHARD F. "Troilus and the Game of Love." ChauR 13 (1979), 201–20.

2298 GRENNEN, JOSEPH E. "'Makyng' in Comedy: 'Troilus and Criseyde', V, 1788." NM 86 (1985), 489–93.

2299 GRIFFIN, SALATHA MARIE. "Chaucer's Troilus and Criseyde from the Perspective of Ralph Strode's Consequences." DAI 39 (1979), 6754–55A. University of Nebraska-Lincoln, 1978.

2300 HANNING, R. W. "The Audience as Co-Creator of the First Chivalric Romances." YES 2 (1981), 1–28.

2301 HANSON, THOMAS B. "The Center of Troilus and Criseyde." ChauR 9 (1975), 297–302. [Boethius, Consolation of Philosophy; Dante, Purgatorio]

2302   HARDIE, J. KEITH. "Structure and Irony in Chaucer's _Troilus and Criseyde_." PAPA 3:2 (1977), 13–19.

2303   HART, THOMAS ELWOOD. "Medieval Structuralism: 'Dulcarnoun' and the Five-Book Design of Chaucer's _Troilus_." ChauR 16 (1981), 129–70. [+Geoffrey of Vinsauf; Euclid]

2304   HAVELY, NICHOLAS. "Tearing or Breathing? Dante's Influence on _Filostrato_ and _Troilus_," in 72, pp. 51–59. [comparison]

2305   HELTERMAN, JEFFREY. "Masks of Love in _Troilus and Criseyde_." CL 26 (1974), 14–31. [+Boccaccio's _Filostrato_, comparison]

2306   HERMANN, JOHN P. "Gesture and Seduction in _Troilus and Criseyde_." SAC 7 (1985), 107–35.

2307   HISCOE, DAVID WINTHROP. "'Equivocations of Kynde': The Medieval Tradition of Nature and Its Use in Chaucer's _Troilus and Criseyde_ and Gower's _Confessio Amantis_." DAI 44 (1983), 1447–48A. Duke University.

2308   HOLLEY, LINDA T. "The Narrative Speculum in _Troilus and Criseyde_." CLAJ 25 (1981), 212–24.

2309   HOUSTON, GAIL TURLEY. "'White by Black': Chaucer's 'Effect Contraire' in _Troilus and Criseyde_." Comitatus 15 (1984), 1–9. [+ambiguity]

2310   HOWARD, DONALD R. "The Philosophies in Chaucer's _Troilus_," in 44, pp. 151–75.

2311   HOWARD, DONALD R. "Renaissance World Alienation," in 64, pp. 47–76. [contemptus mundi theme]

2312   HUGHES, GEOFFREY. "The Sovereignty of Venus: The Problem of Courtly Love." ESA 25 (1982), 61–77. [love potion]

2313   HUPPÉ, BERNARD F. "The Unlikely Narrator: The Narrative Strategy of the _Troilus_," in 61, pp. 179–94.

2314   IERONIM, IOANA. "Troilus şi Cresida" [_Troilus and Criseyde_]. Luceafărul 27 (Bucharest, 1978), 8. In Romanian.

2315   INDICTOR, RINA M. "Fictionalization: The Poetics of Literary Self-Consciousness." DAI 37 (1976), 1531A. New York University.

2316   JENNINGS, MARGARET, C. S. J. "Chaucer's Troilus and the Ruby."

Longer Works other than the Canterbury Tales

N&Q 23 (1976), 533-37. [lapidary symbolism]

2317   JIMURA, AKIYUKI. "The Characterizations of Troilus and Criseyde
       Through Adjectives: 'trewe as stiel' and 'slydynge of
       corage'." PhoenixH 15 (Hiroshima University, 1979), 101-22.

2318   JIMURA, AKIYUKI. "Chaucer's Depiction of Characters Through
       Adjectives: Troilus and Criseyde." The Ohtani Studies (30
       July, 1980), 1-20.

2319   JIMURA, AKIYUKI. "Chaucer's Use of Impersonal Constructions in
       Troilus and Criseyde---by aventure yfalle---." Bulletin of
       Ohtani Women's College 18:2 (Kyoto, 1983), 14-27. In
       English.

2320   JOHNSON, L. STALEY. "The Medieval Hector: A Double Tradition."
       Mediaevalia 5 (1979), 165-82.

2321   KAMINSKY, ALICE R. Chaucer's 'Troilus and Criseyde' and the
       Critics. Athens: Ohio University Press, 1980. 245 pp.
       [evaluation of some 500 items of TC criticism: historical,
       philosophical, formalistic, psychological]
          Reviews: Gay Clifford, TLS (16 January, 1981), 60; S. S.
       Hussey, YES 12 (1982), 234-35; Stephen A. Barney, Speculum 57
       (1982), 351-53; J. Norton-Smith, N&Q 29 (1982), 290; David
       Staines, Speculum 57 (1982), 352-53; A. C. Spearing, RES 34
       (1983), 205-06; Thomas Hahn, SAC 5 (1983), 173-76.

2322   KELLY, HENRY ANSGAR. Love and Marriage in the Age of Chaucer.
       Ithaca and London: Cornell University Press, 1975. 360 pp.
          Reviews: Michael Rudlick, WHR 30 (1976), 66-69; Derek S.
       Brewer, RES 28 (1977), 194-97; Laurence Shook, Speculum 52
       (1977), 701-02; R. T. Davies, MLR 73 (1978), 871-74.

2323   KELLY, HENRY ANSGAR. "Marriage in the Middle Ages: 2:
       Clandestine Marriage and Chaucer's Troilus." Viator 4
       (1973), 435-57.

2324   KIERNAN, K[EVIN] S. "Hector the Second: The Lost Face of
       Troilustratus." AnM 16 (1975), 52-62.

2325   KINNEY, CLARE REGAN. "Strategies of Poetic Narrative: Troilus
       and Criseyde, The Faerie Queene, Book VI, and Paradise Lost."
       DAI 46 (1985), 1285A. Yale University, 1984. [+closure]

2326   KIRK, ELIZABETH D. "'Paradis Stood Formed in Hire Yen': Courtly
       Love and Chaucer's Re-Vision of Dante," in 52, pp. 257-77.

2327   KNAPP, PEGGY A. "The Nature of Nature: Criseyde's 'Slydyng

Corage'." ChauR 13 (1978), 133–40.

2328   KNIGHTEN, MERRELL AUDY, JR. "Chaucer's Troilus and Criseyde:
        Some Implications of the Oral Mode." DAI 36 (1976), 8076A.
        Louisiana State University and Agricultural and Mechanical
        College, 1975.

2329   KNOPP, SHERRON E. "The Narrator and His Audience in Chaucer's
        Troilus and Criseyde." SP 78 (1981), 323–40.

2330   KORETSKY, ALLEN C. "The Heroes of Chaucer's Romances." AnM 17
        (1976), 22–47.

2331   KURTZ, DIANE GRAY. "The Significance of the Tradition of Nature
        in Chaucer's Troilus and Criseyde." DAI 36 (1976), 6116A.
        University of Illinois at Urbana–Champaign, 1975.

2332   LAMBERT, MARK. "Troilus, Books I-III: A Criseydan Reading," in
        2390, pp. 105–25.

2333   LAWTON, DAVID. "Irony and Sympathy in Troilus and Criseyde: A
        Reconsideration." LeedsSE, n. s., 14 (1983), 94–115.
        [+theories of Wayne Clayson Booth, A Rhetoric of Irony] See
        no. 66.

2334   LENTA, MARGARET. "The Mirror of the Mind: A Study of Troilus
        and Criseyde." Theoria 58 (1982), 33–46. [psychological and
        artistic motifs]

2335   LIGGINS, ELIZABETH M. "The Lovers' Swoons in Troilus and
        Criseyde." Parergon 3 (1985), 93–106. [+Boccaccio, Il
        Filostrato]

2336   LONGO, JOSEPH A. "Apropos the Love Plot in Chaucer's Troilus and
        Criseyde and Shakespeare's Troilus and Cressida." CahiersE
        11 (1977), 1–15.

2337   MacCURDY, MARIAN MESROBIAN. "The Polarization of the Feminine in
        Arthurian and Troubadour Literature." DAI 41 (1980), 2596A.
        Syracuse University. [traditions of good and evil]

2338   MAGUIRE, JOHN B. "The Clandestine Marriage of Troilus and
        Criseyde." ChauR 8 (1974), 262–78. [cf. Boccaccio]

2339   MANLOVE, COLIN. "'Rooteless moot grene soone deye': The
        Helplessness of Chaucer's Troilus and Criseyde." ES, n. s.,
        31 (1978), 1–22.

2340   MANN, JILL. "Troilus' Swoon." ChauR 14 (1980), 319–35.

Longer Works other than the Canterbury Tales

[+Boccaccio's Il Filostrato]

2341   MANNING, STEPHEN. "Troilus, Book V: Invention and the Poem as
        Process." ChauR 18 (1984), 288-303. [+poetics; Boethian
        aesthetics; Aquinas]

2342   MARESCA, THOMAS E. Three English Epics: Studies of 'Troilus and
        Criseyde', 'The Faerie Queene', and 'Paradise Lost'.
        Lincoln: University of Nebraska Press, 1979. 222 pp.
          Reviews: Albert C. Labriola, SpenN 11 (1980), 4-7; Michael
        Lieb, Cithara 21:1 (1981), 58-70; John J. O'Connor, RenQ 34
        (1981), 149-51; M. E. McAlpine, Speculum 56 (1981), 457-58;
        John M. Steadman, JEGP 80 (1981), 234-37; Gwenn Davis, SAC 3
        (1981), 156-60; Thomas H. Cain, Clio 11 (1981), 88-91;
        Christina von Nolcken, RES, n. s., 33 (1982), 196-97.

2343   MARTIN, JUNE HALL. Love's Fools: Aucassin, Troilus, Calisto,
        and the Parody of the Courtly Lover. Colección Támesis,
        Serie A: Monografías, 21. London: Tamesis, 1972. 170 pp.
          Reviews: Daniel Eisenberg, MLN 88 (1973), 408-10; Stephen
        G. Nichols, Jr., CL 25 (1973), 171-75; Chauncey Wood,
        Costerus, n. s., 3 (1975), 177-83; Kathleen Kish, RPh 29
        (1976), 344-46.

2344   MATHESON, LISTER M. "Troilus and Criseyde, III.1460,
        'Pourynge'." N&Q 26 (1979), 203.

2345   MAYBURY, JAMES F. "The Character of the Narrator in Troilus and
        Criseyde." NNER 8 (1983), 32-41. [cf. Boccaccio's Il
        Filostrato]

2346   MAYBURY, JAMES F. "Pandarus and Criseyde: The Motif of Incest
        in Chaucer's Troilus." XUS 2:1-2 (1982), 82-89.

2347   McALPINE, MONICA E. The Genre of 'Troilus and Criseyde'.
        Ithaca: Cornell University Press, 1978. 252 pp.
        [Boccaccio, de casibus tragedy; Boethian comedy]
          Reviews: Stephen A. Barney, Speculum 54 (1979), 599-601;
        A. C. Spearing, RES 30 (1979), 458-59; R. T. Davies, N&Q 26
        (1979), 61-62; Gerald Morgan, MLR 75 (1980), 619-20; Robert
        S. Haller, SAC 2 (1980), 172-79; Margaret Schlauch, Style 14
        (1980), 58-60; Thomas A Kirby, ES 62 (1981), 560-61.

2348   McCALL, JOHN P. "Troilus and Criseyde," in 70, pp. 446-63.
        [readings of TC]

2349   McGUNNIGLE, MICHAEL GERARD. "Romanticized History and
        Historicized Romance: Narrative Styles and Strategies in
        Four Middle English Troy Poems." DAI 41 (1980), 2616A.

Northwestern University.

2350   McKINNELL, JOHN. "Letters as a Type of the Formal Level in
        Troilus and Criseyde," in 2390, pp. 73–89. [+Trivet's
        commentary on Seneca's Hercules Furens]

2351   MEDCALF, STEPHEN. "Epilogue: From Troilus to Troilus," in The
        Later Middle Ages. Edited by Stephen Medcalf. New York:
        Holmes and Meier, 1981, pp. 291–305. See no. 2648.

2352   MEHL, DIETER. "The Audience of Chaucer's Troilus and Criseyde,"
        in 69, pp. 173–89.

2353   MIESZKOWSKI, GRETCHEN. "R. K. Gordon and the Troilus and
        Criseyde Story." ChauR 15 (1980), 127–37. [Gordon's
        translation of the Le Roman de Troie of Benoît de
        Sainte-Maure, antifeministic passage]

2354   MILLETT, BELLA. "Chaucer, Lollius, and the Medieval Theory of
        Authorship," in 72, pp. 93–103.

2355   MILOWICKI, EDWARD J. "Characterization in Troilus and Criseyde:
        Some Relationships Centered on Hope." CRCL 11:1 (1984),
        12–24.

2356   MORGAN, GERALD. "The Ending of Troilus and Criseyde." MLR 77
        (1982), 257–71. [+Dante's Paradiso]

2357   MORGAN, GERALD. "The Freedom of the Lovers in Troilus and
        Criseyde," in Literature and Learning in Medieval and
        Renaissance England: Essays Presented to Fitzroy Pyle.
        Edited by John Scattergood. Blackrock, County Dublin,
        Ireland: Irish Academic Press, 1984, pp. 59–102.

2358   MORGAN, GERALD. "The Significance of the Aubades in Troilus and
        Criseyde." YES 9 (1979), 221–35.

2359   MUIR, KENNETH. "A Note on the Text of Troilus and Cressida."
        Library 1 (1979), 168.

2360   NEUMANN, FRITZ-WILHELM. Chaucer: Symbole der Initiation im
        Troilus-Roman. Studien zur Englischen Literatur, hsg. von
        Johannes Kleinstück, Band 17. Bonn: Bouvier Verlag Herbert
        Grundmann, 1977. 126 pp. [initiation, archetypes,
        symbolism]

2361   NEWMAN, BARBARA. "'Feynede Loves', Feigned Love, and Faith in
        Trouthe," in 2222, pp. 257–75.

Longer Works other than the Canterbury Tales

2362   O'DESKY, LEONA. "Chaucer's _Troilus and Criseyde_: Astrology and
the Transference of Power." _DAI_ 35 (1974), 3694-95A.
Rutgers University.

2363   OLMERT, MICHAEL. "Troilus and a Classical Pander: _TC_ III,
729-30." _Chaucer Newsletter_ 1:1 (1979), 18-19. [Troilus'
prayer to Mercury]

2364   O'NEIL, W. M. "The Bente Moone." _AUMLA_ 43 (1975), 50-52. [_TC_
III, 624-25; dating of _TC_]

2365   OSBERG, RICHARD H. "Between the Motion and the Act: Intentions
and Ends in Chaucer's _Troilus._" _ELH_ 48 (1981), 257-70.
[+epilogue]

2366   OWEN, CHARLES A., JR. "Minor Changes in Chaucer's _Troilus and
Criseyde_," in 69, pp. 303-19.

2367   PÂRVU, SORIN. "Chaucer: Troilus şi Cresida" [Chaucer: _Troilus
and Criseyde_]. _Cronica_ (Bucharest, 23 March, 1979), 10. In
Romanian.

2368   PATTERSON, LEE W. "Ambiguity and Interpretation: A
Fifteenth-Century Reading of _Troilus and Criseyda._" _Speculum_
54 (1979), 297-330. [_Disce mori_; +sources]

2369   PEARSALL, DEREK. "The _Troilus_ Frontispiece and Chaucer's
Audience." _YES_ 7 (1977), 68-74. [+Chaucerian audience]

2370   PEED, M. R. "_Troilus and Criseide_: The Narrator and the 'Olde
Bokes'." _AN&Q_ 12 (1973-74), 143-46.

2371   PEYTON, HENRY H., III. "Diomed, the Large-Tongued Greek."
Interpretations 6 (1974), 1-6.

2372   PEYTON, HENRY H., III. "The Roles of Calkas, Helen, and
Cassandra in Chaucer's _Troilus._" _Interpretations_ 7 (1975),
8-12.

2373   PEYTON, HENRY H., III. "Three Minor Characters in Chaucer's
Troilus: Hector, Antigone, and Deiphebus." _Interpretations_
8 (1976), 47-53.

2374   PROVOST, WILLIAM. _The Structure of Chaucer's 'Troilus and
Criseyde'._ Anglistica, 20. Copenhagen: Rosenkilde and
Bagger, 1972, 1974. 120 pp. [structuralist approach:
books, time units, narrative units]
    Reviews: S. S. Hussey, _MLR_ 71 (1976), 372-73; Martin
Lehnert, _ZAA_ 24 (1976), 357-62; G. C. Britton, _N&Q_ 222

(1977), 82–86; F. Diekstra, ES 58 (1977), 159; C. A. Owen,
Speculum 52 (1977), 419–21.

2375   PUHVEL, MARTIN. "Chaucer's Troilus and Criseyde: III.890;
        V.505; V.1174–5." Expl 42:4 (1984), 7–9. [symbolism:
        proverb; English folklore]

2376   REED, GAIL H. V. "Chaucer's Women: Commitment and Submission."
        DAI 34 (1974), 4215–16A. University of Nebraska-Lincoln.

2377   RENOIR, ALAIN. "Bayard and Troilus: Chaucerian Non-Paradox in
        the Reader." OL 36 (1981), 116–40. [images of peacock,
        stairs, Bayard; +Iliad, Aeneid, Chanson des quatre fils
        Amyon]

2378   ROBERTSON, D. W. "The Probable Date and Purpose of Chaucer's
        Troilus." M&H 13 (1985), 143–71.

2379   ROGERS, H. L. "The Beginning (and Ending) of Chaucer's Troilus
        and Criseyde," in Festschrift for Ralph Farrell. Edited by
        Anthony Stephens, H. L. Rogers, and Brian Coghlan. ANSDSL 7.
        Bern: Lang, 1977, pp. 185–200.

2380   ROWE, DONALD W. O Love O Charite! Contraries Harmonized in
        Chaucer's 'Troilus'. Carbondale: Southern Illinois
        University Press; London: Feffer & Simons, 1976. 201 pp.
        [discordia concors tradition]
        Reviews: Hugh T. Keenan, LJ (1 October, 1976), 2065;
        Choice 13 (1976), 1140; Barry Windeatt, MAE 47 (1978),
        156–58; Paul Strohm, Speculum 53 (1978), 188–90; Derek
        Brewer, RES 30 (1979), 334–36; Ralph W. V. Elliot, ES 61
        (1980), 367–69; Jörg O. Fichte, Anglia 98 (1980), 489–92.

2381   ROWLAND, BERYL. "Chaucer's Speaking Voice and Its Effect on His
        Listeners' Perception of Criseyde." ESC 7 (1981), 129–40.

2382   RUDAT, WOLFGANG E. H. "The Character of the Narrator in Troilus
        and Criseyde." NNER 8 (1983), 32–41. [cf. Boccaccio, Il
        Filostrato]

2383   RUDAT, WOLFGANG E. H. "Chaucer's Troilus and Criseyde:
        Narrator-Reader Complicity." AI 40 (1983), 103–13.
        [incestuous suggestions]

2384   RUTHERFORD, CHARLES S. "Troilus' Farewell to Criseyde: The
        Idealist as Clairvoyant and Rhetorician." PLL 17 (1981),
        245–54. [+proverbs]

2385   SADLEK, GREGORY M. "To Wait or to Act? Troilus II, 954." ChauR

Longer Works other than the Canterbury Tales

17 (1982), 62–64.

2386　SADLER, FRANK. "Storm Imagery in Troilus and Criseyde." WGCR 10
(1978), 13–18.

2387　SAKAI, SATOSHI. "Some Women in Middle English Literature (3): A
Portrait of Chaucerian Women." Journal of Tokyo Kasei Gajuin
College (May, 1980).

2388　SALEMI, JOSEPH S. "Playful Fortune and Chaucer's Criseyde."
ChauR 15 (1981), 209–23. [+Boethian determinism]

2389　SALTER, ELIZABETH. "Troilus and Criseyde: Poet and Narrator,"
in 52, pp. 281–91. [Boccaccio, Filostrato, Teseida]

2390　SALU, MARY, ed. Essays on 'Troilus and Criseyde'. Chaucer
Studies 3. Cambridge: D. S. Brewer, Ltd., 1979; Totowa, NJ:
Rowman and Littlefield, 1980. 143 pp. [seven essays on TC]
See nos. 2257, 2277, 2291, 2332, 2350, 2457, 2461.
Reviews: Jill Mann, Encounter (1980), 60–64; Derek
Pearsall, THES (17 October, 1980), 16–17; T. A. Shippey, TLS
(4 July, 1980), 753; Lee W. Patterson, Speculum 56 (1981),
912–14; C. David Benson, SAC 3 (1981), 171–76; Derek
Pearsall, DUJ, n. s., 43 (1981–82), 299–302; Dieter Mehl,
Anglia 100 (1982), 189–92; F. N. M. Diekstra, ES 65 (1984),
555–57.

2391　SCHIBANOFF, SUSAN. "Argus and Argyve: Etymology and
Characterization in Chaucer's Troilus." Speculum 51 (1976),
647–58.

2392　SCHIBANOFF, SUSAN. "Chaucer and 'Stewart's' Pandarus and the
Critics." SSL 13 (1978), 92–99. [development of common
noun]

2393　SCHIBANOFF, SUSAN. "Criseyde's 'Impossible' Aubes." JEGP 76
(1977), 326–33. [dawn-song of Book III]

2394　SCHIBANOFF, SUSAN. "Prudence and Artificial Memory in Chaucer's
Troilus." ELH 42 (1975), 507–17.

2395　SCHMIDT, DIETER. "Das Anredepronomen in Chaucers Troilus and
Criseyde." Archiv 212 (1975), 120–24. ["thou" and "ye"]

2396　SCHROEDER, PETER R. "Hidden Depths: Dialogue and
Characterization in Chaucer and Malory." PMLA 98 (1983),
374–87. [character of Criseyde]

2397　SCHUMAN, SAMUEL. "The Circle of Nature: Patterns of Imagery in

Chaucer's Troilus and Criseyde." ChauR 10 (1975), 99–112.
[+Fortune; astrology, ShT]

2398   SHIKII, KUMIKO. "Researches in Troilus and Criseyde in Japan."
SELLA 13 (1984), 85–97. In Japanese.

2399   SHIRLEY, CHARLES GARRISON, JR. "Verbal Texture and Character in
Chaucer's Troilus and Criseyde: A Computer-Assisted Study."
DAI 39 (1979), 6118A. University of South Carolina, 1978.

2400   SHOAF, R. ALLEN. "Dante's Commedia and Chaucer's Theory of
Mediation: A Preliminary Sketch," in 68, pp. 83–103.
[narcissism; Dante, La Divina Commedia]

2401   SKUBIKOWSKI, KATHLEEN. "Chaucer's Troilus and Criseyde,
IV.29–147." Expl 40:3 (1982), 7–8.

2402   SLOCUM, SALLY K. "How Old Is Chaucer's Pandarus?" PQ 58 (1979),
16–25.

2403   SMITH, NATHANIEL B. and EVAN CARTON. "Chaucer's Art." PMLA 94
(1979), 948–49. Correspondence on no. 2446.

2404   SOMMER, GEORGE J. "Chaucer and the Muse of History: A
Presumption of Objectivity in Troilus and Criseyde." Cithara
23:1 (1983), 38–47. [narrator ambiguity]

2405   SPEARING, A. C. Chaucer: 'Troilus and Criseyde'. Studies in
English Literature, 59. London: Edward Arnold, 1976. 64
pp. [romance, love, feminism]
    Reviews: R. T. Davies, N&Q 24 (1977), 57–58; André Crépin,
EA 30 (1977), 477.

2406   SPECHT, HENRIK. "Some Aspects of the Art of Portraiture in
Medieval Literature: With Special Reference to the Use of
Ethopoeia or Adlocutio," in Proceedings from the Second
Nordic Conference for English Studies. Edited by Håken
Ringbom and Matti Rissanen. Meddelanden Från Stiftelsens för
Åbo Akademi Forskningsinstitut 92. Åbo: Åbo Akademi, 1984,
pp. 403–14.

2407   STANLEY, E. G. "About Troilus." E&S 29 (1976), 84–106. [cf.
Boccaccio's Troilo]

2408   STEADMAN, JOHN M. Disembodied Laughter: 'Troilus' and the
Apotheosis Tradition: A Reexamination of Narrative and
Thematic Contexts. Berkeley, Los Angeles, and London:
University of California Press, 1972. 190 pp.
    Reviews: June Hall Martin, CL 25 (1973), 273–77; Dieter

Longer Works other than the Canterbury Tales

Mehl, Erasmus 26 (1974), 31–34; Bruce Harbert, N&Q 21 (1974), 69; Thomas A. Kirby, ELN 12:1 (1974), 44–46; Theodore A. Stroud, MP 72 (1974), 60–70; W. M. Temple, MAE 43 (1974), 293–95; John B. Friedman, JEGP 74 (1975), 225–28; D. S. Brewer, MLR 70 (1975), 139–41.

2409   STEVENS, MARTIN. "The Double Structure of Chaucer's Troilus and Criseyde," in CUNY English Forum , 1. Edited by Saul N. Brody and Harold Schecter. New York: AMS, 1985, pp. 155–74.

2410   STEVENS, MARTIN. "The Winds of Fortune in the Troilus." ChauR 13 (1979), 285–307.

2411   STILLER, NIKKI. "Civilization and Its Ambivalence: Chaucer's Troilus and Criseyde." JEP 6 (1985), 212–23. [+Boethius, Freud]

2412   STOKES, M[YRA]. "The Moon in Leo in Book V of Troilus and Criseyde." ChauR 17 (1982), 116–29.

2413   STOKES, MYRA. "Recurring Rhymes in Troilus and Criseyde." SN 52 (1980), 287–97.

2414   STOKES, MYRA. "'Wordes White': Disingenuity in Troilus and Criseyde." ES 64 (1983), 18–29.

2415   STORM, MELVIN. "Troilus, Mars, and Late Medieval Chivalry." JMRS 12 (1982), 45–65. [tyranny of Venus over Mars]

2416   STROUD, THEODORE A. "Chaucer's Structural Balancing of Troilus and Knight's Tale." AnM 21 (1981), 31–45. [+Boccaccio, Filostrato, Teseida]

2417   SUDO, J. "Chaucer's Imitation and Innovation in Troilus and Criseyde." PoetT 13 (Tokyo, 1982), 50–74. In English. [cf. Boccaccio's Filostrato]

2418   SUNDWALL, McKAY. "Criseyde's Rein." ChauR 11 (1976), 156–63. [Benoit's Roman de Troie]

2419   SUNDWALL, McKAY. "Deiphobus and Helen: A Tantalizing Hint." MP 73 (1975), 151–56. [influence of Virgil's Aeneid]

2420   TAVORMINA, M. TERESA. "The Moon in Leo: What Chaucer Really Did to Il Filostrato's Calendar." BSUF 22:1 (1981), 14–19.

2421   TAYLOR, ANN M. "Criseyde's 'Thought' in Troilus and Criseyde (II, 598–812)." AN&Q 17 (1978–79), 18–19.

2422   TAYLOR, ANN M. "On Troilus and Criseyde, III, 736–742." AN&Q 13
        (1974-75), 24–25. [Troilus as mouse]

2423   TAYLOR, ANN M. "A Scriptural Echo in the Trojan Parliament of
        Troilus and Criseyde." NMS 24 (1980), 51–56.

2424   TAYLOR, ANN M. "Troilus' Rhetorical Failure (4:1440–1526)." PLL
        15 (1979), 357–69.

2425   TAYLOR, DAVIS. "The Terms of Love: A Study of Troilus's Style."
        Speculum 51 (1976), 69–90. See also no. 2426.

2426   TAYLOR, DAVIS. "The Terms of Love: A Study of Troilus's Style,"
        in 2222, pp. 231–56. [revision of no. 2425]

2427   TAYLOR, KARLA TERESE. "Chaucer Reads the Divine Comedy." DAI 44
        (1983), 1449A. Stanford University.

2428   TAYLOR, KARLA [TERESE]. "Proverbs and the Authentication of
        Convention in Troilus and Criseyde," in 2222, pp. 277–96.

2429   TAYLOR, KARLA [TERESE]. "A Text and Its Afterlife: Dante and
        Chaucer." CL 35 (1983), 1–20. [Dante, La Divina Commedia]

2430   THOMAS, JIMMIE E. "Chaucer's Troilus and Criseyde." Expl 43:1
        (1984), 6–7. [pun; sexual innuendo]

2431   THOMPSON, DIANE PAIGE. "Human Responsibility and the Fall of
        Troy." DAI 42 (1981), 1139A. City University of New York.

2432   THUNDY, ZACHARIAS P. "Chaucer's 'Corones Tweyne' and Matheolus."
        NM 86 (1985), 343–47.

2433   TKACZ, CATHERINE BROWN. "'Troilus the Syke': Boethian Medical
        Imagery in Chaucer's Troilus and Criseyde." BSUF 24:3
        (1983), 3–12.

2434   TOMASCH, SYLVIA. "The Unwritten Dispositio: Principles of Order
        and the Structures of Late Middle English Literature." DAI
        46 (1985), 420A. City University of New York.

2435   TOOLE, WILLIAM B., III. "The Imagery of Fortune and Religion in
        Troilus and Criseyde," in A Fair Day in the Affections:
        Literary Essays in Honor of Robert B. White, Jr. Edited by
        Jack M. Durant and M. Thomas Hester. Raleigh, NC: Winston,
        1980, pp. 25–35.

2436   UTLEY, FRANCIS LEE. "Chaucer's Troilus and St. Paul's Charity,"
        in 69, pp. 272–87.

Longer Works other than the Canterbury Tales

2437   VAN, THOMAS A. "Chaucer's Pandarus as an Earthly Maker." SHR 12
        (1978), 89-97.

2438   VAN, THOMAS A. "Chaucer's Troilus and Criseyde." Expl 34:3
        (1975), 20.

2439   VAN, THOMAS A. "Chaucer's Troilus and Criseyde." Expl 40:3
        (1982), 8-10. [theme of mutability]

2440   VAN, THOMAS A. "Criseyde's Indirections." AN&Q 13 (1974-75),
        34-35.

2441   VAN DYKE, CAROLYNN. "The Errors of Good Men: Hamartia in Two
        Middle English Poems," in Hamartia: The Concept of Error in
        the Western Tradition: Essays in Honor of John M. Crossett.
        Edited by Donald V. Stump, et. al. Texts and Studies in
        Religion, 16. New York: Edwin Mellen, 1983, pp. 171-91.
        [+Poetics of Aristotle and De consolatione philosophiae of
        Boethius]

2442   VANCE, EUGENE. "Chaucer, Spenser, and the Ideology of
        Translation." CRCL 8 (1981), 217-38. [Troy legend]

2443   VANCE, EUGENE. "Mervelous Signals: Poetics, Sign Theory, and
        Politics in Chaucer's Troilus." NLH 10 (1979), 293-337.
        [semiotics; signs; linguistics]

2444   VICARI, PATRICIA. "Sparagmos: Orpheus Among the Christians," in
        Orpheus: The Metamorphoses of a Myth. Edited by John
        Warden. Toronto and Buffalo: University of Toronto Press,
        1982, pp. 63-83. [Troilus's Hymn to Love, Boethius;
        Neoplatonic metaphysics, cosmology, theories of love]

2445   WACK, MARY F[RANCES]. "Lovesickness in Troilus." PCP 19 (1984),
        55-61. [medieval medical view of love]

2446   WACK, MARY FRANCES. "Memory and Love in Chaucer's Troilus and
        Criseyde." DAI 43 (1983), 2343A. Cornell University.
        [+medieval medical writings on lovesickness]

2447   WALLACE, DAVID [J]. "Chaucer's 'Ambages'." AN&Q 23 (1984), 1-4.
        [+Boccaccio, "Lollius"; Virgil]

2447a   WARRINGTON, JOHN, ed. Troilus and Criseyde. London: Dent,
        1974. 337 pp. [revised introduction by Maldwyn Mills]

2448   WASWO, RICHARD. "The Narrator of Troilus and Criseyde." ELH 50
        (1983), 1-25.

2449   WEITZENHOFFER, KENNETH. "Chaucer, Two Planets, and the Moon."
       Sky and Telescope 69 (1985), 278–81. [TC III; date of TC]

2450   WENTERSDORF, KARL P. "Some Observations on the Concept of
       Clandestine Marriage in Troilus and Criseyde." ChauR 15
       (1980), 101–26.

2451   WETHERBEE, WINTHROP. Chaucer and the Poets: An Essay on
       'Troilus and Criseyde'. Ithaca, NY; and London: Cornell
       University Press, 1984. 249 pp. [literary allusion, esp.
       from RR, Virgil, Ovid, Statius, Dante]
         Reviews: John V. Fleming, SAC 7 (1985), 262–67; Bernard
       O'Donoghue, TLS (12 April, 1985), 416; Piero Boitani,
       Speculum 61 (1986), 716–18.

2452   WETHERBEE, WINTHROP. "The Descent from Bliss: Troilus, III,
       1310–1582," in 2222, pp. 297–317.

2453   WETHERBEE, WINTHROP. "'Per te poeta fui, per te cristiano':
       Dante, Statius, and the Narrator of Chaucer's Troilus," in
       57, pp. 153–76. [Dante, Purgatorio; Statius, Thebaid]

2454   WHEELER, BONNIE. "Dante, Chaucer, and the Ending of Troilus and
       Criseyde." PQ 61 (1982), 105–23. [cf. Dante, Paradiso]

2455   WILSON, DOUGLAS B. "The Commerce of Desire: Freudian Narcissism
       in Chaucer's Troilus and Criseyde and Shakespeare's Trolius
       and Cressida." ELN 21:1 (1983), 11–22. [psychoanalytic
       approach]

2456   WIMSATT, JAMES I. "Medieval and Modern in Chaucer's Troilus and
       Criseyde." PMLA 92 (1977), 203–16.

2457   WIMSATT, JAMES I. "Realism in Troilus and Criseyde and the Roman
       de la Rose," in 2390, pp. 43–56. [sources of realism,
       Platonic cosmic fables, Pamphilus]

2458   WINDEATT, BARRY [A]. "'Love That Oughte Ben Secree' in Chaucer's
       Troilus." ChauR 14 (1979), 116–31. [Boccaccio's Il
       Filostrato]

2459   WINDEATT, BARRY [A]. "The 'Paynted Process': Italian to English
       in Chaucer's Troilus." EM 26–27 (1977–78), 79–103.
       [Filostrato]

2460   WINDEATT, B[ARRY] A. "The Scribes as Chaucer's Early Critics."
       SAC 1 (1979), 119–41.

Longer Works other than the Canterbury Tales

2461   WINDEATT, BARRY [A]. "The Text of the Troilus," in 2390, pp.
        1-22.

2462   WOOD, CHAUNCEY. The Elements of Chaucer's 'Troilus'. Durham,
        NC: Duke University Press, 1984. [moral reading]
            Reviews: C. David Benson, AN&Q 23 (1985), 94-95; Ian
        Bishop, SAC 7 (1985), 270-72; Donald F. Chapin, ESC 11
        (1985), 489-91.

2463   WOODS, MARJORIE CURRY. "Chaucer the Rhetorician: Criseyde and
        Her Family." ChauR 20 (1985), 28-39.

2464   YEAGER, R. F. "'O Moral Gower': Chaucer's Dedication of Troilus
        and Criseyde." ChauR 19 (1984), 87-99.

2465   YEARWOOD, STEPHENIE. "The Rhetoric of Narrative Rendering in
        Chaucer's Troilus." ChauR 12 (1977), 27-37.

2466   ZIMBARDO, ROSE A. "Creator and Created: The Generic Perspective
        of Chaucer's Troilus and Criseyde." ChauR 11 (1977), 283-98.

See also: 23, 91, 106, 111, 117, 122, 126, 130, 143, 147, 161, 164, 166,
        176, 182, 184, 185, 200, 211, 212, 224, 225, 227, 242, 243,
        247, 254, 256, 262, 263, 264, 265, 267, 280, 281, 284, 285,
        286, 292, 293, 297, 299, 303, 304, 305, 306, 311, 317, 318,
        326, 331, 333, 335, 342, 349, 355, 357, 363, 364, 370, 373,
        374, 378, 379, 381, 385, 392, 402, 404, 405, 407, 412, 425,
        427, 429, 430, 442, 443, 444, 447, 449, 458, 460, 462, 463,
        474, 478, 483, 485, 488, 497, 501, 504, 505, 524, 532, 536,
        540, 541, 543, 544, 548, 553, 560, 568, 574, 576, 577, 578,
        581, 582, 583, 584, 587, 589, 590, 665, 674, 676, 678, 682,
        683, 685, 688, 699, 706, 709, 719, 720, 721, 747, 748, 756,
        761, 762, 766, 772, 785, 789, 790, 794, 797, 803, 806, 811,
        812, 833, 841, 851, 859, 864, 872, 883, 891, 901, 907, 916,
        983, 992, 1007, 1056, 1076, 1084, 1121, 1168, 1174, 1238,
        1303, 1307, 1311, 1695, 1775, 1874, 1961, 1985, 2058, 2140,
        2147, 2508, 2510, 2680, 2709, 2792, 2844, 2866.

>>> Troilus and Criseyde: Source Studies <<<

2467   BENSON, C. DAVID. The History of Troy in Middle English
        Literature: Guido delle Colonne's 'Historia destructionis
        Troiae' in Medieval England. Cambridge: D. S. Brewer;
        Totowa, NJ: Rowman & Littlefield, 1980. 174 pp.
            Reviews: Jill Mann, Encounter (1980), 60-64; Lois Ebin,
        Speculum 56 (1981), 848-50; McKay Sundwall, SAC 3 (1981),

124–28; F. N. M. Diekstra, ES 65 (1984), 567–69.

2468   BIANCIOTTO, GABRIEL. Edition critique et commentée du 'Roman de Troyle', traduction française du xve siècle du Filostrato de Boccace. Dissertation, Paris, 1977. [refutation of Pratt]

2469   BIGGINS, DENNIS. "A Possible Source for Chaucer's Troilus V 638–44." AN&Q supp. I (1978), 12–14.

2470   BROWN, WILLIAM H., JR. "A Separate Peace: Chaucer and the Troilus of Tradition." JEGP 83 (1984), 492–508. [Benoît de Sainte-Maure, Roman de Troie; Guido delle Colonne, Historia Destructionis Troiae; Joseph of Exeter, Frigii Daretis Ylias; Boccaccio, Il filostrato]

2471   CLAYTON, MARGARET. "A Virgilian Source for Chaucer's 'White Bole'." N&Q 26 (1979), 103–04. [+Mars; Virgil, Georgic I]

2472   CLOGAN, PAUL M. "Two Verse Commentaries on the Ending of Boccaccio's Filostrato." M&H, n. s., 7 (1976), 147–52.

2473   COLLINS, DAVID G. "The Story of Diomede and Criseyde: Changing Relationships in an Evolving Legend." PAPA 7:2 (1981), 9–30. [Benoît de Sainte-Maure; Guido della Colonne; Boccaccio; Shakespeare; Dryden]

2474   DONALDSON, E. TALBOT. "Briseis, Briseida, Criseyde, Cresseid, Cressid: Progress of a Heroine," in 73, pp. 3–12. [Dares; Benoit; Boccaccio; Henryson; Shakespeare]

2475   FROST, WILLIAM. "A Chaucer-Virgil Link in Aeneid XI and Troilus and Criseyde V." N&Q 26 (1979), 104–05.

2476   GLEASON, MARK J. "The Influence of Trevet on Boethian Language and Thought in Chaucer's Troilus and Criseyde." DAI 45 (1985), 2096A. University of Wisconsin-Madison, 1984.

2477   KNAPP, PEGGY ANN. "Boccaccio and Chaucer on Cassandra." PQ 56 (1977), 413–17. [Filostrato]

2478   MATTHEWS, LLOYD J. "Chaucer's Personification of Prudence in Troilus (V.743–749): Sources in the Visual Arts and Manuscript Scholia." ELN 13:4 (1976), 249–55. [+Dante, Purgatorio]

2479   MATTHEWS, LLOYD J. "Troilus and Criseyde, V.743–749: Another Possible Source." NM 82 (1981), 211–13. [Frescobaldi's "Canzone XI"]

Longer Works other than the Canterbury Tales

2480   MIESZKOWSKI, GRETCHEN. "Chaucer's Pandarus and Jean Brasdefer's Houdée." ChauR 20 (1985), 40–60. [Pamphile et Galatée]

2481   WALLACE, D. J. "Some Amendments to the Apparatus of Robinson's Works of Chaucer." N&Q 30 (1983), 202. [+Boccaccio's Il Filostrato]

2482   WIMSATT, JAMES I. "The French Lyric Element in Troilus and Criseyde." YES 15 (1985), 18–32.

2483   WIMSATT, JAMES I. "Guillaume de Machaut and Chaucer's Troilus and Criseyde." MAE 45 (1976), 277–93. [Jugement dou Roy de Behaingne; Remede de Fortune; Mireoir amoureux]

2484   WINDEATT, BARRY. "Chaucer and the Filostrato," in 47, pp. 163–83.

See also: 594, 597, 598, 600, 605, 606, 613, 618, 622, 625, 637, 645, 646, 654, 657, 659, 1311, 2210, 2214, 2216, 2218, 2228, 2229, 2232, 2251, 2256, 2259, 2267, 2268, 2270, 2274, 2275, 2282, 2289, 2295, 2299, 2301, 2304, 2305, 2320, 2326, 2335, 2338, 2340, 2347, 2351, 2355, 2356, 2368, 2389, 2400, 2416, 2418, 2419, 2420, 2429, 2432, 2433, 2441, 2444, 2447, 2450, 2452, 2453, 2454, 2457, 2458, 2459, 2462.

LYRICS AND SHORTER POEMS

GENERAL

2485   CHANCE, JANE. "Chaucerian Irony in the Verse Epistles 'Words
          unto Adam', 'Lenvoy a Scogan', and 'Lenvoy a Bukton'." PLL
          21 (1985), 115-28.

2486   FICHTE, JOERG O. "Womanly Noblesse and To Rosemounde: Point and
          Counterpoint of Chaucerian Love Lyrics," in 72, pp. 181-94.

2487   HAYES, JOSEPH J. "The Court Lyric in the Age of Chaucer." DAI
          34 (1974), 4205-06A. University of Indiana. [+Machaut,
          Deschamps, Hoccleve, Lydgate, Villon]

2488   LAMPE, DAVID. "The Courtly Rhetoric of Chaucer's Advisory
          Poetry." RMSt 9 (1983), 70-83. [Deschamps; Truth, Gent,
          Sted, Wom Nob]

2489   LENAGHAN, R. T. "Chaucer's Circle of Gentlemen and Clerks."
          ChauR 18 (1983), 155-60. [poems to Scogan; Bukton; Vache
          (Truth); Richard II (Sted); Henry IV (Purse)]

2489a   ROBBINS, ROSSELL HOPE. "Chaucer and the Lyric Tradition." PoetT
          15/16 (1983), 107-27.

2490   ROBBINS, ROSSELL HOPE. "The Lyrics," in 70, pp. 380-402.
          [revision of 1969 bibliography]

2491   RUUD, JAY WESLEY. "Tradition and Individuality in Chaucer's
          Lyrics." DAI 42 (1981), 2146A. University of
          Wisconsin-Milwaukee.

2492   SATO, TSUTOMU. Chaucer no Renai Shi: Shiyaku to Kaishaku.
          Tokyo: Kobundo Souppansha, 1976. 230 pp. [Chaucer's love
          poems; +translations]

2493   SHIGEO, HISASHI. "The Meaning of Chaucer's Minor Poems." MeiGR

Lyrics and Shorter Poems

358-60 (1984), 31-47. [ABC, Pity, Lady, and Mars]

2494   STEMMLER, THEO, ed. Medieval English Love Lyrics. English
        Texts, 1. Tübingen: Max Niemeyer Verlag, 1970. 123 pp.
        [anthology]
            Reviews: Horst Oppel, NS 22:2 (1973), 449-50; Martin
        Lehnert, ZAA 24 (1976), 357-62.

2495   STEMMLER, THEO. "My Fair Lady: Parody in Fifteenth-Century
        English Lyrics," in 42, pp. 205-13. [Purse, MerB]

2496   STEVENS, JOHN. "The 'Music' of the Lyric: Machaut, Deschamps,
        Chaucer," in 48, pp. 109-29. [metrics; French sources; Wom
        Nob, Ros]

2497   VARNAITÉ, IRENA. "Lirika Dž. Čosera: Vstanye liričeskie stixi v
        ego poèmax." Literatura 21:3 (1979), 22-32. [+summaries in
        English, Lithuanian]

2498   WIMSATT, JAMES I. "Guillaume de Machaut and Chaucer's Love
        Lyrics." MAE 47 (1978), 66-87. [source study; Lady, Anel,
        Compl d'Am, Ros, Wom Nob, Pity, MercB, Wom Unc; +Graunson]

See also: 22, 103, 110, 156, 175, 176, 210, 263, 417, 543, 669, 692,
            715, 825, 851, 2832.

>>> Lyrics, General: Source Studies <<<

See nos. 597, 615, 634, 643, 645, 654.

AN A B C

2499   BARR, D. J. "Chaucer's 'A. B. C.': Text, Source and Literary
        Context." M.Phil. thesis, University of London (Bedford
        College), 1975.

2500   CRAMPTON, GEORGIA RONAN. "Of Chaucer's ABC." Chaucer Newsletter
        1:1 (1979), 8-9.

2501   DAVID, ALFRED. "An ABC to the Style of the Prioress," in 52, pp.
        147-57. [comparison]

2502   HENRY, AVRIL. "Chaucer's ABC: Line 39 and the Irregular Stanza
         Again." ChauR 18 (1983), 95–99. [The Pilgrimage of the Lyf
         of the Manhode and emendation of ABC]

2503   PACE, GEORGE B. "The Adorned Initials of Chaucer's A B C."
         Manuscripta 23 (1979), 88–98.

2504   REAMES, SHERRY LEE. "The 'A. B. C.' and the 'Second Nun's Tale':
         Translation and Transformation." DAI 36 (1976), 8036–37A.
         Yale University, 1975.

See also: 115, 130, 181, 187, 224, 230, 242, 430, 576, 630, 674, 859,
            866, 891, 2493, 2506, 2866.

CHAUCERS WORDES UNTO ADAM, HIS OWNE SCRIVEYN

2505   KASKE, R. E. "'Clericus Adam' and Chaucer's 'Adam Scriveyn'," in
         73, pp. 114–18. [+sources]

See also: 203, 224, 891, 2485, 2858a.

THE COMPLAINT OF CHAUCER TO HIS PURSE

2506   LUDLUM, CHARLES D. "Heavenly Word-Play in Chaucer's 'Complaint
         to His Purse'." N&Q 23 (1976), 391–92. [+ABC]

2507   RUUD, JAY. "Chaucer's 'Complaint to His Purse'." Expl 41:3
         (1983), 5–6. ["toune" = "predicament"]

See also: 187, 203, 224, 226, 308, 478, 490, 534, 2489, 2495, 2670,
            2883, 2858a.

Lyrics and Shorter Poems

THE COMPLAINT OF MARS

2508   AMSLER, MARK E. "Mad Lovers and Other Hooked Fish: Chaucer's
       Complaint of Mars." Allegorica 4 (1979), 301-14. [+TC]

2509   PARR, JOHNSTONE and NANCY ANN HOLTZ. "The Astronomy-Astrology in
       Chaucer's The Complaint of Mars." ChauR 15 (1981), 255-66.

2510   STORM, MELVIN. "The Mythological Tradition in Chaucer's
       Complaint of Mars." PQ 57 (1978), 323-35.

See also: 180, 187, 188, 224, 269, 311, 339, 474, 483, 597, 654, 859,
       891, 2195, 2471, 2493, 2498, 2792.

THE COMPLAINT OF VENUS

See nos. 187, 188, 224, 293, 474, 582, 597, 859, 891.

A COMPLAINT TO HIS LADY

2511   CLOGAN, PAUL M. "The Textual Reliability of Chaucer's Lyrics: A
       Complaint to His Lady." M&H, n. s., 5 (1974), 183-89.

See also: 110, 224, 654, 859, 2493, 2498.

THE COMPLAINT UNTO PITY

2512   NOLAN, CHARLES J., JR. "Structural Sophistication in 'The
       Complaint Unto Pity'." ChauR 13 (1979), 363-72.

See also: 181, 188, 224, 256, 370, 374, 375, 474, 654, 859, 2493, 2498.

ENVOY TO BUKTON

2513   BREMMER, ROLF, JR. "Friesland and Its Inhabitants in Middle
        English Literature," in Miscellanea Frisica: A New
        Collection of Frisian Studies. Edited by N. R. Arhammar, et
        al. Fryske Akademy 634. Assen: Van Gorcum, 1984, pp.
        357-70. [Frise in Buk 23]

See also: 203, 224, 385, 474, 478, 576, 645, 859, 891, 1434, 2485, 2489,
        2670.

ENVOY TO SCOGAN

2514   HALLMUNDSSON, MAY NEWMAN. "Chaucer's Circle: Henry Scogan and
        His Friends." M&H, n. s., 10 (1981), 129-39.

2515   LENAGHAN, R. T. "Chaucer's Envoy to Scogan: The Uses of
        Literary Conventions." ChauR 10 (1975), 46-61. [+Deschamps]

2516   POLZELLA, MARION L. "'The Craft So Long to Lerne': Poet and
        Lover in Chaucer's 'Envoy to Scogan' and Parliament of
        Fowls." ChauR 10 (1976), 279-86.

See also: 187, 203, 224, 226, 308, 385, 474, 859, 1007, 2485, 2489,
        2654, 2670, 2858a.

THE FORMER AGE

2517   DEAN, JAMES. "The World Grown Old and Genesis in Middle English
        Historical Writings." Speculum 57 (1982), 548-68. [Nimrod]

2518   SCHMIDT, A. V. C. "Chaucer and the Golden Age." EIC 26 (1976),
        99-115. [versification; Boece; sources]

2519   SCHMIDT, A. V. C. "Chaucer's Nembrot: A Note on The Former
        Age." MAE 47 (1978), 304-07. [Walafrid Strabo's Glossa
        Ordinaria; source]

Lyrics and Shorter Poems

2520   WITLIEB, BERNARD. "Jupiter and Nimrod in The Former Age."
            Chaucer Newsletter 2:2 (1980), 12-13. [Ovide Moralisé as
            source]

See also: 203, 629, 654, 859, 891, 2518.

FORTUNE

2521   RUUD, JAY. "Chaucer's 'Fortune'." Expl 43:1 (1984), 8-9.
            [+structure]

See also: 181, 187, 203, 224, 242, 264, 308, 385, 582, 654, 663, 859,
            891.

GENTILESSE

See nos. 203, 242, 629, 654, 859, 2488.

LAK OF STEDFASTNESSE

2522   NORTON-SMITH, J. "Textual Tradition, Monarchy and Chaucer's Lak
            of Stedfastnes." RMSt 8 (1982), 3-10.

See also: 203, 224, 478, 663, 1114, 2488, 2489, 2858a.

PROVERBS

See nos. 203, 1437.

TO ROSEMOUNDE

2523   VASTA, EDWARD. "'To Rosemounde': Chaucer's 'Gentil' Dramatic
        Monologue," in 73, pp. 97-113.

See also: 203, 224, 226, 341, <u>582</u>, 891, <u>2486</u>, <u>2496</u>, <u>2498</u>, <u>2670</u>, 2858a,
        2868.

TRUTH

2524   DAVID, ALFRED. "The Truth about 'Vache'." <u>ChauR</u> 11 (1977),
        334-37.

2525   GILLMEISTER, HEINER. <u>Chaucer's Conversion: Allegorical Thought
        in Medieval Literature</u>. (Aspekte der englischen Geistes- und
        Kulturgeschichte, 2.) Frankfurt-am-Main and New York: Peter
        Lang, 1984. 281 pp. [<u>Truth</u> as exegetical lyric based on 1
        Samuel 6.7-14 and Chaucer's conversion]
        Reviews: James Dean, <u>Speculum</u> 61 (1986), 151-53.

2526   GILLMEISTER, HEINER. "The Whole Truth about <u>Vache</u>." <u>Chaucer
        Newsletter</u> 2:1 (1980), 13-14.

2527   SCATTERGOOD, V. J. "Chaucer's Curial Satire: The <u>Balade de Bon
        Conseyl</u>." <u>Hermathena</u> 133 (1982), 29-45. [+Bible, Boethius]

See also: 115, 187, 203, 242, 269, 478, 629, <u>2488</u>, <u>2489</u>.

WOMANLY NOBLESSE

See nos. 130, 203, 224, 859, <u>2486</u>, 2488, <u>2496</u>, <u>2498</u>.

Lyrics and Shorter Poems

LYRICS NOT ASCRIBED TO CHAUCER IN THE MANUSCRIPTS

AGAINST WOMEN UNCONSTANT

2528   RUUD, JAY. "Against Women Unconstant: The Case for Chaucer's
        Authorship." MP 80 (1982), 161–64. [+Boece]

See also: 2498.

COMPLAYNT D'AMOURS

See nos. 181, 224, 2498.

MERCILES BEAUTE

See nos. 187, 203, 224, 891, 2495, 2498, 2858a.

APOCRYPHA, LOST WORKS, AND WORKS OF DOUBTFUL AUTHORSHIP

GENERAL

2529   ROBBINS, ROSSELL HOPE.   "The Chaucerian Apochrypha," in 28,
        Vol.4, Ch. 11, pp. 1061-1101, with bibliography, pp.
        1285-1306.
           Reviews: Coleman O. Parsons, RenQ 28 (1975), 221-29.

2530   ROBBINS, ROSSELL HOPE.   "The Structure of Longer Middle English
        Court Poems," in 73, pp. 244-64. [dits amoureux, The Court
        of Love, The Flower and the Leaf, The Assembly of Ladies]

See also: 120, 123, 142, 2834.

EQUATORIE OF PLANETIS

See nos. 440, 891, 946, 1986, 1987, 2650.

THE ISLE OF LADIES

2531   JENKINS, ANTHONY, ed. The Isle of Ladies or the Isle of
        Pleasaunce. New York: Garland Publishers, 1980. 195 pp.
        [reproduces the Longleat MS 256 of The Isle of Ladies
        included in Speght]
           Reviews: Vincent Daly, Speculum 55 (1980), 867-68; E. Ruth
        Harvey, SAC 4 (1982), 165-69.

2532   Item cancelled.

Apocrypha, Lost Works, and Works of Doubtful Authorship

See also: 691.

THE ROMAUNT OF THE ROSE

2533   CAIE, GRAHAM D. "An Iconographic Detail in the Roman de la Rose
         and the Middle English Romaunt." ChauR 8 (1974), 320–23.

2534   ECKHARDT, CAROLINE D. "The Art of Translation in The Romaunt of
         the Rose." SAC 6 (1984), 41–63. [comparison, RR]

2535   NORDAHL, HELGE. "Ars fidi interpretis: Un Aspect rhétorique de
         l'art de Chaucer dans sa traduction du Roman de la Rose."
         ArL 9 (1978), 24–31.

See also: 100, 130, 224, 231, 256, 263, 316, 458, 576, 577, 597, 611,
         749, 859, 891, 925, 951, 954, 2140, 2277, 2595, 2598, 2812.

THE TALE OF BERYN

See nos. 694, 739, 978.

THE TALE OF GAMELYN

See no. 686.

BACKGROUNDS

GENERAL BACKGROUNDS INCLUDING HISTORICAL,

AND PHILOSOPHIC BACKGROUNDS

2536   ALFORD, JOHN A. and DENNIS P. SENIFF. <u>Literature and Law in the
        Middle Ages: A Bibliography of Scholarship</u>. Garland
        Reference Library of the Humanities, 378. New York and
        London: Garland, 1984. 292 pp.
        Reviews: Karl H. Van D'Elden, <u>Speculum</u> 60 (1985), 935-36.

2537   ARNOLD, MORRIS S., THOMAS A. GREEN, SALLY A. SCULLY, and STEPHEN
        D. WHITE, eds. <u>On the Laws and Customs of England: Essays
        in Honor of Samuel E. Thorne</u>. Studies in Legal History.
        Chapel Hill: University of North Carolina Press, 1981. 426
        pp.

2538   AULT, WARREN O. <u>Open-Field Farming in Medieval England: A Study
        of English By-Laws</u>. Historical Problems: Studies and
        Documents, 16. London: George Allen and Unwin; New York:
        Barnes and Noble, 1972. 184 pp.
        Reviews: Eleanor Searle, <u>Speculum</u> 49 (1974), 314-16.

2539   BARBER, MALCOLM. <u>The Trial of the Templars</u>. Cambridge, England,
        and New York: Cambridge University Press, 1978. 311 pp.
        Reviews: Gabrielle M. Spiegel, <u>Speculum</u> 55 (1980), 329-32.

2540   BARBER, RICHARD. <u>The Knight and Chivalry</u>. New York: Harper &
        Row, 1982. 399 pp.
        Reviews: Larry D. Benson, <u>Speculum</u> 58 (1983), 546.

2541   BENSON, ROBERT L. and GILES CONSTABLE, eds., with CAROL D.
        LANHAM. <u>Renaissance and Renewal in the Twelfth Century</u>.
        Cambridge, MA: Harvard University Press, 1982. 781 pp.
        [essays by various hands]
        Reviews: John C. Hirsh, <u>SAC</u> 6 (1984), 173-77.

Backgrounds

2542   BOWMAN, LEONARD, ed. Itinerarium: The Idea of a Journey. A
        Collection of Papers Given at the Fifteenth International
        Congress on Medieval Studies, Kalamazoo, Michigan, May 1980.
        Salzburg Studies in English Literature, Elizabethan and
        Renaissance Studies, 92/9. Salzburg: Institut für Anglistik
        und Amerikanistik, 1983. 234 pp.

2543   BOYLE, LEONARD E., O. P. Pastoral Care, Clerical Education and
        Canon Law, 1200-1400. Collected Studies Series, 135.
        London: Variorum Reprints, 1981. 352 pp.

2544   BRINKMANN, HENNIG. Mittelalterliche Hermeneutik. Tübingen: Max
        Niemeyer, 1980. 439 pp.
        Reviews: R. A. Shoaf, Speculum 57 (1982), 123-25.

2545   BRUNDAGE, JAMES A. "Carnal Delight: Canonistic Theories of
        Sexuality," in Proceedings of the Fifth International
        Congress of Medieval Canon Law, Salamanca, 21-25 September
        1976. Monumenta Iuris Canonici, Series C: Subsidia, 6.
        Vatican City: Biblioteca Apostolica Vaticana, 1980.

2546   CARTER, JOHN MARSHALL. Rape in Medieval England: An Historical
        and Sociological Study. Lanham, MD; New York, and London:
        University Press of America, 1985. 185 pp.
        Reviews: James Given, Speculum 61 (1986), 633-35.

2547   CHADWICK, HENRY. Boethius: The Consolations of Music, Logic,
        Theology and Philosophy. Oxford: Clarendon Press; New York:
        Oxford University Press, 1981. 313 pp.
        Reviews: G. H. Allard, Speculum 58 (1983), 742-43.

2548   COBBAN, A. B. The Medieval Universities: Their Development and
        Organization. London: Methuen, 1975. 264 pp.
        Reviews: Astrik L. Gabriel, Speculum 55 (1980), 545-47.

2549   DUGGAN, ANNE. Thomas Becket: A Textual History of His Letters.
        Oxford: Clarendon Press; New York: Oxford University Press,
        1980. 318 pp.
        Reviews: Richard M. Fraher, Speculum 57 (1982), 449-50.

2550   DUGGAN, CHARLES. Canon Law in Medieval England: The Becket
        Dispute and Decretal Collections. Collected Studies, 151.
        London: Variorum Reprints, 1982. 340 pp.

2551   ENNEN, EDITH. The Medieval Town. Trans. Natalie Fryde. Europe
        in the Middle Ages, Selected Studies, 15. Amsterdam and New
        York: North-Holland, 1979. 287 pp.
        Reviews: Richard C. Hoffman, Speculum 55 (1980), 556-57.

General Backgrounds/Historical, Philosophic Backgrounds

2552   FINUCANE, RONALD C. **Miracles and Pilgrims: Popular Beliefs in**
        Medieval England. Totowa, NJ: Rowman and Littlefield, 1977.
        248 pp.
            Reviews: Nancy Partner, Speculum 55 (1980), 865-66.

2553   GIES, FRANCES. **The Knight in History.** New York: Harper & Row,
        1984. 255 pp.
            Reviews: Brigitte Bedos Rezak, Speculum 61 (1986), 654-56.

2554   HARDING, ALAN. "Political Liberty in the Middle Ages," Speculum
        55 (1980), 423-43.

2555   HART, ROGER. **English Life in Chaucer's Day.** English Life. New
        York: Putnam, 1973. 128 pp. [popular; color plates of
        medieval illuminations; historical, sociological, cultural]
            Reviews: Booklist 69 (15 May, 1973), 887; H. T. Keenan, LJ
        98 (1 March, 1973), 738.

2556   HECTOR, L. C. and BARBARA F. HARVEY, eds. and trans. **The**
        Westminster Chronicle, 1381-1394. Oxford Medieval Texts.
        New York: Clarendon Press, Oxford University Press, 1982.
        563 pp. [sources on reign of Richard II]
            Reviews: J. R. Lander, Speculum 59 (1984), 157-59.

2557   HILTON, R. H. **The English Peasantry in the Later Middle Ages.**
        The Ford Lectures for 1973 and Related Studies. Oxford:
        Clarendon Press; New York: Oxford University Press, 1975.
        256 pp.
            Reviews: J. S. Beckerman, Speculum 52 (1977), 989-91.

2558   JEFFREY, DAVID L., ed. **By Things Seen: Reference and**
        Recognition in Medieval Thought. Ottawa: University of
        Ottawa Press, 1979. 270 pp. [medieval idea of referral]
            Reviews: Morton W. Bloomfield, Speculum 55 (1980), 408.

2559   KAEUPER, RICHARD W. "Law and Order in Fourteenth-Century
        England: The Evidence of Special Commissions of Oyer and
        Terminer." Speculum 54 (1979), 734-84.

2560   KEEFE, THOMAS K. **Feudal Assessments and the Political Community**
        under Henry II and His Sons. Publications of the UCLA Center
        for Medieval and Renaissance Studies, 19. Berkeley and Los
        Angeles: University of California Press, 1984. 291 pp.
        [treats the Henry II/Becket disagreement]
            Reviews: Robert B. Patterson, Speculum 61 (1986), 433-34.

2561   KEEN, M. H. **England in the Later Middle Ages: A Political**
        History. London: Methuen; New York: Harper and Row, 1973.

Backgrounds

581 pp.
Reviews: Bertie Wilkinson, Speculum 51 (1976), 144–46.

2562 KIECKHEFFER, RICHARD. European Witch Trials: Their Foundations
in Popular and Learned Culture, 1300–1500. Berkeley and Los
Angeles: University of California Press, 1976. 181 pp.
Reviews: Jeffrey B. Russell, Speculum 53 (1978), 149–51.

2563 KITTELSON, JAMES M. and PAMELA J. TRANSUE, eds. Rebirth, Reform
and Resilience: Universities in Transition 1300–1700.
Columbus: Ohio State University Press, 1984. 367 pp.

2564 KORS, ALAN C. and EDWARD PETERS, eds. Witchcraft in Europe,
1100–1700: A Documentary History. Philadelphia: University
of Pennsylvania Press, 1973. 400 pp.
Reviews: Robert H. West, GaR 27 (1973), 137–41; Lawrence
F. Barmann, S. J., Thought 48 (1973), 314–15.

2565 LEFF, GORDON. The Dissolution of the Medieval Outlook: An Essay
on Intellectual and Spiritual Change in the Fourteenth
Century. New York: New York University Press, 1976. 154
pp.
Reviews: Louis B. Pascoe, S. J., Speculum 53 (1978),
824–26.

2566 LOXTON, HOWARD. Pilgrimage to Canterbury. London: David
Charles; Totowa, NJ: Rowman & Littlefield, 1978. 208 pp.
Reviews: Marjorie Nice Boyer, Speculum 54 (1979), 597–98.

2567 MATE, MAVIS. "The Impact of War on the Economy of Canterbury
Cathedral Priory, 1294–1340." Speculum 57 (1982), 761–78.

2568 McFARLANE, K. B. Lancastrian Kings and Lollard Knights. Oxford,
England: Clarendon Press; New York: Oxford University
Press, 1972. 261 pp.
Reviews: J. M. W. Bean, Speculum 49 (1974), 582–84.

2569 OAKLEY, FRANCIS. The Medieval Experience: Foundations of
Western Cultural Singularity. New York: Charles Scribner's
Sons, 1974. 228 pp.
Reviews: Jeffrey B. Russell, Speculum 52 (1977), 161–62.

2570 ORME, NICHOLAS. English Schools in the Middle Ages. London:
Metheun, 1973. 369 pp.
Reviews: Kenneth Jensen, Speculum 51 (1976), 524–26.

2571 PACKE, MICHAEL ST. JOHN. King Edward III. Ed. L. C. B. Seaman.
London and Boston: Routledge & Kegan Paul, 1983.
Reviews: Richard H. Jones, Speculum 59 (1984), 933–35.

General Backgrounds/Historical, Philosophic Backgrounds

2572   PALMER, J. J. N. England, France and Christendom, 1377-99.
       Chapel Hill: University of North Carolina Press; London:
       Routledge and Kegan Paul, 1972. 282 pp.
       Reviews: G. P. Cuttino, Speculum 49 (1974), 751-52.

2573   PALMER, J. J. N., ed. Froissart: Historian. Woodbridge,
       Suffolk: Boydell & Brewer; Totowa, NJ: Rowman and
       Littlefield, 1981. 203 pp.
       Reviews: Sumner Ferris, SAC 5 (1983), 183-87.

2574   PAYER, PIERRE J. "Prudence and the Principles of Natural Law: A
       Medieval Development." Speculum 54 (1979), 55-70.

2575   PLATT, COLIN. The English Medieval Town. London: Secker and
       Warburg, 1976. 219 pp.
       Reviews: J. M. W. Bean, Speculum 54 (1979), 413-14.

2576   POWELL, JAMES M., ed. Medieval Studies: An Introduction.
       Syracuse: Syracuse University Press, 1976. 389 pp.
       Reviews: Joseph R. Strayer, Speculum 53 (1978), 183-84.

2577   ROBERTS, LAWRENCE D., ed. Approaches to Nature in the Middle
       Ages. Papers of the Tenth Conference of the Center for
       Medieval and Early Renaissance Studies. Medieval and
       Renaissance Texts and Studies, 16. Binghamton: Center for
       Medieval and Early Renaissance Studies, SUNY, 1982. 220 pp.

2578   SCHIFFHORST, GERALD J., ed. The Triumph of Patience: Medieval
       and Renaissance Studies. Orlando, FL: University Presses of
       Florida, 1978. 146 pp.
       Reviews: Lawrence L. Besserman, Speculum 55 (1980),
       606-08.

2579   SCHOFIELD, JOHN H. The Building of London from the Norman
       Conquest to the Great Fire. British Museum Publications for
       the Museum of London. London: Colonnade Books, 1984.
       [Chapter 4 is "The London of Yevele and Chaucer, 1300-1400"]
       Reviews: Kathleen Biddick, Speculum 60 (1985), 1063-64.

2580   SMALLEY, BERYL. The Becket Conflict and the Schools: A Study of
       Intellectuals in Politics. Totowa, NJ: Rowman and
       Littlefield, 1973. 258 pp.
       Reviews: John W. Baldwin, Speculum 51 (1976), 357-59.

2581   SMITH, J. A. CLARENCE. Medieval Law Teachers and Writers,
       Civilian and Canonist. Collection des travaux de la Faculté
       de Droit de l'Universite d'Ottawa, Monographies juridiques,
       9. Ottawa: University of Ottawa Press, 1975. 129 pp.

Bibliography of Chaucer, 1974 - 1985

Backgrounds

Reviews: Peter Weimar, Speculum 54 (1979), 560–61.

2582   STOW, GEORGE B.   "Richard II in Thomas Walsingham's Chronicles."
       Speculum 59 (1984), 68–102.

2583   SWANSON, R. N.   Universities, Academics and the Great Schism.
       Cambridge Studies in Medieval Life and Thought, Third Series,
       12. London and New York: Cambridge University Press, 1979.
       245 pp.
       Reviews: Alan B. Cobban, EHR 95 (1980), 363–65; John E.
       Weakland, AHR 85 (1980), 611.

2584   TIERNEY, BRIAN.   Origins of Papal Infallibility, 1150–1350: A
       Study on the Concepts of Infallibility, Sovereignty, and
       Tradition in the Middle Ages.   Studies in the History of
       Christian Thought, 6. Leiden: E. J. Brill, 1972. 298 pp.
       Reviews: Gaines Post, Speculum 49 (1974), 762–65.

2585   TWIGG, GRAHAM.   The Black Death: A Biological Reappraisal.
       London: Batsford Academic and Educational, 1984. 254 pp.
       Reviews: R. S. Gottfried, Speculum 61 (1986), 217–19.

2586   ULLMANN, WALTER.   Law and Politics in the Middle Ages: An
       Introduction to the Sources of Medieval Political Ideas.   The
       Sources of History: Studies in the Uses of Historical
       Evidence. Ithaca, NY: Cornell University Press, 1975.   320
       pp.
       Reviews: Kenneth Pennington, Speculum 52 (1977), 752.

2587   VAN CAENEGEM, R. C.   The Birth of the English Common Law.
       Cambridge, England, and New York: Cambridge University
       Press, 1973. 160 pp.
       Reviews: R. H. Helmholz, Speculum 51 (1976), 364–65.

2588   VAN CAENEGEM, R. C. with F. L. GANSHOF.   Guide to the Sources of
       Medieval History.   Europe in the Middle Ages, Selected
       Studies, 2. Amsterdam, New York: North-Holland, 1978.   428
       pp.
       Reviews: Paul Meyvaert, Speculum 54 (1979), 872.

2589   VERBEKE, GERARD.   The Presence of Stoicism in Medieval Thought.
       Washington, D. C.: Catholic University Press, 1983. 101 pp.
       Reviews: Marcia L. Colish, Speculum 59 (1984), 449–50;
       Ernest L. Fortin, Review of Metaphysics 38 (1984), 146–47.

2590   WAGNER, DAVID L., ed.   The Seven Liberal Arts in the Middle Ages.
       Bloomington: Indiana University Press, 1983. 282 pp.
       Reviews: Emil Lucki, Speculum 60 (1985), 730–32; John R.
       E. Bliese, QJS 71 (1985), 245–27.

Literary and Aesthetic Backgrounds

2591   WARREN, W. L. Henry II. Berkeley and Los Angeles: University
        of California Press, 1973. 693 pp. [Becket controversy]
        Reviews: Michael Altschul, Speculum 51 (1976), 156-58.

2592   WILLIMAN, DANIEL, ed. The Black Death: The Impact of the
        Fourteenth-Century Plague. Papers of the Eleventh Annual
        Conference of the Center for Medieval and Early Renaissance
        Studies. Medieval and Renaissance Texts and Studies, 13.
        Binghamton: Center for Medieval and Early Renaissance
        Studies, SUNY, 1982. 159 pp.

2593   WOODS, WILLIAM. England in the Age of Chaucer. New York: Stein
        and Day, 1976.
        Reviews: Gabriel Josipovici, NYRB (28 April, 1976), 18-22.

See also: 77, 81, 285, 290, 320, 344, 386, 459, 759, 1184, 1210, 1255,
           1296, 1518, 1636, 1662, 1788, 2059.

LITERARY AND AESTHETIC BACKGROUNDS

2594   ALFORD, JOHN A. "The Grammatical Metaphor: A Survey of Its Use
        in the Middle Ages." Speculum 57 (1982), 728-60. [+PardT]

2595   ANDREAS CAPELLANUS. Andreas Capellanus on Love. Trans. P. G.
        Walsh. Duckworth Classical, Medieval, and Renaissance
        Editions. London: Duckworth, 1982. 329 pp.
        Reviews: David Carlson, Speculum 59 (1984), 608-10.

2596   BADEL, PIERRE-YVES. 'Le Roman de la rose' au XIVe siècle: Etude
        de la réception de l'oeuvre. Publications Romanes et
        Françaises, 153. Geneva: Droz, 1980. 534 pp.
        Reviews: Charles R. Dahlberg, Speculum 56 (1981), 844-47.

2597   BAIRD, JOSEPH L. and LORRAYNE Y. BAIRD. "Fabliau Form and the
        Hegge 'Joseph's Return'." ChauR 8 (1973), 159-69.

2598   BARNEY, STEPHEN A. Allegories of History, Allegories of Love.
        Hamden, CT: Archon Books, Shoe String Press, 1979. 323 pp.
        Reviews: R. T. Davies, MLR 77 (1982), 139-40.

2599   BÄUML, FRANZ H. "Varieties and Consequences of Medieval Literacy
        and Illiteracy." Speculum 55 (1980), 237-65.

2600   BEIDLER, PETER G., ed. John Gower's Literary Transformations in

Backgrounds

the 'Confessio Amantis': Original Articles and Translations.
Washington, D. C.: University Press of America, 1982.
Reviews: Robert Yeager, SAC 5 (1983), 146–52.

2601   BENSON, ROBERT L. and GILES CONSTABLE, eds., with CAROL D.
LANHAM. Renaissance and Renewal in the Twelfth Century.
Cambridge, MA: Harvard University Press, 1982. 781 pp.

2602   BEST, THOMAS W. Reynard the Fox. Twayne's World Author Series,
673. Boston: G. K. Hall, 1983. 178 pp.
Reviews: Jan Ziolkowski, Speculum 59 (1984), 621–23; David
Blamires, MLR 80 (1985), 113.

2603   BOASE, ROGER. The Origin and Meaning of Courtly Love: A
Critical Study of European Scholarship.
Manchester, England: Manchester University Press; Totowa,
NJ: Rowman and Littlefield, 1977. 171 pp.
Reviews: H. A. Kelly, Speculum 54 (1979), 338–42.

2604   BOITANI, PIERO and ANNA TORTI, eds. Literature in
Fourteenth-Century England: The J. A. W. Bennett Memorial
Lectures, Perugia, 1981–1982. Tübinger Beiträge zur
Anglistik 5. Tübingen: Gunter Narr Verlag; Cambridge:
Boydell & Brewer, 1983. 221 pp. See nos. 286, 546a, 1085a,
2074a.

2604a   BOYLE, LEONARD E., O. P. Medieval Latin Paleography: A
Bibliographical Introduction. Toronto Medieval
Bibliographies, 8. Toronto, Buffalo, and London: University
of Toronto Press, 1984. 399 pp.
Reviews: Braxton Ross, Speculum 61 (1986), 623–24.

2605   BRÉMOND, CLAUDE, JACQUES LE GOFF, and JEAN-CLAUDE SCHMITT.
L'"exemplum". Typologie des sources du moyen âge occidental,
40. Turnhout: Brepols, 1982. 166 pp.
Reviews: Charles B. Faulhaber, Speculum 59 (1984), 887–89.

2606   BRODY, SAUL NATHANIEL. The Disease of the Soul: Leprosy in
Medieval Literature. Ithaca, NY, and London: Cornell
University Press, 1974. 223 pp.
Reviews: Denton Fox, Speculum 52 (1977), 126–28.

2607   BROWNLEE, KEVIN. Poetic Identity in Guillaume de Machaut.
Madison: University of Wisconsin Press, 1984. 262 pp.
Reviews: C. M. Reno, Choice 22 (1984), 564; David A. Fein,
FR 59 (1985), 124–25.

2608   BURNLEY, J. D. "Curial Prose in England." Speculum 61 (1986),
593–614.

Literary and Aesthetic Backgrounds

2609   BURNS, NORMAN T. and CHRISTOPHER J. REAGAN, eds. Concepts of the
        Hero in the Middle Ages and the Renaissance. Papers of the
        Fourth and Fifth Annual Conferences of the Center for
        Medieval and Early Renaissance Studies, State University of
        New York at Binghamton, 2-3 May 1970, 1-2 May 1971. Albany:
        State University of New York Press, 1975. 293 pp. [See
        esp.: Morton W. Bloomfield, "The Problem of the Hero in the
        Later Medieval Period," pp. 27-48.]

2610   BURROW, J. A. Medieval Writers and Their Work: Middle English
        Literature and Its Background, 1100-1500. Oxford: Oxford
        University Press, 1982.
            Reviews: J. J. A[nders], CritQ 24 (1982), 92; Tony
        Davenport, English 32 (1983), 155-59; James Simpson, MAE 53
        (1984), 307-11.

2611   BUSBY, KEITH. "Conspicuous by Its Absence: The English
        Fabliau." DQR 12 (1982), 30-41.

2612   COOKE, THOMAS D., ed. The Present State of Scholarship in
        Fourteenth-Century Literature. Columbia and London:
        University of Missouri Press, 1982. 323 pp.
            Reviews: E. D. Blodgett, Speculum 59 (1984), 636-39.

2613   DAVIDOFF, JUDITH M. "The Audience Illuminated, or New Light Shed
        on the Dream Frame of Lydgate's Temple of Glas." SAC 5
        (1983), 103-25.

2614   DAVIDSON, CLIFFORD. A Middle English Treatise on the Playing of
        Miracles. Washington, D. C.: University Press of America,
        1981. [Wycliffite Tretise]

2615   DEMATS, PAULE. Fabula: Trois études de mythographie antique et
        médiévale. Publications romanes et françaises, 122. Geneva:
        Droz, 1973. 194 pp.
            Reviews: John Block Friedman, Speculum 51 (1976), 734-37.

2616   DOOB, PENELOPE B. R. Nebuchadnezzar's Children: Conventions of
        Madness in Middle English Literature. New Haven, CT; London:
        Yale University Press, 1974. 247 pp.
            Reviews: Albert B. Friedman, Speculum 52 (1977), 135-36.

2617   EBERLE, PATRICIA J. "The Politics of Courtly Style at the Court
        of Richard II," in Spirit of the Court: Selected Proceedings
        of the Fourth Congress of the International Courtly
        Literature Society, Toronto 1983. Edited by Glyn S. Burgess
        and Robert A. Taylor. Cambridge: D. S. Brewer, 1985, pp.
        168-78.

Bibliography of Chaucer, 1974 - 1985

Backgrounds

2618   ECKHARDT, CAROLINE D., ed. Essays in the Numerical Criticism of
        Medieval Literature. Lewisburg, PA: Bucknell University
        Press; London: Associated University Presses, 1980. 239 pp.
        Reviews: Edmund Reiss, SAC 4 (1982), 146-49.

2619   FERRANTE, JOAN M., and GEORGE D. ECONOMOU, eds. In Pursuit of
        Perfection. Courtly Love in Medieval Literature. Series in
        Literary Criticism. Port Washington, NY, and London:
        National University Publications, Kennikat Press, 1975. 266
        pp.
        Reviews: R. W. Hanning, Speculum 52 (1977), 965-67.

2620   FINLAYSON, JOHN. "Definitions of Middle English Romance: Part
        I." ChauR 15 (1980), 44-62; Part II, ChauR 15 (1980),
        168-81.

2621   FISCHER, STEVEN R. The Complete Medieval Dreambook: A
        Multilingual, Alphabetical 'Somnia Danielis' Collation.
        Berne and Frankfurt am Main: Verlag Peter Lang, 1982.
        Reviews: Alison M. Peden, MAE 53 (1984), 104.

2622   FLEMING, JOHN V. From Bonaventure to Bellini: An Essay in
        Franciscan Exegesis. Princeton Essays on the Arts.
        Princeton, NJ: Princeton University Press, 1982. 171 pp.
        Reviews: Margaret Harvey, DUJ, n. s., 46 (1984), 95;
        Ronald B. Herzman, SAC 6 (1984), 189-92.

2623   FLEMING, JOHN V. An Introduction to the Franciscan Literature of
        the Middle Ages. Chicago: Franciscan Herald Press, 1977.
        274 pp.
        Reviews: Williell R. Thompson, Speculum 54 (1979), 126-27.

2624   FLEMING, JOHN V. Reason and the Lover. Princeton, NJ:
        Princeton University Press, 1984. [RR]
        Reviews: Helen Cooper, SAC 7 (1985), 194-97.

2625   FORD, BORIS, ed. Medieval Literature: The European Inheritance.
        The New Pelican Guide to English Literature, I, 2.
        Harmondsworth: Penguin, 1982. 623 pp. [essays by various
        hands]
        Reviews: S. S. Hussey, MLR 80 (1985), 111.

2626   GALLO, ERNEST. The 'Poetria Nova' and Its Sources in Early
        Rhetorical Doctrine. De proprietatibus litterarum, Series
        Maior, 10. The Hague, Paris: Mouton, 1971. 241 pp.
        Reviews: James J. Murphy, Speculum 49 (1974), 116-18.

2627   GINSBERG, WARREN. The Cast of Character: The Representation of

Literary and Aesthetic Backgrounds

Personality in Ancient and Medieval Literature. Toronto: University of Toronto Press, 1983. 202 pp. See no. 368.

2628 GRABES, HERBERT. _The Mutable Glass: Mirror-Imagery in Titles and Texts of the Middle Ages and English Renaissance_. Trans. Gordon Collier. Cambridge: Cambridge University Press, 1982. 414 pp. [references to Chaucer]
Reviews: A. Fowler, _TLS_ (19 August, 1983), 872; Cecily Clark, _ES_ 65 (1984), 370–71; Dennis Kay, _RES_ 36 (1985), 398–401; Marie-Madeleine Martinet, _EA_ 38 (1985), 315–16.

2629 GRAY, DOUGLAS. "Notes on some Middle English Charms," in 69, pp. 56–71.

2630 GREEN, D. H. "On Recognizing Medieval Irony," in _The Uses of Criticism_. Edited by A. P. Foulkes. Literaturwissenschaftliche Texte, Theorie und Kritik, 3. Frankfurt: Peter Lang; Bern: Herbert Lang, 1976, pp. 11–55. [chiefly on French and German literature]

2631 HAAS, RENATE. _Die mittelenglische Totenklage: Realitätsbezug, abendländische Tradition und individuelle Gestaltung_. Sprache und Literatur, 16. Frankfurt am Main, Bern, and Cirencester: Peter D. Lang, 1980. 363 pp.
Review: Velma Bourgeois Richmond, _Speculum_ 58 (1983), 186–88.

2632 HANNA, RALPH, III. _The Index of Middle English Prose. Handlist I: A Handlist of Manuscripts Containing Middle English Prose in the Henry E. Huntington Library_. Totowa, NJ: Boydell & Brewer; Cambridge: D. S. Brewer, 1984. 81 pp. [HM 144, Ellesmere, _CT_, _Mel_, _Lady_] See no. 2644 below.
Reviews: Mark Y. Herring, _ARBA_ 16 (1985), 395–96.

2633 HESS, URSULA. _Heinrich Steinhöwels 'Griseldis': Studien zur Text- und Überlieferungsgeschichte einer frühhumanistischen Prosanovelle_. Münchener Texte und Untersuchungen zur deutschen Literatur des Mittelalters, 43. Munich: C. H. Beck, 1975. 270 pp.
Reviews: Winder McConnell, _Speculum_ 54 (1979), 384–86.

2634 HIMMELFARB, MARTHA. _Tours of Hell: An Apocalyptic Form in Jewish and Christian Literature_. Philadelphia: University of Pennsylvania Press, 1983. 198 pp.
Reviews: Susan Niditch, _Speculum_ 60 (1985), 479–80.

2635 IKEGAMI, TADAHIRO. "Some Features of Medieval English Literature." _SeijoB_ 99 (Tokyo, 1982), 1–23. In Japanese.

Backgrounds

2636   JAUSS, HANS ROBERT. Alterität und Modernität der
mittelalterlichen Literatur. Gesammelte Aufsätze 1956–1976.
Munich: Wilhelm Fink, 1977. 450 pp.
Reviews: W. Rothwell, FS 34:2 (1980), 85.

2637   KIBLER, WILLIAM W. and JAMES I. WIMSATT, eds. "The Development
of the Pastourelle in the Fourteenth Century: An Edition of
Fifteen Poems with an Analysis." MS 45 (1983), 22–78.
[University of Pennsylvania MS French 15]

2638   KIBLER, WILLIAM W., ed. Eleanor of Aquataine: Patron and
Politician. Symposia in Arts & Humanities 3. Austin:
University of Texas Press, 1976. 183 pp. See also no. 511.
Reviews: VQR 52:4 (1976), 112; John C. Moore, Speculum 53
(1978), 148–49.

2639   KNIGHT, STEPHEN. Arthurian Literature and Society. New York:
St. Martin's Press, 1983. 229 pp.
Reviews: Choice 22 (1984), 268; British Book News (July,
1984), 435.

2640   LADNER, GERHART B. "Medieval and Modern Understanding of
Symbolism: A Comparison." Speculum 54 (1979), 223–56.

2641   LAWLER, TRAUGOTT, ed. and trans. The 'Parisiana Poetria' of John
of Garland. With Introduction and Notes. Yale Studies in
English, 182. New Haven, CT; London: Yale University Press,
1974. 352 pp.
Reviews: Douglas Kelly, Speculum 52 (1977), 707–09.

2642   LAWTON, DAVID A., ed. Middle English Alliterative Poetry and Its
Literary Background: Seven Essays. Woodbridge, Suffolk:
Boydell & Brewer, 1982. 168 pp.
Reviews: Hoyt N. Duggan, Speculum 60 (1985), 170–73.

2643   LEE, BRIAN S. "This is no fable": Historical Residues in Two
Medieval Exempla." Speculum 56 (1981), 728–60. [+CT, PhyT,
ParsT]

2644   LESTER, G. A. The Index of Middle English Prose. Handlist II:
A Handlist of Manuscripts Containing Middle Enlgish Prose in
the John Rylands University Library of Manchester and
Chetham's Library, Manchester. Cambridge: D. S. Brewer,
1985. See no. 2632.
Reviews: Mark Y. Herring, ARBA 17 (1986), 453.

2645   LEWIS, C. S. Studies in Medieval and Renaissance Literature.
Collected by Walter Hooper. Cambridge: Cambridge University
Press, 1966, 1980.

BIBLIOGRAPHY OF CHAUCER, 1974 - 1985

Literary and Aesthetic Backgrounds

Reviews: Jill Mann, Encounter (1980), 60–64.

2646   LEWIS, R. E., N. F. BLAKE, and A. S. G. EDWARDS. Index of
Printed Middle English Prose. New York: Garland, 1985.
400 pp. [first-line index of prose appearing in printed
editions, 1480—; bibliography covers books, anthologies,
articles]
Reviews: Mark Y. Herring, ARBA 17 (1986), 453–54; Choice
23 (1986), 1038.

2647   LURIA, MAXWELL. A Reader's Guide to the 'Roman de la Rose'.
Hamden, CT: Archon, 1982. 282 pp.
Reviews: Alfred David, Speculum 59 (1984), 404–06.

2648   MEDCALF, STEPHEN, ed. The Later Middle Ages. The Context of
English Literature, 4. New York: Holmes & Meier, 1981. 312
pp. See no. 2351.
Reviews: Lois Ebin, Speculum 58 (1983), 509–11; James
Simpson, MAE 53 (1984), 307–11.

2649   MÉNARD, PHILIPPE. Les fabliaux: Contes à rire du moyen âge.
Littératures modernes, 32. Paris: Presses Universitaires de
France, 1983. 252 pp.
Reviews: M. A. Bossy, Speculum 60 (1985), 439–40.

2650   METLITZKI, DOROTHEE. The Matter of Araby in Medieval England.
New Haven, CT: Yale University Press, 1977. 320 pp.
Reviews: M. C. Seymour, ES 61 (1980), 556–59.

2651   MIDDLETON, ANNE. "The Idea of Public Poetry in the Reign of
Richard II." Speculum 53 (1978), 94–114. [persona, poetic
voice]

2652   MINER, EARL, ed. Literary Uses of Typology from the Late Middle
Ages to the Present. Princeton, NJ: Princeton University
Press, 1977. 403 pp.

2653   MINNIS, A. J., ed. Gower's 'Confessio Amantis': Responses and
Reassessments. Cambridge: Boydell & Brewer, 1983. 202 pp.
[eight essays by various hands]
Reviews: John H. Fisher, SAC 7 (1985), 221–24.

2654   MOORMAN, CHARLES. Editing the Middle English Manuscript.
Jackson: University Press of Mississippi, 1975. 107 pp. [a
guide]
Reviews: R. J. Schoeck, Speculum 55 (1980), 410–11.

2655   MÖSKE, BIRGIT. Caritas: Ihre figurative Darstellung in der
englischen Literatur des 14. bis 16. Jahrhunderts. Bonn:

Backgrounds

Bouvier, 1977. 208 pp.
Reviews: Stephen L. Wailes, SAC 2 (1980), 194-96.

2656   MURPHY, JAMES J. "Literary Implications of Instruction in the
        Verbal Arts in Fourteenth-Century England." LeedsSE 1
        (1967), 119-35.

2657   MURPHY, JAMES J., ed. Medieval Eloquence: Studies in the Theory
        and Practice of Medieval Rhetoric. Berkeley; Los Angeles;
        London: University of California Press, 1978. 354 pp. See
        no. 856.
        Reviews: George Kennedy, SSI 44 (1979), 201-04; Stephen
        Knight, AUMLA 52 (1979), 311-13; Richard L. Hoffman, SAC 1
        (1979), 183-87.

2658   MURPHY, JAMES J. Rhetoric in the Middle Ages: A History of
        Rhetorical Theory from St. Augustine to the Renaissance.
        Berkeley, Los Angeles, London: University of California
        Press, 1974. 395 pp.
        Reviews: Judson Boyce Allen, Speculum 52 (1977), 411-14.

2659   NICHOLSON, PETER. "The Two Versions of Sercambi's 'Novelle'."
        Italica 53 (1976), 201-13.

2660   NOOMEN, WILLEM and NICO VAN DEN BOOGAARD, eds. Nouveau recueil
        complet des fabliaux (N. R. C. F.). Assen (Low Countries):
        Van Gorcum; New York: Garland Publishing, Inc., 1983-84. 2
        vols. 870 pp.
        Reviews: Elina Suomela-Härmä, NM 86 (1985), 428-29; Roy J.
        Pearcy, Speculum 61 (1986), 448-50.

2661   NWUNELI, M. L. "Satire and the Manipulation of Conventions in
        the Middle English Chanson d'aventure." Lagos Rev. of Eng.
        Studies 1:1 (1979), 45-58.

2662   OBRIST, BARBARA. Les débuts de l'imagerie alchimique (XIVe - XVe
        siècles). Paris: Le Sycomore, 1982. 328 pp.
        Reviews: William Newman, Speculum 60 (1985), 188-90.

2663   O'DONOGHUE, BERNARD. The Courtly Love Tradition. Literature in
        Context Series. Manchester, England: Manchester University
        Press; Totowa, NJ.: Barnes and Noble, 1982. 314 pp.
        [anthology of 12th and 13th century extracts]
        Reviews: Avril Bruten, TLS (6 January, 1984), 20; Marcelle
        Thiebaux, SAC 6 (1984), 208-13; F. R. P. Akehurst, Speculum
        60 (1985), 224-25.

2664   PEARSALL, DEREK. Manuscripts and Readers in Fifteenth-Century
        England: The Literary Implications of Manuscript Study.

Literary and Aesthetic Backgrounds

Essays from the 1981 Conference at the University of York.
Cambridge and Totowa, NJ: Boydell and Brewer, 1983. 146 pp.
[nine essays by various hands]
Reviews: Basil Cottle, TLS (13 July, 1984), 795; Vincent
Gillespie, Library 7 (1985), 363-66.

2665 PELEN, MARC M. "The Marriage Journey: Dream Vision Romance
Structures and Epithalamic Conventions in Medieval Latin and
French Poems and in Middle English Dream Poems." DAI 34
(1974), 7242A. Princeton University.

2666 PETERS, EDWARD. The Magician, the Witch, and the Law. The
Middle Ages. Philadelphia: University of Pennsylvania
Press, 1978. 218 pp. [sheds light on magic in literature]
Reviews: Richard Kieckhefer, Speculum 55 (1980), 828-29;
Brian P. Copehaver, JHP, 19 (1981), 502-06.

2667 PFANNKUCHE, ANTHONY VOSS. "Dreams and Fictions: Essays on
Medieval Dream Visions." DAI 35 (1975), 4449-50A.
University of Iowa, 1974.

2668 PINBORG, JAN. Medieval Semantics: Selected Studies on Medieval
Logic and Grammar. Ed. Sten Ebbesen. CS 195. London:
Variorum Reprints, 1984. 358 pp.
Reviews: P. Osmund Lewry, Speculum 60 (1985), 488.

2669 QUILLIGAN, MAUREEN. The Language of Allegory: Defining the
Genre. Ithaca, NY; and London: Cornell University Press,
1979. 305 pp.
Reviews: Paul Strohm, SAC 3 (1981), 169-71; J. D. Burnley,
RES, n. s., 33 (1982), 238-40.

2670 RANSOM, DANIEL J. Poets at Play: Irony and Parody in the Harley
Lyrics. Norman, OK: Pilgrim Books, 1985. 160 pp. [+Buk,
Purse, Ros, Scog]

2671 ROLLINSON, PHILIP. Classical Theories of Allegory and Christian
Culture. Appendix on primary Greek sources by Patricia
Matsen. Duquesne Studies in Language and Literature 3.
Pittsburgh, PA: Duqeusne University Press; Binghamton:
Harvester Press, 1981. 175 pp. [+Robertsonianism]
Reviews: George D. Economou, SAC 5 (1983), 197-200.

2672 ROMBAUTS, A. and A. WELKENHUYSEN, eds. Aspects of the Medieval
Animal Epic. Proceedings of the International Conference,
Louvain, May 15-17, 1972. Mediaevalia Lovaniensia, I, 3.
Louvain: Louvain University Press; The Hague: Martinus
Nijhoff, 1975. 268 pp.
Reviews: Frank R. Jacoby, Speculum 52 (1977), 736-40.

BIBLIOGRAPHY OF CHAUCER, 1974 - 1985

Backgrounds

2673   ROTH, NORMAN. "'Deal gently with the young man': Love of Boys in
        Medieval Hebrew Poetry of Spain." Speculum 57 (1982), 20–51.

2674   RUGGIERS, PAUL G., ed. Versions of Medieval Comedy. Norman:
        University of Oklahoma Press, 1977. 252 pp. See no. 361.
        Reviews: John L. Grigsby, RPh 36 (1983), 584–88.

2675   SCHMIDT, A. V. C. and NICOLAS JACOBS, eds. Medieval English
        Romances. New York: Holmes & Meier, 1980. 2 vols., 1: 206
        pp., 2: 282 pp.
        Reviews: Anthony S. G. Edwards, Speculum 57 (1982), 660–63.

2676   SCHOLLER, HARALD, ed. The Epic in Medieval Society: Aesthetic
        and Moral Values. Tübingen: Max Niemeyer, 1977. 410 pp.
        See no. 1299.

2677   SCHULTZ, JAMES A. "Classical Rhetoric, Medieval Poetics, and the
        Medieval Vernacular Prologue." Speculum 59 (1984), 1–15.

2678   SMITH, NATHANIEL B., and JOSEPH T. SNOW, eds. The Expansion and
        Transformation of Courtly Literature. Athens: University of
        Georgia Press, 1980. 235 pp. [twelve essays by various
        hands] See nos. 310, 2235.
        Reviews: Douglas Kelly, Speculum 56 (1981), 440–41; H. A.
        Kelly, SAC 3 (1981), 179–83; Barbara N. Sargent-Baur, RPh 36
        (1982), 94–98.

2679   SPECHT, HENRIK. Poetry and the Iconography of the Peasant: The
        Attitude to the Peasant in Late Medieval English Literature
        and in Contemporary Calendar Illustrations. Anglica et
        Americana, 19. Copenhagen: Department of English,
        University of Copenhagen, 1983. 103 pp.
        Reviews: R. F. Yeager, Speculum 60 (1985), 1022–24.

2680   STEVENS, JOHN. Medieval Romance: Themes and Approaches.
        English Literature. London: Hutchinson, 1973. 255 pp.
        [WBT, FranT, KnT, TC]
        Reviews: Helaine Newstead, Speculum 51 (1976), 359–61.

2681   SUCHOMSKI, JOACHIM. "Delectatio" und "Utilitas": Ein Beitrag
        zum Verständnis mittelalterlicher komischer Literatur.
        Bibliotheca Germanica, 18. Bern and Munich: Francke, 1975.
        336 pp.
        Reviews: Michael Curschmann, Speculum 53 (1978), 195–97.

2682   SZARMACH, PAUL E. and BERNARD LEVY, eds. The Alliterative
        Tradition in the Fourteenth Century. (Middle-English Texts &
        Contexts Series, 3.) New York: Burt Franklin, 1979; Kent,
        OH: Kent State University Press, 1981. 230 pp. [9 essays

Literary and Aesthetic Backgrounds

by various hands]

2683   TRIPP, RAYMOND P., JR. "On the Continuity of English Poetry."
PoetT (Fall, 1976), 1-21. [comments on Chaucer]

2684   TRISTRAM, PHILIPPA. Figures of Life and Death in Medieval
English Literature. New York: New York University Press,
1976. 245 pp.
Reviews: Siegfried Wenzel, Speculum 53 (1978), 638-40.

2685   TYDEMAN, WILLIAM. The Theatre in the Middle Ages: Western
European Stage Companies, c. 800-1576. Cambridge, England,
and New York: Cambridge University Press, 1978. 298 pp.
Reviews: Stanley J. Kahrl, Speculum 55 (1980), 851-53.

2686   VAN DYKE, CAROLYNN. The Fiction of Truth: Structures of Meaning
in Narrative and Dramatic Allegory. Ithaca, NY: Cornell
University Press, 1985. 315 pp.
Reviews: L. L. Bronson, Choice 23 (1985), 104.

2686a   WAWN, ANDREW N. "Chaucer, The Plowman's Tale and Reformation
Propaganda: The Testimonies of Thomas Godfray and I Playne
Piers." BJRL 56 (1973), 174-92. [Lollardy] See no. 807.

2687   WENZEL, SIEGFRIED. Verses in Sermons: 'Fasciculus Morum' and
Its Middle English Poems. Cambridge, MA: Medieval Academy
of America, 1978. 234 pp.
Reviews: James J. Wilhelm, SAC 3 (1981), 183-85.

2688   WICKERT, MARIA. Studies in John Gower. Trans. Robert J. Meindl.
Washington, D.C.: University Press of America, 1982. 249 pp.
Reviews: Robert Yeager, SAC 5 (1983), 146-52.

2689   WILSON, KATHARINA MARGIT. "Wikked wyves and blythe bachelers:
Secular Misogamy from Juvenal to Chaucer." DAI 41 (1981),
4707A. University of Illinois at Urbana-Champaign, 1980.

2690   WOODS, MARJORIE CURRY, ed. and trans. An Early Commentary on the
'Poetria Nova' of Geoffrey of Vinsauf. Garland Medieval
Texts 12. New York: Garland, 1985.

2691   ZACHER, CHRISTIAN K. Curiosity and Pilgrimage: The Literature
of Discovery in Fourteenth-Century England. Baltimore:
Johns Hopkins University Press, 1976. 196 pp.
Reviews: V. J. Scattergood, ELN 15:2 (1977), 125-27;
Gillis Kristensson, ES 59 (1978), 373-74; M. C. Seymour, RES
29 (1978), 79-81.

2692   ZUMTHOR, PAUL. Essai de poétique médiévale. Poétique 4. Paris:

Backgrounds

Editions du Seuil, 1972.
Reviews: Morton W. Bloomfield, Speculum 49 (1974), 388–90.

2693   ZUMTHOR, PAUL. La poésie et la voix dans la civilisation
médiévale. Collège de France: Essais et Conférences.
Paris: Presses Universitaires de France, 1984. 117 pp. [in
opposition to Derrida; on orality]
Reviews: William D. Paden, Speculum 61 (1986), 721–23.

See also: 12, 374, 413, 418, 440, 451, 495, 511, 530, 562, 2058, 2059,
2203, 2487, 2525, 2552, 2696, 2705 2709, 2728, 2731, 2735,
2775, 2781.

SOCIAL BACKGROUNDS

2694   BELLAMY, JOHN. Crime and Public Order in England in the Later
Middle Ages. Studies in Social History. London: Routledge
& Kegan Paul; Toronto: University of Toronto Press, 1973.
229 pp.
Reviews: R. H. Helmholz, Speculum 50 (1975), 716–17.

2695   BENNETT, MICHAEL J. Community, Class and Careerism: Cheshire
and Lancashire Society in the Age of 'Sir Gawain and the
Green Knight'. Cambridge Studies in Medieval Life and
Thought, Third Series, 18. Cambridge: Cambridge University
Press, 1983. 286 pp.
Reviews: Joel T. Rosenthal, Speculum 59 (1984), 619–21;
Paul Strohm, SAC 6 (1984), 170–73.

2696   BENSON, LARRY D. and JOHN LEYERLE, eds. Chivalric Literature:
Essays on Relations Between Literature and Life in the Later
Middle Ages. Kalamazoo: Western Michigan University, 1980.
See no. 2704.
Reviews: Richard Firth Green, Speculum 58 (1983), 1027–28.

2697   BORNSTEIN, DIANE. The Lady in the Tower: Medieval Courtesy
Literature for Women. Hamden, CT: Shoe String Press, 1983.
149 pp.
Reviews: John F. Plummer, SAC 6 (1984), 177–80.

2698   BOSWELL, JOHN. Christianity, Social Tolerance, and
Homosexuality: Gay People in Western Europe from the
Beginning of the Christian Era to the Fourteenth Century.
Chicago and London: University of Chicago Press, 1980. 424

Social Backgrounds

pp.
Reviews: Jeremy DuQ. Adams, Speculum 56 (1981), 350-55.

2699   BRAET, HERMAN and WERNER VERBEKE, eds. Death in the Middle Ages.
        Mediaevalia Lovaniensia, Ser. 1, Studia 9. Leuven: Leuven
        University Press, 1983. 291 pp.

2700   BRITTON, EDWARD. The Community of the Vill: A Study in the
        History of the Family and Village Life in Fourteenth-Century
        England. Toronto: Macmillan of Canada, 1977. 291 pp.
        Reviews: John S. Beckerman, Speculum 54 (1979), 551-53.

2701   BULLOUGH, VERN L. and JAMES BRUNDAGE. Sexual Practices and the
        Medieval Church. Buffalo: Prometheus, 1982. 289 pp.
        Reviews: Charles T. Wood, Speculum 61 (1986), 386-87.

2702   DAMIAN, PETER. Book of Gomorrah: An Eleventh-Century Treatise
        Against Clerical Homosexual Practices. Trans. Pierre J.
        Payer. Waterloo, Ontario: Wilfrid Laurier University Press,
        1982. 108 pp.
        Reviews: Ralph J. Hexter, Speculum 59 (1984), 642-45.

2703   DEAN, KITTY CHEN. "'Maritalis affectus': Attitudes Towards
        Marriage in English and French Medieval Literature." DAI 40
        (1980), 5044-45A. University of California, Davis, 1979.

2704   FERRIS, SUMNER. "Chronicle, Chivalric Biography and Family
        Tradition in Fourteenth-Century England," in 2696, pp. 25-38.

2705   GREEN, RICHARD FIRTH. Poets and Princepleasers: Literature and
        the English Court in the Late Middle Ages. Toronto:
        University of Toronto Press, 1980.
        Reviews: Diane Bornstein, Speculum 56 (1981), 874-76;
        Nicholas Jacobs, SAC 4 (1982), 154-59; Helen Houghton, CL 36
        (1984), 85-87.

2706   HELMHOLZ, R. H. Marriage Litigation in Medieval England.
        Cambridge Studies in English Legal History. Cambridge,
        England, and New York: Cambridge University Press, 1974.
        246 pp.
        Reviews: M. M. Sheehan, Speculum 52 (1977), 983-87.

2707   HILTON, R. H., ed. Peasants, Knights and Heretics: Studies in
        Medieval English Social History. Past and Present
        Publications. London, New York: Cambridge University Press,
        1976. 330 pp.
        Reviews: Bernhard W. Scholz, History 5 (May, 1977), 157;
        R. M. Haines, DalR 57 (1977), 176; Steven Epstein, JEconHist
        37 (1977), 815-16.

Backgrounds

2708   JACKSON, W. H., ed. Knighthood in Medieval Literature.
        Woodbridge, Suffolk: D. S. Brewer, 1981. 105 pp. [6 essays
        by various hands]
            Reviews: C. Blair, British Book News (October, 1982), 634;
        C. Lee, MedR 9 (August, 1984), 315.

2709   KELLY, HENRY ANSGAR. Love and Marriage in the Age of Chaucer.
        Ithaca: Cornell University Press, 1975. 359 pp. [+TC]
            Reviews: Kevin J. Harty, CEA 37:4 (1975), 36; Michael
        Rudick, WHR 30:1 (1976), 66-69.

2710   NEWTON, STELLA MARY. Fashion in the Age of the Black Prince: A
        Study of the Years 1340-1365. Woodbridge: Boydell Press;
        Totowa, NJ: Rowman and Littlefield, 1980. 151 pp.
            Reviews: J. A. Meisel, Speculum 57 (1982), 398-400.

2711   NICHOLLS, Jonathan W. The Matter of Courtesy: A Study of
        Medieval Courtesy Books and the Gawain-Poet. Woodbridge,
        Suffolk: D. S. Brewer, 1985. 241 pp.

2712   NOONAN, JOHN T. "Marriage in the Middle Ages, I: Power to
        Choose." Viator 4 (1973), 419-34.

2713   PALMER, ROBERT C. "Contexts of Marriage in Medieval England:
        Evidence from the King's Court circa 1300." Speculum 59
        (1984), 42-67.

2714   PAYER, PIERRE J. Sex and the Penitentials: The Formation and
        Transmission of a Sexual Code 550-1150. Toronto, Buffalo,
        and London: University of Toronto Press, 1984. 219 pp.
            Reviews: Susan A. Keefe, Speculum 61 (1986), 453-55.

2715   SAUL, NIGEL. Knights and Esquires: The Gloucestershire Gentry
        in the Fourteenth Century. Oxford Historical Monographs.
        Oxford: Clarendon Press; New York: Oxford University Press,
        1981. 316 pp.
            Reviews: E. Miller, TLS (22 January, 1982), 70; J. M. W.
        Bean, Speculum 58 (1983), 535-37; C. Dyer, MAE 52 (1983),
        121-23.

2716   SCATTERGOOD, V. J. and J. W. SHERBORNE, eds. English Court
        Culture in the Later Middle Ages. New York: St. Martin's
        Press, 1983. 364 pp. [ten essays by various hands] See no.
        1211.
            Reviews: Janet Backhouse, The Library 6 (1984), 406-408;
        Ruth Morse, SAC 6 (1984), 219-23; Jeremy Griffiths, MAE 54
        (1985), 299-301.

2717   SCHMITT, JEAN-CLAUDE. The Holy Greyhound: Guinefort, Healer of Children Since the Thirteenth Century. Cambridge: Cambridge University Press, 1983. 215 pp.
      Reviews: Bruce A. Rosenberg, SAC 6 (1984), 223-26.

2718   VALE, JULIET. Edward III and Chivalry: Chivalric Society and Its Context, 1270-1350. Woodbridge, Suffolk: Boydell; Totowa, NJ: Rowman and Littlefield, 1982. 207 pp.
      Reviews: Richard H. Jones, Speculum 59 (1984), 933-35.

2719   WENZEL, SIEGFRIED. "Pestilence and Middle English Literature: Friar John Grimestone's Poems on Death," in 2721, pp. 131-59.

2720   WHITE, LYNN, JR. "Death and the Devil," in 64, pp. 25-46.

2721   WILLIMAN, DANIEL, ed. The Black Death: The Impact of the Fourteenth-Century Plague. Medieval and Renaissance Texts and Studies, 13. Binghamton: Center for Medieval and Early Renaissance Studies, 1982. 159 pp. [1977 conference papers] See no. 2719.

2722   WOODS, WILLIAM. England in the Age of Chaucer. New York: Stein & Day, 1976. 230 pp.
      Reviews: LJ 101 (1976), 2280; Choice 14 (1977), 257.

See also: 77, 81, 290, 344, 396, 413, 480, 587, 1203, 1210, 1253, 1478, 1812, 2322, 2545, 2568, 2616, 2673, 2731, 2741.

MEDIEVAL WOMEN'S STUDIES

2723   ATKINSON, CLARISSA W. Mystic and Pilgrim: The 'Book' and the World of Margery Kempe. Ithaca, NY; and London: Cornell University Press, 1983. 241 pp.
      Reviews: A. Daniel Frankforter, AHR 89 (1984), 749; Christian K. Zacher, Speculum 60 (1985), 469-70.

2724   BAKER, DEREK, ed. Medieval Women. Dedicated and Presented to Rosalind M. T. Hill on the Occasion of Her Seventieth Birthday. Studies in Church History, Subsidia, 1. Oxford: Basil Blackwell, for the Ecclesiastical History Society, 1978. 399 pp.
      Reviews: Speculum 55 (1980), 184.

2725   BERMAN, CONSTANCE H., CHARLES W. CONNELL, and JUDITH RICE

Backgrounds

ROTHSCHILD, eds. The Worlds of Medieval Women: Creativity, Influence, and Imagination. Literary and Historical Perspectives of the Middle Ages, 2. In Memory of Marjorie M. Malvern. Morgantown: West Virginia University Press, 1985. See nos. 1456, 2145.

2726 DICKINSON, JEAN G. "The Role of Woman in the Late Medieval Tale." DAI 46 (1985), 145A. New York University.

2727 DRONKE, PETER. Women Writers of the Middle Ages: A Critical Study of Texts from Perpetua (+203) to Marguerite Porete (+1310). Cambridge and New York: Cambridge University Press, 1984.
  Reviews: Alison Hennegan, NSt 108 (1984), 23-24; Ralph Hexter, Speculum 62 (1987), 131-33.

2728 FERRANTE, JOAN M. Woman as Image in Medieval Literature from the Twelfth Century to Dante. New York, London: Columbia University Press, 1975. 166 pp.
  Reviews: H. A. Kelly, Speculum 52 (1977), 715-21.

2729 KING, MARGARET L. and ALBERT RABIL, JR., transs. Her Immaculate Hand: Selected Works. MRTS, 20. Binghamton, NY: CEMERS, 1984. 167 pp.

2730 KRAUS, HENRY. "Eve and Mary: Conflicting Images of Medieval Women," Chapter 3 in The Living Theatre of Medieval Art, no. 2809, pp. 41-62.

2731 LUCAS, ANGELA M. Women in the Middle Ages. New York: St. Martin's Press, 1983. 187 pp.
  Reviews: Ute Stargardt, SAC 6 (1984), 202-05.

2732 McGOWAN, RICHARD J. "Thomas's Doctrine of Woman and Thirteenth-Century Thought," in Proceedings of the Illinois Medieval Association, 2. Edited by Mark D. Johnston and Samuel M. Riley, et al. Normal: The Graduate School, Illinois State University, 1985, pp. 209-26.

2733 METZ, RENE. La femme et l'enfant dans le droit canonique mediéval. Collected Studies, 222. London: Variorum Reprints, 1985. 342 pp.

2734 MOREWEDGE, ROSMARIE THEE, ed. The Role of Women in the Middle Ages. Papers of the Sixth Annual Conference of the Center for Medieval and Early Renaissance Studies, State University of New York at Binghamton, 6-7 May 1972. Albany: State University of New York Press, 1975. 195 pp.
  Reviews: H. A. Kelly, Speculum 52 (1977), 715-21.

2735   ROSE, MARY BETH, ed. Women in the Middle Ages and the
       Renaissance: Literary and Historical Perspectives.
       Syracuse, NY: Syracuse University Press, 1986. 288 pp.
       [eleven essays by various hands]

2736   SHAHAR, SHULAMITH. The Fourth Estate: A History of Women in the
       Middle Ages. Trans. Chaya Galai. London and New York:
       Methuen, 1983. 351 pp.
          Reviews: Suzanne P. Wemple, Speculum 61 (1986), 204–06.

2737   STILLER, NIKKI. Eve's Orphans: Mothers and Daughters in
       Medieval English Literature. Contributions in Women's
       Studies 16. Westport, CT: Greenwood Press, 1980. 152 pp.
          Reviews: Choice 18 (1981), 954.

2738   STUARD, SUSAN MOSHER, ed., et al. Women in Medieval Society.
       Philadelphia: University of Pennsylvania Press, 1976. 219
       pp.
          Reviews: Mary Beth W. Marvin, FR 51 (1977), 311–13.

2739   WEMPLE, SUZANNE FONAY. Women in Frankish Society. Marriage and
       the Cloister, 500 to 900. The Middle Ages. Philadelphia:
       University of Pennsylvania Press, 1981. 348 pp.
          Reviews: Valerie M. Lagorio, Manuscripta (St. Louis, July,
       1982), 115–17.

2740   WILSON, KATHARINA M., ed. Medieval Women Writers. Athens:
       University of Georgia Press, 1984.
          Reviews: Alison Hennegan, NSt 108 (1984), 23–34; H. P.
       Weissman, Choice 22 (1984), 86–87; Jeanette M. Beer, CML 5
       (1985), 326–27; Judith J. Killman, CML 5 (1985), 323–25.

2741   WOOD, CHARLES T. "The Doctors' Dilemma: Sin, Salvation and the
       Menstrual Cycle in Medieval Thought." Speculum 56 (1981),
       710–27.

See also: 56, 245, 248, 250, 252, 253, 371, 378, 381, 1001, 1002, 1006,
           1009, 1090, 1097, 1113, 1138, 1160, 1164, 1303, 1346, 1395,
           1426, 1431, 1436, 1438, 1455, 1456, 1471, 1478, 1480, 1487,
           1491, 1494, 1496, 1509, 1552, 1553, 1582, 1586, 1611, 1633,
           1641, 1645, 1697, 1822, 2033, 2138, 2146, 2211, 2279, 2322,
           2376, 2405, 2545, 2546, 2562, 2564, 2649, 2666, 2697, 2701,
           2703, 2706, 2709, 2712, 2713, 2714, 2789, 2800.

Backgrounds

ECONOMIC BACKGROUNDS

2742   BOLTON, J. L. The Medieval English Economy, 1150-1500. London:
        J. M. Dent; Totowa, NJ: Rowman & Littlefield, 1980. 400 pp.
        Reviews: Joel T. Rosenthal, Speculum 56 (1981), 348-50.

2743   CROSSLEY, D. W., ed. Medieval Industry. Research Report, 40.
        London: Council for British Archaeology, 1981. 156 pp.

2744   DE ROOVER, RAYMOND. Business, Banking, and Economic Thought in
        Late Medieval and Early Modern Europe. Ed. Julius Kirshner.
        Chicago and London: University of Chicago Press, 1974. 383
        pp.
        Reviews: Archibald R. Lewis, History 3:1 (1974), 116;
        Thomas W. Bloomquist, JEconHist 35 (1975), 821-30.

2745   GIMPEL, JEAN. The Medieval Machine: The Industrial Revolution
        of the Middle Ages. New York: Holt, Rinehart and Winston,
        1976. 274 pp.
        Reviews: Bert S. Hall, Speculum 53 (1978), 266-68.

2746   LITTLE, LESTER K. Religious Poverty and the Profit Economy in
        Medieval Europe. Ithaca, NY: Cornell University Press,
        1978. 267 pp.
        Reviews: Richard C. Trexler, Speculum 55 (1980), 809-12.

2747   LLOYD, T. H. The English Wool Trade in the Middle Ages.
        Cambridge, England, and New York: Cambridge University
        Press, 1977. 351 pp.
        Reviews: Sylvia L. Thrupp, Speculum 53 (1978), 826-27.

2748   POSTAN, M. M. Essays on Medieval Agriculture and General
        Problems of the Medieval Economy and Medieval Trade and
        Finance. Cambridge, England: University Press, 1973. 302
        pp.
        Reviews: TLS (17 August, 1973), 94; David Knowles, AHR 79
        (1974), 1165-67; Richard Roehl, JEH 36 (1976), 725-28.

2749   RICHARDS, J. F., ed. Precious Metals in the Later Medieval and
        Early Modern Worlds. Durham, NC: Carolina Academic Press,
        1983. 502 pp. See esp. pp. 79-96, 97-158.
        Reviews: Mavis E. Mate, Business History Review 58 (1984),
        457-58.

2750   UNGER, RICHARD W. The Ship in the Medieval Economy, 600-1600.
        London: Croom Helm; Montreal: McGill-Queen's University
        Press, 1980. 304 pp.

Reviews: Timothy J. Runyan, Speculum 57 (1982), 671–73.

2751 YOUNG, CHARLES R. The Royal Forests of Medieval England.
Philadelphia: University of Pennsylvania Press, 1979.
Reviews: Sumner Ferris, SAC 3 (1981), 185–88.

See also: 290, 413, 587, 2763.

RELIGIOUS BACKGROUNDS

2752 BERKHOUT, CARL T. and JEFFREY B. RUSSELL. Medieval Heresies: A
Bibliography 1960–1979. Subsidia Mediaevalia 11. Toronto:
Pontifical Institute of Medieval Studies, 1981.
Reviews: Anne Hudson, MAE 53 (1984), 149–50.

2753 BLAKE, NORMAN F. "Varieties of Middle English Religious Prose,"
in 69, pp. 348–56.

2754 BOYLE, LEONARD E., O. P. "Aspects of Clerical Education in
Fourteenth-Century England," in 72a, 19–32.

2755 BRASWELL, MARY FLOWERS. The Medieval Sinner: Characterization
and Confession in the Literature of the English Middle Ages.
Rutherford, NJ: Fairleigh Dickinson University Press; London
and Toronto: Associated University Presses, 1983. 160 pp.
[penitential motifs; Langland, Gower, the Pearl poet]
Reviews: Charles R. Sleeth, TLS (13 April, 1984), 408;
John V. Fleming, Speculum 60 (1985), 649–50.

2756 BROWN, PETER. The Cult of the Saints: Its Rise and Function in
Latin Christianity. Haskell Lectures on History of
Religions, n. s., 2. Chicago: University of Chicago Press,
1981. 187 pp.
Reviews: John M. McCulloh, Speculum 58 (1983), 152–54.

2757 CHENEY, C. R. The Papacy and England, 12th–14th Centuries:
Historical and Legal Studies. Collected Studies, 154.
London: Variorum Reprints, 1982. 346 pp.

2758 COHEN, JEREMY. The Friars and the Jews: The Evolution of
Medieval Anti-Judaism. Ithaca, NY; and London: Cornell
University Press, 1982. 301 pp.
Reviews: Daniel J. Lasker, Speculum 58 (1983), 743–45.

Backgrounds

2759   EMMERSON, RICHARD KENNETH. Antichrist in the Middle Ages: A
        Study of Medieval Apocalypticism, Art, and Literature.
        Seattle: University of Washington Press, 1981. 366 pp.
        [+CYT]
        Reviews: Robert E. Lerner, Speculum 57 (1982), 601-04;
        Ronald B. Herzman, SAC 5 (1983), 164-66.

2760   FOWLER, DAVID C. The Bible in Early English Literature. Seattle
        and London: University of Washington Press, 1976. 263 pp.
        Reviews: Lawrence L. Besserman, Speculum 53 (1978),
        572-73.

2761   FOWLER, DAVID C. The Bible in Middle English Literature.
        Seattle: University of Washington Press, 1984. 326 pp. See
        no. 2175.
        Reviews: A. J. Minnis, TLS (9 August, 1985), 884.

2762   GEARY, PATRICK J. Furta Sacra: Thefts of Relics in the Central
        Middle Ages. Princeton, NJ: Princeton University Press,
        1978. 227 pp.
        Reviews: Roger E. Reynolds, Speculum 54 (1979), 570-72.

2763   HELMHOLZ, R. H. "Usury and the Medieval English Church Courts."
        Speculum 61 (1986), 364-80.

2764   HERRMANN-MASCARD, NICOLE. Les Reliques des saints. Formation
        coutumière d'un droit. Société d'histoire du droit:
        Collection d'histoire institutionelle et sociale, 6. Paris:
        Klincksieck, 1975. 446 pp.
        Reviews: Patrick J. Geary, Speculum 52 (1977), 694-96.

2765   HUDSON, ANNE, ed. English Wycliffite Sermons. Vol. 1. Oxford:
        Clarendon Press, 1983.
        Reviews: Cecily Clark, ES 65 (1984), 467-68; N. F. Blake,
        MLR 79 (1984), 664-65.

2766   KIECKHEFER, RICHARD. Unquiet Souls: Fourteenth-Century Saints
        and Their Religious Milieu. Chicago and London: University
        of Chicago Press, 1984. 238 pp.
        Reviews: Donald Weinstein, Speculum 61 (1986), 672-74.

2767   LAMBERT, MALCOM. Medieval Heresy: Popular Movements from
        Bogomil to Hus. New York: Holmes & Meier, 1977. 430 pp.
        Reviews: Robert L. Lerner, Speculum 53 (1978), 821-24.

2768   LERNER, ROBERT E. The Heresy of the Free Spirit in the Later
        Middle Ages. Berkeley, Los Angeles, London: University of
        California Press, 1972. 257 pp.
        Reviews: Eleanor L. McLaughlin, Speculum 49 (1974),

747-51.

2769   LOURDAUX, W. and D. VERHELST, eds. The Concept of Heresy in the
        Middle Ages (11th-13th C.). Proceedings of the International
        Conference, Louvain, May 13-16, 1973. Mediaevalia
        Lovaniensia, Series I, Studia IV. Louvain: University
        Press; The Hague: Martinus Nijhoff, 1976. 232 pp.
        Reviews: Jeffrey B. Russell, Speculum 53 (1978), 161-63.

2770   MULDOON, JAMES. Popes, Lawyers, and Infidels: The Church and
        the Non-Christian World, 1250-1550. The Middle Ages.
        Philadelphia: University of Pennsylvania Press, 1979.   212
        pp.
        Reviews: Thomas M. Izbicki, Speculum 55 (1980), 818-20

2771   OBERMAN, HEIKO A. "Fourteenth-Century Religious Thought: A
        Premature Profile." Speculum 53 (1978), 80-93.

2772   PAGE, CORNELIUS ALBERT, ed. and trans. 'The myrrour of
        synneres': A Critical Edition with Reprint and Translation
        of the 'Speculum peccatoris'. Monograph Series, Institute of
        Medieval and Renaissance Studies. Dobbs Ferry, NY: Mercy
        College, 1976. 94 pp.
        Reviews: Choice 14 (1977), 1215.

2773   PETERS, EDWARD, ed. Heresy and Authority in Medieval Europe.
        Philadelphia: University of Pennsylvania Press, 1980.   312
        pp.
        Reviews: Edward K. Burger, Manuscripta 25 (1981), 180-81;
        Alexander Murray, MAE 52 (1983), 358-59.

2774   REEVES, MARJORIE. The Influence of Prophecy in the Later Middle
        Ages: A Study in Joachism. Oxford, England: Clarendon
        Press; New York: Oxford University Press, 1969. 574 pp.
        Reviews: Charles T. Davis, Speculum 50 (1975), 347-49.

2775   REYNOLDS, ROGER E. "'Sixes and Sevens'—And Eights and Nines:
        The Sacred Mathematics of Sacred Orders in the Early Middle
        Ages." Speculum 54 (1979), 669-84.

2776   RICHE, PIERRE and GUY LOBRICHON, eds. Le moyen âge et la Bible.
        Bible de Tous les Temps, 4. Paris: Beauchesne, 1984.   639
        pp.
        Reviews: Jerry H. Bentley, Speculum 61 (1986), 744-45.

2777   RIEHLE, WOLFGANG. The Middle English Mystics. Trans. Bernard
        Standring. London and Boston: Routledge & Kegan Paul, 1981.
        Reviews: William F. Pollard, SAC 5 (1983), 193-96.

Backgrounds

2778   ROBERTSON, D. W., JR.   "Chaucer and Christian Tradition," in 63,
        pp. 3-32.

2779   RUSSELL, JEFFREY BURTON. Satan: The Early Christian Tradition.
        Ithaca and London: Cornell University Press, 1981. 258 pp.
        [Patristic, Gnostic traditions]
        Reviews: John Boswell, Speculum 60 (1985), 458-61.

2780   SHEPHERD, GEOFFREY. "Religion and Philosophy in Chaucer," in 49,
        pp. 262-89. [general]

2781   SUMPTION, JONATHAN. Pilgrimage, An Image of Mediaeval Religion.
        London: Faber and Faber, 1975. 391 pp.
        Reviews: Giles Constable, TLS (22 August, 1975), 949;
        Enoch J. Powell, Spectator (10 May, 1975), 576; Lester K.
        Little, Speculum 54 (1979), 194.

2782   SZITTYA, PENN R.   "The Antifraternal Tradition in Middle English
        Literature." Speculum 52 (1977), 287-313.

2783   TUCK, ANTHONY J. "Carthusian Monks and Lollard Knights:
        Religious Attitude at the Court of Richard II," in 72, pp.
        149-61.

2784   WAKEFIELD, WALTER L. "Heretics as Physicians in the Thirteenth
        Century." Speculum 57 (1982), 328-31.

2785   WARD, BENEDICTA. Miracles and the Medieval Mind: Theory, Record
        and Event, 1000-1215. The Middle Ages. Philadelphia:
        University of Pennsylvania Press, 1982. 321 pp. [St.
        Frideswide, St. William of Norwich; Compostela, Rome,
        Jerusalem as pilgrimage centers]
        Reviews: Joseph-Claude Poulin, Speculum 59 (1984), 450-53;
        N. Tanner, MAE 53 (1984), 148-49.

2786   WILSON, STEPHEN, ed. Saints and Their Cults: Studies in
        Religious Sociology, Folklore and History. Cambridge,
        England, and New York: Cambridge University Press, 1983.
        435 pp.
        Reviews: Clare Stancliffe, TLS (24 August, 1984), 955.

See also: 247, 249, 274, 290, 334, 413, 528, 538, 589, 729 1118, 1518,
        2545, 2568, 2583, 2584, 2622, 2623, 2707, 2714, 2731, 2741,
        2746.

SCIENTIFIC BACKGROUNDS

2787   ARNALD OF VILLANOVA. 'Opera Medica Omnia', II: Aphorismi de
        gradibus. Ed. Michael R. McVaugh. Adsidua Opera, Seminarii
        Historiae Medicae Granatensis et Amplissima Munificentia,
        Universidad de Barcelona, University of North Carolina.
        Granada-Barcelona: Universidad de Barcelona, 1975. 338 pp.
        [pharmaceuticals]
            Reviews: John M. Riddle, Speculum 53 (1978), 115-16.

2788   BROWN, P. "Chaucer's Visual World: A Study of His Poetry and
        the Medieval Optical Tradition." DAI 43 (1982), 4284C.
        University of York, England, 1981. [CT Fragments I, VIII,
        Jean de Meun, Dante, Boccaccio] See also no. 301.

2789   BULLOUGH, VERN L. "Marriage in the Middle Ages, 3: Medieval
        Medical and Scientific Views of Women." Viator 4 (1973),
        485-501.

2790   CONSTANTINE THE AFRICAN. 'Liber de coitu': El tratado de
        andrología, estudio y edición crítica. Ed. and trans. into
        Spanish by Enrique Montero Cartelle. Monografias, 77.
        Santiago de Compostela: Universidad de Santiago de
        Compostela, 1983. 223 pp.
            Reviews: Luke Demaitre, Speculum 61 (1986), 229.

2791   DALES, RICHARD C. The Scientific Achievement of the Middle Ages.
        Pennsylvania Paperback, 47. Philadelphia: University of
        Pennsylvania Press, 1973. 182 pp.
            Reviews: Bruce S. Eastwood, Speculum 51 (1976), 731-32.

2792   EADE, J. C. The Forgotten Sky: A Guide to Astrology in English
        Literature. New York and Oxford: Oxford University Press,
        1984. [Mars, TC, GP, FranT, KnT, MLP, MerT, NPT, ParsP, SqT,
        WBP]
            Reviews: Sigmund Eisner, SAC 7 (1985), 181-83.

2793   FRIEDMAN, JOHN B. "John Siferwas and the Mythological
        Illustrations in the Liber cosmographiae of John de Foxton."
        Speculum 58 (1983), 391-418.

2794   FRIEDMAN, JOHN B. "Richard de Thorpe's Astronomical Kalendar and
        the Luxury Book Trade at York." SAC 7 (1985), 137-60.

2795   GRYMONPREZ, POL, ed. 'Here men may se the vertues off herbes':
        A Middle English Herbal (MS. Bodley 483, ff. 57r-67V).
        Scripta, 3. Brussels: Omirel, 1981. 148 pp.

277

Backgrounds

Reviews: Henry Hargreaves, <u>Speculum</u> 57 (1982), 684.

2796   LINDBERG, DAVID C., ed. <u>Science in the Middle Ages</u>. The Chicago
       History of Science and Medicine. Chicago and London:
       University of Chicago Press, 1978. 549 pp.
       Reviews: Richard C. Dales, <u>Speculum</u> 56 (1981), 932–33.

2797   LINDBERG, DAVID C. <u>Studies in the History of Medieval Optics</u>.
       CS 186. London: Variorum Reprints, 1983. 302 pp.

2798   MANZALAOUI, M. "Chaucer and Science," in 49, pp. 224–61.
       [general]

2799   NEWTON, ROBERT R. <u>The Moon's Acceleration and Its Physical
       Origins, 1: As Deduced from Solar Eclipses</u>. Baltimore and
       London: The Johns Hopkins University Press, 1979. 583 pp.
       Reviews: Claudia Kren, <u>Speculum</u> 55 (1980), 820–21.

2800   ROWLAND, BERYL, ed. <u>Medieval Woman's Guide to Health: The First
       English Gynecological Handbook</u>. Middle English text with
       Modern English translation on facing page. Kent, OH: Kent
       State University Press, 1981. 192 pp.
       Reviews: Jerry Stannard and Linda Ehrsam Voigts, <u>Speculum</u>
       57 (1982), 422–26.

2801   RUBIN, STANLEY. <u>Medieval English Medicine, A. D. 500–1300</u>.
       London: David & Charles; New York: Barnes & Noble, 1974.
       232 pp.
       Reviews: John J. Contreni, <u>Speculum</u> 52 (1977), 743–44.

2802   TEMKIN, OWSEI. <u>Galenism: Rise and Decline of a Medical
       Philosophy</u>. Cornell Publications in the History of Science.
       Ithaca and London: Cornell University Press, 1973. 240 pp.
       Reviews: Michael McVaugh, <u>Speculum</u> 51 (1976), 545–46.

2803   USSERY, HULING E. <u>Chaucer's Physician: Medicine and Literature
       in Fourteenth-Century England</u>. Tulane Studies in English,
       19. New Orleans, LA: Tulane University, 1971. 158 pp.
       Reviews: Joseph E. Grennen, <u>Speculum</u> 49 (1974), 158–59.

2804   VOIGTS, LINDA E. and MICHAEL R. McVAUGH, eds. <u>A Latin Technical
       Phlebotomy and Its Middle English Translation</u>. Transactions,
       74/2. Philadelphia: American Philosophical Society, 1984.
       66 pp.
       Reviews: Faye Marie Getz, <u>Speculum</u> 60 (1985), 1030–32.

2805   WHITE, LYNN, JR. <u>Medieval Religion and Technology: Collected
       Essays</u>. Publications of The Center for Medieval and
       Renaissance Studies, 13. Berkeley: University of California

Press, 1978. 384 pp. [19 previously published essays]
Reviews: G. Leff, TLS (21 December, 1979), 169.

See also: 258, 366, 459, 561, 588, 1589, 1647, 1916-29, 1986-92, 2038, 2095, 2585, 2606, 2616, 2741, 2745.

ARTISTIC BACKGROUNDS

2806   FORSYTH, ILENE H. "The Theme of Cockfighting in Burgundian Romanesque Sculpture." Speculum 53 (1978), 252-82.

2807   FRIEDMAN, JOHN BLOCK. The Monstrous Races in Medieval Art and Thought. Cambridge, MA; and London: Harvard University Press, 1981. 268 pp.
Reviews: Peter Riesenberg, Speculum 57 (1982), 882-83; Lee W. Patterson, Criticism 24 (1982), 70-73.

2808   KLINGENDER, FRANCIS. Animals in Art and Thought to the End of the Middle Ages. Ed. Evelyn and John Harthan. Cambridge, MA: The M. I. T. Press, 1971. 580 pp.
Reviews: Gerhart B. Ladner, Speculum 50 (1975), 732-38.

2809   KRAUS, HENRY. The Living Theatre of Medieval Art. Bloomington and London: Indiana University Press, 1967, 1972. 272 pp. [iconography; social factors, class system, popular impact, art used against heresy, anti-Semitism; Iconoclasm; attitudes toward women] See no. 2730.
Reviews: TLS (18 January, 1968), 722.

2810   McLEAN, TERESA. Medieval English Gardens. New York: Viking Press, 1980. 298 pp. [includes "Love Gardens"]
Reviews: Jerry Stannard, Speculum 57 (1982), 971.

2811   PEARSALL, DEREK and ELIZABETH SALTER. Landscapes and Seasons of the Medieval World. London: Paul Elek, 1973. 252 pp.
Reviews: Kenneth Bleeth, Speculum 51 (1976), 345-48.

2812   SALTER, ELIZABETH and DEREK PEARSALL. "Pictorial Illustration of Late Medieval Poetic Texts: The Role of the Frontispiece or Prefatory Picture," in Medieval Iconography and Narrative: A Symposium. Edited by Flemming G. Andersen, Esther Nyholm, Marianne Powell, and Flemming Talbo Stubkjaer. Proceedings of the Fourth International Symposium organized by the Centre for the Study of Vernacular Literature, held at Odense

Backgrounds

University on 19–20 November, 1979. Odense, Denmark: Odense
University Press, 1980. 225 pp.

2813   SWAAN, WIM. The Late Middle Ages: Art and Architecture from
1350 to the Advent of the Renaissance. Ithaca, NY: Cornell
University Press, 1977. 232 pp.
Reviews: Whitney S. Stoddard, Speculum 54 (1979), 428–29.

2814   WOODMAN, FRANCIS. The Architectural History of Canterbury
Cathedral. London and Boston: Routledge & Kegan Paul, 1981.
282 pp.
Reviews: Peter Fergusson, Speculum 59 (1984), 220–22.

See also: 105, 113, 136, 143, 164, 166, 169, 184, 352, 422, 431, 514,
1055, 1073, 1533, 1852, 1853, 1907, 2142, 2478, 2622.

MUSIC BACKGROUNDS

2815   BERNHARD, MICHAEL. Wortkonkordanz zu Anicius Manlius Severinus
Boethius 'De institutione musica'. Bayerische Akademie der
Wissenschaften, Veröffentlichungen der Musikhistorischen
Kommission. Band 4. München: C. H. Beck, 1979. 813 pp.
Reviews: Claire Maitre, RdeMus 66 (1980), 96–97; Peter
Cahn, MF 34 (1981), 380–81.

2816   BULLOCK-DAVIES, CONSTANCE. Menestrellorum multitudo: Minstrels
at a Royal Feast. Cardiff: University of Wales Press, 1978.
180 pp. [+musical instruments]
Reviews: Edmund A. Bowles, Speculum 54 (1979), 349–53.

2817   CHADWICK, HENRY. Boethius: The Consolations of Music, Logic,
Theology, and Philosophy. Oxford: Clarendon Press, Oxford
University Press, 1981. 313 pp.
Reviews: Andrew Hughes, Mus&Let 64 (1983), 267–69; Alison
M. Peden, MAE 53 (1984), 99–100.

2818   CRANE, FREDERICK. Extant Medieval Musical Instruments: A
Provisional Catalogue by Types. Iowa City: University of
Iowa Press, 1972. 105 pp.
Reviews: Edmund A. Bowles, Speculum 49 (1974), 324–26.

2819   EDMISTON, JEAN. "Boethius on Pythagorian Music." MusR 35
(1974), 179–84. [tetrachord and the four elements;
heptachord and planetary order; therapeutic use of music;

theory of sound and hearing]

2820 FALLOWS, DAVID. "Early English Song." MusT 124: no. 1689
(November, 1983), 679–80. [review article]

2821 GROUT, DONALD J. "La Griselda di Zeno e il libretto dell'opera
di Scarlatti" [Zeno's Griselda and the Libretto of the Opera
by Scarlatti]. NRMI 2 (1968), 207–25. [Griselda tradition,
including ClT]

2822 HOPPIN, RICHARD H. Medieval Music. The Norton Introduction to
Music History. New York: W. W. Norton, 1978. 566 pp.
Reviews: Andrew Hughes, Speculum 55 (1980), 539–42.

2823 HUGHES, ANDREW. Medieval Music: The Sixth Liberal Art. Toronto
Medieval Bibliographies, 4. Toronto: University of Toronto
Press, in association with the Centre for Medieval Studies,
1974. 326 pp.
Reviews: Thomas H. Connolly, Speculum 52 (1977), 381–82.

2824 MAHER, TERENCE JAMES. "On a Contemporary Boethian Musical
Theory." DAI 41 (1980), 2347A. University of Iowa.
[quadrivium of Boethius; musica mundana; Scholastic education
and Realism]

2825 REANEY, GILBERT. "The Irrational and Late Medieval Music," in
64, pp. 197–219.

2826 REIMER, ERICH. "Musicus und Cantor: Zur Sozialgeschichte eines
musikalischen Lehrstücks." ArchMus 35 (1978), 1–32.
[+Boethius, De institutione musica]

2827 SADIE, STANLEY, ed. The New Grove Dictionary of Music and
Musicians. London: Macmillan, 1980. 20 vols.
Reviews: Joseph Dyer, Speculum 58 (1983), 528–35.

2828 WILKINS, NIGEL. Music in the Age of Chaucer. Cambridge: D. S.
Brewer, 1979. 174 pp. [See also Wilkins, Chaucer Songs, no.
582.]
Reviews: John Caldwell, Mus&Let 61 (1980), 410–11; Peter
Phillips, Mus&Mus 28 (August, 1980), 41; Richard Rastall,
EarlyMus 8 (1980), 531–33; Barbara R. Hanning, MusQ 67
(1981), 285–89; Nick Sandon, Consort 37 (Canada, 1981),
422–23; Karl Reichl, Anglia 100 (1982), 501–04; David
Fallows, MusT 124 (1983), 679–80; F. N. M. Diekstra, ES 65
(1984), 555.

2829 WILSON, EDWARD and IAN FENLON, eds. The Winchester Anthology: A
Facsimile of British Library Additional Manuscript 60577.

Backgrounds

> Introduction and list of contents by Edward Wilson, an
> account of the music by Ian Fenlon. Cambridge: D. S.
> Brewer, 1981. 47 pp. + 225 leaves.
> Reviews: A. S. G. Edwards, <u>SAC</u> 5 (1983), 208–10.

See also: 288a, 311, 437, <u>582</u>, 1336, 1366, <u>2273</u>, <u>2547</u>.

DICTIONARIES AND INDEXES

2830 DAVIS, NORMAN, DOUGLAS GRAY, PATRICIA INGHAM, and ANNE
   WALLACE-HADRILL, comps. A Chaucer Glossary. Oxford:
   Clarendon, 1979. 185 pp.
    Reviews: T. A. Shippey, TLS (30 November, 1979), 73; Basil
   Cottle, RES 31 (1980), 445-46; J. J. Anderson, CritQ 23
   (1981), 82-83; W. Bruce Finnie, SAC 3 (1981), 134-37; Stephen
   A. Barney, MLR 77 (1982), 920-21.

2831 DILLON, BERT. A Chaucer Dictionary: Proper Names and Allusions,
   Excluding Place Names. Boston: G. K. Hall; London: Prior,
   1974. 266 pp.
    Reviews: Wilson Library Bulletin 49 (1975), 670; Choice 12
   (1975), 978; RSR 3 (1975), 144; LJ 100 (1975), 382.

2832 KERLING, JOHAN. Chaucer in Early English Dictionaries: The
   Old-World Tradition in English Lexicography Down to 1721 and
   Speght's Chaucer Glossaries. Germanic and Anglistic Studies
   of the University of Leiden, 18. Netherlands: Leiden
   University Press; Boston: Kluwer, 1979. 360 pp. [Appendix:
   "Chaucer, The Plowman's Tale, and Henry VIII."]
    Reviews: H. H. Meier, DQR 12 (1982), 153-56.

2833 KERLING, JOHAN. "Franciscus Junius, 17th-Century Lexicography
   and Middle English," in LEXeter '83 Proceedings. Papers from
   the International Conference on Lexicography at Exeter, 9-12
   September, 1983. Edited by Reinhard R. K. Hartmann.
   Lexicographica Ser. Maior, 1. Tübingen: Niemeyer, 1984, pp.
   92-100.

2834 LYONS, THOMAS R. and MICHAEL J. PRESTON. A Complete Concordance
   to Two "Chaucerian" Poems: 'The Floure and the Leafe' and
   'The Assembly of Ladies'. Ann Arbor, MI: Xerox University
   Microfilms, 1974.

2835 SCHÄFER, JÜRGEN. "Chaucer in Shakespeare's Dictionaries: The
   Beginning." ChauR 17 (1982), 182-92. [Speght's influence on
   Jacobean dictionaries]

Dictionaries and Indexes

2836   SCOTT, A. F. Who's Who in Chaucer. London: Elm Tree Books; New York: Taplinger, 1974. 145 pp. [glossary of personal names, including animals]
Reviews: Wilson Library Bull. 49 (May, 1975), 669; ARBA 7 (1976), 612.

2837   TSUCHIYA, TADAYUKI. "A Concordance and Glossary to the General Prologue of the Canterbury Tales." Bulletin of the Faculty of General Education, Utsunomiya University (1984), 89-108.

See also: 2032.

RECORDINGS, FILMS, AND FILMSTRIPS

DISTRIBUTORS

APPLAS Applause Productions, Inc. 85 Longview Rd., Port Washington, NY 11050.

CAED Caedmon. 1995 Broadway, New York, NY 10023.

CORT Coronet. Division of Esquire, Inc., 65 E. South Water St., Chicago, IL 60601.

EAV Educational Audio-Visual. 29 Marble Ave., Pleasantville, NY 10570.

EBEC Encyclopedia Britannica Educational Corporation. 425 North Michigan Ave., Chicago, IL 60611.

KLISET Thomas S. Klise. Box 3418, Peoria, IL 61614.

MCINVP McIntyre Visual Publications. 716 Center St., Lewiston, NY 14092.

NCAT National Center for Audio-Tapes. University of Colorado, 348 Stadium Bldg., Boulder, CO 80309.

NICEM National Information Center for Educational Media. University of Southern California, Los Angeles, CA 90007.

GENERAL STUDIES

2838 BOWDEN, BETSY. "The Chaucer Tapes." Chaucer Newsletter 6:2 (1984). [GP: Prioress, PardT, MerT, WBT, NPT]

Recordings, Films, and Filmstrips

2839   GREEN, MARTIN. "The Dialectic of Adaptation: 'The Canterbury
        Tales' of Pier Paolo Pasolini." LFQ 4 (1976), 46-53.
        [review]

RECORDINGS

2840   BLAKE, N. F. and J. D. BURNLEY. Life in Chaucer's England (and)
        Courtly Love. Cassette. Cited in Audio Learning, Inc.
        Catalogue (Manhasset, NY, 1986). No. ELA085.

2841   BLAKE, N. F. and J. D. BURNLEY. The Miller's Tale—A Discussion
        (and) The Miller's Tale—A Further Discussion. Cassette.
        Cited in Audio Learning, Inc. Catalogue (Manhasset, NY,
        1986). No. ELA086.

2841a   BORNSTEIN, DIANE and JOHN H. FISHER. A History of the English
        Language. 3 Casettes. CAED 3008. [performance by J. B.
        Bessinger, Jr.; includes selections from General Prologue to
        the Canterbury Tales and Treatise on the Astrolabe]

2842   BREWER, DEREK and A. C. SPEARING. Chaucer: The Merchant's Tale
        (and) Chaucer: The Franklin's Tale. Cassette. Cited in
        Audio Learning, Inc. Catalogue (Manhasset, NY, 1986). No.
        ELA018.

2843   BREWER, DEREK and A. C. SPEARING. Chaucer: The Nun's Priest's
        Tale (and) Chaucer: The Pardoner's Tale. Cassette. Cited
        in Audio Learning, Inc. Catalogue (Manhasset, NY, 1986). No.
        ELA019.

2844   BREWER, DEREK and A. C. SPEARING. Troilus and Criseyde: The
        Poem in Relation to Its Age (and) An Analysis of Troilus and
        Criseyde. Cassette. Cited in Audio Learning, Inc. Catalogue
        (Manhasset, NY, 1986). No. ELA017.

2845   BROWN, DEREK and DEREK PEARSALL. Some Problems in Reading the
        Canterbury Tales. Cassette. Queue, Inc. 562 Boston Ave.,
        Bridgeport, CT 06610.

2846   BROWN, PETER and DEREK PEARSALL. Some Problems in Reading the
        Canterbury Tales. Cassette. Cited in Audio Learning, Inc.
        Catalogue (Manhasset, NY, 1986). No. A42.

2847   CANTERBURY TALES. Cassettes, 2 parts, 15 min. ea. University of
        Connecticut, 1961. Cited in NCAT Literature Catalogue

(Boulder, CO). No. 0023-00.
Part 1: No. 0023-01, "Introduction to Chaucer"; Part 2: No. 0023-02, "Comments on the Prologue of the Canterbury Tales."

2848   CANTERBURY TALES. Cassette, 90 min. Cited in Medieval Sounds Catalogue (New York). [contains Prologue and more in Middle English]

2849   THE CANTERBURY TALES. Phonodisc, 33-1/3 rpm, 12 in., 4 sides. APPLAS. Cited in NICEM, 1980. [read by Peggy Ashcroft (in Modern English) and others; includes the Pardoner's Tale, the Miller's Tale, the Wife of Bath, and others]

2850   THE CANTERBURY TALES. Phonodisc, 33-1/3 rpm, 12 in., 4 sides. APPLAS. Cited in NICEM, 1980. [read by J. B. Bessinger (in Middle English) and others; includes the Miller's Tale, the Reeve's Tale, the Pardoner's Prologue and Tale, and the Nun's Priest's Tale]

2851   THE CANTERBURY TALES. Phonodisc, 33-1/3 rpm, 12 in., 2 sides. APPLAS. Cited in NICEM, 1980. [read (in Middle English) by John Burrow and others; contains the "outstanding excerpts"]

2852   THE CANTERBURY TALES. Phonodisc, 33-1/3 rpm, 12 in., 8 sides. APPLAS. Cited in NICEM, 1980. [read by Nevill Coghill (Modern English); includes the Pardoner's Tale, the Prologue, the Reeve's Tale, and the Man of Law's Tale]

2853   CHAUCER. Phonodisc, 33-1/3 rpm, 12 in., 2 sides. EBEC. Cited in NICEM, 1980. [selections from the Prologue and the Pardoner's Tale of the Canterbury Tales read (in Middle English) by Coghill and Davis]

2853a   CHAUCER, GEOFFREY. The Canterbury Tales: "The Miller's Tale" and "The Pardoner's Tale." Cassette. CAED. No. 1130. [read by Michaél MacLiammóir and Stanley Holloway]

2854   CHAUCER, GEOFFREY. The Canterbury Tales: "The Nun's Priest's Tale" and "The Pardoner's Tale." Cassette. CAED. No. 1008. [read by Robert Ross (in Middle English)]

2855   CHAUCER, GEOFFREY. The Canterbury Tales: General Prologue, Prologue to the Parson's Tale, Chaucer's Retraction. Cassette and/or phonodisc. CAED. No. 1151. [read by J. B. Bessinger, Jr. (in Middle English)]

2856   CHAUCER, GEOFFREY. The Canterbury Tales: The Wife of Bath. Cassette. LC No. R66-1803. CAED. SWC 1102. Cited in CAED Catalog. [translated by J. U. Nicholson and performed by

Recordings, Films, and Filmstrips

Dame Peggy Ashcroft]

2857   CHAUCER'S CANTERBURY TALES. Cassette, 2 parts, 15 min. ea.
        Cited in NCAT Literature Catalogue (Boulder, CO). No.
        0514-00.
            Part 1: No. 0514-01; Part 2: No. 0514-02.

2857a   CHAUCER'S CANTERBURY PILGRIMS. Phonodisc, 33-1/3 rpm, 12 in., 2
        sides. EAV. Cited in NICEM, 1980. [includes excerpts from
        the Prologue; one side read in Modern English, the other in
        Middle English]

2858   CHAUCER, GEOFFREY. Two Canterbury Tales in Middle English: "The
        Miller's Tale" and "The Reeve's Tale." Cassette. CAED. No.
        1223. [read by J. B. Bessinger, Jr.]

2858a   CHAUCER, GEOFFREY. "The Parliament of Fowls" abd Six Lyric Poems
        (in Middle English). Cassette. CAED. No. 1226. [read by
        J. B. Bessinger, Jr.]

2859   COYLE, MARTIN and WILLIAM O. EVANS. Chaucer: The Art of the
        General Prologue (and) Chaucer: Art, Order, and Justice in
        "The Knight's Tale." Cassette. Cited in Audio Learning,
        Inc. Catalogue (Manhasset, NY, 1986). No. ELA082.

2860   COYLE, MARTIN and WILLIAM O. EVANS. Chaucer: The Marriage
        Group--"The Wife of Bath's Tale" and "The Clerk's Tale" (and)
        Chaucer: The Marriage Group--"The Merchant's Tale" and "The
        Franklin's Tale." Cassette. Cited in Audio Learning, Inc.
        Catalogue (Manhasset, NY, 1986). No. ELA081.

2861   ENGLISH POETRY FROM CHAUCER TO MILTON. Phonodisc, 33-1/3 rpm, 12
        in., 2 sides. APPLAS. Cited in NICEM, 1980. [selections
        read by Mark Van Doren and others]

2862   HEARING POETRY: CHAUCER TO MILTON. Cassette. LC No. RA55-196.
        CAED. SWC 1021. Cited in CAED Catalog. [Chaucer, Geoffrey:
        Prologue to the Legend of Good Women (Selections);
        performances by Mark Van Doren, Hurd Hatfield, Frank Silvera,
        and Jo Van Fleet]

2863   INTRODUCTION TO CANTERBURY TALES. Cassette (in two parts). Part
        1: No. NT016; Part 2: No. NT017. Cited in Gould Media
        Catalogue (Mount Vernon, NY, 1986). [read by Felicity
        Currie]

2864   PEARSALL, DEREK and ELIZABETH SALTER. Chaucer and the Difficulty
        of Medieval Poetry. Cassette. Cited in Audio Learning, Inc.
        Catalogue (Manhasset, NY, 1986). No. A1.

2865 PEARSALL, DEREK and ELIZABETH SALTER. Chaucer and the Difficulty
of Medieval Poetry. Cassette. Queue, Inc. Side One:
Problems of Reading and Understanding Chaucer. Side Two:
Realism and Convention in the Canterbury Tales.

2866 THE PROSODY OF CHAUCER. Cassette, 2 parts, 60 min. ea.
International Tape Exchange, 1961. Cited in NCAT Literature
Catalogue (Boulder, CO). No. 0207-00. [read by James G.
Southworth]
Part 1: No. 0207-01, "Prologue . . .," "House of Fame,"
"Parlement of Briddes," and "Troilus and Criseyde"; Part 2:
No. 0207-02, "The Pardoner's Tale," "ABC," and "Boke of the
Duchess."

2867 ROULSTON, MICHAEL. Geoffrey Chaucer. Cassette. Cited in Audio
Learning, Inc. Catalogue (Manhasset, NY, 1986). No. GW01.
[narrated by Richard Klee]

2868 SELECTED SHORT POEMS. Phonodisc, 33-1/3 rpm, 12 in., 2 sides.
APPLAS. Cited in NICEM, 1980. [read by J. Bessinger (in
Midddle English); includes the Parliament of Fowls, To
Rosamund, etc.]

FILMS AND FILMSTRIPS

2869 CANTERBURY TALES, THE. Filmstrip with cassette/script. 83
frames. LC No. 81-730174. KLISET, 1980. [presents a
version of Chaucer's Tales and explains their stories and
characters]

2870 CHAUCER. Filmstrip with cassette. 83 frames, color, 35 mm. +
script. KLISET, 1980. Cited in Library of Congress
Catalogs: Audiovisual Materials, 1982, p. 90.

2871 CHAUCER. Filmstrip with cassette/script. 88 frames. LC No.
81-730175. KLISET, 1980. [covers life of Chaucer and
discusses his major work]

2872 CHAUCER AND THE MEDIEVAL PERIOD. Color/black and white. 13
min., 16 mm. CORT, 1957. Cited in EDUCATIONAL FILM LOCATOR
(1980), p. 763. [uses Canterbury Tales to present three
classes of Medieval society]

2873 ENGLISH LITERATURE: A SURVEY. Filmstrip. [15 filmstrips]

Recordings, Films, and Filmstrips

Cited in Films for the Humanities Catalogue (Princeton, NJ, 1982).
Unit 2:1, Middle English Literature; Unit 2:2, Chaucer.

2874 CHAUCER'S ENGLAND: WITH A SPECIAL PRESENTATION OF THE PARDONER'S TALE. Color/black and white, 30 min., 16 mm. EBEC, 1958. Cited in EDUCATIONAL FILM LOCATOR (1980), p. 763. [presents the conditions under which Chaucer's Canterbury Tales were originally told, dramatized by the Pardoner]

2875 GEOFFREY CHAUCER AND MIDDLE ENGLISH LITERATURE. Motion picture, 35 min. Available on VHS, Beta, or U-Matic. Cited in Films for the Humanities Catalogue (Princeton, NJ, 1986), No. 906.

2876 MEDIEVAL ENGLAND. Filmstrip with Cassette. 150 frames. LC No. 75-733119. MCINVP, 1974. Cited in NICEM, 1980.

2877 THE PARDONER'S TALE. 16 mm. film. 15 min. Black and white. Optical Sound. Cited in NICEM, 1969. [from the On Stage series]

2878 RICHMOND, VELMA B. A Prologue to Chaucer. Video cassette (VHS, Beta, and U-Matic), 29 min., color. Princeton, NJ: Films for the Humanities.

2879 A SURVEY OF ENGLISH LITERATURE. Filmstrips. With cassette. Cited in Cassettes Unlimited Catalog.
31a. Old English and the Middle English Periods.

PEDAGOGY

2880   ANDERSON J[OHN] J., ed. <u>Chaucer, 'The Canterbury Tales': A</u>
        <u>Casebook</u>. Casebook Series. London and Basingstoke:
        Macmillan, 1974. 255 pp. [critical articles and excerpts]
          Reviews: R. M. Wilson, <u>MLR</u> 70 (1975), 389–90.

2880a   BRECKENRIDGE, JAY RANKIN. "A Visit with Geoffrey Chaucer: The
        Medieval Poet Characterized for a Modern Audience." <u>DAI</u> 45
        (1985), 2868A. Carnegie–Mellon University, 1984.
        [commentary, playscript, and video-taped reading for
        beginning students of Chaucer]

2881   CHICKERING, HOWELL, ed., with Frederic Cheyette and Margaret
        Switten. <u>1983 NEH Institute Resource Book for the Teaching</u>
        <u>of Medieval Civilization</u>. Amherst, MA: Five Colleges, 1984.
        284 pp. [+Boethius, St. Augustine, Dante] See Clasby, <u>KnT</u>,
        no. 1277.

2882   FABIAN, BERNHARD. <u>Von Chaucer bis Pinter: Ausgewählte</u>
        <u>Autorenbibliographien zur englischen Literatur</u>. Athenäum–
        Taschenbücher Literaturwissenschaft. Königstein/Ts:
        Athenäum–Verlag, 1980. [brief bibliographical sketches]

2883   GARBÁTY, THOMAS. <u>Medieval English Literature</u>. Lexington, MA:
        D. C. Heath, 1984. [anthology by genres; <u>MilT</u>, <u>Th</u>, <u>Purse</u>]
          Reviews: J. Dickenson, <u>Lore&L</u> 4 (1985), 97.

2884   GIBALDI, JOSEPH, ed. <u>Approaches to Teaching Chaucer's</u>
        <u>'Canterbury Tales'</u>. Consultant Ed. Florence H. Ridley.
        Approaches to Teaching Masterpieces of World Literature, 1.
        New York: Modern Language Association, 1980. 175 pp.
          Reviews: John Kelly, <u>CollL</u> 8 (1981), 192; Gerald L. Evans,
        <u>SAC</u> 4 (1982), 152–53; Sumner Ferris, <u>LRN</u> 7 (1982), 170–71.

2885   GRENNEN, JOSEPH E. <u>Chaucer's 'Canterbury Tales'</u>. Monarch Notes
        and Study Guides. New York: Monarch Press, 1964. 83 pp.

2886   LEHNERT, MARTIN, ed. and trans. <u>Hier hatte ich einst viel</u>
        <u>Pläsier: Volkstümliche englische Dichtung des Mittelalters</u>.

Pedagogy

Parallel-Text ed. Leipzig: Insel Verlag Anton Kippenberg, 1980. 351 pp. [women; nature; students; scholars; death; medicine; coinage; books; Chaucer's friar; Hoccleve; thematic anthology including excerpts from Chaucer]
Reviews: George Seehase, ZAA 31 (1983), 353-55.

2887 McDERMOTT, JOHN J. "Teaching Students to Read Chaucer Aloud." CE 37 (1975), 402-04. [use of Knapp and Snortum, The Sounds of Chaucer's English]

2888 NORTON-SMITH, JOHN. Geoffrey Chaucer. Medieval Authors Series. London: Routledge, 1974. 274 pp.
Reviews: R. M. Wilson, MLR 70 (1975), 389-90.

2889 PARTRIDGE, A. C. A Companion to Old and Middle English Studies. Totowa, NJ: Barnes and Noble; London: Andre Deutsch, 1982.
Reviews: Carl T. Berkhout, Speculum 60 (1985), 448-49.

2890 REINECKE, GEORGE F. "Speculation, Intention, and the Teaching of Chaucer," in 43, pp. 81-93.

2891 SATŌ, TSUTOMU and SEIZŌ SUKAGAWA. Chaucer: Sono Jidai, Bungaku, Gengo [An Approach to Chaucer]. Tokyo: Seibido, 1982. 150 pp. In Japanese. [primer: Chaucer's age, life, works]

2892 THOMAS, NIGEL and RICHARD SWAN. The Prologue to 'The Canterbury Tales' by Geoffrey Chaucer. Macmillan Master Guides. London: Macmillan Education, Ltd., 1985. 80 pp.

2893 WEISSMAN, HOPE PHYLLIS. "One Way to End a Chaucer Course." Chaucer Newsletter 2:2 (1980), 3-7. [+Très Riches Heures]

2894 WILLMOTT, MICHAEL. "Chaucer is Alive and Kicking." TES 3374 (20 February, 1981), 34-35. [teaching Chaucer]

See also: 191, 198, 200, 482, 898, 1277, 1464, 2625, 2647, 2654, 2663, 2838-79.

AUTHOR INDEX

293

Author Index

Author Index

Author Index

AUTHOR INDEX

Author Index

AUTHOR INDEX

AUTHOR INDEX

Author Index

AUTHOR INDEX

Author Index

Author Index

Author Index

Author Index

Author Index

Author Index

SUBJECT INDEX

Subject Index

Subject Index

Subject Index

Subject Index

Subject Index

Subject Index

Subject Index

Epic: 2230, 2676
  conventions: 1296, 1299, 1304, 1883
  animal epic: 1900, 2672
Epicureanism: 1653
Epideictic discourse: 2010
Epilogue (TC): 2351, 2365
Epistemology of art: 2017
  Boethian: 2268
  of love: 2085
Epistola Valerii Rufino ne Ducat Uxorem: 1844
Epithalamic conventions: 2665
EQUATORIE OF PLANETIS: 440, 891, 946, 1986, 1987, 2650
Equivocation: 833
Erasmus, Desiderius: 710
Ernest and game: 741, 1076, 1106, 1124, 1133, 2183, see Game
Eroticism: 415, 560, 1036, 1853, 1891
Eschatology: 1954, 2185
Esther (Queen): 1600
Ethics: 603, 1921, 2192
Ethology: 1020
Ethopoeia: 551, 2406
Eucharist: 1250
Euclid: 2303
Eunuch: 1463
Evil: 2337
Exchange (foreign): 986
Exegesis: 249, 960, 1556, 1718, see Patristic criticism
  antifraternal: 1537
  patristic: 469, 1706
  Scriptural: 970, 1175, 2525
  typological: 1536
Exempla: 280, 528, 589, 1397, 1529, 1556, 1680, 1719, 1885, 2605, 2643
Exorcism: 1328, 1537
Experience (as philosophic concept): 1161

Fableau dou Dieu d'Amors: 2196
Fables: 330, 1112
  beast: 1873, 1883
  satiric: 1877
Fabliaux: 288, 360, 486, 595, 694,

713, 779, 959, 981, 993, 1029, 1127, 1346, 1349, 1383, 1539, 1769, 2597, 2611, 2649, 2660, see Bawdry, Dirty Joke
  Old French: 993
Facial expression: 1541
Fairies: 913
  fairy land: 1435
  fairy tale: 1346
Fall, the: 1774, 2517
Fals felicite: 2001
False appearances: 2078, 2079
Falstaff: 708, 740, 743
Fame, Book of Fame: 2070, see HF
  world of: 2073
Family: 2700, 2704
Fantasy: 1353
Fare-carte: 2271
Fasciculus morum: 2687
Fashion: 2710, see Costume
Fate: 1301
Father figures: 546a
Faulkner, William: 684
Feast, Feasting: see Food
Female Tatler, The: 785
Femininity: 579
Feminism: 1586, 2405
  polarization of: 2337
Feminist, Criseyde as: 2279
  nun: 1908
Feminist criticism: 56, 245, 248, 1006
Feudalism: 1519, 2560
Fevre, Jean le: 1475
Fibonacci (Lombard mathematician): 1061
Fiction (Chaucerian): 305, 365, 1107
  fictionalizations: 2315
Fielding, Henry: 847
Figmenta vs. veritas: 1509
Figura: 445, 1167
  figure: 979
Figurative meanings: 2055
  negation: 861
  patterns: 2236
Il Filocolo: see Boccaccio
Il Filostrato: see Boccaccio
Fin amor: 2149, see Courtly love,

Love
Final -e: 865, 878, 953
Finance (medieval): 986, 1244
Finnian: 552
Fish: 1237, 1840
  hooked fish: 2508
Fistula in ano: 1369
Fitzgerald, F. Scott: 709
Flattery: 1734
Florent, Tale of (Gower): 1450,
  1454
Floure and the Leaf, The: 2530,
  2834
Flower (service of the): 2140
Folklore: 1081, 1852, 2375
Folktale: 1561, 1704a
Food (including feasts, feasting):
  526, 1080, 1250, 1251, 1257,
  1870, 2816
Fool: 536, 2072, 2343
  archetypal: 2064
Foreign exchange: 986, 1244, 1766
Foreknowledge: 1880
Forests (royal): 2751
Form: 1876, see Structure
Formalist criticism: 1650, 1768,
  2321
FORMER AGE: 2517-2520+
Formulaic diction: 999
Fortitude: 1547
Fortuna: 2278
Fortune: 663, 1062, 1681, 1682,
  1708, 2388, 2397, 2410, 2435
FORTUNE: 2521+
Foucault, Michel: 365
Fountain of Love: 2066, 2067
Fox and Pitt: 775
Foxton, John de: 2793
Fragments of CT: see CT,
  Fragments
Frame tale: 633, 976, 1003, 1016,
  1032, 1091, 1105, 1107, 1033,
  1040, 1154, 1851
  framework: 2168, 2170, 2256
Francis of Assisi, St.: 1242
Franciscans (literature and
  exegesis): 2622, 2623
Franciscus Junius: 2833
FRANKLIN'S TALE: 1632-1673+

Free spirit (heresy): 2768
Free will: 537, 1281, 1880
Freedom (human): 590, 1301, 2357
  fredom: 1058
French influence on Chaucer: 599,
  607, 662
French language: 1228
  loan words: 702, 879, 881, 889,
  910, 951
French lyric element(TC): 2482
Frescobaldi, Matteo, "Canzone a
  Ballo": 2479
Freud, Sigmund: 349, 1563, 2015,
  2411, 2455
FRIAR'S PROLOGUE and TALE:
  1514-1529+
Friars: 1178, 1239, 2758, 2782
Friday: 1289
Frideswide, St.: 2785
Friendship motif: 358
Friesland: 2513
Frigii Daretis Ylias (Joseph of
  Exeter): 2470
Froissart, Jean: 453, 478, 583,
  664, 2041, 2101, 2143, 2573
  Paradys d'amour: 2066
Fronstispiece (in medieval poetic
  texts): 2812
Fruit-chaff metaphor: 1113
Fruitfulness (and sterility): 1674
Fulgentius (Fabius Planciades
  Fulgentius): 635
Furnivall, Frederick James: 89

Game: 502, 1086
  game and ernest: 741, 1106,
  1124, 1133, 2183
  game of love: 2297
  game and play: 1101
  games: 1327, 1609, 1963
  games and high seriousness: 741,
  1076
  Canterbury game: 1707
  May games: 1612
Game in myn hood: 952
GAMELYN, TALE OF: 686
Gardens in Chaucer: 383, 780, 1640,
  1667, 1884
  medieval: 2810, 2811

SUBJECT INDEX

Subject Index

Subject Index

Subject Index

Subject Index

2310, 2321
Phislyas: 1414
Phoebus, Gaston (Count of Foix):
    1930
Phyllis (legend of): 2151
PHYSICIAN'S TALE: 1674-1690+
Physiognomy: 356, 402, 1208, 1241
Physiology (medieval): 372
Pierides (muses): 1404
Piers Plowman: see Langland
Pilgrimage: 407, 739, 802, 962,
    988, 1007, 1020, 1022, 1026,
    1049, 1051, 1106, 1124, 1156,
    1159, 2552, 2691
  Canterbury: 2566
  motif: 710, 1965, 2078, 2781
  narratives: 1053
Pilgrimage of the Lyf of the
    Manhode: 2502
Pilgrim's Tale: 807
Pilgrims, no. of in GP: 1186, see
    GENERAL PROLOGUE, Pilgrimage
Pirandello, Luigi: 722
Pitt and Fox: 775
Pity: 370
PITY: 2512-2513+
Plague: 1694, 2585, 2592, 2720
De Planctu Naturae (Alanus de
    Insulis): 1209, 2017, 2208
Planctus Mariae: 1067
Planets: 2449
  order of: 2819
Plato and Platonic tradition: 613,
    1048, 1153, 1902, 2120
  in cosmic fables: 2457
  Timaeus: 2120
Play: 526, 1024, 1101
Pleonasm: 859
Plowman's Tale, The: 807, 2686a,
    2832
Pluma Sardanapalli: 2278
Plutarch: 1317
Pluto and Proserpina: 1593
Poet (as image): 1660
  Chaucer's idea of: 414
Poetics: 246, 297, 305, 420, 961,
    1023, 1098, 1150, 2111, 2692,
    2443, 2667
  Chaucerian: 348, 2124, 2341

of classical myth: 453
of court lyric: 478
of inflation: 2117
Renaissance: 697
of romance: 527
of translation: 542
Poetria nova (Geoffrey de
    Vinsauf): 264, 591, 828, 841,
    2303, 2626, 2690
Poetry, art of: 2111
  and crisis: 470
  difficulty of medieval: 2864,
    2865
Poison: 1037, 1285
  lore: 1754
Polarities: 2164, 2181
Polarization (of feminine): 2337
Polish analogue: 653
Politeness: 1364, 1365
Politics (14th c.): 1296, 2586
  in Chaucer: 428
  in TC: 2443
Pomeroy (place name): 1527
Pope, Alexander: 148, 678, 730,
    749, 783
Popular literature: 60, 657, 1081,
    1395
Portraits of Chaucer: 113, 136,
    143, 164, 166
Portraiture (by Chaucer): 264, 854,
    1624, 2381, 2406, see
    Characterization
  of Fame: 2104
  GP: 1200, 1202, 1203, 1204,
    1206, 1223, 1254, 1263, 1267
  of January: 1595
Portuguese analogues: 610
Postillae litteralis et moralis
    super totam Bibliam: 1182
Postmodernism: 2097
Potentia absoluta: 1566
Pound, Ezra: 716
Poverty: 1158
  religious: 2746
Power: 1097, 1455, 2362
Praeteritio: 840
Pratt, Robert: 2468
Preaching, preachers: 1028, 1168,
    1698, 1706, see Sermon, Homily

Subject Index

Subject Index

SUBJECT INDEX

Speght, Thomas: 155, 173, 686, 815, 2531, 2832, 2835
Spelling: 90, 869, 949
Spenser, Edmund: 324, 330, 387, 391, 445, 455, 669, 670, 671, 680, 686, 700, 720, 724, 725, 726, 742, 750, 769, 777, 778, 1877, 2325, 2342, 2442
  Daphnaida: 2021
  "E. K.": 686
Spiced conscience: 937
Spiritual sickness: 1687
  vision: 1198
Spirituality: 1096, 1198, 2565
Spring (season of): 1207
Squeamishness: 1328
SQUIRE'S TALE: 1623-1631+
Stag of love: 2058
Stair (image of): 2377
Stars: 1290, 1411
Statius: 627, 2451
  Thebaid: 1309, 1317, 2157, 2267, 2453
Steel (true as): 2317
Stereotypes (female): 1487, 2144
Sterility: 1674
Stoicism: 2589
Storm imagery: 2386
Stothard, Thomas: 144, 714
Stow, John: 120, 123, 127, 155, 2016
Strabo, Walafrid, Glossa ordinaria: 2519
Stratford atte Bowe: 1228
Straw, Jack: 1886
Strode, Ralph: 258
  Consequences: 2299
Structural analysis: 404, 2202
Structuralism, structuralist approaches: 265, 272, 1305, 1340, 1768, 1801, 2321, 2374
  medieval: 2303
Structure: 295, 369, 427, 835, 847, 903, 982, 995, 1100, 1101, 1103, 1118, 1160, 1165, 1189, 1272, 1288, 1329, 1491, 1539, 1645, 1697, 1721, 1758, 1851, 1862, 1982, 2025, 2043, 2061, 2092, 2093, 2125, 2164, 2166,

2181, 2189, 2204, 2236, 2302, 2409, 2416, 2434, 2512, 2521, 2530, 2686
  semiological: 114
  verbal: 1581
Style: 823-867+
  levels of: 892, 1548
Suetonius (Gaius Suetonius Tranquillus): 1844
Suffering: 323, 1170
Summa de Vitiis (Peraldus): 1957
Summa Virtutum de Remediis Anime: 1978
SUMMONER'S TALE: 1530-1540+
Summoners: 1518
Supernaturalism: 2136
Surgery: 1291
Surrealism: 2104
Suspended judgement: 460
Swoons: 2335, 2340
Sword (healing): 612
Symbolism: 61, 265, 296, 364, 458, 633, 1061, 1063, 1159, 1241, 1578, 1701, 1765, 1821, 1852, 1853, 1891, 1894, 1959, 2058, 2316, 2360, 2375, 2640
Syntax: 859, 877, 906, 932, 1344, 1990
  and lexis: 972, 1218

Taboo-words: 943, 1838, see Bawdry, Obscenity, Scatology, Vulgarity
Tail-rhyme romances: 1817
Taillynge: 1772
TALE OF BERYN: 694, 739, 978
Tartarye (place): 1629
Tattle's Well's Faire: 817
Technical writer (Chaucer as): 1987, 1991
Technology: 2805
Templars: 2539
Template (testamental): 1428
Temple of Glas: 2200, 2613
Temporality: 555, see Time
Temptation: 1614
Tercelet: 1628, see PF: 2163-2209+
Il Teseida: see Boccaccio
Testament of Cresseid: 185, 678, 719, 2287

SUBJECT INDEX

SUBJECT INDEX

Subject Index

SUBJECT INDEX

El prevenido engañado: 1088
Zeno, Apostolo (Griselda): 2821
Zephirus: 1207

Zodiac: 1154, 1578
  of tales: 1132